Visualizing Spanish Modernity

Edited by
Susan Larson and Eva Woods

Oxford • New York

English edition
First published in 2005 by
Berg
Editorial offices:
First Floor, Angel Court, 81 St Clements Street, Oxford OX4 1AW, UK
175 Fifth Avenue, New York, NY 10010, USA

Berg is the imprint of Oxford International Publishers Ltd.

Library of Congress Cataloging-in-Publication Data
Visualizing Spanish modernity / edited by Susan Larson and Eva Woods.— English ed.
p. cm.
Includes bibliographical references and index.
ISBN 1-85973-801-X (cloth) — ISBN 1-85973-806-0 (pbk.)
1. Popular culture—Spain—History—19th century. 2. Visual communication—Spain—History—19th century. 3. Spain—Intellectual life—19th century. 4. Popular culture—Spain—History—20th century. 5. Visual communication—Spain—History—20th century. 6. Spain—Intellectual life—20th century. 7. Spain—In art. I. Larson, Susan, 1968- II. Woods, Eva.

DP203.5.V58 2005
306'.0946'09034—dc22 2005017026

British Library Cataloguing-in-Publication Data
A catalogue record for this book is available from the British Library.

ISBN-13 978 1 85973 801 6 (Cloth)
978 1 85973 806 1 (Paper)
ISBN-10 1 85973 801 X (Cloth)
1 85973 806 0 (Paper)

Typeset by Avocet Typeset, Chilton, Aylesbury, Bucks
Printed in the United Kingdom by Biddles Ltd, King's Lynn.

www.bergpublishers.com

For Marc and Oscar

For Jesse

Contents

List of Illustrations ix

Acknowledgments xiii

Notes on Contributors xv

1 Visualizing Spanish Modernity: Introduction 1
Susan Larson and Eva Woods

2 Visibly Modern Madrid: Mesonero, Visual Culture, and the Apparatus of Urban Reform 24
Rebecca Haidt

3 Foresight, Blindness or Illusion? Women and Citizenship in the Second Series of Galdós's *Episodios nacionales* 46
David R. George, Jr

4 Horror, Spectacle and Nation-formation: Historical Painting in Late-nineteenth-century Spain 64
Jo Labanyi

5 Isidora in the Museum 81
Luis Fernández Cifuentes

6 Thresholds of Visibility at the Borders of Madrid: Benjamin, Gómez de la Serna, Mesonero 94
Andrew Bush

7 Seeing the Dead: Manual and Mechanical Specters in Modern Spain (1893–1939) 112
Brad Epps

8 Santiago Rusiñol's *Impresiones de arte* in the Age of Tourism: Seeing Andalusia after Seeing Paris 142
Elena Cueto Asín

9 Landscape in the Photography of Spain 163
Lee Fontanella

10 From Engraving to Photo: Cross-cut Technologies in the Spanish Illustrated Press 178
Lou Charnon-Deutsch

11 Spain's Image and Regional Dress: From Everyday Object to Museum Piece and Tourist Attraction 207
Jesusa Vega

12 Observing the City, Mediating the Mountain: *Mirador* and the 1929 International Exposition of Barcelona 228
Robert A. Davidson

13 Joan Miró, 1929: High and Low Culture in Barcelona and Paris 245
Félix Fanès

14 Stages of Modernity: The Uneasy Symbiosis of the *género chico* and Early Cinema in Madrid 263
Susan Larson

15 Visualizing the Time-space of Otherness: Digression and Distraction in Spanish Silent Film 283
Eva M. Woods

16 Modern Anxiety and Documentary Cinema in Republican Spain 301
Geoffrey B. Pingree

17 The Last Look from the Border 329
Joan Ramon Resina

Index 349

Illustrations

2.1 Anonymous, "Titi." *The Penny Magazine* (December 1835), *Semanario Pintoresco* (September 1836) 28
2.2 Artist unknown, "Termómetro." *Semanario Pintoresco* 1839 37
2.3 Artist unknown, "La Iglesia de San Justo, Madrid." *Semanario Pintoresco* 1839 38
2.4 Artist unknown, "Lectura de las familias." *Semanario Pintoresco* frontispiece, 1839 41
4.1 Francisco Pradilla y Ortiz, *Doña Juana la Loca* 1877 65
4.2 José Casado del Alisal, *Leyenda del rey monje* 1880 65
7.1 Santiago Rusiñol, *Caps d'anarquistes I and II* 1894 114
7.2 Santiago Rusiñol, *Caps d'anarquistes III and IV* 1894 115
7.3 Agustí Centelles, *Morts a la plaça [de] Catalunya* July 19, 1936 116
8.1 Miguel Utrillo, "Los cármenes de Granada." *Impresiones de arte*, date unknown 155
8.2 Miguel Utrillo, "Carrer de la miseria." *Impresiones de arte*, date unknown 158
8.3 Santiago Rusiñol, "Noia de Consuegra." *Impresiones de arte*, date unknown 159
9.1 José Ortiz Echagüe, "Paisaje el el río." 1905 172
9.2 José Ortiz Echagüe, "El Duero por Soria." 1910 173
10.1 "General Prim, jefe del cuarto cuerpo del ejército de África." *El Museo Universal* 4 (February 5, 1860): 18 183
10.2 "Unas segadoras en la campiña de Córdoba." *Ilustración Española y Americana* 20 (July 15, 1876): 24 184
10.3 Alfonse Legros, "La pequeña María." *Ilustración Española y Americana* 21 (January 30, 1877): 69 185
10.4 "Iglesia de Santa María del Mar." *Ilustración Española y Americana* 22 (April 22, 1878): 257 186
10.5 "Segovia, Estado actual del Alcázar." *Ilustración Española y Americana* 22 (August 8, 1878): 76 186
10.6 R.P. Napper, "Grupo de gitanos en Andalucia hacia 1863." In López Mondéjar (1997) *Historia de la fotografía en España*, p. 42 187

10.7 Jules Lefebre, "Mignon." *Ilustración Española y Americana* 22 (October 15, 1878): n.p. 187
10.8 "Vista de un campamento marroquí – El sultán en marcha – Fantasía – Realidad." *Ilustración Española y Americana* 49 (July 8, 1905):12 188
10.9 Alfredo Orillac, "Panamá. Individuos que compenen la comisión de estudios, presidida por Mr. de Lesseps." *Ilustración Española y Americana* 24 (February 22, 1880): 117 189
10.10 Victoriano Otero, "Cuba. Grupo de soldados que defendieron valerosamente el poblado de 'Dos Caminos' premiados con la Cruz del Mérito Militar." *Ilustración Española y Americana* 39 (May 30, 1895): 329 190
10.11 Chute and Brook, "Antes de la salida." "Adiós al Río de la Plata. Motevideo. Embarco de voluntarios españoles para la guerra de Cuba, en el vapor "San Francisco" de la Compañía transatlántica." *Ilustración Española y Americana* (October 22, 1895): 228 191
10.12 Vicente Echavarri, Gonzalo Arregui. "Entusiasta despedida hecha por el pueblo y las autoridades a las tropas del Segundo Regimiento de Artillería de Montana a su partida para Melilla, el 3 del Actual." *Ilustración Española y Americana* 37 (November 15, 1893): 300 192
10.13 "La salida. Madrid. Banquete de las armas de infantería (del natural)." *Ilustración Española y Americana* 38 (March 15, 1894): 144 193
10.14 "La guerra en Cuba – guerrilla de tropas españolas en manigua." *Ilustración Española y Americana* 39 (December 15, 1895): 353 194
10.15 "La guerra en Cuba – Guerrilla defendiendo el paso de un convoy en Santiago de Cuba" *Ilustración Española y Americana* 41 (December 22, 1897): 392 195
10.16 "Campamento de Alto Songo (Santiago de Cuba) – Una guerrilla de descanso." *Ilustración Española y Americana* 43 (November 22, 1895): 293 195
10.17 Corcos, "Fiel mensajera" *Ilustración Española y Americana* 35 (July 30, 1891): n.p. 196
10.18 "La miseria en Andalucía" *Blanco y Negro* 4 (June 9, 1894): cover 199
10.19 Lebrón, "Dolores Cisnero, Cantinera del Bataillón de Pavía. *Blanco y Negro* 5 (November 30, 1895): n.p. 200
10.20 "El hombre del día. Rafael Guerra (Guerrita)." *Blanco y Negro* 4 (July 7, 1894): n.p. 201
10.21 Untitled. *Ilustración Española y Americana* 51 (December 8, 1907): 336 202
10.22 Sánchez Germona. "Nueva vida." *Ilustración Española y Americana* 49 (January 8, 1905): n.p. 203

12.1	Artist unknown, *Mirador* banner, 1929	231
13.1	Joan Miró, *Collage*, 1929, Museum of Modern Art, New York	246
13.2	Detail from Joan Miró, *Collage*, 1929, Museum of Modern Art, New York	247
13.3	Gaietà Cornet, Caricature of the politicians Alejandro Lerroux and Melquiades Álvarez, published in *Cu-cut!* (September 5, 1907)	250
13.4	Joan Miró, *The Kerosene Lamp*, 1924, The Art Institute of Chicago	251
13.5	Joan Miró, *Still Life – Glove and Newspaper*, 1921, Museum of Modern Art, New York	252
13.6	First version of *Collage*, 1929, photographed in 1930 in the foyer of the cinema Studio 28 in Paris, where Luis Buñuel's *L'Age d'Or* was premiered	253
13.7	Pablo Picasso, *La guitarra*, 1913, Museum of Modern Art, New York	254
17.1	Robert Capa, "Barcelona, January 1939." *Spain. Spanish Civil War (1936–9)*	330
17.2	Robert Capa, "Barcelona, January 1939." *Spain. Spanish Civil War (1936–9)*	341
17.3	Robert Capa, "Barcelona, January 1939." *Spain. Spanish Civil War (1936–9)*	342

Acknowledgments

Visualizing Spanish Modernity is the product of several years of collaboration with friends and colleagues. It has taken many turns in its trajectory from the abstract to the real and has been made possible because of generous grants from several institutions. We received essential publication and permissions subsidies through the Research Committee at Vassar College and were awarded a grant from the University of Minnesota's Program for Cultural Cooperation Between Spain's Ministry of Education, Culture and Sports and United States Universities. We will always be grateful to Malcolm A. Compitello and Arnaldo Cruz-Malavé for their assistance in securing this aid even before the collection had taken shape. David Bird lent a helping hand at a critical time with the permissions. We are also indebted to L. Elena Delgado, Jordana Mendelson and Oscar E. Vázquez, the organizers of the *Recalcitrant Modernities: Spain, Difference and the Construction of European Modernism* conference at the University of Illinois in Urbana-Champaign for inviting us to share an early version of our introduction with an exceptionally creative and supportive group of established interdisciplinary scholars.

We would like to thank Enrique Blanco Arroyo and Josefira Martínez for the cover image and their solidarity with our project. Jane Livingston of Vassar's Computer Instructional Services provided the essential technical know-how to create the cover, and Ian Critchley from the Production Department at Berg guided us through the artistic decisions. Kathleen May and Francesca Martin, also at Berg, were consistently supportive and encouraging editors. We feel very fortunate to have worked with them. We received invaluable advice from Andrew Bush, Lisa Paravisini, Jeffrey Schneider, and Sherry Velasco. Many thanks also go to those who read portions of the manuscript: Lou Charnon-Deutsch, Dianna Niebylski, Ana Rueda, and especially William F. Woods. Thanks to Gabe Milner for his translation

Most of all, we take this opportunity to thank all of the contributors who have entrusted their work to us and given us the incredibly stimulating experience of theorizing Spain's modern period through the lens of visual studies. The frequent contact we had with the authors of the chapters included here immersed us for a time in a provisional, virtual scholarly community that we will genuinely miss.

Notes on Contributors

Andrew Bush is Professor of Hispanic Studies and Jewish Studies at Vassar College, Poughkeepsie, New York. He has published widely in both fields, and served as the editor of the *Revista de Estudios Hispánicos*. Most recently he has written essays on American Jewish poetry, the philosophy of María Zambrano, and Golden Age drama. He is also the author of *The Routes of Modernity: Spanish American Poetry from the Early Eighteenth to the Mid-Nineteenth Century* (Bucknell UP, 2000).

Lou Charnon-Deutsch is Professor of Spanish and Women's Studies at State University of New York Stony Brook. Her recent books include *Narratives of Desire: Nineteenth-Century Spanish Fiction by Women* (Pennsylvania State UP, 1994), *Culture and Gender in Nineteenth-Century Spain* (co-edited with Jo Labanyi: Oxford UP, 1995), *Fictions of the Feminine in the Nineteenth-Century Spanish Press* (Pennsylvania State UP, 2000), and *The Spanish Gypsy: History of a European Obsession* (Pennsylvania State UP 2004). She serves on the editorial board of the *Revista de Estudios Hispánicos*, *Decimonónica*, and *Letras Femeninas* and is American Editor of *The Hispanic Research Journal*.

Elena Cueto Asín is Assistant Professor of Spanish at Bowdoin College, Maine. Her field of research includes the relationships between literature and the visual arts in Spain, especially in the area of theater, as well as the connections between Spanish and French cultural production. Her work appears in various journals including *ALEC*, *Catalan Review*, *Revista de Estudios Hispánicos*, and *Romance Language Annual*.

Robert A. Davidson is Assistant Professor of Spanish at the University of Toronto. He works on the avant-garde, architecture, and cinema and is currently preparing two books: *Jazz Age Barcelona: Text, Rhythm and Violence* as well as a second project that deals with the space of the modern hotel. He is co-editor of "New Coordinates: Spatial Mappings, National Trajectories," a forthcoming double issue of *Diacritics* and is Book Review Editor for the *Revista Canadiense de Estudios Hispánicos*.

Brad Epps is Professor of Romance Languages and Literatures and Studies in Women, Gender, and Sexuality at Harvard University. He has published over fifty articles on modern literature, film, art, architecture, and immigration from Spain, Latin America, Catalonia, and France and is the author of *Significant Violence: Oppression and Resistance in the Narratives of Juan Goytisolo* (Oxford UP, 1996). He is currently preparing two books: *Daring to Write*, on gay and lesbian issues in Latin America, Spain, and Latino cultures in the United States, and *Barcelona and Beyond*, on the transformations of the Catalan capital. He is also co-editing two volumes, one with Luis Fernández Cifuentes, *Spain Beyond Spain: Modernity, Literary History, and National Identity*, and another with Keja Valens, *Passing Lines: Immigration and (Homo)sexuality*.

Félix Fanès is Professor of Contemporary Art at the Universitat Autònoma of Barcelona and the Director of the Salvador Dalí Institute. He has published extensively on art, literature and film (*El cas Cifesa: vint anys de cine espanyol*) and has lectured at the Centre Georges Pompidou in Paris and the New York Institute of Fine Arts. His most recent publication is *Salvador Dalí: The Making of an Image (1925–1930)* (Yale UP, 2003).

Luis Fernández Cifuentes has been the Robert S. and Ilse Friend Professor of Romance Languages and Literatures at Harvard University since 1988. He has published two books, two critical editions, over sixty articles and over seventy book reviews. He has been the editor or co-editor of three books of essays, and given more than fifty lectures in Europe and the United States. His area of specialization is contemporary Spanish literature (eighteenth, nineteenth and twentieth centuries) with frequent incursions in Latin American literatures.

Lee Fontanella is currently Head of Humanities and Arts at Worcester Polytechnic Institute, Massachusetts. He has written a dozen books on photography, one on Spanish literature, delivered about 70 lectures and written nearly as many articles, book chapters, prefaces and reviews. His published books include: *Fillos da terra* (2001), *Lleida 1871: la visita del rei: Amadeu I de Savoia* (2000), *Charles Clifford: Fotógrafo en la Corte de Isabel II* (1997), *Charles Thurston Thompson e o proxecto fotográfico ibérico* (1996), *Diaphanoramas románticos* (1994), *Fotógrafos en la Sevilla del Siglo XIX* (1994), *Open Spain/España Abierta* (1992), *"Sem": Los Borbones en pelota* (1991) and *La historia de la fotografía en España, desde sus orígenes hasta 1900* (1981). His work is primarily in nineteenth-century cultural history, literary and visual sources.

David R. George, Jr. received a Ph.D. from the University of Minnesota-Twin Cities in September 2003. He is Lecturer at Bates College, Maine, where he teaches Spanish language, literature and culture. He has read and published papers on various aspects of nineteenth-century Peninsular literature and visual arts, as well as on film and popular culture of the early twentieth century. His recent work examines the role of Galdós's Second Series of the *Episodios nacionales* in citizen education and political socialization during the early Restoration period (1876–81).

Rebecca Haidt is Associate Professor of Spanish Literature at Ohio State University. Her book *Embodying Enlightenment: Knowing the Body in Eighteenth-Century Spanish Literature and Culture* (St. Martin's Press, 1998) was awarded the Modern Language Association's Katherine Singer Kovacs Prize for Outstanding Book published in the field of Latin American and Spanish Literature and Culture for 1999. Her latest publication is *Seduction and Sacrilege: Rhetorical Power in "Fray Gerundio de Campazas"* (Bucknell UP, 2002). She is currently finishing a book on women, work and the luxury marketplace in eighteenth-century Madrid, and her latest project is a study of visual cultures and early-nineteenth-century modernity.

Jo Labanyi is Professor of Spanish and Cultural Studies at the University of Southampton, UK, and a founding editor of the *Journal of Spanish Cultural Studies*. Her most recent books are *Gender and Modernization in the Spanish Realist Novel* (Oxford UP, 2000) and the edited volume *Constructing Identity in Contemporary Spain: Theoretical Debates and Cultural Practice* (Oxford UP, 2002). She is currently writing a book on 1940s Spanish cinema, and coordinating a five-year collaborative project *An Oral History of Cinema in 1940s and 1950s Spain*.

Susan Larson is Assistant Professor of Spanish at the University of Kentucky and managing editor of the *Arizona Journal of Hispanic Cultural Studies*. She has published articles in the areas of twentieth-century Spanish literature and urban studies and is currently studying the reciprocal relationship between urban planning, popular culture and the avant-garde during Madrid's early industrial period.

Geoffrey B. Pingree is Associate Professor of Cinema Studies and English at Oberlin College, Ohio. He received his Ph.D. from the University of Chicago in 1996 and taught at George Washington University, where he was director of the Institute for Documentary Filmmaking, and at Catholic University, where he was director of the Program in Media Studies. He has written on documentary cinema, film and history, and Spanish cinema, and he co-edited *New Media, 1740–1915* (MIT Press 2004). He is currently finishing a book on documentary cinema and the idea of Spain.

Joan Ramon Resina is Professor of Romance Studies and Comparative Literature at Cornell University, Ithaca, New York. He is the author of *La búsqueda del Grial* (Anthropos, 1988), *Un sueño de piedra: Ensayos sobre la literatura del modernismo europeo* (Anthropos, 1990), *Los usos del clásico* (Anthropos, 1991) and *El cadáver en la cocina: La novela policiaca en la cultura del desencanto* (Anthropos, 1997). He has edited six volumes: *Mythopoesis: Literatura, Totalidad, Ideología* (Anthropos, 1992), *El aeroplano y la estrella: El movimiento vanguardista en los Países Catalanes (1904–1936)* (Rodopi, 1997), *Disremembering the Dictatorship: The Politics of Memory since the Spanish Transition to Democracy*. (Rodopi, 2000), *Iberian Cities* (Routledge, 2001), *After-Images of the City*, co-edited with Dieter Ingenschay (Cornell UP, 2003), and *Casa encantada: Lugares de memoria en la España constitucional (1978–2004)*, co-edited with Ulrich Winter (Vervuert, 2005). Among his distinctions are the Fulbright Fellowship and the Alexander von Humboldt Fellowship.

Jesusa Vega is Lecturer in Modern and Contemporary Art in Madrid's Universidad Autónoma. Her research interests include the history of prints in Spain, Francisco de Goya especially works on paper and Spanish art in the eighteenth and nineteenth centuries. Her most recent publication is *Vestir la identidad, construir la apariencia. La cuestión del traje en la España del siglo XVIII* (Ayuntamiento de Madrid, 2005). She is currently directing the subsidized research project, *Visual Culture: The Construction of Memory and Identity in Contemporary Spain*.

Eva Woods is Assistant Professor at Vassar College, Poughkeepsie, New York, in Hispanic Studies and Media Studies. She is currently finishing the book *White "Gypsies": Racing for Modernity in Spanish Stardom and Folkloric Musical Films, 1923–1954* (Minnesota UP, 2006). She is also involved in the collaborative book project, *Cinema and the Mediation of Everyday Life: An Oral History of Cinema-Going in 1940s and 1950s Spain* (Berghahn 2006), led by Jo Labanyi. With a grant from the Delmas fund she is investigating the role of visual media in portraying the border between Spain and Africa since the late nineteenth century.

–1–

Visualizing Spanish Modernity: Introduction

Susan Larson and Eva Woods

> History decays into images, not into stories.
>
> Walter Benjamin[1]

Benjamin's prophetic words remind us that history is less a narrative than a series of visual moments or scenes which inescapably permeate the present as well as the past. We see with modern eyes: the way history "looked" is lost to us, yet at the same time reborn through our present-day vision. Historicizing Spain's visual culture is, therefore, a task of historical perception, of making out constellations of dialectical images that hover between the past and the present and making them our own.[2] For Benjamin, the material culture of the past is recognizable only through fleeting and instantaneous images that, when unrecognized as constitutive of the present, "threaten to disappear irretrievably" (*Illuminations* 255). Although we can never see the past as it really was, we must, according to Benjamin, "seize hold of a memory as it flashes up [unexpectedly] at a moment of danger" (255). The urgency conveyed by Benjamin's theory of history could not have been more acute. Fascism's power to manipulate images and the meanings of history needed to be countered by a critical historical materialism that could "brush history against the grain" (257). One of the primary aims of this collection is to excavate the visuality of Spain's past in order to better ground interpretations of Spain's mid- to late-twentieth-century cultures of fascism, dictatorship, democracy, and late capitalism. Benjamin's concerns echo throughout these chapters as they interrogate how we visualize modernity in Spain, and more specifically, how our understanding of Spain has been mediated and shaped by modern technologies of vision since the nineteenth century.[3]

These chapters offer a series of views into the past that describe the modern experience in Spain as varied, discontinuous, inescapably plural and consisting of mixed speeds and spaces. Perception in modernity, as Benjamin described it, entailed jolts, distractions, and the constant shock of the new, all provoked by the mechanized world. Developments in train technology, trolleys, and eventually subways required individuals to accustom their senses to different experiences of motion, space, and time. As elsewhere, the emergence of panoramic or filmic vision compounded with these other sensory onslaughts provoked an attitude that was at once blasé and defensive.[4] Through photography and cinema, the current of subjective experience could now be mobilized and reconfigured onto a filmic image that reanimated the frozen image, promising seemingly infinite possibilities for the spectator. Visionaries such as Etienne-Jules Marey and Edward Muybridge endeavored to atomize time itself through experiments with chronophotography, "the photography of time."[5] As the history of European philosophy has shown through its consistent use of visual metaphors, Western culture has been driven to visualize, and images of motion in space and time seemed to capture the very essence of modern life.[6]

In Spain, in the period between 1830 and 1936, dramatic technological advances allowed for greater reproducibility of the image and the corresponding growth of visual culture.[7] Commonly heard expressions such as "cinema is the motor of modernity" place our present moment in an historical context, while making the nineteenth century an "indispensable starting point" for visual culture studies (Schwartz and Przyblyski xxi). Since we now live in a "visual age" and are more visually literate than at any preceding time, it is essential to incorporate the study of visual culture, practices of looking, and visuality into the methodologies of Spanish Peninsular Studies.[8] This volume has grown out of a desire to address this issue. It is a collaborative, interdisciplinary project concerned with engaging the meaning of what Benjamin called the "Age of Mechanical Reproduction" in Spain, an age which went hand in hand with shifts in practices of consumption, urban growth, changing gender roles, new ideas of race, nation and ethnicity, the expansion of leisure, and the creation of a new entertainment industry and information technologies.

The chapters in this collection map the relationship between the visual and modernity in Spain, starting with the objects and practices of mass culture that interact or comment upon the production and consumption of images. Each chapter contains arguments about various media that are informed by theories developed in a wide variety of disciplines. These references to diverse media and visual practices support Jonathan Crary's assertion that "[t]he circulation and reception of *all* visual imagery [was] so closely interrelated by the middle of the [nineteenth] century that any single medium or form of visual representation no longer had a significant autonomous identity" (23). Nowadays, the "collapse of the media into each other" can be seen in the juxtaposition of music, text, video and image on the Internet, or the conflation of video, multimedia performance and installation art (Elkins 42). But this collapse was already beginning to occur in the nineteenth century. Many of the chapters collected here reflect on the blurred boundaries between high and low culture, both of which were increasingly subject to commodification, or absorbed by commercial culture. Postmodern aesthetics were already partially visible. Now as then, distinctions between high and low are being superseded. At the level of production and distribution, "cultural workers today actually or potentially rely on much the same technologies and institutions" while at the level of reception, "the meanings of all products of contemporary culture tend to be cut from much the same cloth [...]. As there are no longer any definitively separate realms of cultural production, it follows that there can be no islands of counterhegemonic purity" (Burgin 20).

The chapters in this collection also examine the spaces in which these practices of vision existed, the complicit and contestatory modes that they provided, and their role in forming viewing subjects into modern Spanish citizens. Our contributors describe the social, political, and cultural meanings of urban spaces (Davidson, Haidt, Fernández Cifuentes, Larson), railroads (Haidt, Woods), museums (Fernández Cifuentes, Labanyi, Vega), photography (Charnon-Deutsch, Epps, Fontanella, Resina), illustrated magazines (Charnon-Deutsch, Davidson, Cueto Asín, Haidt), painting (Fanès, Labanyi), international exhibits and fairs (Davidson, Vega), serialized or popular literature (George, Fernández Cifuentes, Bush, Resina), cinema (Larson, Woods, Pingree, Resina), and popular theater (Larson). The chapters differ in their methodologies and disciplinary assumptions, but all acknowledge a modern optic by means of overlapping visual media at different scales – the high and the low, the national and the micronational, the public and the private, and the gendered male and female. Spain is seen both from within and without, represented in very different ways to itself and for itself, and from in and outside of its geographical borders.[9]

Many of the chapters in *Visualizing Spanish Modernity* identify a common polemic. In their interpretations of modernity and the changing notions of subjectivity and viewership in Spain, these authors locate an anxiety over the desire to represent a coherent vision of Spanish modernity through artistic means, a desire that was frustrated by the difficulty of expressing the material realities of Spain's modernization and its utopian dream of modernity through mass-produced media. How would the different viewing publics react to these conflicted images? More than one reading was certainly possible in Madrid's Prado Museum in the late nineteenth century, for example, which had opened to the public following its nationalization in 1868. Museum-goers who entered on Sunday, the day free of charge to the general public, tended to read the artwork differently from those who paid full price during the rest of the week (Labanyi, Fernández Cifuentes). Spanish popular audiences had been schooled to read visual images in terms of religious allegory. As a result, economically disadvantaged spectators who could not afford the museum's catalogue often mistook Velázquez's *La rendición de Breda* for St. Peter proffering the keys to the pearly gates because the Prado did not display the titles of the paintings until the start of the twentieth century. Traveling sideshows, exhibitions and fairs showcased historical paintings as larger-than-life wax tableaux, further reinforcing popular interpretations of high art and the mixing of high and low.

Several studies examine how cultural artifacts such as painting, photography, lithography, or collage belonged to a conventional, familiar genre or defined new generic boundaries, as did so much mass-produced culture in the "Age of Mechanical Reproduction". Collage, for example, confronted observers with a foregrounded medium, while the object in question receded from view. The aura of the object, which created the traditionally intimate relationship between spectator and artwork, was consciously destabilized in the collages of Miró, who refused the cultural hierarchies of high and low art by ritualizing the popular (Fanès). Indeed, the nature of audiences and their expectations were undergoing major shifts as modes of production and consumption continued to shift. It was clear that realism could not satisfy the visual expectations and desires that were developing in the Spanish nation.[10]

Contributors to this volume seek to avoid the commonly held assumption that Spain's modernity was radically different from that of the rest of Europe. Instead, they attempt to historicize the relationship between vision and modernity as existing within the larger processes of European and Western modernity, and as accompanied by the many ambivalences and contradictions that sustain it. Simplistic and sometimes demonized concepts of Spanish modernity serve only to justify a fervent defense of a postmodern condition that fails to fully explain the heterogeneous social, political and cultural dynamics of the nineteenth and early twentieth centuries. Such arguments attempt to demonstrate a clear progression from the modern to the postmodern, from the technologically ignorant and easily manipulated to the media-savvy citizen of the present world. Anxious to break with their Francoist past, enthusiasts of the postmodern aesthetic have oftentimes produced a grand narrative of their own, distorting and simplifying the nature of Spanish modernism. There is a tendency to see the modern observer in general and the Spanish in particular as primitive, backward and naïve compared to the supposedly culturally aware postmodern global citizen. In *A Singular Modernity* (2002), however, Frederic Jameson (2–5) questions whether the features of the modern – asceticism, phallocentrism, logocentrism, to name a few – were as undesirable, repressive, or omnipresent as the postmodernists thought they were. He now admits that he and other postmodernists may not have done modernism justice.

Studies of European modernity, modernization and modernism have traditionally relied on an inadequate number of European examples.[11] The chapters here provide a corrective to such descriptions, envisioning an exchange of cultural practices between the center and margin, between Spain and the rest of Europe, and among Spain's wide array of regions, cultural communities and colonies. [12] This fluid interaction is an inherent characteristic of the chaotic and tumultuous process of modernity everywhere. Even the most hegemonic of modernities draws on the peripheral or the marginal (Geist and Monleón). The specificity of Spain's modernity does not mean that it lies outside of a larger European modernity (France, Germany, England) or that Spain arrives "late" to modernity, as is so often assumed. Nineteenth- and early-twentieth-century Spanish imperialism in Africa has been explained as a strategy to "catch up" with Europe's advance into the African continent, yet France and Britain relied on Spain's participation in suppressing Moroccan resistance in order to offset German expansion into the area. [13] Spain was therefore materially and symbolically necessary to the larger European claims that capitalist modernity was a justification for imperialism.[14]

Not surprisingly, a general definition of Spanish modernity as quixotic or recalcitrant collapses in the face of a serious consideration of Spain's colonial subjects and what can be termed Castile's "internal regional others." Robert A. Davidson, for instance, examines *Mirador*, the literary and *modernista* Catalonian journal published from 1929 to 1932, which battled censorship from Madrid and took an intense interest in the cultural specificity of Barcelona. His Chapter 12 presents an alternate vision of the city's development and resistance to hegemonic Castilian culture. In her study of Santiago Rusiñol's travel writing, Elena Cueto Asín demonstrates in Chapter 8 how Catalans like the painter Rusiñol fall into the trap of culturally colonizing the southern Andalusian region, while Jesusa Vega documents in Chapter 11 the efforts of liberal, secular-minded intellectuals to preserve regional, popular ways of dressing against a homogenizing modernity imposed from without. Eva Woods explains in Chapter 15 how seemingly gratuitous plot digressions in silent films depicted traumatizing yet adventurous journeys to "exotic" lands, offering glimpses at what lay "outside" of modernity, and thereby justifying Spain's modernization. These chapters and others explore how race and class collide with the fears and hopes of advancing technological progress, and consider the new modes of social organization that accompany modernization. Paying close attention to the tendentious power relations between Spain's now autonomous regions – Catalonia and Andalusia in particular – as well as to the shadow of its former colonies, this collection reframes the debate on Spanish modernity: Spain is a European "other" *and* dependent upon its own internal and colonial "others."[15]

How we conceptualize Spain's modernity as we draw the line between the present and the past, however, is generally bound up with Enlightenment understandings of progress and social development and with nineteenth-century historicism, which saw Spain as a unified entity within a specific historical development (Chakrabarty x). Seen thus, Spanish history has been articulated as both subject and object of modernity and has assumed a unified body called the Spanish people, which was nevertheless split into a forward looking and modern elite, and an unmodern peasantry (Chakrabarty 40). Historicism made capitalist modernity "look not just global but global over time, by originating in [central] Europe and then spreading out." Historical time, as a measure of the cultural distance assumed to exist between that center and its periphery (Chakrabarty 47), was thus used to define Spain's time as coeval with that of Europe's, and to deny the possibility of "other" times, especially those of the former Spanish colonies. For these and other reasons, Hispanic Studies must question the legacy of nineteenth-century historicism by engaging in close study of Spain's visual discourses of modernity, which cross constraining disciplinary boundaries yet retain a dialectical understanding of the modern.

Capitalist modernity and its philosophy of liberalism are based on what many, inspired by Marx, have termed "creative destruction": the process by which technological progress and human emancipation for the few go hand in hand with instability, alienation, injustice and violence for many. Benjamin was also troubled by modernity's dark side: "There is no document of culture that is not at the same time a document of barbarism" (*Illuminations* 256). Modern culture is never any one thing or even a set of fixed objects. Culture exists only as an idea, yet an idea developed and deployed in the modern (and postmodern) world as a means of ordering, controlling and defining "others" in the name of power and profit. Much recent work in the field of visual studies cites Benjamin, sometimes uncritically celebrating the "liberating effects" of early consumer culture's "spectacular Woman," for example, while avoiding any mention of the concurrent exploitation of female workers. In Spain, the imposition of modernity led to a brutal, chaotic industrial development and an accelerated rhythm of life, exacerbated by mass media images that seemed to legitimate modernity's empty promises of a new world (Subirats, *Después de la lluvia* 27). Many Spaniards ran headlong towards this idealized future, basing their hopes on images from more industrially developed countries while denying or wishing away their own surroundings. Modernity's promise of salvation was not always grounded in Spanish historical or material reality.

The dates framing this collection – roughly the 1830s to 1939, the end of the Spanish Civil War – mark the beginning of a modern economy in Spain and the consolidation of the liberal nation state, as well as the growth of the urban centers and spaces of public leisure and spectacle made possible by electricity, transportation, mass production and an entertainment industry. The liberal revolution of 1868 galvanized Spain's transition to modernity (Fusi and Palafox 20–65) and fundamentally altered visuality. The trappings of the modern state expanded into all areas of national life through the standardization of an educational system, a national press, the centralized railway, suffrage, the central state's attempt to incorporate, organize and monitor independent-minded regions, universities, academies and learned societies, the legal codification of the public sphere, the drafting of a national anthem, a uniform tax system, a regular national census, and the creation of the Guardia Civil. These social and economic reforms were designed to bring the whole of the national territory under state jurisdiction and into a single market economy, affecting private as well as public life. As many of the chapters point out, the general reorganization of society in nineteenth-century Spain transformed the experience of looking and the concept of the visual, thereby requiring the formation of new kinds of viewers capable of processing and assimilating a new sense of nation and citizenship.

To be sure, Western culture had become decidedly ocularcentric well before the nineteenth century. Vision had been privileged at least as early as Plato's notion that ethical universals must be accessible to "the mind's eye." In the Renaissance, Cartesian perspectivalism, the invention of printing, devices such as the camera obscura, and the development of the modern sciences reinforced the hegemony of vision (Jay 186–189). More modern notions of vision began to evolve with the institutional arrangements of the eighteenth century, in which "looking and the gaze became central to the production of knowledge and the regulation of subjects" (Evans 15). Foucault's analysis of Jeremy Bentham's architectural model of the panopticon, originally designed in 1787 for a prison, for example, shows how the power of surveillance, whether constant or sporadic, produces self-regulating behavior from individuals (Jay 195–228). The visual had become instrumental to the systematic acquisition of power and knowledge over the body. With capitalist modernity, vision and the laboring body became mechanized, measurable and thus exchangeable. Likewise, new optical devices and their practices and spaces of observation made viewers of both high and low culture into consumers of commodities.

In Spain and elsewhere, the normalization of observation fitted modern citizens for the task of consuming images. It is therefore ironic that as technologies of vision became more advanced in the nineteenth and twentieth centuries, the privileging of sight began to inspire deep mistrust. When in the mid-nineteenth century, vast improvements in the microscope offered a new view of the world, rendering the naked eye insufficient for observing or knowing "truth," reality no longer seemed as controllable or visually knowable as previously thought. Lack of confidence in the visual was mirrored by the decentering of the subject, now conceived as a split entity divided by Freud's discovery of the unconscious and by a greater intellectual understanding of economy and class as outlined by Marx. Ideology, as Marx and Engels described it in *The German Ideology*, seemed more like a visual illusion than true consciousness: "If in all ideology men and their circumstances appear upside down as in a *camera obscura*, this phenomenon arises just as much from their historical life-process as the inversion of objects on the retina does from their physical life-process" (Marx and Engels 46). Thinkers from Marx to Foucault would later launch critiques of the disciplining of the subject under capitalism, with pointed references to the normalization of vision and the training of the modern spectator for purposes of surveillance and control.

Such rethinking of the subject and questioning of the authority of vision is critical to an understanding of Spanish writers and thinkers such as José Ortega y Gasset, who by 1910 had begun to outline his ideas on perspectivism. In contrast to rationalist thinking that asserted one truth or one reality after subjective points of view had been factored out, Ortega y Gassett argued that individual points of view were valid perspectives on reality, and that "there were as many spaces of reality as there were perspectives on it" (Kern 151). Philosophers of vision after Ortega y Gasset would use similar insights to analyze modern surveillance techniques, and to critique the society of the spectacle, ocular metaphors such as the "gaze," and the objectification of women. The visual would become suspect and even threatening as a form of control, a manipulative inversion on both individual and collective, real and symbolic levels.

With the twentieth century, changes including the increasing mechanization of Spanish life, the concentration of an organized working class in the city centers, new definitions of womanhood, and the secularization of education during the Second Republic aggravated ambivalent feelings about Spain's uncomfortable and irregular encounters with modernization. This tension only increased with the additional economic, political and social strain imposed by the colonial wars in Africa. Photography and later cinema, through both private and government sponsored documentary films, brought the war home, assaulting the Spanish national imagination at a critical time when Spain was losing its most valued colonies (Cuba, Puerto Rico, the Philippines and Guam) and pursuing colonialist expansion into Africa. Class tensions that would culminate in the 1936 Spanish Civil War and the dictatorship of General Francisco Franco would bear witness to other shifts in perception, such as the formation of a viewership in the service of the ever more inward-looking, centralized state, buttressed by National Catholic ideology.

Yet fascism and Francoism in Spain were far from pre-modern. Despite the fact that they appropriated pre-Enlightenment rhetoric and consistently returned to previous aesthetic styles such as Herreran neo-classicism, they skillfully manipulated the newest forms of media. By many historical accounts, the Nationalists were far more successful than the Republicans in utilizing radio and film through government subsidies and censorship.[16] Many historians have cited fascism as the highest (and most terrifying and reactionary) form of aesthetic modernism and modernity.[17] Benjamin's urgent call to understand images in their context and their relationship to the present is one that has been answered by many Hispanic Studies scholars, but it remains for us to more fully understand the period leading up to fascism and dictatorship in Spain – that is, the nineteenth century up through the 1930s.[18]

To illustrate the complexity of nineteenth- and early-twentieth-century viewership, we cite a dilemma faced by scholars of visual culture and modernity in Spain that derives from some widely held beliefs about the introduction of cinema to turn-of-the-century spectators. Film historians uniformly hold that early cinema (usually actualities, or short clips of real-life events such as the release of factory workers from their place of work, and other urban activities) projected an image of modernity to viewers who experienced their nation as anything but modern, but were nevertheless drawn to the dynamic images on the screen. The attraction to film came both from seeing the image itself and from the radically different type of viewing experience made possible by film technology. Cinema projected modernity, and was, for film's first spectators, an instance of modernity itself, thereby complicating, enriching or double-coding every instance of the visual in modern society.

In nearly every nation's film history there is an anecdote that tells the story of the birth of its cinema. In Spain, the story goes something like this: in 1896, the widely circulated Lumière brothers' actuality of a train pulling into the station in Lyon, *La llegada de un tren* (The Arrival of a Train), terrified Spanish audiences, who believed the image would continue its trajectory right through the screen (Torres 16; López Serrano 87; Lorenzo Díaz 26). In Spain, this initial sensationalistic media event created a demand for more such actualities.[19] Film historians have repeatedly used these events to demonstrate what they believe to be the naïveté and visual innocence of the first moviegoers. With no discussion of pre-cinematic practices, they leave the reader with the impression that film audiences were perpetually stunned by images of the real world captured within the confines of the flat screen. Spanish film histories consistently cite the same anecdote about *La llegada de un tren*, registering the irony of the backward Spaniard who watches modern train technology through the very device that epitomizes modernity, the cinema. The audience's astonishment and fear are seen as a metaphor for Spain's anxiety over its decidedly unmodern status; another well-known image of two trains crashing into one another is said to suggest that Spanish modernity is inevitably doomed, if not entirely impossible.

But there is another way of interpreting this event that problematizes the all-too-familiar notions of Spanish backwardness that obscure a deeper understanding of Spain's modernity. Against the standard view of the film's viewers as uneducated, pre-modern spectators, Tom Gunning doubts that their astonishment came from confusing the representation of the train with reality. Instead he suggests that viewers experienced what in Media Studies is called an "immediacy with the image." Spectators watched the film but were unaware of it as a product of technology because the film erased the traces of its own medium. Despite the image's mediation by cinema – despite the knowledge that the film was just a film and not a real train crashing through the screen – their belief was momentarily suspended, or perhaps held in parallel suspension along with their belief in the reality of their location in the nickelodeon or alternative viewing space. What astonished them was the discrepancy between what they knew and what they saw with their eyes.

Audiences were aware of this gap and even became conscious of their desire for immediacy and their simultaneous need to experience that immediacy through media. It was this desire that created the demand for more sensationalist images. At the core of this common anecdote and our questioning of its cultural meaning, then, is the challenge and even the necessity to rethink and rehistoricize our assumptions about observers and viewing practices of this period. Many of the chapters here reconsider the simplistic notion of a naïve pre-modern audience by emphasizing the idea that visuality is a social process, one "informed by the various interests and desires of the viewer, and by the social relations that exist between the perceiver and the perceived" (Chaplin and Walker 22). Viewers and spectators are not simple entities, neither stable nor fixed across time, and they function within a social and psychic process: their "subjective desires and capacities" inform their reading of texts while simultaneously enabling them "to take up positions of identification in relation to [a text's] meaning" (Hall 310–11).

The following descriptions of the chapters emphasize the individuality of each contribution and point out their many interconnections. Avoiding the disciplinary boundaries of literary studies, art history, or history, they offer a network of ideas, approaches, and case studies whose differences often complement one another, informing the debate about the nature of modernity in Spain and the role of visuality in its evolution. We see the case studies as useful historical and cultural background for understanding Spain's modernity, while the cultural theories they employ serve as a grid for discussions of other cultural texts. Most of all, these contributions are an invitation to future interdisciplinarity in their attempt to break out of commonly held assumptions about Spain's modern culture in the nineteenth and early twentieth centuries.

The Chapters

Rebecca Haidt historicizes the writer and journalist Mesonero Romanos' attempts to make ideas more "perceptible" through printed images and their juxtaposition with written narrative. According to him, increased perceptibility would improve Spain's access to the advantages of modernity. Haidt's Chapter 2, "Visibly Modern Madrid: Mesonero, Visual Culture, and the Apparatus of Urban Reform," sets Mesonero's urban reform initiatives within the contexts of Madrid's visual cultures in the 1830s and 1840s, such as magic lantern shows, fashion displays, urban guides and the ever-pervasive coexistence of text and image. She considers how the paired discourses of sight and modernity were present in Mesonero's work with illustrated newspapers (such as *Semanario Pintoresco Español*), with journalistic media (*Diario de Avisos de Madrid* and the *Semanario*), and with tourism-oriented publishing ventures such as his repeatedly re-edited *Manual de Madrid* (1831). At stake for Mesonero Romanos was the question of how to draw visitors and investment to Madrid when it was not widely considered to be a site of worldwide cultural or economic importance. Yet by training viewers to perceive their city – new urban development projects, for example – through the latest developments in visual information technologies, citizens not only would become more literate in rational modes of viewing, but also would be instilled with a spirit of "public prosperity and civic awareness."

In light of nineteenth-century theories of vision and contemporary work in the field of visual culture, David R. George, Jr. traces in Chapter 3 how the metaphorical and literal uses of vision in the novel provide Restoration Spain with a mapping of political citizenship based on the model of the spectator. He asserts that the nineteenth-century realist novel, exemplified by Benito Pérez Galdós's Second Series of *Episodios nacionales*, was thoroughly invested in debates on the subjective nature of vision and its relation to the political problem of educating and controlling Spain's middle-class urban and especially female citizens. The discourses of vision are particularly salient in the treatment of female protagonists, whose experiences are narrated with ample references to the faculty of sight, blindness, optical illusions and delusions caused by dementia, obsession, ignorance or loss of consciousness. As observers of the political spectacle of the Fernandine period, the success of these women as citizens is directly tied to the positioning of their bodies before an appropriate "optical device" that would allow them to see reality clearly. Such locating renders them visible and therefore makes them available as potential subjects to be represented and controlled as citizens in the political public sphere. Through the description of how women see, Galdós comments upon the relationship between attempts to normalize sight and the creation of a consensus necessary to transform Spanish society.

The training of citizens-as-spectators is fundamentally tied to the construction and evolution of popular spectatorship and burgeoning mass culture in the late nineteenth and early twentieth centuries in Spain. In Chapter 4 "Horror, Spectacle and Nation-formation: Historical Painting in Late-nineteenth-century Spain," Jo Labanyi studies the slippage between high cultural and mass cultural modes of spectatorship, showing how museums and painting not only were mediated by practices of consumption but also relied on realist modes of representation to educate viewers about democracy and modern citizenship. Reading two paintings – Francisco Pradilla y Ortiz's (1877) *Doña Juana la Loca* and José Casado del Alisal's (1880) *Leyenda del rey monje* (reproduced in 1880s waxwork shows and concurrently in National Art Exhibitions at the Prado Museum) – Labanyi shows how particular representations of the nation's past incorporated sensationalist images of horror and death even while they functioned as a pedagogy of citizenship via spectatorship. By analyzing the politics of looking, class relations, and notions of justice represented in the paintings, and by historicizing the reality of their viewing context, Labanyi gives us access to a new view of historical painting characterized not as an elitist cultural experience, but as a complex popular practice that attempted to instill responsible civic relations and modes of viewing appropriate to modern citizens.

The museum, like printed matter, archives the historical emphasis of vision, and was one of the most distinctive features of the visual experience at the turn of the century. In Chapter 5 "Isidora in the Museum," Luis Fernández Cifuentes discusses the nature of visuality and how Benito Pérez Galdós's realist novel *La desheredada* (1909) interfaces with the visual logic and appeal of the museum, as well as with issues of corporeality and narrativity. The museum joins an array of new modes of technology, representation, spectacle, distraction, consumerism and entertainment crucial to the training of the modern urban gaze. Programs, guidebooks, souvenir biographies, promotional material, and popular serialized novels like *La desheredada* all influenced the viewing expectations of the public, and linked institutions of the visible by steering interpretations of visual attractions in directions acceptable to middle-class viewers. At the same time, viewing habits were fluid and not always uniform. As the fictional character Isidora's experience of the Prado Museum demonstrates, the disjunction between an institution's ostensible purpose and the variety of its uses by spectators highlights the contradiction that a museum's founding definition and its eventual social function were not necessarily identical.

Andrew Bush reflects in Chapter 6 on the writings of Walter Benjamin, Ramón Gómez de la Serna, and Mesonero Romanos. He structures his discussion with the motif of the camera obscura in Benjamin, microscopes and glasses in Gómez de la Serna's description of Madrid's Rastro (flea market), and the significance of the telescope to Mesonero Romanos's musings on Madrid's important monument, the Puerta de Toledo. Central to his interpretation of these three space-times is the idea of receptive vision: a kind of vision that is neither passive nor active but located, as he puts it, at a threshold that is both welcoming and receiving. This alternative vision disrupts the subject-centered and egocentric viewpoint. By examining this in-between space, Bush explores how objects can momentarily acquire values that lie beyond the homogenous time of capitalism (beyond exchange and use value), and instead become "precious," or collectable, visibly different to the glimpse of the receptive eye. It is significant that this transformation occurs at the border of Madrid, a place of entrance and exit, and a place that accumulates the detritus of society. Here, among the market activities, spaces of preciousness might appear, even if only in the form of fragments, shocks, or glimpses of an incomplete object. Finally, Bush grounds this visual ambivalence in Romanticism, showing how the Romantic vision of the threshold provided grounding for turn-of-the-century modes of seeing inanimate objects.

Visions of the past or of the nation that are partial constitute another alternative mode of seeing. In Chapter 7 "Seeing the Dead: Manual and Mechanical Specters in Modern Spain (1893–1939)," Brad Epps considers the ties and tensions between manual and mechanical representations of death and those condemned to death in four 1894 drawings of Anarchists by Santiago Rusiñol, and a 1936 photograph by Agustí Centelles of the victims of street fighting at the outbreak of the Spanish Civil War. Epps connects the importance of death for the national imagination to the tendency of writers (Barthes, Sontag and Derrida) to see photography in terms of death and its obliteration of meaning, arguing that the sketch should also be considered in light of cultural and national drives to ascribe meaning to death. Reassessing the status of the sketch alongside photography, Epps reads it through a theory of vision that is historically attuned to the medium's violent national context. For Epps, the differences between the two mediums yield a fractured picture of a fragmented place (Catalonia, not "sovereign Spain"), calling into question the viability of "seeing" (a) culture, with its objective and subjective turns, its necessities and accidents. Only in the particularities can we see a tearing apart of homogenous Spanish identity into an infinite difference that makes other nationalisms visible in Spain. Epps thus calls for a history of the nation enabled by partial vision, a binocular vision that embraces shared viewings, which are crucial for feeling compassion in art. Only a vision that employs glances and partial views as opposed to "necessary" monocular vision will be able to move beyond the apparent differences between the drawings, in order to see how both are prone to blind spots, omissions, and chance.

In Chapter 8, Elena Cueto Asín looks at a different aspect of Santiago Rusiñol's artistic production in "Santiago Rusiñol's *Impresiones de arte* in the Age of Tourism: Seeing Andalusia after Seeing Paris." Like Labanyi and Fernández Cifuentes, Cueto Asín studies the breakdown of the aura of the Romantic artist, distanced and cosmopolitan, and the inevitable, necessary mixing of this "legitimate" observer with the fledgling, yet already highly commercialized practice of tourism that marketed new ways of seeing monuments, cities, and travel to larger sectors of the population. Rusiñol's critique of a prosaic, rational modernity is only possible, however, through technological developments such as trains, urban planning, and guidebooks that provide the material for his cosmopolitan travels. Cueto Asín focuses her discussion on a series of articles collected in the volume *Impresiones de arte*, written when Rusiñol traveled to Paris and Italy, and the *Cartas de Andalucía* (*Letters from Andalusia*), that Rusiñol was commissioned to write by the Barcelona daily *La Vanguardia*. As literature and as cultural testimonial, these articles, argues Cueto Asín, are as worthy of critical attention as his paintings, and contribute valuable information to an understanding of the figure of the tourist as a significant element of modern culture. In these journalistic chronicles, Rusiñol adopts the model of the international travel writer whose intellectual activity distances him from the figure of the conventional tourist. While in the cultural capitals of Europe, the artist strives to see himself as the impressionistic explorer, mediating the foreign through his exploration of the self, and defining that self against the multitude. When this Catalan travels to Andalusia, however, his view becomes imbued with colonialist overtones: his interest in the architectural "riches" of the south, coupled with his reformist concern for abject social conditions, betray a more ambivalent attitude toward marginality and the external forces of modernity.

Lee Fontanella in Chapter 9 "Landscape in the Photography of Spain," also discusses the importance of the traveling Romantic artist, but in relation to pictorialist, or "painterly" landscape photography and its development through the nineteenth and twentieth centuries. Contrary to many assumptions about the inherent objectivity of photography, he argues, photography, more than painting, expressed the subjective potential of landscape. In much Spanish landscape photography, landscape is invented as if the artists had fallen upon a scene and then subjectively interpreted it, personalizing landscape and the artist's affective encounter with it. As photography matures, then, it moves towards a subjective artistry more often associated with painting. Fontanella draws upon examples in which landscape was photographed because it had an affective value, evoking the Romantic idea of the individual in concert with nature. Rather than the details of landscape, the viewing subject became the object of contemplation, implied by the human experience with the land, such as the difficulty of climbing to a vantage point to scope the terrain. At the Spanish border where the sea threatens to engulf the land, for instance, photography per se "mattered" to Spanish photographers. In nineteenth-century peripatetic photographic excursions, however, the photographer felt less of a connection to the landscape, and relied instead on a realist mode that focused on exotic details at the expense of landscape. For this reason, a touristic mode of seeing predominated in nineteenth-century landscape photography until its collusion with a pictorialist vision that coincided with modernism in Spain. This later impressionistic focus on mood and atmosphere was also seen in the work of the pictorialist photographer Ortiz Echagüe, who attempted to make sense of Spain's political chaos through personalized landscapes, in contrast to the journalistic realism that became dominant around the time of the Civil War.

Shedding light on the evolution of photography in relation to the illustrated newspaper is Chapter 10, "From Engraving to Photo: Cross-cut Technologies in the Spanish Illustrated Press." Lou Charnon-Deutsch outlines the introduction of photography and subsequent photomechanical technologies and the images that they produced for publication in late-nineteenth-century illustrated magazines, which evolved from upscale, limited-run productions to mass-produced periodicals targeting a middle-class readership. She examines this transformation in two of Madrid's most popular periodicals during the thirty-year period from 1880 to 1910, widely considered the heyday of the Spanish illustrated weeklies: *El Museo Universal*, which would eventually become Abelardo de Carlos's *La Ilustración*

Española y Americana, the most lavish and prestigious of Spanish illustrated magazines, and the more affordable and widely read *Blanco y Negro*. Charnon-Deutsch traces important changes in compositional techniques and print quality, editorial comments about new photo technologies, the explosion of photographic reporting in the 1890s, and the reasons for the eclipse of the large-format illustrated weeklies. Addressing these issues, she concludes that engraving and photography were codependent technologies; that photography impacted the engravers as a workforce prior to and following the invention of photomechanical reproduction, and that engraving influenced the thematic and political content of the first photographs.

Jesusa Vega in Chapter 11, "Spain's Image in Regional Dress: From Everyday Object to Museum Piece and Tourist Attraction" argues that reform initiatives arose in opposition to cultural directives that strove to safeguard regional ways of dressing that seemed threatened by modernity. Liberal intellectuals recognized the development of mass communication and industrialization as agents of change, yet were concerned over this irretrievable loss of regional culture. Paradoxically, some of these same intellectuals criticized foreign writers who obsessively catalogued the singularities of Spanish attire in their need to construct an exotic Spain. But this recuperation of the past paired with a colonial nostalgia required uplifting social narratives that would project confidence onto a population ravaged by wars and economic hardship. The spectacle of past traditions (in this case, dress) could ironically promote much-needed icons of national or regional identity that would last into an unstable and unknown future. Traditional dress would acquire new meanings and values because of the production of visions of the past and the construction of subjects in order to read that past. Clothing would remain in museums, deemed worthy of exhibition and study. This new role for popular or folk dress was showcased in the first large exhibit of Spanish traditional dress, organized between 1921 and 1925 in Madrid and highlighted in articles and photographs in the national and regional press, in the creation of the Museum of Dress (Museo del Traje, later the Museo del Pueblo Español), and in El Pueblo Español at the International Exposition in Barcelona in 1929.

To this day, El Pueblo Español is touted as an educational space for cultural edification and leisure, the jewel in the crown of the Spanish heritage industry that offers visitors the possibility of getting to know all seventeen autonomous communities through handicraft markets, cultural displays, samples of food and folk shows – a symbolic tour through the cultural diversity of the Spanish state. But what has this space meant for the inhabitants of Barcelona? Robert A. Davidson describes how literary journals and newspapers have historically played an important role in the consolidation of Catalan culture in "Observing the City, Mediating the Mountain: *Mirador* and the 1929 International Exposition of Barcelona" (Chapter 12). Optics, politics and the competing national subjectivities of a modernizing country under a dictatorship combined to make the Barcelona Fair much more than a simple trade show or celebration of a utopian future. Sizeable meetings, international exhibitions drew together the latest products of ingenuity and labor and exposed them to the public gaze in vast modern pavilions. Once the disparate components of a fair were in place, the exposition became a fantasy world of economic possibilities, a carnival of reification and visual extravagance. *Mirador* enhanced the relationship between the exposition and its local spectators. First appearing in 1929, it marked the transition between Barcelona's past and future, ironically projecting a new urban and cultural vision from where the restrictive medieval wall had stood, as if holding the city and its inhabitants captive, until the 1850s.

In Chapter 13, art historian Félix Fanès confronts essential questions about visual representation and the relationship to high and low culture in the modern, industrial age in "Joan Miró, 1929: High and Low Culture in Barcelona and Paris." Miró moved in two distinct but overlapping circles during the late 1920s: the Catalan anti-artists of *L'Amic de les Arts* on the one hand, and Bataille's group of dissident surrealists on the other. Both were resistant to hierarchies within the world of artistic expression, and both fiercely proposed the use of "bad taste" in their search for what Gasch termed "unexpected forms of sudden intensity." In his close analysis of Miró's untitled 1929 collage, Fanès employs the concept of concealment as outlined by Michael Leiris and Walter Benjamin. An essential characteristic of the image in the industrial age, concealment, they wrote, responded to the desire to preserve images by literally hiding them within a medium. Miró's use of concealment, according to Fanès, recalls Benjamin's distinction between "cult value" and "exhibition value" in works of art. "Cult value" holds clear connotations of magic and religion for Benjamin: the image's strength lies in its concealment precisely because it does not have to be seen in order to perform its function. It is enough for it to come into contact with a priest or some other go-between. Although this evokes an earlier social system, the concept helps us see how images in Miró's collages seem to avoid deterioration. Nevertheless, preservation is ultimately futile. Exhibition, as the basis for any relationship with images, allows for an inevitable fading: images tend to deteriorate, regardless of their use value.

In a sense, the myth of modernist rupture has depended fundamentally on the binary model of realism versus experimentation, an opposition that is questioned when one analyzes the practice of vision as it was resisted or deflected by popular or mass culture. Many of the chapters here urge scholars of the modern, industrial period in Spain to historicize the experience of the turn-of-the-century urban observer, and to treat it as a constantly changing and evolving, even potentially contradictory subjectivity. In a careful case study of the 1907 performance of a *zarzuela* entitled *Cinematógrafo Nacional* in Madrid's Apollo Theater "Stages of Modernity: The Uneasy Symbiosis of the *género chico* and Early Cinema in

Madrid" (Chapter 14), Susan Larson describes how the *género chico*, however fearful it may have been in the face of its new cinematic rival, effectively represented film as an art in its urban and political context, serving as a chronicle of the reception of silent film in Madrid just as it was beginning to attract a wide audience. It is clear that early cinema did not produce any new forms, concepts or techniques that were not already available in other genres, instead consisting of a coming-together in a new way of other aspects of modern culture, outpacing these other forms, ultimately becoming much more than just another scientific novelty.

Modernism is oftentimes presented as the appearance of the new for an observer who remains perpetually the same, or whose historical status is never interrogated. Eva Woods's Chapter 15, "Visualizing the Time-space of Otherness: Digression and Distraction in Spanish Silent Films," looks at two feature-length silent films, *La gitana blanca* (The White Gypsy, 1923) and *La Condesa María* (The Countess María, 1927) whose plot digressions occupy a central place in their expositions of modernity and race for a public deeply troubled by Spain's colonialist incursions in North Africa. A prevalent technique in silent cinema was the narrative digression of a character journeying to distant lands, which offered spectacular exterior shots of foreign locations, capitalizing on the audience's desire for thrills and the exotic. Digressions were also useful for propaganda purposes since footage was often lifted from other films, in particular government-sponsored military documentaries. In the case studies here, characters travel to Morocco to fight against Rifian rebels or board trains to travel to Gypsy camps. These trajectories, more complex than the simple notion of traveling to the "past" or returning to "civilization," offered characters and spectators glimpses of contingent temporalities, of what it might be like to see a time and space not standardized by capitalist modernity, a desirable albeit anxiety-producing vision. The cinema screen often stood in for the train window, transporting passenger/citizens/spectators through increasingly porous boundaries of time and vision.

Geoffrey B. Pingree in "Modern Anxiety and Documentary Cinema in Republican Spain" (Chapter 16) discusses the struggle of Spain's Second Republic to create a distinct and compelling national identity that would repudiate Spain's monarchical and ecclesiastic past in order to provide a unified vision of the newly democratic nation. Cinema was a critical part of this campaign, for its documentary production supported the Republic's bold move to herald a new public culture and project a new vision of Spain. Within this collective national discussion, documentary film emerged as a privileged form, a genre that seemed uniquely poised to effect the sort of wide-ranging social and political change that Republicans believed the nation required. Documentary film was, after all, not only a medium that could visually represent Spain, but also a mode that promised a unique purchase on the truth. Indeed, the Republic looked primarily to documentary rather than to fiction film as the best means of capturing and projecting a new and "truer," more "real" sense of Spanish national identity. Yet the documentary films produced during the Second Republic reflect a nagging ambivalence, an instability that characterized the government and betrayed its failure to create a symbolic identity that could distinguish and unify the struggling nation. Documentary cinema seemed to function as a contradictory discourse within the Second Republic, a popular art form that was effectively used to preserve high culture. In this sense, documentary cinema embodies an essential and paradoxical element of the Second Republic – a desire for liberation often expressed through the recuperation of a traditional past.

Like so many of the authors presented here, Joan Ramon Resina explores vision while contemplating the significance of borders. His Chapter 17, "The Last Look from the Border," argues that "seeing" Spain depends on the existence of a political horizon. What does it mean to "see" the nation from its border, from the perspective of the exilic eye, otherness, or loss? How does a nation look as it recedes into history? For Resina, seeing from these liminal spaces both binds our vision and enables the condition for our perception of objects. Resina analyzes a series of looks that occur in close spatial and temporal proximity to one another, looks embedded within the nation's violent history: two photographs in Robert Capa's "Barcelona" series, Antoni Rovira i Virgili's written account of the last days of Republican Catalonia, and the mysterious glance between Falangist ideologue Rafael Sánchez Mazas and an anonymous Republican militiaman poised to kill him that functions as the central enigma of Javier Cercas' novel *Soldados de Salamina* (2001). Noting the ambiguity of the images of looks in these texts, he questions how one can read such images before they are subordinated to a political narrative, especially when they provide no written captions (see Capa's photos) that would assign specific meanings to the looks.

Critiquing Jameson's notion of the political as the horizon of all reading and interpretation, as this dissolves political specificity and creates a political metalanguage that ultimately becomes meaningless, Resina maintains that we must see these images as symptoms which ultimately resist meaning and are irreducible to language. If photography contains an inherent violence, then to append signs to it tames its poignancy. Resina expands on the theme (also taken up in the chapters by Epps and Woods) of how the photographic medium constitutes a commentary on the impossibility of representing time, or recapturing the truth of any moment. Informed by Edmund Husserl's ideas about how we experience the world through vision, he explains how alterity, or otherness, is inherent in vision: we cannot surmount the fact that ultimately we look at the world from the other side of a horizon. From this vantage point, Resina convincingly explodes the commonly held assumption that nations are imagined, arguing that nations can be eminently visual and may reveal themselves to a particular form of attention – a viewer who is receptive, or who "oversteps her ideal bubble and exposes herself to a different regime of visibility." By insisting on the border as both the limit and the nation's very horizon of possibility, he simultaneously reminds us of the inadequacies of vision and yet its indispensability to our understanding of nation and subjectivity.

Notes

1. *The Arcades Project* (Benjamin 1999: 476).
2. According to Elkins (2003), the term "visual culture" was first used in 1972 by Baxandall (1972). Somewhat younger than British cultural studies (it becomes a discipline, for instance, in the 1990s), it is primarily a movement centered in the U.S. (Elkins 2003: 2–4). Visual culture, as defined by Schwartz and Przyblyski (2004: 7), "has a particular investment in vision as a historical specific experience, mediated by new technologies and the individual and social formations that they enable." It "includes the study of image/objects and also reaches beyond them to include the history of vision, visual experience, and its historical construction" (2004: 7).
3. See Elkins (2003: 31–7) for a useful series of lists of theorists and historians who are taken as models by scholars of visual culture. In this categorization, Benjamin ranks as one of the most important theorists. That one is compelled to list and categorize in this way is a telling symptom of our disciplinary training.
4. See Simmel (1995).
5. See Kern (1983: 21) and Doane (2002: 33–68) for more on Marey's studies of chronophotography.
6. For a history and analysis of the representability of time, see Kern and Doane (2002). Regarding visual metaphors in philosophy or the intersection of vision and philosophy or critical theory, see Jay (1994); Levin (1988, 1993, 1997), Mitchell (1994), Fuery and Fuery (2003), Brennan and Jay (1996) and Virilio (1994).
7. Graham and Labanyi (1995: 11) describe the relationship between modernity and modernization in the last quarter of the nineteenth century in the following terms: "It was capital-driven modernization which produced both modernity and modernism: modernity understood as the condition of life subjectively experienced as a consequence of the changes wrought by modernization and modernism as an artistic/cultural response (across literature, theatre, painting, architecture, music, and later cinema and design) to that subjective experience".
8. It is telling that a highly publicized reader on nineteenth-century visual culture (Schwartz and Przyblyski 2004) contains only the most tangential references to Spain or Latin America, apparently considering them peripheral to

European and North American modernity. Although also influential to our study, the somewhat earlier collection, Charney and Schwartz (1995), again fails to include references to countries outside the "first world."

9. For more on ocular regimes, see Jay (1994); Virilio (1994: 24–30) discusses "regimes of the visual" and a new "logistics of the image."
10. See Chakrabarty (2000: 149–79) for a fuller discussion of the national, vision, and imagination.
11. See note 5.
12. Geist and Monleón (1997) explain the marginal case of Spanish modernism by showing that understandings of hegemonic modernism rely on a reduced number of artistic examples. The result is a distorted canon that stubbornly excludes Hispanic production (xix). Theirs is an invitation to include Spain's modernism within its broader European context, as a fluid exchange between the center and margin.
13. See Balfour (2002: 7–9) for a discussion of the international Conference of Algeciras in 1906 and the Cartagena Pact of 1907. The Spanish Liberals were far more receptive to European colonialism than the Conservatives, even spearheading business initiatives in Morocco.
14. "The Disaster [of 1898] and the challenge of modernization encouraged a renewal of traditional views about Spanish history and the nature of Spanishness. One such view laid stress on a universalist mission of Spain to bring spirituality to an increasingly materialistic world. According to this vision, the source of Spain's new resurgence lay in the Hispanic traditions it had created in its former Empire; by increasing trade and cultural contacts with its ex-colonies, Spain could create a new cultural empire as counterweight to the Anglo-Saxon world" (Balfour 1995: 30).
15. For more on the destabilization of the European narrative of modernity, see Mitchell (2000).
16. See Balsebre (2001). For a detailed account of Spanish film directors invited to Nazi Germany by Joseph Goebbels, then Minister of Information and Propaganda, see Álvarez Berciano and Sala Noguer (2000: 203–43).
17. For an example of reactionary aesthetic modernism, see Benjamin's (1969: 241–2) citation of Marinetti in "The Work of Art in the Age of Mechanical Reproduction" in *Illuminations*. For more on the making of Spanish modernity under Francoism, see Richards (1995).
18. Some excellent cultural histories that contextualize their objects of study within modernity do exist in the entertainment industry, popular spectacles and theatre, and the early cinema: See Salaün (1990), Gubern (1997), Subirats (1997), Mendelson (2005) and Díaz (1999).
19. In 1899, in Barcelona, Fructuoso Gelabert made the first national production, *Choque de dos transatlánticos* (Two Transatlantic Liners Crashing), using

miniature toy boats in a tank. In 1902, also in Barcelona, one of early film's most renowned special effects artists, Segundo de Chomón, made *Choque de trenes* (Trains Crashing) by combining two takes of real trains moving at high speeds in opposite directions with takes of two toy trains against a miniature landscape (Sánchez Vidal 1992: 41–2).

Works Cited

Álvarez Berciano, Rosa and Ramón Sala Noguer. *El cine en la zona nacional 1936–1939*. Bilbao: Mensajero, 2000.

Balfour, Sebastian. *Deadly Embrace: Morocco and the Road to the Spanish Civil War*. London: Oxford University Press, 2002.

—— "The Loss of Empire, Regenerationism and the Forging of a Myth of National Identity." In *Spanish Cultural Studies: An Introduction*. Eds. Helen Graham and Jo Labanyi. London: Oxford, 1995. 29–31.

Balsebre, Armand. *Historia de la Radio en España Vol. I (1874–1939)*. Madrid: Cátedra, 2001.

Baxandall, Michael. *Painting and Experience in Fifteenth-Century Italy: A Primer in the History of Pictorial Style*. Oxford: Clarendon Press, 1972.

Benjamin, Walter. *Illuminations*. Trans. Harry Zohn. New York: Schocken, 1969/1955.

—— *The Arcades Project*. Trans. Howard Eiland and Kevin McLaughlin. Cambridge, MA and London: Harvard University Press, 1999.

Brennan, Teresa and Martin Jay. *Vision in Context: Historical and Contemporary Perspectives on Sight*. New York: Routledge, 1996.

Burgin, Victor. *In/Different Spaces: Place and Memory in Visual Culture*. Berkeley: University of California Press, 1996.

Chakrabarty, Dipesh. *Provincializing Europe: Postcolonial Thought and Historical Difference*. Princeton, NJ: Princeton University Press, 2000.

Chaplin, Sarah and John A. Walker. *Visual Culture: An Introduction*. Manchester: Manchester University Press, 1997.

Charney, Leo and Vanessa R. Schwartz, eds. *Cinema and the Invention of Modern Life*. Berkeley: University of California Press, 1995.

Crary, Jonathan. *Techniques of the Observer: On Vision and Modernity in the Nineteenth Century*. Cambridge, MA and London: MIT Press, 1990.

Díaz, Lorenzo. *La España alegre: Ocio y diversión en el siglo XIX*. Madrid: Espasa Calpe, 1999.

Doane, Mary Anne. *The Emergence of Cinematic Time: Modernity, Contingency, the Archive*. Cambridge, MA: Harvard University Press, 2002.

Elkins, James. *Visual Studies: A Skeptical Introduction*. New York: Routledge, 2003.

Evans, Jessica. "Introduction." In *Visual Culture: The Reader*. Eds. Jessica Evans and Stuart Hall. London: Sage, 1999. 11–20.
Foucault, Michel. *Discipline and Punish*. London: Penguin, 1977.
Fuery, Patrick and Kelli Fuery. *Visual Cultures and Critical Theory*. London: Arnold, 2003.
Fusi, Juan Pablo and Jordi Palafox. *España 1808–1996. El desafío de la modernidad*. Madrid: Espasa-Calpe, 1997.
Geist, Anthony L. and José B. Monleón, eds. *Modernism and its Margins: Reinscribing Cultural Modernity from Spain and Latin America*. New York: Garland, 1999.
Graham, Helen and Jo Labanyi. "Culture and Modernity: The Case of Spain." In *Spanish Cultural Studies: An Introduction*. Eds. Helen Graham and Jo Labanyi. London: Oxford, 1995. 1–19.
Gubern, Román. *Medios icónicos de masas*. Madrid: Historia 16, 1997.
Gunning, Tom. "An Aesthetic of Astonishment." In *Viewing Positions: Ways of Seeing Film*. Ed. Linda Williams. New Brunswick, NJ: Rutgers University Press, 1995. 114–33.
Hall, Stuart. "Introduction [to Looking and Subjectivity]." In *Visual Culture: The Reader*. Eds. Jessica Evans and Stuart Hall. London: Sage, 1999. 309–14.
Jameson, Fredric. *A Singular Modernity: Essay on the Ontology of the Present*. London and New York: Verso, 2002.
Jay, Martin. *Downcast Eyes: The Denigration of Vision in Twentieth-Century French Thought*. Berkeley: University of California Press, 1993.
Kern, Stephen. *The Culture of Time and Space, 1880–1918*. Cambridge, MA: Harvard University Press, 1983.
Levin, David Michael. *Modernity and the Hegemony of Vision*. Berkeley: University of California Press, 1993.
—— *Sites of Vision: The Discursive Construction of Sight in the History of Philosophy*. Cambridge, MA: MIT Press, 1997.
—— *The Opening of Vision: Nihilism and the Postmodern Situation*. New York: Routledge, 1988.
López Serrano, Fernando. *Madrid, figuras y sombras: De los teatros de títeres a los salones de cine*. Madrid: Complutense, 1999.
Marx, Karl and Frederick Engels. *The German Ideology*. Trans. S. Ryazanskaya. Moscow: Progress, 1964.
Mendelson, Jordana. *Documenting Spain: Artists, Exhibition Culture, and the Modern Nation, 1929–1939*. University Park, PA: Pennsylvania State University Press, 2005.
Mitchell, Timothy. *Questions of Modernity*. Minneapolis, MN: University of Minnesota Press, 2000.
Mitchell, W.J.T. *Picture Theory*. Chicago: University of Chicago Press, 1994.

Richards, Mike. "'Terror and Progress': Industrialization, Modernity, and the Making of Francoism." In *Spanish Cultural Studies: An Introduction*. Eds. Helen Graham and Jo Labanyi. London: Oxford, 1995. 173–82.

Salaun, Serge. *El cuplé*. Madrid: Espasa-Calpe, 1990.

Sánchez Vidal, Augustín. *El cine de Chomón*. Zaragoza: Caja de Ahorros de la Inmaculada Aragón, 1992.

Schwartz, Vanessa R. and Jeannene M. Przyblyski, eds. *The Nineteenth-Century Visual Culture Reader*. New York and London: Routledge, 2004.

Simmel, Georg. "The Metropolis and Mental Life." In *Metropolis: Center and Symbol of our Times*. Ed. Philip Kasinitz. New York: New York University Press, 1995.

Subirats, Eduardo. *Después de la lluvia*. Madrid: Taurus, 1981.

—— *Linterna mágica: Vanguardia, media y cultura tardomoderna*. Madrid: Siruela, 1997.

Torres, Augusto M., ed. *Spanish Cinema 1896–1983*. Trans. E. Nelson Modlin III. Madrid: Editorial Nacional, 1986.

Virilio, Paul. *The Vision Machine*. Trans. Julie Rose. Bloomington, IN: Indiana University Press, 1994.

–2–

Visibly Modern Madrid: Mesonero, Visual Culture, and the Apparatus of Urban Reform

Rebecca Haidt

In the introduction to the inaugural issue (1836) of the *Semanario Pintoresco Espanol*, Ramón Mesonero Romanos informed readers that the journal will provide *dibujos* (sketches or diagrams; generally, images) and *grabados* (stereotyped and/or engraved woodblock prints) to "hace[r] más perceptible el objeto de que se trata" (make the object in question more perceptible). Mesonero affirms at least two propositions in this statement: first, that his readers would find graphic "perceptibility" more attractive than that possible through narrative or descriptive linguistic accounts of things; and also, that there are differing degrees to which diverse representations can convey information. Simply, visual depictions provide the *Semanario's* readership with a higher order of information ("más perceptible") than usually made possible through only verbal text. Mesonero points out that in offering such enhanced information delivery to its readers, the *Semanario* is following the lead of "países más adelantados que el nuestro" (countries more advanced than our own) – for example, England and France.[1] In those nations, interest in and understanding of the information channeled through cheap and accessible instruments of the press (e.g., *The Penny Magazine*) have served to extend "la lectura a todas las clases del pueblo" and contribute "notablemente a la prosperidad" (extend reading to all classes of people and notably contribute to prosperity).[2] Through the medium of the illustrated periodical, ideas can be extended among a diverse audience due to graphic iteration of verbally encoded information, and through the expanded repertoire of meanings possible in assemblages of images, texts, columns and typefaces. Mesonero links the negotiation of these new contingencies and juxtapositions to economic and cultural advancement. Making things more "perceptible" brings with it the likelihood of increasing a nation's access to the advantages of modernity.

This chapter sets several of Mesonero's urban reform initiatives within some of the contexts of Madrid's visual cultures in the period spanning roughly the 1830s and 1840s, and considers the twinned ideologies of sight and modernity opened to audiences by illustrated papers such as the *Semanario Pintoresco Español*.

Mesonero's work with journalistic media (such as the *Diario de Avisos de Madrid* and the *Semanario*), municipal administrators (e.g., the *alcalde* the Marqués Viudo de Pontejos), and tourism-oriented publishing ventures (such as his repeatedly re-edited *Manual de Madrid*, first published in 1831) addressed the question of how to draw visitors and investment to a city regarded by few as a site of worldwide importance.[3] Madrid was neither a center of luxury consumption (as was Paris) nor a powerful showplace of industry (as was London). Many saw it, with the genteel tourist Ferrer, as exotic in its "curious contrasts," (48), a place centered around the court yet diverse in population, and lacking cultural capital. But in fact Madrid was a complicated and unsettled place during the period of Ferrer's visit.[4] In the 1830s and 1840s, following the war of independence, years of famine and cholera, and the first *desamortizaciones* (property disentailments), the capital saw new waves of immigration from the provinces and a boom in housing construction for the wealthy, even as inhabitants trod dirty, crowded, narrow roadways, and counted among themselves legions of abandoned children and indigent. At the same time, the capital was more a seat of privilege and bureaucracy than a symbol of the nation. Edward Baker points out that during these years Mesonero projects "la transformación de la villa coronada y señorial en capital nacional, en representación simbólica de la historia y la cultura nacionales" (the transformation of the royal and seigneurial city into a national capital, into a symbolic representation of national history and culture) ("Introducción" xix). Mesonero devoted these decades to urbanization and publishing projects geared toward getting not only monied tourists (like Ferrer), but also *madrileños* themselves to perceive the historical streets and buildings of Madrid as rich channels of power and global cultural influence.[5] Conceived of as distinct from the majority of visual recreations available to audiences, the illustrated periodical was crucial to the larger project of training readers and citizens in viewing practices informed by ideas of prosperity and public spirit. Yet Mesonero's particular conceptualization of the city's perceptibility is situated at the cusp of technological developments, such as stereotype printing, the railway, and photography, which would profoundly alter urban understandings of history, actuality, and the meanings of the modern.

What did Mesonero have in mind when he used the word *perceptible*? The answer will have something to do with the kind of spectacles and images available to readers and viewers during the period. For example, city texts were increasingly popular from the 1830s to the 1860s across Europe. The *guía urbana* or urban guide, such as *Paseo por Madrid, o Guia del forastero en la corte* (Stroll through Madrid, or Guide to the Visitor in the Court) (1815), with its listing of streets, enumeration of local customs and feast days, and tabulation of local statistics, was a genre long established as useful to merchants, travelers and residents.[6] At mid-century, urban guides focusing on artistic, historical and monumental sights – that is, reflecting particularly the interests of consuming tourists – shared generic terrain (and popularity among readers) with travel accounts and memoirs of voyages. By the late 1840s the daguerreotype's popularity made it possible for many *madrileños* to see landscapes, buildings and their own images captured on dark, silvery glass plates.[7] Broadsheet accounts of scandals and crimes, often accompanied by crude woodblock prints, offered city readers a patchwork guide to human horrors. Peepshows, shadow plays, magic lantern exhibits and other extra-theatrical spectacles provided recreational visions to urban residents of different classes; and the daily sights of traffic and movement in streets, or fashionable display near the Prado, provided a variety of viewing pleasures to those who had the time to stand and observe.

During the first half of the nineteenth century, one of the most marketable of image-genres was that of "authentic" Spain, captured under rubrics ranging from the picturesque to *costumbrismo*. As the developing exchange economy contributed to the currency of literary and artistic tropes of authenticity of experience, what Stewart has called "the nostalgic myth of contact and presence" (133) became particularly attractive to large urban audiences whose individual perceptive fields in the growing metropolis no longer could capture the dimensions of cities' wide-ranging and complex places. The emergence of *costumbrismo* in European periodicals from the 1830s onward marks the development of a literary and graphic art market for local accounts of city experiences, in which key *topoi* – "the crowd", "the street" and the "type" – feed audience desire for the experience of presence.[8] They provide readerships with what Boym calls "contexts for remembrances and debates around the future" (77), in which the rapidly changing city is the proving ground for the connection between recollection and loss.

Nostalgia for the recognizably "Spanish" informs various visual and textual modes ranging from the record to the recuperation, from periodical *costumbrismo* to early documentary photography, from romantic reworkings of regional legends to illustrated periodicals such as the *Semanario* – all of which, as Fontanella has pointed out, share the aim of "sintetizar una visión problemática y confusa" (synthesize a problematic and confusing vision) (*La imprenta* 68). The narrator of a typical Mesoneran *costumbrista* essay (for example) and the eye of court photographer Charles Clifford (who took scores of photographs documenting royal processions, public works, and national historic sites during the reign of Isabel II) equally claim readers' and viewers' affinities with a larger project of cultural memory, for the observed types, edifices and landscapes serve as both evidence of the actual, and signs of "lo antiguo español" (venerable Spanish heritage); that is, as a source of cultural capital accessible to citizens in need of means to remember, and thus represent to themselves, a more coherent national past.[9]

Signal personages, historic episodes and cultural values were purveyed in a variety of visual media, from paintings to photographs to lithographs. Readers comfortable with the conventions of academic painting regularly subscribed to print collections of royal and religious themes advertised in periodicals such as the *Gaceta de Madrid* and *El Diario de Madrid*, and made possible a steady second-hand market in fine-art *grabados* as advertised in the papers' classified columns (Vega 344–6). For these viewers, the pleasure of an image was that of seeing not only forms or light effects achieved through masterful technique, but also inscriptions whose interpretation might shift depending on political vicissitudes: Vega observes that print collectors and viewers of the period negotiated the "recuperación de imágenes y láminas que habían circulado anteriormente" (recuperation of images and prints that had circulated previously) which bore changed inscriptions "para adecuarla[s] a las nuevas circunstancias históricas" (to adjust them to new historical circumstances) (Vega 345). Such changes were a factor in Mesonero's stated desire to avoid the inclusion, in the *Semanario*, of images related to politics (Rubio Cremades 14).

Thus many readers would have brought to their use of illustrated periodicals the capacity to discern various levels on which imagery circulated and recirculated. In fact, the *Semanario* recuperated images used in European papers such as *The Penny Magazine*. For example, in September 1836 the *Semanario* ran a large image of a marmoset or "Titi" on the second page of a naturalist article on the species (no. 23: 192) (Figure 2.1); yet this same print had run in *The Penny Magazine* in December 1835 (no. 238), on the front page, at the head of an article on the "Ouistiti" (489). In the editor's introduction to the first issue of the *Semanario*, Mesonero (1836: 6) acknowledged that the paper was following standard practice in "reproducir los dibujos y artículos de los que de esta clase se publican en el estrangero" (reproducing the sketches and articles of this type of material published abroad). Indeed, early *Semanario* issues mimicked not only individual images, but also formatting and juxtapositions of elements as found in *The Penny Magazine*. This reproduction would have been understood by readers as an up-to-the-minute, modern feature of the *Semanario.* And *The Penny Magazine* informed its English-language readers in 1833 that stereotyping enabled the producers to "assist foreign nations in the production of 'Penny Magazines,'" noting that the editors sell stereotyped pages and casts of woodcuts internationally, thereby enabling them to direct "the popular reading of four great countries into the same channels" and leaving "some capital free in each to be devoted to other objects" (*Paper and Printing* 31).

The recuperation of *dibujos* and replication of layouts served to create a traveling archive or library of imagery shared across Europe by consumers of illustrated periodicals and of prints. Yet despite the modernity of acquaintance with such an archive, recognition was not the sort of seeing Mesonero had in mind when he wrote of making his periodical's discussed objects more *perceptible*; for Mesonero was speaking of a material synergy among text, illustration, readership, and the cultural sphere of civic praxis. One proof of this is found in remarks in the

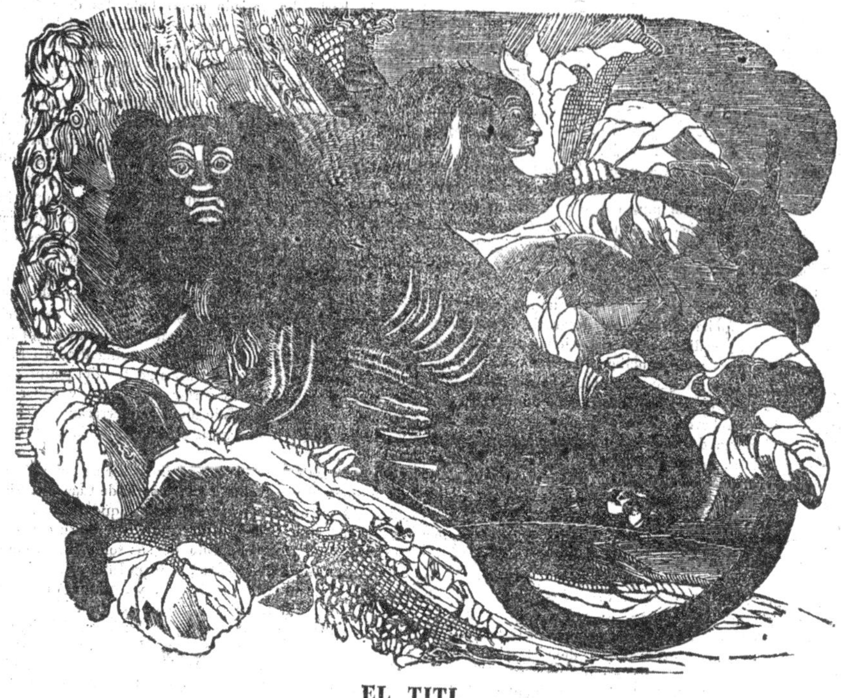

Figure 2.1 Anonymous, "Titi." *The Penny Magazine* (December 1835), *Semanario Pintoresco* (September 1836).

preface to the 1839 issue of the *Semanario*, in which Mesonero reviews the paper's contributions to public life over the preceding three years, and notes as particularly important the paper's having "[promoted] con toda intención el deseo de conocer nuestro país" (expressly [promoted] the desire to know our country) ("A nuestros lectores" 3) and "facilitado en fin por la introducción del grabado en Madera, la publicación de mil dibujos originales, dando … alguna aplicación a los trabajos de nuestros apreciables artistas" (ultimately facilitated, through the introduction of woodblock engraving, the publication of a thousand original images and giving … some incentive to work to our appreciable artists) as opposed to only "haber copiado de los extranjeros" (having copied from foreigners) (4). The autocthonous production of *dibujos* is integral to the goal of opening ideas to a range of classes in society who "absolutely lacked the means and pleasure" of learning (3).

As the Church understood from at least the time of the Council of Trent, the visual conveyance of information was important in any attempt to educate or lead a largely illiterate populace. Whether for purposes of instruction or diversion, "the image had been used … even before the development of sequential narrative" to communicate ideas (Gombrich 231). From the late eighteenth century through the

1840s, the number of persons capable of participating in popular visual diversions was vastly greater than that of persons able to entertain themselves through reading media such as books or newspapers. Yet newspapers and books were themselves visual experiences reliant on frameworks that safely set the verbal content off from "reality"; that is, they disseminated information in accordance with certain graphic conventions. For example, the newspaper, in both Spain and Europe, had long-established layout structures that were part of the staging of semantics. The specificity and accessibility of particular content were enhanced by the dividing of the page into columns and sections, by the insertion of graphic boxes around content, and by the further division of regions of the page into subsections. Readers had the opportunity to skip over sections and choose to read one part of an exposition rather than another; or they could read in a linear fashion, following a section from beginning to end through successive pages or numbers. Readers also could expect certain consistent hierarchies of information as conveyed by layout on a page: the most important discussions, expositions or subjects generally would appear on the first page or toward the top of a page or column, while less compelling subjects, such as classified advertisements, would more likely merit placement toward the bottom or the back.[10]

From their experiences with magic lantern and panorama exhibitions, readers understood a medium in which image and text or commentary could illustrate one another directly; they were familiar with print–image relationships from broadsides dealing with current events and crimes. But most often the illustrations heading such broadsheets were images not created expressly to explicate the information in the text: most printers had a limited roster of crude woodcut images to include at the top of broadsheet texts, and frequently reused them. The new and directly referential graphic modalities that appeared from the 1820s to the 1840s in England, France and Spain established the kinds of relationships present-day readers still have with the information conveyed through mass press culture: content was communicated not just through text, but also through (for example) "images divided between the editorial and the illustrational" (de la Motte and Przblyski 5). In particular, the inclusion of explicative imagery served to render the overall content of the periodical more persuasive: European readers of the period understood, along with the editor of the French *L'Illustration*, that written descriptions seem "inanimate, always incomplete and hard to understand, in comparison to the representation of such things."[11] That is, visual transcription (de la Motte and Przblyski 1999: 6) served best to convey ideas and animate the minds of readers toward understanding of ideological content – which is exactly what Mesonero claimed when he argued that images served to make content more "perceptible."

The trope of the magic lantern (and, toward mid-century, the daguerreotype) as an instrument of perception or visibility was a popular print device during the late eighteenth and early nineteenth centuries, permitting authors to emphasize to readers either the supposed truth, or the proposed fiction, of verbal content. For example, in the 1820 Madrid periodical *La Linterna Mágica*, each issue is structured as an imaginary scene in a magic lantern show, in which contemporary Madrid characters engage in behavior interpreted by an announcer or guide named Maese Pedro.[12] But the *idea* of lantern illumination is not equivalent to the actual experience of seeing illustrations. Visual transcription in print periodicals placed imagery with relation to texts as a means of enhancing the actual conveyance of targeted information. Thus the inclusion of visual imagery implied changes in the techniques of semantic structuring within the medium. Readers were now invited to condition their practice of recreational witness to the particular viewpoint or perspective elaborated through a paper's assemblage of ideas within blocked columns, divided sections, and carefully placed illustrations. Readers would be encouraged, through the proximity of images to text, to discern relationships between the objects portrayed and the ideas conveyed through the surrounding verbal text – that is, to produce "propositional interpretations" of connections between juxtaposed or closely-featured elements in a given medium (Messaris 110–11). And for the first time, audiences unable to read would have access to the newspaper's graphic semantic structurings through their consumption of the featured illustrations and images. In other words, as never before, through the multi-technique, multi-practice vehicle of the illustrated periodical, readers and non-readers would be invited to engage in the apprehension of an informing ideology, such that the overall experience of various kinds of looking and envisioning would bring the user, through concerted semantic structures, toward knowledge of the connection between image and civic awareness. And *that* was the particularly modern connotation of Mesonero's *perceptible*.

When Mesonero assumed directorship of the *Diario de Avisos de Madrid* in 1835, he did so with the express intention of popularizing his reform projects for the capital.[13] In his first "letter from the editor" of April 1, 1835, he informed his audience that he would often make some space in the periodical to "llenar" (fill) the public mind with data concerning "datos estadísticos de la población de la capital, las variaciones en la salud pública, el movimiento mercantil e industrial del vecindario, las mejoras de policía urbana, los progresos de la instrucción y demás objetos análogos" (statistical data about the population of the capital, variations in public health, commercial and industrial movement in the area, improvements in public policy, progress in education and other similar topics) ("Boletín" *Trabajos no coleccionados* 5).[14] Writing within a long line of urban reformers (such as Casimiro de Uztáriz) whose plans did not fully materialize due to the difficulty of bringing together royal, ecclesiastical and private interests, Mesonero's early *Diario de Avisos* project was part of an intended synergy among the Ayuntamiento (led by the Marqués Viudo de Pontejos), private investors, aristocratic benefactors and the periodical press, oriented toward expanding the spatial and conceptual boundaries of *madrileños* and instilling in them a new public awareness of the city.[15] Mesonero saw his editorship of the periodical as an opportunity to present data while exercising his readers in strategies for interpreting it within a rational, civic-minded program of urban development.

The *Diario de Avisos* did not contain graphic or explicitly referential illustrations of the printed data content, but Mesonero understood that the public – of which he conceived broadly – must first be taught to feel comfortable with, and learn to interpret, information converted into statistics and annexed in summaries, all under the rubric of "municipal development." For example, a June 1835 "Boletín" piece instructed a wide range of readers that they should familiarize themselves with Madrid's "códigos municipales" (municipal codes) so that "cada uno de sus vecinos conozca sus derechos y obligaciones como jefe de familia, como amo, como criado, como dueño de tienda o establecimiento público, como casero, como inquilino, como forastero" (each one of her [i.e., Madrid's] neighbors might know his rights and obligations as head of household, as master, as servant, as owner of a shop or public establishment, as a landlord, as a tenant, as a visitor) (43). After summarizing the sections of the municipal code and giving readers an overview of its order and rationale, Mesonero explains how a *madrileño* might best construe the applicability of certain codes to his or her individual situation. He particularly approves, for example, of the codes pertaining to construction and housing, for it can only redound to the benefit of the city's development that landlords clearly envision the applicability of rules concerning "elevación, forma, dimensiones de las puertas, ventanas, medianerías, buhardillas, comunes, tejados … el color de las fachadas" (elevation, form, the dimensions of entryways, windows, subdivisions, attics, water closets, roof tiling … the color of façades) and other structural specifics (45–6). In this rehearsal of the parts of an edifice, he walks readers through an exercise in envisioning buildings in accordance with, not general semantic categories such as "house," "palace" or "convent," but the details that may be seen when one takes time to notice them, the details that normally a passerby might not observe, but that contribute to the effect made by any structure on the overall aesthetics of a street's appearance.

Mesonero's 1835 essays in the *Diario de Avisos* present readers with an insistent and serialized case for envisioning the city as a complex of infrastructural elements, linking human and residential to constructed and textual components of the urban environment. As he points out in "Aguas" (water piping) in June, the need for a "plano general de la población en que se marque el desnivel respectivo de cada calle" (general map of the population, indicating the respective gradient of each street) easily could be satisfied by first undertaking a survey to precisely indicate "los acueductos o canerías públicas o particulares, conocer exactamente la altura subterránea a que caminan … clasificar por cuadrículas los diversos terrenos" (aqueducts and public or private water pipes, to know precisely the subterrean depth at which they run … to classify diverse parcels in *quadrillé*), etc. (54). The need to control the city's street vendors is related, in a piece published in the same month, to the need for improvement in legal infrastructure, for the presence of *puestos ambulantes* (itinerant vendors' stands) in the streets exacerbates already existing problems of inconsistency in laws concerning property ownership, upkeep and uniformity of appearance ("Puestos ambulantes" 48). That issue referred in turn to the concerns aired (also in June) in a prior article on property regulations, in which the author asserts that one of the most important goals of creating a responsible populace aware of municipal ordinances is their instruction in the need for visual regularity, clarity, and taste in the appearance of city properties ("Boletín," *TNC* 45–6). In two previous articles from that year on "Policía urbana," Mesonero had observed (in April) that *puestos ambulantes* block pedestrians' way in the streets (18), a problem linked (as he pointed out in May) to the need to convert main thoroughfares (such as the calle de Alcalá) into spacious boulevards of pleasing and imposingly tasteful appearance, consistent with the aspect offered by other capital cities (38).

As Mesonero pointed out in an 1851 article published in *La Ilustración*, Madrid is the most modern court in Europe ("Estátuas y monumentos públicos" 129), in that it is not as many centuries old as are the "antiquísimas metropolis de Francia, Inglaterra, Alemania" (the ancient metropolises of France, England and Germany) (129). Madrid "carece por lo tanto de aquella grandiosidad de detalles, de aquella magnificencia del conjunto" (therefore lacks that greatness of details, that totalized magnificence) visible in those older cities; it cannot boast of the "grandeza y material ostentación" (grandeur and material ostentation) visible in long-established European capitals' streets and buildings (130). This lack is problematic for two reasons, according to Mesonero. Monuments and statues beautify city streets and lend them an aspect of grandeur, a quality that visitors (such as Ferrer) did not tend to associate with Madrid; and they also function as "páginas históricas y artísticas que revelan al forastero la vida de un pueblo y las fases sucesivas de su civilización y cultura" (artistic and historical pages that reveal to the foreigner the life of a people and the successive phases of its civilization and culture) (134). They function, in other words, as elements in not only a concerted municipal effort at ideological orientation with regard to the cultural values of the nation, but also a larger project of attracting tourists and visitors ("que revelan al forastero") to see the capital as such.

One of Mesonero's central concerns in his tireless circulation of proposals concerning municipal ordinances, building reforms, or proposed expansions of city limits was to promote changes that would markedly affect the perception of Madrid by both foreigners and residents.[16] Not only decorative elements such as statues and monuments, but also structural components such as improved city lighting or the creation of commercial districts replete with shopping arcades, were conceived with a mind toward enhancing the city's *aspecto* or perceptibility as a modern urban complex of pleasant and grand spaces.[17] Further, by means of serialized discussion in outlets such as the *Diario de Avisos* and the *Semanario*, Mesonero projected mass public familiarization with the city's legacy of grandeur and future of development, knowledge of which was crucial to proper perception of the *aspecto* of the capital.

Traditionally, the city core or center was the place of first presentation of that *aspecto* to tourists and travelers. The entrance to the city led from venerable, centuries-old overland routes, and the principal point of departure and depot for non-rail public transportation (i.e. coaches) was the center of the city (as was the case in Madrid). In fact, Mesonero generated his early urbanization work (with its focus on the city center) at the cusp of momentous change in urban residents' experience of notions such as "periphery" and "center," brought by the spread of the railroad from the 1840s onward. Though cities welcomed construction of new railway depots, across Europe tensions were raised by the question of the urban core's accommodation to the possibilities of the railway. The railroad "is not an integral part of the city; it is located outside the traditional city walls" and its new peripheral situation "terminates the intimate relationship between the means of transport and its destination" (Schivelbusch 161). Visitors arriving by railway would neither pass through, nor disembark near, the historic grandeur and renovations in and around the city's core.

In 1842 a group of Madrid *comerciantes*, anxious to capitalize on the possibilities presented by a railway network to the city, petitioned the municipal government to create a ministry of *obras públicas* (public works) (González Yánci 19); over a decade earlier, the Marqués de Pontejos (a tireless advocate of progress in the capital) had formulated one of the earliest proposals for rail lines to Madrid, in 1830 (González Yánci 21). Nonetheless, the introduction of the railway seemed to Mesonero to pose the problem of the shifting of sight lines and the displacement of sites of prime visibility, away from the Retiro, the Prado, the Calle de Alcalá and the Puerta del Sol, and toward Atocha. Mesonero opposed the expansion of city limits near Atocha for the purpose of granting the railroad company's request to have its offices and new terminal within the city limits, citing the enormous sums required to build new roadways, new city walls, and public spaces at a far edge of the city and arguing (in the 1851 "Proyecto de nueva barrera y paseo de Atocha") (Project for a new gate and avenue at Atocha) that it were better to invest money in enhancing the avenues "de la izquierda del Salón, entre la esquina del Retiro y el monumento del 2 de Mayo" (to the left of the Salón, between the corner of Retiro park and the monument to May 2nd) – in a more central location, a key space of daily pedestrian traffic, and thus a focus of visual consumerism for urban and foreign strollers (146). (As an alternative, Mesonero argued, at the very least the city should be investing the money in improving infrastructure, such as the "traída de aguas, sin cuya adquisición pronta y abundante serán inútiles todos los planes proyectados para engrandecimiento de Madrid" [channeling of water, without the prompt and abundant acquisition of which all projected plans for the enlargement of Madrid will be rendered useless]) (147). Mesonero's focus on the city's core impeded his ability to envision the different kinds of seeing, and experiences of entry, that would be created by rail travel: the steam-powered arrivals and departures and streaming-through of passengers (in greater numbers and with greater frequency than possible in coaches) facilitated a circulation of goods and persons without precedent in speed or numbers, and in previously peripheral or extramural zones.[18]

In his 1835 *Rápida ojeada sobre el estado de la capital*, Mesonero stated the need for the city to have an "aspecto más lisonjero" (more pleasing aspect) (9) and reminded his compatriots that "la cultura y el esplendor de la capital son un termómetro seguro para conocer el grado de civilización de cada pueblo" (the culture and splendor of the capital are a secure thermometer for measuring the degree of civilization of a given people) (7). Insisting on "culture" and "splendor" (which, in the case of Madrid, were sited in the core between the palace and the Prado), Mesonero seems to sideline major new forces in urban development (such as planning for railroads, which within a generation would render the city a node within pan-continental networks of investment and consumption possibilities). But he was not eschewing industrialization so much as focusing on a different industry altogether: that of tourism. Mesonero argued in his 1841 *Recuerdos de viaje por Francia y Bélgica* that tourists are key to the modernity of Paris: the spectacular edifices and streets in the French capital attracted the "manantial inagotable de riquezas" (endless flow of riches) that come with "centenarios, miles de … ricos huéspedes, que … en busca de nuevas y gratas sensaciones" (hundreds, thousands of … rich visitors, who … in search of new and pleasurable sensations) disembark daily to spend their "guineas" in the pursuit of fantasies and pleasure (69). In elaborating Madrid's *aspecto*, Mesonero lay claim to modernizing the perceptibility of Madrid as a European showplace and emphasized the urgency of attracting (British) tourists' guineas to the capital.[19] The enhancement of not only citizens', but also *tourists*' perceptions are the point of urban reforms, and any specific, concrete projects undertaken by municipal authorities should be oriented toward this end. Thus the importance of informing the public regularly about the details of what is needed for the city's improvement, while simultaneously reminding readers that the point of improvements is the reclamation of the grandeur, authority and imposing tastefulness that is the birthright of not only the capital of one of the world's greatest (former) empires, but of a modern European city.

From the first issue of the *Semanario* in 1836, modernity looms large as a rationale for the illustrated periodical. The use of woodcut images to directly illuminate text is a contemporary and progressive means of extending popular education and "useful knowledge" (Mesonero "Introducción" 4). The public clamors currently for the illustrated press, consumption of which is furiously in vogue across Europe (4). In the introduction to the 1839 volume, the *Semanario*'s director notes that woodblock engravings are very modern and "sobresalen en todas las publicaciones extranjeras" (are notable in all the foreign publications) (3). Not only is the technology modern, but also the impetus given to Spanish craftspersons and artists is new and progressive, remedying "el atraso lamentable de nuestras artes" (the lamentable backwardness of our arts) (3). One of the most modern aspects of the *Semanario*, then (according to Mesonero), is the fact that its generation of a body or storehouse of autocthonous Spanish imagery having to do with Spanish themes, places and interests, has at the same time served to advance Spain economically – by giving work to Spanish artists in need of *aplicación* (application) (4) – and industrially, through the stimulation of progress in print technologies.

No matter how many inventions, machines, or industrial advances a country might produce, none of them is of benefit if the public lacks access to ideas and readings; thus "las publicaciones baratas" (inexpensive publications) render the greatest advantage in modern culture, as "la lectura es la base de la instrucción, la instrucción es la primera rueda de todas las máquinas, el móvil de todas las riquezas; un pueblo que no lee opondrá siempre una fuerza invincible a su prosperidad" (reading is the base of instruction, education is the primary wheel of all machinery, the motivating force behind all riches; a people that does not read will always pose an invincible force against its own prosperity) (3) and the greatest benefit is generated by affordable *illustrated* publications, as they can capture "la atención general" (general attention) and put ideas and initiatives "en tan inmediato contacto con el pueblo" (in such immediate contact with the people) (4).

The illustrations in the *Semanario* during the period under discussion ranged from tiny cartoon vignettes, to impressive architectural views, to portrait busts, to picturesque and sublime renderings of landscapes. Notable are the numerous tables, charts and graphics devoted to topics in natural history, hygiene, economics and engineering. For example, over the course of several months the 1839 volume featured anatomical drawings to illustrate an article on the restrictive effects of corsets, brief tables of statistics in short blurbs such as "tarifa de multas en tiempos de Luis X" (price-list of fines at the time of Louis X), a depiction of a thermometer in an article on "el Termómetro," and so on (pages 36, 98 and 104 respectively). The use of such illustrations for this kind of material had been standard since the middle of the eighteenth century, from the 1751 launching of Diderot's and D'Alembert's massive, illustrated encyclopedic publishing venture, the *Encyclopèdie*, through the 1820s transatlantic periodical

Museo Universal de Ciencias y Artes, and on to the *Penny Magazine* and the *Semanario*.

Under Mesonero's editorship the *Semanario* explicitly engaged in a two-pronged initiative concerning the modernization of the city by pairing rationalized visual practices and the orderly mustering of information, with text content designed to emphasize key ideas concerning imperial glory and enlightened urban progress. For example (again from the 1839 volume), two articles on the Caja de ahorros (savings bank) extolled the bank's "halagueño espectáculo" (pleasing spectacle) of Christian charity and sensible morals (no. 8: 64), while at the same time assuring readers that participation in the Caja, "verdadero blasón del siglo actual" (truly the glory of the century we live in) (no. 7: 56), was a progressive act that would "propagar el amor al trabajo, único manantial de la riqueza pública y privada" (propagate love of work, the sole source of public and private riches) (no. 7: 56).[20] A few months later, a full-page "estado demostrativo" (display chart) utilized the table and column format to convey to readers exact figures concerning deposits and receipts in the Caja. As the editor notes in a comment below the table, the *estado demostrativo* format is intended to help the reader "formar idea a un golpe de vista de la marcha y progreso de este filantrópico establecimiento" (form at a glance an idea of the progress and growth of this philanthropic establishment) (no. 18: 144). Mesonero's Caja de Ahorros initiative was one among several urbanization projects intended to "marcar una gran distinción entre el antiguo y el moderno Madrid" (distinguish clearly between the old and the new Madrid) (Maluquer y Salvador 4). Thus the *Semanario* employs modern representational modes to best transmit progressive ideas such as the role of widespread capital accumulation in the reform of urban life.

As Mesonero signaled in the prospectus to the *Semanario*, texts would be paired, for purposes of clarity, with "sus correspondientes ilustraciones" (their corresponding illustrations), such as "sendas viñetas que reproducen con exactitud los personajes, sitios, monumentos y producciones naturales" (discrete vignettes that reproduce with exactitude the characters, places, monuments and natural products).[21] The "exactitude" of correspondence between text and image was a factor in the truth-telling function of the kinds of prints used to disseminate information in certain series of articles. In the case of the 1839 "Termómetro" article, for example, the register of the verbal content is that of factual explanation of the device, and the accompanying illustration serves precisely to refer to the discussed content concerning the instrument's workings. (Figure 2.2). Prominent in each issue of the *Semanario* (beginning in 1839) were articles on "España pintoresca," and "Madrid artístico," whose accompanying images effected representation within the register of architectural plans, official city views, and the portrait – all of which serve documentary rather than fictional functions. (Figure 2.3). Nor were the images in these series paired with *costumbrista* articles that dealt in imaginary or satirical scenarios concerning place. The juxtaposition of portraits or factual images, and narrative texts relaying scientific or historical data, proposed their mutually reinforced truthfulness and argued for the subjects' position in a modernity made explicit through the modern medium of illustrated serialization itself.[22]

104 **SEMANARIO PINTORESCO.**

dores de tan espantoso *repique*, dice un autor, levantaron el sitio y emprendieron la ?uga. La mayor campana que se conoce es la de un convento situado en Moscou, la que aseguran tiene 41 pies de circunferencia, y pesa 1409 quintales.

—

LAS 2734 LENGUAS.

El sabio aleman Adelung, ha calculado que el número de lenguas que se hablan en Europa es 387 : en Asia 987: en Africa 276; en América 1084 : total 2734. La confusion hace progresos.

—

LAS DOS MITADES.

Un poetrasto que acababa de componer un largo poema preguntó á un amigo de qué modo se valdria para hacerle mas agradable al público. Quitàndole la mitad, contestó aquel, y suprimiendo la otra.

—

La poesía de las cuatro naciones.

La poesía italíana (decia el Papa Ganganelli), es un *fuego que chispea;* la poesía española un *fuego que enciende*; la poesía francesa un *fuego que ilumina*, y la poesía inglesa un *fuego que ennegrece*.

—

TAPICES.

Los primeros fueron fabricados por los sarracenos en el Mediodia de la Francia en 742, bajo el imperio de su 17.º rey Childerico II.

EL TERMOMETRO.

Al tratar del termómetro no intentamos entrar en pormenores cuya esplicacion pertenece mas bien á un estenso tratado elemental de física que á un sucinto artículo de periódico. Limitarémonos pues à decir que este instrumento inventado à fines del siglo XVI, y cuyo autor no se sabe con certeza, no se divide en igual número de grados en los diferentes paises en que se halla puesto en uso. Distínguense los termómetros *Centigrado*, *Reaumur* y *Farenheit.* La unidad de la medida es en los dos primeros el intérvalo comprendido entre la temperatura del hielo cuando se derrite, y la del agua cociendo bajo 0m, 76 de presion atmosférica; este intérvalo se divide en 100 partes en el termómetro *centigrado*, y en 80 en el de *Reaumur.* De aqui se deduce que para transformar, por ejemplo, 20 grados de Reaumur en los centigrados que los corresponden basta multiplicar 20 por 5 | 4 y nos producirà 25. Si el número 20 representase los grados del centigrado habria que multiplicarlos por 4 | 5 y nos daria 16. Puede ejecutarse la operacion sobre la figura que à continuacion estampamos.

El termómetro Farenheit, usado particularmente en los paises en que prevalece el idioma inglés, no tiene por unidad de medida el mismo intérvalo que los dos primeros: sus dos estremos fijos son la temperatura del agua cociendo, y la que se obtiene por la mezcla de iguales porciones de sal marina y de nieve, mezcla que produce un frio mayor que el de la nieve sola. Este intervalo està dividido en 212 partes: el yelo derritiéndose corresponde al grado 32, de lo que resulta que el intervalo que media entre esta temperatura y la del agua cociendo se divide en 180 partes. Por consiguiente si se quiere transformar un número de grados Farenheit, por ejemblo, 92, en centígrados habrá de comenzarse por separar 32 ° para colocarle al punto de marca del centigrado, en seguida se tomaràn los 5 | 9 del resultado, y producirà 33, ° 3 : para el termómetro Reaumur se tomarán los cuatro 4 | 9 y darà 26, ° 7,: que asimismo puede comprobarse en la figura.

De aqni se deduce lo importante que es cuando se cita una temperatura no omitir la designacion de termómetro de que se toma.

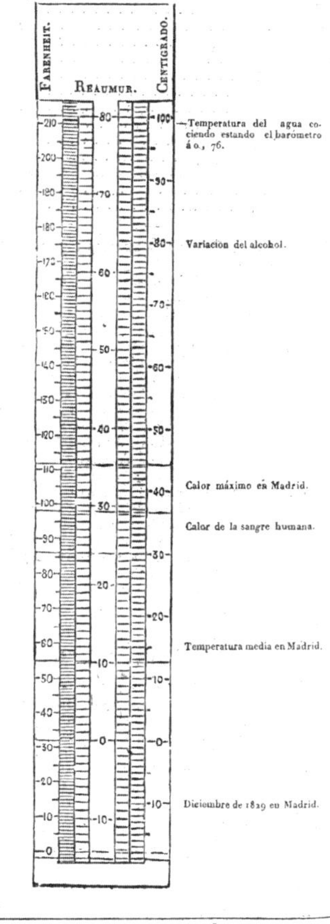

MADRID: IMPRENTA DE OMAÑA, 1840.

Figure 2.2 Artist unknown, "Termómetro." *Semanario Pintoresco* 1839.

Figure 2.3 Artist unknown, "La Iglesia de San Justo, Madrid." *Semanario Pintoresco* 1839.

Conclusion

In the *Proyecto de mejoras generales*, Mesonero claimed that the more visible, easily manageable and hospitable to circulation Madrid became, the less "barbarous" it would be (19), for the "suntuosas puertas y arcos de triunfo que antes ostentaban a su ingreso las grandes capitales, parecen hoy ridículas cuando sirven a limitar su progreso, o han venido a quedar sólo como monumentos artísticos, colocados muchas veces en lo que es hoy centro de la ciudad" (sumptuous gates and triumphal arches that great capitals previously boasted at their entrances, now appear ridiculous when they serve to limit progress, or have become little more than artistic monuments, often placed in what is today the center of the city) (8). Rather (he held), any reform projects should be undertaken to let the grandeur of the city center and of the capital's past shine through without the obstacle of such ostentation: the city's authorities should focus on "necessity" and "convenience," and should "trazar un camino que a ellos conduzca; a fomentar y utilizar lo existente; a neutralizar los obstáculos que se opongan; a impulsar, en fin, y promover la industria privada y su justo y racional galardón" (trace a path that leads to them; to foment and utilize that which already is constructed; to neutralize obstacles that might be placed in the way of progress; to push, ultimately, and promote private industry and its just and rational reward) (10). The point was not to create Madrid as "artistic," "monumental," or "civilized" *ex nihilo*, but rather to effect the selective demolitions, rehabbings and installations that would bring an authentic yet invisible inheritance of splendor into plain view.

Carlos Reyero observes that beginning in the mid-1830s, "figuras históricas universalmente reconocidas comenzaron a encarnar el orgullo nacional, por encima de las controversias políticas de los tiempos … [y] más allá de la dependencia de un presente incierto" (universally recognized historic figures began to embody national pride, beyond the political controversies of the times … [and] removed from dependence on an uncertain present) (35) – a consideration appealing to those desiring commemorative statuary in a city rife with social and political instability. The first monument accordingly erected was that to Cervantes, installed 1835 in the Plaza de las Cortes. Mesonero praised it in his *Rápida ojeada* (32); yet a decade after the statue's installation, Mesonero clarified (in the *Proyecto de mejoras*) that such projects make sense only as part of a larger program of "progress" (8), which meant the selective combination of the city's past glories with advances in industrial techniques (such as iron and glass architecture, or improved street lighting). Thus even as he acknowledged the role played in other historic cities by commemorative sculptures, Mesonero insisted that Madrid's relative youth as a capital invited an urban planning praxis that might selectively highlight imperial grandeur through the installation of not monuments or triumphal arches, but a modern program of economic and industrial development.

In a cultural context of constant change (political, proprietary, technological) and representational innovation (e.g., the diorama, the daguerreotype), the *Semanario* took up-to-the-minute visual information technology – the cultivation of national artists; the latest mode of aligning data in tables and charts – and utilized it as a tool to enhance narrative information concerning the modernization of both Madrid and the nation. In this regard Mesonero pointed explicitly to the importance of the illustrated periodical in the editor's "Advertencia" to the January 1, 1837 issue of the *Semanario.* "Nos lisonjeamos de que muy en breve podremos ofrecer" (we are pleased to announce that we quite soon will be able to offer) the reader a text that can compete with "las numerosas publicaciones de este género que ven cada día nacer las capitales más adelantadas" (the numerous publications of this type that are launched every day in the most advanced capital cities), he informed the reader, promising "una publicación beneficiosa al pais" (a publication beneficial to the nation) (Mesonero 1837: 1). Two years later, the frontispiece to the 1839 volume of the *Semanario*, featuring a woodblock print titled "Lectura de las familias" (reading for families) conveys the benefits accruing to the country through illustrated reading. (Figure 2.4) Several groupings of persons are interacting with text: some are reading, and some listening or watching. All of them are referring to visual imagery in their activities. Three groupings use pages bearing text and printed illustrations, and one is occupied by consultation of a printed page with reference to a globe. Clearly, what they are discussing is rendered more "perceptible" (as Mesonero had theorized the function of illustrations) and rewarding than it would be through the medium of print alone; and this is inextricably bound up with the fact that they are discussing and looking communally, their intimate interactions a synecdoche of the larger gathering of persons and interests that is the nation. These groupings seem to configure a clarity of purpose extending beyond an unstable present. They represent the readers and visitors in whom Mesonero hoped that a training in propositional frameworks around the notion of progress, and an awareness of the glories of Spanish history, might trigger recognition of a Madrid newly visible as a modern European capital.

Notes

1. In *Memorias de un setentón*, Mesonero informs readers that he wanted to found a periodical "nueva absolutamente entre nosotros en la esencia y en su forma, y a semejanza de las que con los títulos *Penny Magazine* y *Magasin Pittoresque* había visto nacer en Londres y París" (absolutely new to us in essence and form, and resembling those with the titles *Penny Magazine* and *Magasin Pittoresque*, which I had seen appear daily in London and Paris) (II, 180). For convenience, in subsequent references to the journal I will abbreviate the title to *Semanario.*
2. For more on *The Penny Magazine*, see *Paper and Printing*; and William David Washington, "The Penny Magazine: A Study of the Genesis and Utilitarian Application of the Popular Miscellany" (Ph.D. thesis, Ohio State University, 1967).

Figure 2.4 Artist unknown, "Lectura de las familias." *Semanario Pintoresco* frontispiece, 1839.

3. *Manual de Madrid: Descripción de la Corte y la Villa de Madrid* (Madrid: Imprenta de D.M. de Burgos) went through several re-editions through the 1830s, and then significant expansion in the following two decades, as *Manual histórico-topográfico, administrativo y artístico de Madrid* (Madrid: Imprenta de D. Antonio Yenes, 1844, 1854).
4. For more on Madrid during the period, see Baker *Materiales*; Juliá et al.; and Parsons.
5. For more on Mesonero and his urbanization work, see Baker "Introducción"; Maluquer y Salvador; Martín Muñoz; Romero; Ruiz Palomeque; and the contributions in *Mesonero Romanos (1803–1882)*.
6. Mesonero himself produced one of the most important of nineteenth-century European urban guides, the 1831 *Manual de Madrid*.
7. For more on the first years of photography in Spain, see Fontanella *Photography*; López Mondejar; and Riego *La introducción*.
8. For more on *costumbrismo*, see Fontanella *La imprenta*; Fernández de Montesinos; and Varela.
9. For more on the work of Clifford, see Fontanella *Clifford en España*.
10. An interesting discussion of the ideological staging of content through graphic column format is found in Henkin (Chapter 5).

11. Cited in de la Motte and Przblyski (6).
12. A reference to a character in Cervantes's *Don Quixote*. Maese Pedro was both a puppet master and a master of deception (II, 25 and 26).
13. *Trabajos no coleccionados*, 3; citing from *Memorias de un setentón*.
14. For convenience I will abbreviate the title *Trabajos no coleccionados* to *TNC* in subsequent references.
15. Uztáriz, in his *Discurso sobre el gobierno de Madrid*, had many of the same complaints as did Mesonero a century later: the difficulty of passing uniform building codes, the need for municipal and private interests to work in concert, and advances in other European cities that never seem to take root in Madrid. Mesonero possessed the Uztáriz manuscript and consulted it (Molas Ribalta xvi).
16. To take two examples from 1846, the *Memoria Explicativa del Plano General de Mejoras*, *TNC* 265–85; the "Proyecto de Ordenanzas de Policía Urbana y Rural," *TNC* 219–32.
17. For example, the 1851 "Traída de aguas a Madrid" *TNC* 196–210; or, from the same year, "Mercados cubiertos" *TNC* 211–18.
18. González Yánci (26) points out the exponential increase in passenger traffic made possible by rail travel: before the introduction of the railway there had been one coach a day to Aranjuez from Madrid, which carried a maximum of twenty passengers on the six-hour journey; but by rail there were three departures a day to Aranjuez, carrying up to 690 passengers on a ninety-minute hour trip that cost 25 per cent less.
19. Indeed, his insistence on the connection between a visible *aspecto* and civilization was current ideology across Europe: for example, in 1838 the House of Commons Select Committee argued that London's lower classes had to be able to *observe* their "better-educated neighbors" in order to improve themselves (Urry 80), and Baron Hausmann's large-scale Parisian demolitions were explicitly undertaken to ensure the orderliness of *policía* that comes through visibility.
20. The Caja de Ahorros was founded in 1838 and opened its doors in early 1839. For more on the Caja see Sanz García.
21. Cited in Rubio Cremades (72).
22. Further discussion of such relationships is found in Riego, *La construcción social*.

Works Cited

Baker, Edward. "Introducción." In R. Mesonero Romanos. *Rápida ojeada sobre el estado de la Capital y los medios de mejorarla*. Ed. E. Baker. Madrid: CIDUR, 1989. i–xxiv.

—— *Materiales para escribir Madrid: Literatura y espacio urbano de Moratín a Galdós*. Madrid: Siglo Veintiuno, 1999.

Boym, Svetlana. *The Future of Nostalgia*. New York: Basic Books, 2001.

De la Motte, Dean, and Jeannene M. Przblyski. "Introduction." In *Making the News: Modernity and the Mass Press in Nineteenth-Century France*. Eds. D. de la Motte and J.M. Przblyski. Amherst: University of Massachusetts Press, 1999. 1–14.

Diderot, Denis, and Jean D'Alembert, eds. *Encyclopèdie, ou Dictionnaire raisonné des Sciences, des arts et des métiers*. Paris: Briasson, 1751–65. 17 vols.

Fernández de Montesinos, José. *Costumbrismo y novela: ensayo sobre el redescubrimiento de la realidad española*. Berkeley: University of California Press, 1960.

Ferrer y Herrera, Antonio Carlos. *Paseo por Madrid 1835*. Ed. J.M. Pita Andrade. Madrid: Colección Almenara, 1952.

Fontanella, Lee. *La imprenta y las letras en la España romántica*. Berne: Peter Lang, 1982.

—— *Photography in Spain in the Nineteenth Century*. Dallas, TX: Delahunty Gallery; San Francisco, CA: Fraenkel Gallery, 1983.

—— *Clifford en España. Un fotógrafo en la Corte de Isabel II*. Madrid: El Viso, 1999.

Gombrich, E.H. *The Uses of Images: Studies in the Social Function of Art and Visual Communication*. London: Phaidon, 1999.

González Yánci, María Pilar. *Los inicios del ferrocarril en Madrid*. Madrid: Artes Gráficas Municipales, 1994.

Henkin, David. *City Reading: Written Words and Public Spaces in Antebellum New York*. New York: Columbia University Press, 1995.

Juliá, Santos. *Madrid: Historia de una capital*. Madrid: Alianza, 1994.

La Linterna Mágica. Madrid: Imprenta de Doña Rosa Sanz, 1820.

López Mondejar, Publio. *Historia de la fotografía en España*. Barcelona: Lunwerg, 1997.

Maluquer y Salvador, José. *Ahorro popular: Efemérides de Madrid del 17 de Febrero de 1839. Iniciativas de Pontejos y Mesonero Romanos*. Madrid: Sucesora de M. Minuesa de los Ríos, 1914.

Martín Muñoz, José. *La política local en el Madrid de Pontejos (1834-1836)*. Madrid: Caja de Madrid, 1995.

Mesonero Romanos, Ramón. *Manual de Madrid: Descripción de la Corte y la Villa de Madrid*. Madrid: Imprenta de D.M. de Burgos, 1831.

—— "Boletín." *Diario de Avisos de Madrid* (April 1, 1835): 5. In *Trabajos no coleccionados*. Vol. I. Madrid: Imprenta de los Hijos de M.G. Hernández, 1903. 2 vols.

—— "Policía urbana." *Diario de Avisos de Madrid* (April 20, 1835): 15–18. In *Trabajos no coleccionados*. Vol. I. Madrid: Imprenta de los Hijos de M.G. Hernández, 1903. 2 vols.

—— "Policía urbana." *Diario de Avisos de Madrid* (May 24, 1835): 36–42. In *Trabajos no coleccionados*. Vol. I. Madrid: Imprenta de los Hijos de M.G. Hernández, 1903. 2 vols.

—— "Boletín." *Diario de Avisos de Madrid* (June 4 J, 1835): 43–7. In *Trabajos no coleccionados*. Vol. I. Madrid: Imprenta de los Hijos de M.G. Hernández, 1903. 2 vols.

—— "Puestos ambulantes." *Diario de Avisos de Madrid* (9 Junio 1835): 48–52. In *Trabajos no coleccionados*. Vol. I. Madrid: Imprenta de los Hijos de M.G. Hernández, 1903. 2 vols.

—— "Aguas." *Diario de Avisos de Madrid* (June 24, 1835): 53-7. In *Trabajos no coleccionados*. Vol. I. Madrid: Imprenta de los Hijos de M.G. Hernández, 1903. 2 vols.

—— "Introducción." *Semanario Pintoresco Español* (April 3, 1836): 3–6.

—— "Advertencia." *Semanario Pintoresco Español* (January 1, 1837): 1.

—— "A nuestros lectores." *Semanario Pintoresco Español* (January 6, 1839): 3–4.

—— *Proyecto de mejoras generales de Madrid, presentado al excelentísimo Ayuntamiento Constitucional.* Madrid: Imprenta de D. Agustín Espinosa y Compañía, 1846.

—— "Estátuas y monumentos públicos." *La Ilustración.* (March 8, 1851): 129–37. In *Trabajos no coleccionados*. Vol. I. Madrid: Imprenta de los Hijos de M. G. Hernández, 1903. 2 vols.

—— "Proyecto de nueva barrera y paseo de Atocha." *La Ilustración* (April 5, 1851): 138–47. In *Trabajos no coleccionados*. Vol. I. Madrid: Imprenta de los Hijos de M.G. Hernández, 1903. 2 vols.

—— *Memorias de un setentón: Natural y vecino de Madrid.* Madrid: Oficinas de la Ilustración Española y Americana, 1881. 2 vols.

—— *Recuerdos de viaje por Francia y Bélgica en 1840 a 1841.* Nueva edición. Madrid: Oficinas de la Ilustración Española y Americana, 1881.

—— *Trabajos no coleccionados*. Vol. I. Reformas de Madrid y de su administración. Madrid: Imprenta de los Hijos de M.G. Hernández, 1903. 2 vols.

—— *Rápida ojeada sobre el estado de la capital, y los medios de mejorarla* (1835). Ed. Edward Baker. Madrid: CIDUR, 1989.

Mesonero Romanos (1803-1882). Madrid: Ayuntamiento/Delegación de Cultura, 1982.

Messaris, Paul. *Visual Literacy: Image, Mind and Reality.* Boulder, CO: Westview, 1994.

Molas Ribalta, Pedro. "El Marqués de Uztáriz y el *Discurso sobre el Gobierno de*

Madrid." C. Uztáriz. *Discurso sobre el gobierno de Madrid.* Ed. Pedro Molas Ribalta. Oviedo: Instituto Feijoo de Estudios del Siglo XVIII. IX–XXVIII, 2000.

Museo Universal de Ciencias y Artes. London, Mexico, Colombia, 1825–6.

Paper and Printing: The New Technology of the 1830s. Taken from the Monthly Supplement of *The Penny Magazine of the Society for the Diffusion of Useful Knowledge*. Ed. Colin Cohen. Oxford: Plough Press, 1982.

Parsons, Deborah. *A Cultural History of Madrid.* Oxford and New York: Berg, 2003.

Paseo por Madrid, o Guía del forastero en la Corte. Madrid: Repullés, 1820.

The Penny Magazine of the Society for the Diffusion of Useful Knowledge. London, 1832–45.

Reyero, Carlos. *La escultura conmemorativa en España: La edad de oro del monumento público, 1820–1914.* Madrid: Cátedra, 1999.

Riego, Bernardo. *La introducción de la fotografía en España: Un reto científico y cultural.* Girona: CCG Ediciones/Ajuntament de Girona, 2000.

—— *La construcción social de la realidad a través de la fotografía y el grabado informativo en la España del siglo XIX.* Santander: Universidad de Cantabria, 2001.

Romero, Federico. *Mesonero Romanos, activista del Madrileñismo.* Madrid: Instituto de Estudios Madrileños, 1968.

Rubio Cremades, Enrique. *Periodismo y literatura: Ramón de Mesonero Romanos y El Semanario Pintoresco Español.* Valencia: Institut de Cultura Juan Gil-Albert/Generalitat de Valencia, 1995.

Ruiz Palomeque, Eulalia. *Ordenación y transformaciones urbanas del casco antiguo madrileño durante los siglos XIX y XX.* Madrid: Instituto de Estudios Madrileños, 1976.

Sanz García, José María. *El Monte de Piedad y la Caja de Ahorros de Madrid (1702–1942).* Madrid: Artes Gráficas Municipales, 1972.

Schivelbusch, Wolfgang. *The Railway Journey: Trains and Train Travel in the Nineteenth Century.* Trans. Anselm Hollo. New York: Urizen Books, 1980.

Semanario Pintoresco Español. Madrid, 1836–57.

Stewart, Susan. *On Longing: Narratives of the Miniature, the Gigantic, the Souvenir, the Collection.* Baltimore, MD: Johns Hopkins University Press, 1984.

Urry, John. "Sensing the City." In *The Tourist City.* Eds. D. Judd and S. Fainstein. New Haven, CT: Yale University Press, 1999. 71–86.

Uztáriz, Casimiro de. *Discurso sobre el gobierno de Madrid* (1746). Ed. Pedro Molas Ribalta. Oviedo: Instituto Feijoo de Estudios del Siglo XVIII, 2000.

Varela, José, ed. *El costumbrismo romántico*. Madrid: EMESA, 1969.

Vega, Jesusa. "Estampas calcográficas de la Década Ominosa entre la devoción, la Propaganda política y lo popular." *Archivo Español de Arte* 67.268 (October–December 1994): 343–58.

–3–

Foresight, Blindness or Illusion? Women and Citizenship in the Second Series of Galdós's *Episodios nacionales*

David R. George, Jr

The nineteenth century was characterized by the proliferation of images in the enormous range of popular and intellectual publications that contributed to the rise of mass culture. Pictures were an important means of supplementing narrative, and in Spain, as elsewhere in Europe, readers – especially new readers – were trained in the techniques of reading images and texts together in illustrated newspapers, novels, and advertisements. The widespread use of imagery reflected a more generalized cultural practice of picturing and visualizing, even in the absence of concrete or material images, as a mode of understanding the world. By mid-century, the application of positivistic methods in almost every field of scientific and social investigation, as well as in the literary and visual arts, caused seeing to become the principal mode of discerning truths, and for representing existence and bodies of knowledge (Fabian 106–9).

Benito Pérez Galdós's adoption of the Realist and Naturalist aesthetics in the late 1870s, and the use of themes related to vision and blindness in several of his novels, most notably *Marianela* (1878) and *Cánovas* (1912), situate the author's literary production plainly within a mass culture that was increasingly concerned with seeing Spain's present and envisioning its future. While only twenty of Galdós's novels were ever illustrated (the First and Second Series of his *Episodios nacionales* in 1882–4), sight as a metaphor of interpretation is prevalent throughout his writings as readers are frequently invited to "see" what the author or his narrators describe. This reliance on visualization and the invitation to see are the common denominators that tie together the great variety of historiographic discourses Galdós employs in the early *Episodios nacionales*, published between 1873 and 1879, to represent contemporary Spanish history to readers in the late 1870s. The evidence presented by the different voices that directly and indirectly narrate the twenty historical novels, and the principle of authority that allows the characters to speak and to be "heard," is based on the fact that they have seen and bore witness to the main events of Spanish history in the first three decades of the nineteenth century. Galdós's citizen-historians use vision both literally (through the description of things seen) and metaphorically (through the evocation of images) to narrate the past and to organize individual and national experiences. Vision and common lines of sight construct an internal coherence within each series of novels by integrating a chorus of characters into a resonating collective "we saw" that is fundamental to the legitimatization of the short historical fictions as representative of national experience (Lozano 18–19).

The use of vision in the early *Episodios*, specifically in the Second Series, binds the historical novels to the broader visual culture of the early Restoration period (1875–81), when official as well as popular art was dominated by academic history painting. The publication of the Second Series coincides almost exactly with the consolidation of Antonio Cánovas del Castillo's political system and the key years of his first tenure as Prime Minister. The drive to normalize sight through the constitution of a common visual field found in the *Episodios* is underpinned by the moderate liberal project to redefine the proper citizen of the new Spanish state into a mere observer of political and social realities rather than as an instigator of action. The novels in many ways seem to reinforce the Cánovas regime's desire to pacify society through the normalization and institutionalization of political behaviors conducive to the creation of an ordered liberal civil society. In response to the Restoration's search for historical continuity, the second cycle of historical novels that began to appear in 1875 exchange the violence and upheaval depicted in the First Series for the ordinary, quotidian conditions of what the narrator refers to as "el vivir lento y casi siempre doloroso de la sociedad" under the notorious reign of Ferdinand VII, from 1814 to 1833 (Galdós 163). By embedding the narration of history into the everyday conversations and discussions of private individuals who share their visions of Spanish society, the fictionalized depictions of the Liberal Triennium (1820 to 1823), and the repression of the Ominous Decade (1823 to 1833), the collective experiences of the past are offered to readers of the late 1870s as a backdrop against which to envision the political realities of the Restoration and of assessing their own behavior as observers and citizens.

The mental and physical capacities and incapacities of observation associated with the characters of the Second Series, along with the techniques employed by them to see and to be seen – and represented – bear directly upon the narrator's explicit and implicit assessments of their fitness to act as citizens and, ultimately, to make positive contributions to the construction of a future liberal state in Spain. References to vision, blindness, optical illusions, and hallucinations caused by dementia, madness, obsession, ignorance, or the loss of consciousness, are signposts in the selection process through which the ten novels of the Second Series promote an image of the citizen as political spectator rather than actor. Allusions to vision, visibility, and ways of seeing are particularly striking in the presentation and subsequent treatment of the female protagonists of the novels. While characters of both genders suffer from visual maladies, the use of visual metaphors and scientific references to sight are particularly salient in descriptions of how the women in the novels see and experience history. From their first appearance, the personalities of main female protagonists, Jenara Baraona, Sola Gil de la Cuadra, and Sor Teodora de Aransis y Peñafort are framed by detailed references to their capacities as observers and to the physiological conditions that make their sight possible.

The three women exemplify the different avenues of public visibility available to middle-class women in late-nineteenth-century Spain and the ways in which each incarnates a different modality of female vision. Their qualities, successes, and failures as observers of political and historical realities can be studied as indicators of late-nineteenth-century perceptions of women's aptitudes for engaging the public sphere, as well as the dangers that their unchecked participation might pose for society at large. My study focuses on the descriptions of the way each woman sees and how this presentation predicates the way she is subsequently seen by readers in the historical and imaginary society they inhabit. I explore two possible explanations for the attention given to women as observers in the Second Series. From a clinical perspective based on the scientific discoveries of the nineteenth century, the focus on women's vision as a problem further corroborates theories of the "weaker sex" upon which much social and political theory was based. In this sense, the symptoms found in Galdós's female characters simply lend further credence to the policy of excluding women from the public sphere. On another level, the descriptions of how women see provided the novelist Galdós with a mechanism for exposing the difficulties implied in the drive to normalize and rationalize sight as a metaphor for the creation of the consensus necessary to transform Spanish society.

Over the course of the century, vision passed from being a privileged form of accessing knowledge to becoming itself an object of scrutiny and study (Crary 1990: 3). The discovery that the human body played a pivotal role in the production of optical experience gave rise to a subjective model of vision that had an unsettling effect on classical models of knowledge. The body could no longer be considered a neutral site of representation for the reflection of external truths. Instead, vision was shown to occur at the nexus between the body's anatomical and physiological conditions, and data drawn from the exterior world. With the notion that optical truth was inseparable from whatever the healthy corporal eye experienced, new theories of knowledge and technologies of observation had to be designed around the regulation and normalization of sight as a way of regaining access to objective reality. The result was the emergence of a new kind of observer whose sight had to be limited to a prescribed set of possibilities determined by the positioning of the body before an apparatus that isolated the eye. Jonathan Crary observes that such devices and techniques "are the outcome of a complex remaking of the individual as observer in something calculable and regularizable and of human vision into something measurable and thus exchangeable" (Crary 1990: 17).

The problem of managing the subjective vision of the observer has its correlate in nineteenth-century political theory in the difficulties of containing Romantic individualism in the form of the private citizen and the creation of a liberal public sphere. By the middle of the century, debates on the nature of liberty and on ideal forms of political participation increasingly turned away from the idealization of direct engagement modeled on the democracies of Antiquity, and toward the creation of representative institutions that regulate and organize the individual and collective demands on the state from within the private sphere. From this shift, the spectator/observer soon emerged as the dominant model of political participation and citizenship. "The spectator," Hannah Arendt writes, "because he is not involved, can perceive [the] design of providence or nature, which is hidden from the actor" (52). The splitting of the subject between the disinterested judge and the interested agent, bestows on the former the capacity "to grasp individual actions as parts of a totality" and on the latter, the insight to act accordingly (Arendt 52). Through the demarcation of the limits of individual autonomy and public responsibility, the subject as citizen is divided and positioned as a distanced, yet active observer before the spectacle of the state. Chris Otter remarks that in the nineteenth century, bourgeois "Respectability involved a certain distancing, and sight, as the primary sense of distance, played a critical role in its performance" (2). Vision was privileged as a denial of the immediacy and proximity associated with the other senses like taste and smell. With the proper degree of self-control, sight was assumed to be more rational and less visceral. The all-important division of social space into realms of public and private that underpinned liberal governments is made possible by a system of representation-based technologies of "social envisioning" that allowed the individual to "see" the public from within the private sphere – the private familial home or the various spaces of informal bourgeois sociability (Durham Peters 79). Likewise, a consequent transformation of urban spaces also allowed for the performance or staging of privacy, making it visibly quantifiable in public (Otter 6).

In the context of the emerging liberal state in Europe, the concept of female citizenship is better understood as a civic duty, since it was theorized almost universally as an extension of male citizenship and the patriarchal household. Together with property ownership, marriage and family were seen as crucial elements for the maintenance of private existence that, as Jürgen Habermas has identified, were necessary in order for men to enter into the public sphere as citizens (29). The institution of marriage secured an appropriately productive and safe place for middle-class women within society, while excluding them from its power structure. The marriage contract made women subject to the society's rigid code of social obligations, but it also obliged them to relinquish most of their social rights as a condition of their inclusion. As a consequence, female citizenship could be practiced only from within the marriage contract and the domestic space that it safeguarded. Only from the legitimate positions of wife and mother were women rendered visible and made available as potential subjects to be represented by the bourgeois order of the liberal state.

Jo Labanyi writes that for nineteenth-century political theorists "women were a special problem since … [they] were incapable of transcending subjective emotion" (43). Weakness is an adjective applied to describe both women's potential practice of public space and their capacity to see and discern the truth. The female observer and the female gaze are marked as dangerous for the establishment, for the maintenance of optical truth, and for the overall functional order of a public sphere in which individuals are obliged to look beyond private, subjective interests in order to measure their actions and become conscious of how these affect the good of the whole community. In the reconfiguration of social space that arises from the ascendancy of the bourgeoisie, the home and its intimate realm comes to function in a manner similar to the plethora of optical gadgets that filled the European city arcades as well as the salons of many middle-class houses. The domestic sphere can be seen as an optical device designed to limit the reach of women's vision and to restrict their visibility within society. The result: female citizen's civic duties are contained within the scope of the husband and family's immediate interests. Crary studies in detail the various optical devices and techniques of observation that develop in response to the need to control the eye, separating it from the body of the observer, in order to assure a proper perception of reality. Apparatuses like the stereoscope and zoetrope isolate the eye and therefore limit vision to only the very specific range of visual effects allowed by the machine. In the case of the female observer, the need to isolate eyesight and to create distance becomes even more urgent: women's capacities to see and to judge properly are seen as a function of the appropriate positioning of their bodies and their eyes before "devices" like the family and the institutions of marriage that not only control their ability to see but also regulate their reproductive function in bourgeois society.

The plot of the Second Series is built around seven main characters: Salvador Monsalud, Sola Gil de la Cuadra, Jenara Baraona, Carlos Navarro, Patricio Sarmiento, Benigno Cordero, and Juan Pipaón. The ten volumes follow these individuals through two decades of Spanish history, from 1813 to 1834. The series opens with the retreat of the French armies and Joseph Bonaparte in 1813–14, and follows the course of the notorious reign of Ferdinand VII that ended with his death in 1833. The period depicted is one marked by great tumult and political repression, the rise of the middle class, and the normalization of the basic tenets of early-nineteenth-century liberalism. The lives of these seven individuals are interconnected on two levels: first, and most obviously, by a shared historical experience; and second, by the set of love triangles and intrigues that develop around the hero of the series: Salvador Monsalud. As a liberal and Francophile, he is the catalyst for a great many conflicts and rivalries; the most lasting of which arises in the first volume, *El equipaje del rey José* (1875), between him and his half-brother Carlos Navarro. Navarro is Monsalud's diametric opposite: fervent Catholic, reactionary and Absolutist, with an eye on preserving the Spanish tradition against foreign influences and liberalism.

The ideological enmity between the two men is personified in the astute and seductive figure, Jenara Baraona, who marries Navarro but remains hopelessly in love with Monsalud. Jenara's first appearance in *El equipaje del rey José* plays a key role in the narrator's description of the rivalry and hatred between Monsalud and Navarro. Her introduction could take many forms, but the text focuses very explicitly on the way she sees. The narrator begins, "Jenarita o Generosa, a pesar de su belleza virginal, tenía en ocasiones un ceño algo sombrío y un modo de mirar que no indicaba diafanidad o, mejor el perfecto equilibrio de espíritu de un ángel celeste" (Galdós 226). Eyes are not directly mentioned, yet they are suggested in the reference made to her "ceño" (brow) and "modo de mirar" (way of looking). The use of the adjective "sombrío" (gloomy) or (shadowy), seems to be more than purely functional. In *Theory of Colours*, Johann Wolfgang von Goethe reverses the Enlightenment's emphasis on transparency by claiming that visual perception occurs in "the realm of … the turbid, cloudy and gloomy" (quoted in Crary 1990: 71). By setting Jenara's eyes in the shadow of a creased brow, an expression that indicates contemplation of and reaction to the world around her, the text very subtly alludes to the processes of visual perception that take place, not in full view, but in the internal eye of the mind. The "weightiness" of her way of looking, the lack of *diafanidad*, defines the character as an active and autonomous observer of the world.

Jenara's "gaze," to use the psychoanalytical term, appears in contrast of her beauty, as the narrator notes, and detracts from it by betraying in fundamental ways the innocence and balance of the feminine "nature" announced by her virginal appearance. Film critic Laura Mulvey writes, "In their traditional exhibitionist role women are simultaneously looked at and displayed, with their appearance coded for strong visual and erotic impact so that they can be said to connote *to-be-looked-at-ness*" (203). In a formulation of female beauty that long predates the cinema, women are idealized as silent, passive objects, seen but never returning the gaze of male admirers. The processes of perception rendered in the description of Jenara's sight cause the figure to challenge such traditionalist notions, and put her at odds with the bourgeois order of the Restoration. In spite of her attractiveness, by looking (back) she undoes the fundamental norms that structure the visual field from a male perspective and so, comes to represent those forces in society that must be contained and disciplined if individual will is to be subjugated to the good of the whole. Her inherent resistance to such norms further aligns her sight with an alternative observer model, theorized as "both the site and the producer of sensation" (Crary 1990: 75). Jenara occupies a position of power vis-à-vis the other characters, on an almost equal footing with her male counterparts. At the same time, by virtue of her sex, she is marked as a potential danger to those around her (Monsalud, Navarro, and the other women characters) as well as to the emerging liberal social order.

The presentation of Jenara continues: "Sus sentimientos, siempre en lucha, se manifestaban de improviso y de una manera torrencial y borrascosa. Cualquier accidente externo, impresionándola como impresiona el rayo, podía hacerlos cambiar en un instante" (Galdós 227). Alone, the observation implies that her behavior is unpredictable, and, indeed, throughout the novels the reader and the other characters are forever trying to understand the true motives that lie behind her actions. However, when put together with the torrential changes in her feelings, the text further highlights the manner in which her vision (and vision in general) functions: external stimuli are processed within the internal systems of the psyche such that reality and its perception can be two entirely different things. Jenara's capacity to see properly is under constant threat by storms of sentiment that cloud over her eyes and that randomly redirect her attention or cause her to misinterpret or overinterpret the events happening around her. As mentioned above, it is precisely in the opaque and cloudy regions that visual perception occurs, yet the problem the text brings out here is something else. For the moderate Liberals of the Restoration, as well as those of the late 1820s, what is problematic is the immediacy and spontaneity that define the relationship between Jenara's actions and her sight. The Jacobin tradition in Spain, as it was represented by the *Exaltado* Liberals, idealized immediacy and direct participation of citizens in the public sphere. For moderates, by contrast, a lack of distance and immediacy was largely responsible for the collapse of previous liberal experiments and was deemed wholly incompatible with so-called rational forms government.

The consequences of Jenara's irrational sight are a primary force driving the series' fictional plot development. Because of her relatively high social position, Jenara is freed from the obligations of conventional bourgeois matrimony and occupies an almost exclusively public position in Spanish society. For much of the ten volumes, she almost never disappears from the public "eye"; a position that is presented ambiguously as both the cause and the effect of her estrangement from her husband. Her frequent comings and goings as she attends the *tertulias* of 1820s Madrid only heightens the tension that exists between her beauty and her curious eyes, and accelerates the dissolution of the stable domestic sphere that would rein her in by isolating her vision, controlling and limiting her gaze. Without a center in the home, her subjective view remains unchecked by the physical and psychological constraints of motherhood and marriage, and she responds only to the whims of her most immediate desires. Jenara's introduction in *El equipaje del rey José* places her outside of the range of accepted behaviors for women imagined by the bourgeois order of the Restoration. Catherine Jagoe observes how the social behavior of women associated with the eighteenth century, like Jenara, came to be counterpoised in Galdós's fiction to that of the nineteenth-century middle-class ideal of the domestic angel (21). However, it can also be argued that the character not only is used to provide a point of contrast to the exalted figure of the angel, but also serves to illustrate the destructive behavior of the male protagonists. The irrational torrents of emotion that determine Jenara's vision throughout the 1820s are replicated in Monsalud's Romantic melancholy and angst at seeing a Spain that fails to correspond to his idealized vision, and in Navarro's fanatical adherence to the reactionary *Apostolicos* and the nascent Carlist movement.

By the conclusion of the Second Series in *Un faccioso más y algunos frailes menos* (1879), both Monsalud and Jenara seek to reinvent themselves in the private sphere once the liberal future of Spain appears to be secure under the regency of María Cristina. This is a key moment in the novel because it demonstrates that the complicity of the observer is necessary for the construction of a new consensus of sight upon which to base the truths of the new political reality. Jenara's retreat from public visibility is signaled by the transformation of her highly politicized salon into an intimate *tertulia* where art and literature are discussed. The move suggests her acceptance of the system of representation to be implanted by the coming liberal regime, and is further confirmed when readers recall that in her new residence in the countryside she would eventually write the memories that the narrator employs in the composition of the sixth volume, *Los cien mil hijos de San Luis* (1877). In the end, she never relinquishes her gaze, and once she is free of her troublesome marriage to Navarro following his death, and after she accepts the impossibility of her relationship with Monsalud, she represents the strongest prospect as a model for the full practice of female citizenship offered to early Restoration society in the Second Series.

Even though Jenara Baraona occupies a central position in the plot of the Second Series, the true heroine of the ten novels is Soledad (Solita) Gil de la Cuadra. Cast as the silent victim of historical circumstance who has little or no interest in the events of history beyond their immediate impact on her desire to be brought together with her protector/guardian Salvador Monsalud. Her innate goodness and humanity is a contrast to the political calculations that motivate the actions of people around her – most notably the social climbing civil servant Juan Braga Pipaón, and Jenara Baraona. Her relationship with Monsalud, following the incarceration of her father by the authorities of the liberal government at the end of the novel, causes her to come into conflict with Jenara, giving form to the second triangulation that structures the plot of the Series. Unlike Jenara, Sola is rarely, if ever, presented outside the private sphere or actively engaging in the many political discussions that connect the lives of the fictional characters to the political and social realities of the 1820s. Attached to the domestic sphere, Sola is offered as representative of the ideal angel of the house whose virtues are explored over the course of the Series via her struggle to secure the roles of wife and mother in a future liberal society.

As in the presentation of Jenara, the introduction of Sola also directs the reader's attention to the character's capacities for visual perception. In Chapter 3 of *El Grande Oriente* (1876), the main action of the story is temporarily interrupted in order to describe the neighbors who inhabit the building on Madrid's narrow Calle Coloreros where Monsalud, his mother, and Patricio Sarmiento, the Jacobin schoolteacher, reside. The narrator catalogues the members of each household, moving from floor to floor. Upon reaching the second apartment on the fourth floor, the narration takes on a mysterious, even sinister tone: an old man of 50, who keeps to himself and who seldom goes out after dark, and a pair of eyes. The narrator chooses to allude at first, indirectly, to the gentleman's sole companion, explaining how "Antes de que penetrara en ella [la vivienda] cualquier extraño, tómabanse minuciosas precauciones, y dos ojos negros miraban por la cruz del ventanillo examinando atentamente al inoportuno" (Galdós 421). Here, attention is drawn to the character's eyes, and even though they are framed by the peephole, readers know from the start that they are black. Such a descriptive detail is completely lacking in the presentation and subsequent information readers learn about Jenara. The eyes are immediately identified as being attached to "una señorita, hija del señor Gil de la Cuadra," the Absolutist functionary/conspirator (Galdós 421). The figure remains nameless for several lines, as the narrator describes her virtues and how she is loved by the neighbors of the building.

A physical description of Sola is not given until several paragraphs later, but when it is, her formal introduction is prefaced by a confession: "Como cronistas, sentimos tener que decir que Solita era fea. Fuera de los ojos negros … no había en su facción ni parte alguna que aisladamente no fuese imperfectísima" (Galdós 422). That only Sola's eyes are seen at first, and that they are later revealed to be her only notable physical attribute, underscore her positioning in the novels and the type of observer that she represents. Like Jenara, Sola also looks. Yet she does so from within her father's home, therefore the potential dangers of her autonomous vision are reined in and controlled. Peering through the cross-shaped peephole (that emphasizes the weight of her Catholic faith) of the door, the young woman's capacity to see is limited to the spatially prescribed possibilities of the interior domestic space. The peephole, like so many optical devices of the nineteenth century, isolates the eyes, and disarticulates them from the body so the world on the other side can be properly distanced and ascertained as truth. Sola's person becomes indistinguishable from the paternal home; therefore, her vision is inseparable from this essential point of reference on the social map. The door of the home functions here as a mask and a filter, as an optical device that protects her and corrects her subjective vision by limiting perceptions of the public sphere to that which is only immediately relevant to the maintenance of the internal sanctity of the familial sphere. As seen through the peephole, society is divided into friends and foes of her family and of her domestic bliss. By placing Sola behind the door, her vision is set up to conform to the liberal ideal of female civic duty widely diffused through Restoration culture in which women's role was limited to the private sphere. It is not surprising that she is affectively referred to by the narrator and the other male characters as *ángel*. Her friend and later suitor, Benigno Cordero, also likes to call her "Hormiguita" to emphasize her industriousness and her "natural" predilection for domestic chores. The result of these appellations is to identify Sola's disposition as model and her potential contribution as a female citizen, as ideal.

In light of her father's political affiliation, Sola's enclosure in the apartment is initially understood as a form of imprisonment perpetuated by the sinister forces of Spain's Absolutist factions. However, her perspective on the world changes very little once she is "freed" from the house following Don Urbano Gil de la Cuadra's unfortunate death at the end of the novel. On her own in the world, "Sola y Monda" (as she refers to herself) spends much of the rest of the series seeking to regain the security of the paternal home, nostalgic for the clarity and stability that the structure provided her eyesight. The character displays a great degree of self-discipline by continuing to see within the parameters of the domestic sphere even though she no longer resides within such a space. "[T]he self-government necessary for liberalism as a technology of rule to operate," Otter remarks, "was precluded by socio-sensual environments within which the human organism was denied the possibility of forming a certain relationship with the senses" (3). The trials and tribulations that Sola faces over the course of the last six volumes of the Series are presented to underscore the strength of her self-control, and to redirect the blame of her inability to see clearly at times, underscores not only towards the inherent weakness of Sola's eyesight, but also that associated with the male vision or lack of vision upon which she seeks to depend for stability and future happiness.

In the seventh novel, *El terror de 1824* (1877), Sola finds herself caring for the exalted liberal Patricio Sarmiento, who has succumbed to hunger and poverty in the early days of the period of political repression known as the Ominous Decade. When, in his delirium, he reaffirms his dream of a glorious death on the gallows in the name of Liberty and demands to be allowed to hand himself over to the police, Sola is horrified at the persistence of the same kind of irrational thought that had led to her father's death and the exile of Monsalud. She responds to his declaration, saying that "La libertad no necesita más víctimas sino hombres que la sepan entender" (Galdós 669). With this statement, she not only ties her own future liberty to the will and acts of men, but also makes an appeal for a rationalized vision of the public sphere. Distance, as noted above in the words of Arendt, is the key to understanding freedom and to using it wisely. In this scene the author makes explicit the interdependencies that tie together men's and women's visions of the world and that determine the different roles they are to carry out in society. John Durham Peters notes that at a certain point in the nineteenth century, "Immediate experience of the local, long prized by common sense as the only experience worth having is, for people in certain class positions, no longer a trustworthy guide to practical life in the modern world" since it no could no longer provide a general vision of the social world (81). In the division of social space along gender lines, middle-class women's vision is theorized within the confines of the localized necessities of the family and the home. In the context of the private/public divide, the bifocality that Durham Peters associates with modern society is constituted by the juxtaposition of the visual capacities of men and women as husband and wife (79). Sola finds that while she maintains her highly localized, but not myoptic, vision of the problems of Spain, she comes to realize that the men in her life, driven by liberal idealism, suffer from hyperopia: while they act with immediacy, they are only capable of seeing the global impact of their actions.

As long as her hopes for the future remain intact, she continues to see as if she were still behind the door of her father's apartment. But when her future as mother and wife is threatened by the events of history or the actions of other characters, the toll of her predicament is registered in hallucinations and the temporary loss of vision as the bases that make possible her ability to rationalize the visual environment deteriorate. Two such moments occur in *Los Apostólicos* (1879), when Sola dreams of marrying Monsalud whom she has not seen or heard from for several years. Early in the novel, which opens in December of 1829, readers overhear a conversation between Sola and her new protector, Benigno Cordero. The two discuss the momentous event of the day: the arrival of María Cristina of Naples in Madrid to wed Ferdinand VII. Sola's perception of the import of the marriage is filtered entirely through her own desire to be reunited with Monsalud. A single detail of the vast changes announced by the royal wedding captures her attention: the promise of amnesty for the liberal exiles. For the young woman, this translates into the return of her lover and the restoration of her happiness through the founding of a home and a family. Later the same day, as she is watching the parade down the Calle Mayor from the balcony of a friend's home, she finds herself within earshot of a conversation between her rival Jenara Baraona and another guest at the gathering. Upon hearing Jenara's news of Monsalud (that he has no plans of returning from abroad and is even considering marriage) causes Sola's vision of the spectacle in the street to become cloudy and muddled: "no veía nada, sino una confusa corriente de colorines y formas … todo en tropel y borrosamente, al modo de nube formada de la disolución de todas las visiones humanas" (Galdós 887). The narrator explains the phenomenon stating that, "Un cerebro que desfallece, permitiendo la alteración de las sensaciones ópticas, suele producir desvanecimiento y síncope" (Galdós 887). Her eyesight suffers as her mind loses control over her senses and the frame through which she views the world collapses.

Later in the novel, Monsalud does in fact return only to find that Sola has resigned herself to marrying Benigno Cordero, certain that she would never see her lover again. When he appears, she loses her composure while struggling to respect the promise she has made to Cordero. After a brief conversation, the two part, perhaps forever. The narrator describes the effect that seeing Monsalud disappear has on Sola's eyes, "Ni tampoco es digno de mención el fenómeno (que no sabemos si será óptica o qué será) de que Sola le siguiese viendo aún después de que las ramas de los olivas y la creciente penumbra de la tarde ocultaran completamente su persona" (Galdós 959). The narrator presents the phenomenon that Sola experiences as a trivial detail not worth mentioning, still it is included in the text. The character suffers from an after-image; she continues to see the figure of Monsalud even though he is no longer present. The existence of the after-image, as Crary (1988: 35) points out, was one of the central discoveries which led to the collapse of the observer model based on the camera obscura, which relocated the production of visual experience from outside to inside the body. The fact that the viewer continued to see light and color after the camera obscura's opening had been closed, led scientists and philosophers (like Goethe) to rethink the body's role in the activity of optical perception. The inclusion of such an incident in Galdós's text further reconfirms the author's awareness of contemporary debates on the nature of vision and optics. On the one hand, by showing that Sola's vision is prone to such illusions, the text underlines the delicate mental state associated with women's behavior in the nineteenth century and confirms the necessity to exclude them from engaging in the public sphere. On the other, the presence of an after-image marks her eyesight as autonomous and therefore deserving of the attention of the liberal architects of the new state. It stresses the necessity of institutions like the home and the family as fundamental to the ordering of women's optical experience in the establishment of consensus and the basic truth upon which bourgeois society depends.

Of the ten volumes of the Second Series, *Un voluntario realista* (1878) (A Royalist Volunteer), stands somewhat apart from the unfolding drama of that which links the lives of the main characters. The novel provides an alternative setting in which to explore the violence that characterizes the relationship between Carlos Navarro and Salvador Monsalud. The historical backdrop is the *Malcontents* uprising of 1827 against Ferdinand VII in the interior of the northwestern province of Catalonia. Monsalud returns to Spain as a liberal spy and coincides with Navarro in the midst of the armed conflict between rebel factions of the

Royalist Volunteers and troops loyal to the king. After being taken prisoner by Navarro, the hero of the series narrowly escapes execution when the young Pepet Armengol takes his place before the firing squad.

Sor Teodora de Aransis y Peñafort, the protagonist of *Un voluntario realista*, provides an important point of contrast to both Sola and Jenara: of the three her sight is the only one marked by a well-defined political position. The novel takes place in a rather remote area in the small medieval town of Solsona in the interior of the Catalan province of Lleida. Sor Teodora lives in the Dominican convent of San Salomó that occupies a prominent position at one extreme of the city and is one of the last vestiges of the former prominence of the city as a seat of religious power. The narrator employs visualization techniques to present location and describe the structure of the convent. The bird's-eye view of the town establishes in the imagination of the reader a tangible separation between the world inside and outside of San Salomó. The structure that encloses the women who take their vows isolates them from the mundane preoccupations of everyday life by blocking their vision: "Su estructura no permitía a los curiosos ojos monjiles ver la calle" (Galdós 776). The nuns' eyes are described as "curiosos" or mischievous, and thus in need of the control afforded by the stone walls of the convent that prevent them from wandering. The edifice limits their vision to a single image of the outside world: the empty countryside that spreads out at the western edge of Solsona and extends towards the foot of the Pyrenees. The structure is thus situated such that it blinds the nuns to everything except the greatness of God as it is manifested in the wonders of the natural world.

The nuns' eyesight is not simply limited by architectural space; implied in the description of the convent is a suggestion that the reduction of their visual field to a single landscape results in the debilitation of the overall capacity to see. Upon arriving at San Salomó to begin his training as a *sacristan*, the young Pepet Armengol (the royalist volunteer referred to in the novel's title) is frightened by "las pálidas caras de ojos mortecinos" that circulate in and around the cloister. The eyes he sees appear to be dead, as if made of glass, reinforcing an idea of blindness that is associated with the world inside of the convent. Admittance into the community requires the young woman to reject worldly possessions, vision and visibility within society. The ultimate act of self-abnegation, it involves the denial of autonomy in favor of the religious order. The sisters' eyes can be looked upon as pure optical devices, divested completely of their capacity to see, that is, to produce optical truth. As they are positioned within the cloister, they are programmed only to reflect the absolute truth of God.

The effect of the cloister on the way the nuns see the world can be compared to pre-nineteenth-century models of the observer based on the camera obscura. As Crary (1988: 31) points out, the device "guaranteed access to an objective truth about the world" by placing the viewing subject in a passive role as receiver." The camera obscura functioned to maintain the direct correspondence between external reality and interior representations by supposedly blocking all of the senses except for sight, and essentially erasing the presence of the body from the activity of seeing. The opening, which allowed light into the dark chamber, constituted a singular and authoritative, as well as measurable, point from which to establish an objective view of the world. Like the convent, the camera obscura downplays the role of the body and was thought to allow the mind to directly access the fundamental truths of the world. Crary notes (1988: 32) that for Descartes the apparatus also afforded the viewer a space for "introspection and self-observation." The description of the convent as a setting for the novel already begins to uncover the problems associated with this model of human vision and the objective truth that it supposedly upheld.

Galdós questions the Church's claim to truth and its role in the creation of new social and political reality in late-nineteenth-century Spain by introducing a body into the institutionalized structure that had hitherto maintained absolute authority over the psyche of the nation. Teodora's initial appearance in the novel is focalized through the eyes of the young Pepet as he watches the induction ceremony during which the young woman enters the convent. From this vantage point, the narrator describes the scene and the effect that it has upon the male observer, providing the reader with a striking description of the young woman: "No alzaba del suelo los ojos, no movía ni las cejas ni los descoloridos labios, ni las negras pestañas que velaban sus miradas como vela el pudor a la hermosura, ni parte alguna del cuerpo. Parecía una estatua, una mujer muerta que, acababa de morir en aquel instante, se conservara derecha y de rodillas por milagroso don" (Galdós 778).

The novitiate's downcast eyes are mentioned in the narration as if to emphasize her submission to the order and to announce the relinquishment of her vision as part of the process of accepting the Dominican order. Every aspect of her body is perfectly still as it becomes aligned with the spatial and social coordinates of the convent and the religious order. As in the case of Jenara, in this presentation there are no eyes, rather only the suggestion of eyes that are protected by her black eyelashes. There is however a gaze that these same eyelashes are designed to censor, regulate, and protect. Veiled in this fashion, Teodora's eyesight is seemingly made available for idealization in the moment that it begins to turn inward and is fixed on the internal contemplations of the self and of God. The narrator projects onto Pepet's experience of the ceremony the perception that she is like a statue in order to solidify the characterization of the nun in the mind of male readers as a perfectly apolitical and otherworldly being. Her physical appearance in this scene places her *fuera del siglo* or outside of the world and free from the problems that effect society and completely blind to the mundane passions of men (Galdós 869–70).

Nevertheless, an inherent tension is suggested in the mention of Teodora's gaze: by looking away and down she apparently submits to the order; however, the action might also be interpreted as an act of resistance. In spite of the stillness of the rest of her body, Teodora's eyes are the only part of her that remains active: they are not blank, nor glassy, nor dead. The eyelashes provide a cover for the truth, that she is not wholly engaged in what is taking place before her at the altar. Here then, as in the case of Jenara, outer appearances are deceiving. In spite of the convent's thick walls, the narrator advises the readers that "[e]s probable que no reinara dentro de San Salomó la paz más perfecta … pero también es probable que los solsoneses no supiesen nada de esto" (Galdós 776). Likewise, the reader soon learns that Teodora also hides a secret: later in the novel she confesses that she entered the convent, not to escape the world, but as a way of engaging it more fully in the hope of saving her brother who is lost to the perverse liberal cause. The statue-like image that permits Teodora to be idealized as a figure of absolute innocence and purity is soon dissipated as the underlying plot of the novel is revealed: certain members of the Dominican community are deeply involved in the royalist volunteer's instigation of the revolt.

Teodora's religious and political fanaticisms involve a rejection of vision that goes beyond the innocent abnegation of the nun who decides to dedicate her life to the contemplation of God. Teodora is cast as a non-citizen because she comes to incarnate the mentality of the *ancien regime* under which the public sphere was the exclusive arena of the aristocracy and the Church. In spite of her angelic appearance, Teodora is far from apolitical. It is not the walls of the convent or the irrationality of her faith that blind Teodora, but her ultra-conservative, reactionary ideology and her support of the *Apostólicos*. Departing from the model of the view inside the camera obscura, the strength of these convictions makes it unnecessary for her to see in order to access the truth. For her the world is black and white, divided into good and evil, legitimate and illegitimate. The frustrated Pepet laments the fact that he has been born too late; when he looks around he realizes that he lives in an uneventful and antiheroic time. On the contrary, Teodora disagrees: "Yo no veo sino guerra – dijo después de una pausa, durante la cual miraba delante de sí como se mira a un espejo" (Galdós 784). She has no need to see in order to interpret the events that have put into doubt the historical integrity of the Spanish monarchy and the preponderance of the Catholic Church.

Towards the end of *Un voluntario realista*, Teodora becomes the victim of an optical illusion as the framework that organized her (lack of) vision of the world literally crumbles in flames. Pepet, distraught by the failure of the *Malcontents*' revolt and being rejected by Teodora after he declares his love for her, sets fire to San Salomó and kidnaps the nun. Their flight into the Pyrenees is cut short thought by a broken axle and they seek refuge in the remote and quasi-abandoned Regina Coeli monastery. Forced to face the violent results of her rejection of vision (Teodora incites Pepet to seek glory and to fight for the absolutist cause) incarnated by her abductor, the nun suffers a hallucination that forces her to explore her conscience and to question her actions. Alone in a doorless cell Teodora engages in a dialogue with an eerie specter, "sombra interior, proyectada por la íntima luz del alma" (Galdós 868). Unlike the incident of Sola's experience with the after-image of Monsalud, the narrator is careful to remind readers, "No justo decir que lo vió [el espectro], sino que lo sintió dentro de sí, levantándose y saliendo majestuosamente de su corazón como de una tumba" (Galdós 868). It cannot be said that the nun's experience is optical, yet its effects are just as real from her perspective. At this point in the text, the false objectivity and claims to truth sustained by the structure of the convent in Solsona and the religious order are revealed to be an optical delusion that covers over the projection of individual will over the world, coloring perceptions and leading to misinterpretations.

Through the exploration of the ways the three women see, the Second Series of *Episodios nacionales* offer readers a model of the observation that involves a balance between the immediate and the distant. It requires an observer who is able to see and comprehend Spain in all of its historical vicissitudes without losing sight of the present moment, with its specific conditions and possibilities. The model emphasizes the presence of the body and the need to control it in the processes of perception, through the division of social space into institutional structures that rationalize sight. Indeed, the overall effect of the texts is to reaffirm previously held views of women in Spanish (and European) society and to justify their positioning within the visual framework of the Restoration. With this in mind, however, the texts also expose difficulties and dangers involved in the creation of the type of continuum that Cánovas del Castillo promoted when he openly declared his intentions before the *Cortes* in March of 1876: "continuamos lo que no podemos menos de continuar, que es la historia de España. Es inevitable que lo pasado se incorpore en lo presente" (345). While the characters studied do not represent the full spectrum of perspectives present in nineteenth-century Spain, the focus on eyesight brings into relief the principal conflicting modes of approaching the world that contributed to the meltdown of civil society at various moments in the recent past. The association between women and weakness, reconfirmed in the way that they see, is employed to expose the inherent weaknesses of Spanish society.

The modality of sight represented by Teodora is linked to that of the anti-citizen and the mentality of the *ancien régime* under which the public sphere was the exclusive arena of the aristocracy and the Church. Alternatively, the kind of citizenship that the novels promote through the exploration of women's vision is based on the acceptance of mediation and representation. While it is true the Church functioned as a mediating institution, its function was not necessarily questioned since it maintained a monopoly on truth. However, when access to the public sphere and the bases of truth are put into flux by the conflicting interests of a broader group of private individuals, representation and mediation become the accepted mechanisms of self-governance for the achievement of consensus. For male readers of the late 1870s, Sola clearly embodies the model of ideal female citizenship propagated in the political discourses of nineteenth-century liberalism promoted by Restoration culture. She never questions or resists the positioning of her body and the rectification of her sight through the institutions of home and marriage. In her character and through her harmless "to-be-looked-at-ness," the responsibilities of male citizenship are reflected and promoted as an essential part of middle-class men's access to the public sphere. By contrast, in the figure of Jenara Barona, the series confronts the same readers with the problem that women also see. On the surface, the dangers of the female gaze as a potential position from which to practice female citizenship are diffused through the rejection of Jenara's independent vision and her engagement of public space. The figure of Jenara represents how a lack of emotional distance, while not as destructive as its falsification as represented by Teodora, is no less problematic for the proper functioning of society. However, as has been noted here, it is also crucial to bear in mind how over the course of the series her character and her vision evolve in ways very similar to those of her male counterparts, Monsalud and Navarro. Unlike Teodora's eyesight, which is denied all legitimacy, Jenara's is a vision that simply needs to be re-centered away from the public sphere and re-prioritized by the pursuit of privacy for it to make a positive contribution to the advancement of the liberal project. The use of Jenara and Sola as mechanisms to explore the weakness of men's vision does not preclude the fact that through these figures, Galdós also speculates on the shape and form of female citizenship in a future liberal Spain. The conclusion, if seen strictly through the optic of nineteenth-century liberalism, is disheartening: if the men in the series need to start seeing like men, then for the women to be considered as citizens they too must see like men.

Works Cited

Arendt, Hannah. *Lectures on Kant's Political Philosophy*. Ed. Ronald Beiner. Chicago: University of Chicago Press, 1982.

Cánovas del Castillo, Antonio. *Discursos políticos y parlamentarios*, *Obras completas*, Vol. 2. CD-Rom. Madrid: Fundación Cánovas del Castillo and Boletín Oficial del Estado, 2000.

Crary, Jonathan. "Modernizing Vision." In *Vision and Visuality*. Ed. Hal Foster. Seattle, WA: Bay Press, 1988.

—— *Techniques of the Observer: On Vision and Modernity on the Twentieth Century*. Cambridge, MA: MIT Press, 1990.

Durham Peters, John. "Seeing Bifocally." In *Culture, Power, Place: Explorations in Critical Anthropology*. Eds. Akhil Gupta and James Ferguson. Durham, NC: Duke University Press, 1997. 75–92.

Fabian, Johannes. *Time and the Other: How Anthropology Makes its Object*. New York: Columbia University Press, 1983.

Habermas, Jürgen. *The Structural Transformation of the Public Sphere*. Cambridge, MA: MIT Press, 1994.

Jagoe, Catherine. *Ambiguous Angels: Gender in the Novels of Galdós*. Berkeley: University of California Press, 1994.

Labanyi, Jo. *Gender and Modernization in the Spanish Realist Novel*. Oxford and New York: Oxford University Press, 2000.

Lozano, Jorge. *El discurso histórico*, Madrid: Alianza, 1987.

Mulvey, Laura. "Visual Pleasure and Narrative Cinema." In *Narrative, Apparatus, Ideology: A Film Theory Reader*. Ed. Phillip Rosen. New York: Columbia University Press, 1986. 198–209.

Otter, Chris. "Making Liberalism Durable: Vision and Civility in the Late Victorian City." *Social History* 27(1) (2002): 1–15.

Pérez Galdós, Benito. *Episodios nacionales*. Vol. 2. Madrid: Aguilar, 1993.

—— *El equipaje del rey José*. *Episodios nacionales*. Vol. 2. 147–236. 1875.

—— *El Grande Oriente*. Vol 2. 237–590. 1876.

—— *Los cien mil hijos de San Luis*. *Episodios nacionales*. Vol. 2. 591–674. 1877.

—— *El Terror de 1824*. *Episodios nacionales*. Vol. 2. 675–774. 1878.

—— *Un voluntario realista*. *Episodios nacionales*. Vol. 2. 775–872. 1878.

—— *Los Apostólicos*. *Episodios nacionales*. Vol. 2. 873–982. 1879.

—— *Un faccioso más y algunos frailes menos*. *Episodios nacionales*. Vol. 2. 983–1092. 1879.

–4–

Horror, Spectacle and Nation-formation: Historical Painting in Late-nineteenth-century Spain

Jo Labanyi

On viewing the catalogue of the Museo del Prado's 1992 exhibition of nineteenth-century Spanish historical painting (Díez), I was struck by the frequency, in a pictorial genre promoted by the Spanish state as a tool of nation-formation, of melodramatic – even Gothic – sensationalism.[1] What kind of image of the nation, I wondered, would these scenes of death and madness have produced in the broad public who viewed these paintings at the Exposiciones Nacionales de Bellas Artes mounted from 1856 by the Ministerio de Fomento, which included education in its modernizing agenda? My wonderment increased when I discovered, thanks to Sánchez Vidal's research into the Gimeno family (which pioneered cinema in Spain while running a flourishing waxworks business) that in the 1880s waxwork shows started to reproduce historical paintings shown at the National Art Exhibitions. The two examples cited by Sánchez Vidal (114–16) are, precisely, the two paintings that had most struck me as being at odds with any nation-formation mission: Francisco Pradilla y Ortiz's (1877) *Doña Juana la Loca* (Figure 4.1) and José Casado del Alisal's (1880) *Leyenda del rey monje* (Figure 4.2), reproduced as wax tableaux by the Galería de Figuras de Cera La Universal at the Fiesta del Pilar in Zaragoza in 1883 (repeated 1884 and 1882, respectively).[2] That images produced as part of the state's attempt to foster a national school of painting of the highest quality, winning prizes at international as well as national exhibitions, should also be money-makers at fairground displays suggests that, in at least some cases, they held considerable potential for slippage between high cultural and mass cultural modes of spectatorship. In this chapter I will focus on these two paintings, while discussing late-nineteenth-century historical painting generally. I shall read these paintings through Mark B. Sandberg's thesis, in his book on waxworks and folk museums in 1880s and 1890s Scandinavia, that such spectacles constituted a pedagogy of spectatorship: that is, by exposing the public to representations of the past organized in a particular way, they schooled them in modes of viewing appropriate to modern citizens.[3]

Figure 4.1 Francisco Pradilla y Ortiz (1848–1921), *Doña Juana la Loca con el féretro de Felipe el Hermoso* 1877. Oil on canvas. 3.4 × 5.0 m. © 2004 Museo Nacional del Prado.

Figure 4.2 José Casado del Alisal (1832–86), *Leyenda del rey monje* 1880. Oil on canvas. 3.56 × 4.74 m. © 2004 Museo Nacional del Prado.

I have argued previously (Labanyi) that the nation-formation process that occurred in Spain – as elsewhere in Europe – in the late nineteenth century, intensifying from 1875 under the Restoration, took the form not only of central state legislation but also of the debates on national life that took place in the public sphere. I use the term "public sphere" in Habermas's sense of public opinion, whose role was to provide a forum for debate among members of civil society, in order to keep a democratic check on the actions of the state. The nation-formation project contained a considerable amount of heterogeneity, for public disagreement on what the nation was and should be was considerable. As Boyd notes, these debates were, among other things, a "dispute over the right to define and transmit the meaning of history" (xv). In his article in the catalogue of the 1992 Prado exhibition *La pintura de historia en el siglo XIX en España* (Díez 35), Pérez Sánchez observes that late-nineteenth-century Spanish historical painting does not propose a single, celebratory model of the nation but a "duplicidad interpretativa." The National Art Exhibitions were a site of struggle between competing interpretations of the national past in which artists, members of the jury that awarded the prizes, reviewers in the national press, and the educated and mass public all played a part. The stakes were considerable, in terms of both financial reward (the top prizes consistently went to historical paintings) and public dissemination (through engravings in the national press, not to mention school textbooks, postage stamps, calendars, and brand labels: Álvarez Junco 283).

Although these exhibitions were sponsored by the state and held in Madrid, and although many of the prize-winning paintings were bought by the state for the National Art Museum (amalgamated with the Prado when the latter passed from crown to state ownership with the 1868 revolution) or for the Congress or Senate, painters from the periphery increasingly won the major prizes (Gutiérrez Burón vol. 1: 24–5). A high proportion of prize-winning entries were painted at the Spanish Academy in Rome by artists on state or local government scholarships. All writers on the subject stress the importance of historical painting in fostering local as well as national identities. Despite the overwhelming prestige of the National Art Exhibitions, local exhibitions, also privileging historical paintings, continued to be held in many provinces, sponsored by local governments or private cultural associations (Arias Anglés et al. 41, 50; Gutiérrez Burón vol. 1: 147; Pantorba 3). Provincial Diputaciones, as well as the Congress and Senate, commissioned historical paintings – often on local topics – for display on their walls. The Valencian and Catalan local governments played a major role as patrons, commissioning many works which were awarded prizes at the National Art Exhibitions. Favorite subjects – with painters and patrons from other regions too – included Jaume I el Conquistador (who conquered Valencia and Mallorca from the Moors) and the Príncipe de Viana (heir to Juan II of Aragón, proclaimed king by the Catalans when he was arrested by his father under pressure from the latter's second wife, the mother of Fernando el Católico) (Reyero 1987: 141–8, 213–20). Paintings on this last subject not only catered to Catalan regionalist sentiment but also disputed the legality of the Reyes Católicos' accession to the throne of a unified Spain. Private provincial cultural associations also commissioned works that celebrated a local past: for example, the painting of Abderrahmán III commissioned for the Salón Liceo del Círculo de la Amistad of Córdoba (Reyero 1987: 80), contrasting with the celebration of the Catholic Kings' conquest of Granada that was a favourite topic in paintings commissioned by the central state – for example, Pradilla's (1882) *La rendición de Granada*, contracted by the Senate in 1878 after the spectacular success of *Doña Juana la Loca* (Reyero 1989: 23).

If historical painting in the 1850s and 1860s had largely followed French Republican neo-classical models, it was in order to construct a secular genealogy of the nation, countering the celebration of religious fervour found in, for example, the various paintings of Columbus's exploits (Reyero 1987: 267–97). This secularizing classicism was developed from the early 1860s, by Gisbert in particular, into a statuesque hyper-realism that recreated the execution of martyrs fighting for local or liberal freedoms, in order to support progressive political agendas. Gisbert's famous painting of the execution of the Comuneros was bought by the Congress in 1861, and his equally famous 1888 painting of the Romantic revolutionary Torrijos facing the firing squad was commissioned for the Congress in 1886 by Sagasta's Progressive government, as part of its campaign against Cánovas's centralizing measures (Reyero 1989: 26). The role of the Republican leader Castelar in championing historical painting is notable: in 1873, as president of the First Spanish Republic, he set up the Spanish Academy in Rome which would produce so many prize-winning historical works (Pradilla painted his *Doña Juana la Loca* while studying there, and Casado was its president from its inception until his resignation in 1881 when his *Leyenda del rey monje* failed to win the top prize at that year's National Art Exhibition). Castelar headed the parliamentary commission that secured state funds to buy Pradilla's painting for a record 40,000 pesetas, and gave an impassioned speech to the Congress in defence of Casado's painting (whose depiction of Ramiro II of Aragón with the heads of the nobles he had slaughtered could be read as a statement of anti-monarchist sentiment), again securing state funds (35,000 pesetas, second only to the sum paid for Pradilla's painting) to buy it for the nation (Salvá Herán 83–4; Gutiérrez Burón vol. 1: 397; Arias Anglés et al. 55).

I will be most interested here in the dominant move in the late 1870s and 1880s to more expressive, dynamic artistic forms, which rendered history not in the form of the statuesque but in that of the (often sensationalist) theatrical tableau. This new concern with theatrical spectacle does not seem to have been identified with any particular political agenda – it equally served the purpose of glorifying national unification (as in Pradilla's 1882 *La rendición de Granada*) or of denouncing the religious intolerance that formed its basis (as in Vicente Cutanda y Toraya's *¡A los pies del Salvador! (Episodio de una matanza de judíos en la edad media)*, awarded third prize at the 1887 National Art Exhibition). But its emphasis on dramatic effect produces a disconcerting freezing of time, which disturbs any providentialist notion of history moving inexorably towards a present thereby constructed as the realization of a manifest destiny. In many cases, the moment of time that is frozen is a scene of individual or (more often) collective death, presented not as stoic triumph (as so often in the earlier neo-classical paintings), but as a source of horror. The freezing of time eternally prolongs the moment of dying or the moment of horror of those who, within the painting, contemplate the already (but only just, or possibly not quite) dead. Any transcendental or redemptive message is undone by this very physical focus on gore and horror: the contorted or dismembered corpses, the bodily reaction of the diegetic onlookers. Álvarez Junco titles a section of his book on Spanish nation-formation "La pintura histórica les pone rostro" (249–58), but what stands out in these historical paintings is not the faces but the bodies.

One must remember here the emphasis on physical mutilation in Christian religious painting: Spanish audiences (especially the illiterate whose education was imparted largely by religious images) would have been used to contemplating gruesome scenes of martyrdom, and would have been trained to inscribe these gory scenes in a teleological narrative of redemption. That Spanish popular audiences were schooled to read visual images in terms of religious allegory is shown by contemporary complaints that the lower classes who flocked to the Prado on non-rainy Sundays – the only time that attendance was free, after it was opened to the public following its nationalization with the 1868 Revolution (Gil and Romea 119) – mistook Velázquez's *La rendición de Breda* for St. Peter proferring the keys to the pearly gates: a forgivable mistake given that the Prado did not display the titles of paintings till the start of the twentieth century (lower-class spectators could hardly be expected to buy the catalogue). Indeed, the restriction of free access to Sundays constructed a visit to the Prado as something one did after mass.[4] However, even the most gruesome Christian iconography contains signals that invite the degradation of the flesh to be read as spiritual triumph: not least the omnipresent heavenwards gaze of the sufferer and/or bystanders. In Pradilla's painting, the upwards gaze of the seated ladies-in-waiting is trained on the vacant gaze of Juana la Loca looking downwards at the coffin of Felipe I; while, in Casado's painting, the *rey monje* is looking up at the horrified nobles who are looking down at the severed heads of his victims. Any upwards gaze is redirected downwards to the spectacle of death. In Pradilla's painting, the priest's face, buried in his prayerbook, is almost hidden by his cowl, as if disowning what is going on. In Casado's painting, the only representative of the Church is the bishop whose severed head forms the gruesome bell clapper proferred by the *rey monje* to his rebellious nobles. Although the foremost noble has a Christ-like countenance and posture – Jacinto Octavio Picón, reviewing the 1881 National Art Exhibition, complained that he looked like a "Cristo enfurruñado" (Díez 358) – his gaze is fixated on the bleeding heads on the ground (not even on the bishop's head dangling to the left). A redemptive reading of either of these paintings requires considerable ingenuity.

Popular audiences were, however, used to forms of spectacle other than the religious. We should not forget the public executions that drew large crowds, albeit moved ever further to the city outskirts in the mid-century (Fernández de los Ríos 156). Marginally less gruesome but equally sensationalist were the mass cultural entertainments proliferating with the acceleration of urbanization from the 1870s on. This is precisely the time when the historical paintings exhibited at the National Art Exhibitions developed a penchant for the spectacular. If these paintings were reproduced in mass cultural forms such as calendars and brand labels, it is because they shared the representational codes of contemporary mass culture – including waxworks, and (from 1895) the cinema which critics have seen as an articulation of the modern habits of mass cultural consumption articulated by the "living pictures" of the wax tableaux (Charney and Schwartz; Schwartz; Singer; Sandberg). Indeed, several of these historical paintings were painstakingly recreated in a number of historical films of 1944–52, many (but not all) directed for CIFESA by Juan de Orduña with the pre-war avant-garde stage designer Sigfrido Burmann as artistic director (Díez 113–18; Hernández Ruiz). The best known example is Burmann's meticulous reproduction in tableau form of Pradilla's *Doña Juana la Loca* at the end of Orduña's *Locura de amor* (1948), massively popular as Pradilla's painting had been in its day.

The nation-formation project of early Francoism differed from that of the Restoration not only in that it was not allowed debate in the public sphere, but also because its privileged vehicle was the mass cultural medium of cinema – whereas painting is a high cultural medium. With the development during the nineteenth century of forms of public exhibition, however, it became increasingly unclear who the public for paintings was – a problem that mirrored contemporary political debates about who exactly constituted the nation. The Academia de Bellas Artes de San Fernando had been founded in 1753 with the mission of educating national taste, so as to produce citizens worthy to be members of civil society (Álvarez Junco 81). It must be remembered that political liberalism was based on the notion of representative government, whereby elected representatives acted on behalf of the interests of the less able, who in turn voted for these representatives in the name of those who were excluded from suffrage on the grounds that they were not capable of independent judgement, because of lack of education or lack of economic independence. Late-nineteenth-century Spanish politics were riven by disagreements about who constituted the nation. The 1869 Constitution, for instance, following the 1868 revolution which deposed Isabel II, placed sovereignty in the nation rather than the crown and introduced universal suffrage (males over 25). The draft constitution (never instituted) of the 1873–4 First Republic replaced national with popular sovereignty, opening the way for inclusion of the lower classes. The Krausist reformers of the 1870s and 1880s supported national rather than popular sovereignty, with suffrage based on a limited property qualification since they felt the masses needed to be educated before being enfranchised. The 1876 Restoration Constitution, drafted under the conservative liberal leader Cánovas del Castillo, revoked universal suffrage, reintroducing a substantial property qualification and placing sovereignty in the hands, not of the nation or the people, but of the monarchy and parliament. In 1890, universal suffrage was reintroduced by the progressive leader Sagasta (Labanyi 24, 108).

These renegotations of sovereignty find their cultural counterpart in the hesitations regarding the appropriate public for the National Art Exhibitions. The historical paintings showcased by these exhibitions constructed the nation not only by inviting citizens to internalize particular versions of the national past, but – more importantly – by developing certain kinds of taste, as Gutiérrez Burón (vol. 1: 87) has noted. Bourdieu has argued that taste is not the product of class but constructs class in the first place. That is: one is labelled as belonging to a particular social class according to what cultural products one consumes and – especially – the manner in which one consumes them. Bourdieu's key insight is that cultural products are labelled "high culture" or "popular culture" (he uses the latter term in its late-twentieth-century sense of "mass culture") not because of their intrinsic qualities but because of the manner in which they are consumed. High cultural products are those which are consumed in a detached, disinterested, aesthetic manner; while popular cultural products are those consumed through forms of emotional and bodily involvement. Bourdieu assumes that popular culture, unconcerned with aesthetic considerations, is largely realist, and that high culture is aligned with an avant-garde scorn for realism, since the latter supposes audience identification. Bourdieu is discussing France in 1963; his analysis overlooks the earlier history of taste. For, in the mid to late nineteenth century, popular audiences mostly consumed a diet of spectacle (narrative and non-narrative), which in the growing urban centres, as it became enmeshed with a proliferating mass culture of commercial performance and mechanical reproduction, adopted increasingly sensationalist forms. Whereas realism was the privileged art form of the bourgeoisie, seen as a vehicle of nation-formation since, on the one hand, it invited the audience identification necessary to construct national citizens as a "we," while, on the other, it served as a forum for public debate, parallel to the national press, airing a common fund of concerns about what "national society" was and should be. Realism's combination of intellectual reflection with audience identification made it always prone to tip into the melodramatic sensationalism of popular culture, from which it partly extricates itself (in the case of the realist novel, at least) through self-reflexive critique. This ambivalence allowed realism to serve as the basis of nation formation, since the modes of response it permitted were all-inclusive: the realist novel could function as an apprenticeship in citizenship by emotionally engaging the untutored reader, who would then be invited to partake in intellectual reflection (and thus "elevated" to a higher cultural plane) through its metafictional commentary on its own processes.

What, however, of the visual arts? Sandberg observes a complementary process whereby, in the 1880s, popular spectacles like waxworks started to mimic the representational techniques of realism in order to acquire a higher cultural status. Previously, waxworks were associated with sensationalist displays of diseased or dismembered bodies, of an often morbid or pornographic nature – as in the Venus figures that could be taken apart to show their inner organs (Pilbeam 1–16). This was true both of the "anatomical cabinets" of wax figures that toured the fairground circuit (which proclaimed their wares among a motley assortment of freak shows) and of the anatomical collections, which included figures modelled in wax, of medical schools and anthropological museums (both open to public display for "educational" but often prurient purposes).[5] Pilbeam has shown how Madame Tussaud, after moving her waxwork display to England in 1802, trod a difficult path between the popular touring circuit and the more upmarket museum, building her reputation on the *frisson* of authenticity derived from the fact that she had, during the French Revolution, made casts of guillotined heads or murdered leaders *in situ* (Marat stabbed in his bath was, and still is, a favorite), but at the same time insisting on her respectable connections with the French royalty and aristocracy. Tussaud's wax "museum" – as she called it even during its touring days – contained a mix of displays of great historical figures from the past and present, increasingly legitimized by authentic material props and costumes; and the "Adjacent Room" which in 1846 became dubbed the "Chamber of Horrors," depicting the acts of notorious criminals. The concern with authentic props and costumes had, by the 1880s, developed into the creation of tableaux, sometimes arranged in a developmental narrative sequence, involving a number of wax figures arranged in a play of body movements and gazes that bound them together in an "event," located in a recreation of the original environment. This new vogue for tableaux became the basis of the displays in the new Paris wax museum – the Musée Grévin – when it opened in 1882 (Schwartz 89–148).

As Sandberg argues in his discussion of how these techniques were developed by the upmarket wax museums created in Scandinavia in the 1880s, these tableaux – whether recreating historical scenes or famous crimes – schooled spectators in causal logic (through their perception of the relations between figures and their environment), and in the limits of what constituted acceptable voyeurism (through visual jokes which subjected the unreflective viewer to private if not public embarrassment). Unlike Tussaud's earlier displays, which invited spectators to mingle with and touch the wax figures, the construction of these tableaux in the form of a self-contained environment, viewed through a glass or imaginary fourth wall, encouraged the spectator to gaze, but from a distance. Most importantly, such tableaux abandoned the emphasis on isolated body-parts typical of the disreputable early history of waxworks, insisting on the incorporation of bodies into a socially constituted whole. The pedagogy of spectatorship constituted by such tableaux functioned by inviting visitors to knowingly have it both ways: that is, to enjoy the sensationalism of the scenes depicted, but to reflect on the mechanics of the illusion created. Via a different route, the wax museums of the 1880s come to coincide with the contemporaneous strategies of the realist novel which, in Spain at least, borrows from sensationalist popular fiction while inviting the reader to reflect critically on its effects.

The other gentrification strategy used by wax museums in the 1880s was the construction of tableaux recreating scenes from realist novels (for example, those of Zola reproduced in the Musée Grévin) or – more frequently – historical paintings, showing that the popular cultural medium of wax figures was capable of creating the effects of high culture. This was possible only because the high cultural works that were imitated themselves contained the sensationalist effects on which popular culture relied. The 1880s can thus be defined as the period when realism (bourgeois culture) and spectacle (popular culture) come together, in a shifting and uneasy alliance that attempts to work through the various possible definitions of who is eligible for national citizenship (perhaps we should say "national spectatorship"). As Sandberg notes (69–116), the modern nation-formation process takes place not only via the Foucauldian subjection of citizens to surveillance, but also via the construction of certain legitimate forms of looking. In urban modernity, to be is to look as well as to be looked at. Indeed, "being-looked-at" can construct one as an individual or as a member of the mass, but looking necessarily constructs one as an individual. This is particularly true when the looking takes place within the confines of a high cultural event like a state-run National Art Exhibition, with the paintings viewed at a distance on a wall. The massive dimensions of many of these historical paintings (the bigger canvases tended to win the prizes: Pradilla's *Doña Juana la Loca* measured 2.38 × 3.13 meters, Casado's *La leyenda del rey monje* 3.36 × 4.74 meters), while forcing a direct involvement in the painting, also obliged one to stand back to take the whole thing in.

It is clear that the organizers of the National Art Exhibitions were ambivalent about who their intended audience was (just as the Prado opened its doors to the masses on Sundays provided it was a dry day so they would not muddy the floor). Entry was initially free to encourage cross-class attendance, and from 1871 railway companies offered substantial discounts (45 per cent in 1881) so people could travel from the provinces. In 1864 the press reported traffic jams in the surrounding streets and extra members of the Guardia Civil were brought in. To counter the threat of crowd disorder, from 1861 the state increasingly reduced the number of days with free entry; by 1884 it was limited to Sundays. The number of tickets sold in 1884 was 15,386, peaking at 21,396 in 1887, which was also the year when the largest number of historical paintings were exhibited (no attendance figures are available for days when access was free). In 1860 an anonymous reviewer in *La Época* had waxed lyrical about the innate artistic vocation of the "pueblo español" that flocked to that year's National Art Exhibition, making it difficult to get in; and in 1864 even the conservative novelist Alarcón claimed that "el pueblo por antonomasia, la plebe de la villa, la gente que habla a voces en las calles y plazas constituye, por decirlo así, la vanguardia de la opinion pública." By contrast in 1884 Jacinto Octavio Picón complained about the ignorance of uneducated viewers (Gutiérrez Burón vol. 1: 617–21, 625; vol. 2: 703–4, 710; Reyero 1989: 100). Gutiérrez Burón cites two press articles of 1881 (the year when the refusal to award top prize to Casado's *Leyenda del rey monje* caused a public outcry, and when Sagasta's progressives returned to power, reinstating educational freedom) which defend popular taste against the decision of the jury, on opposing grounds. The first (in *La Gaceta Universal*) insisted that "las obras de arte caen de lleno bajo la jurisdicción del *sufragio universal*" (original emphasis), making it clear that the definition of who was fit to form the national art public was a definition of who was fit to enjoy civil rights: this supposes that artistic taste is based on a capacity for intellectual discrimination (Gutiérrez Burón vol. 1: 622). The second (in the *Revista de Madrid*) defended the lower classes' artistic taste on the basis of their emotional response: "En cuestiones de estética, el corazón es el que mejor juzga, es, por lo menos, juez inapelable. ¿Conmueve la obra? ¿Hiere las fibras ignoradas en que duerme el sentimiento? Pues la obra es buena, es hermosa, y merece aplauso incondicional … ¿No conmueve? ¿No arranca un grito involuntario a los labios o una lágrima a los ojos? Pues entonces ¿Qué importa que la crítica la halle perfecta? (Gutiérrez Burón vol. 1: 623). The same defence of popular taste on the basis of its emotional engagement is found in an 1887 article in *La Ilustración Artística* (Gutiérrez Burón vol. 1: 622–3).

These press articles suggest that popular and bourgeois taste, based on emotional involvement and intellectual discrimination respectively, had become inextricably entangled – and that the historical paintings privileged at the National Art Exhibitions played a role in this process. The requirement to appeal to a broad public seems to have produced a contamination of bourgeois art by the sensationalism characteristic of popular taste. As an 1867 article in *La España* commenting on the mass attendance at the National Art Exhibitions stated: "donde quiera que haya un espectáculo allí está Madrid. El espectáculo es para Madrid absolutamente necesario" (Gutiérrez Burón vol. 2: 719).

At this point it becomes necessary to discuss the implications of the fact that, in late-nineteenth-century Spain, waxworks remained an itinerant fairground attraction, rather than being incorporated into bourgeois culture through the creation of elegant wax museums. While this did not stop Spanish waxworks from starting in the 1880s to recreate historical paintings, as happened contemporaneously in the wax museums of northern Europe, one cannot help wondering if the public exhibition of historical paintings took on in Spain some of the functions fulfilled by the new sophisticated wax museums elsewhere: specifically, the use of a sensationalist mode of realism that appealed to popular tastes while educating those tastes in bourgeois decorum – and conversely allowing bourgeois viewers to indulge popular tastes they might not confess to at home. Puente notes that no bourgeois would have bought for his home paintings with the gruesome subject matter of those exhibited at the National Art Exhibitions (Arias Anglés et al. 28). Interestingly, the pre-1856 exhibitions of the Academia de San Fernando in the Calle de Alcalá had coincided with Madrid's September Feria celebrated in the same locality, producing a hugely mixed public. Indeed, there were complaints that the public for the September Feria regarded these exhibitions as an extension of the fairground stalls (Arias Anglés et al. 77). This led to the transfer of the exhibitions to the Ministerio de Fomento (now Teatro Calderón) in the Calle de Atocha, where they remained after their conversion into the National Art Exhibitions till their 1867 relocation to the Palacio de la Fuente de la Castellana (popularly known as the Barracón del Indo, since the pavilion was installed much like a fairground barracks in the garden of the private mansion of Señor Indo). This was the locale where Pradilla's and Casado's paintings were exhibited, in both cases attracting huge crowds (Díez 312; Pantorba 111; Gil and Romea 216). In 1887 the exhibitions were relocated to what is now the Museo de Historia Nacional (Pantorba 10). We may also note that, just as the gentrified wax museums of northern Europe located their "Chamber of Horrors" in a different space from the respectable historical tableaux, so too the National Art Exhibitions had their "Sala del Crimen" where paintings judged unworthy of acceptance were hung (Gutiérrez Burón vol. 1: 575–7).

Pantorba, writing at the time of the early Francoist nation-formation project, notes the gruesome nature of the majority of historical paintings exhibited – and awarded prizes – at the National Art Exhibitions: "Todas las notas negras de la historia de España, que no son pocas [...]. No se buscaba sino lo convulso [...] cadáveres y féretros, puñales y fusiles, miradas de horror, ojos de llanto, ademanes amenazadores" (35). Pantorba could be describing the contexts of a wax museum. He rightly picks up the theatricality and play of gazes, again typical of the wax tableaux that came into vogue in the 1880s. Significantly, Pradilla – the painter of the most successful historical painting of them all, that of Juana la Loca gazing ashen-faced and blank-eyed (like a wax effigy) at the coffin of Felipe I – had trained with a stage designer in Zaragoza and subsequently worked in Madrid with two Italian stage designers (Arias Anglés et al. 205). Just as contemporary wax museums elsewhere filled their tableaux with historically authentic accessories, so Pradilla worked from props and costumes constructed by him from descriptions of the time (Díez 313, 316). Casado also drew on his studio wardrobe of historical costumes to paint *Leyenda del rey monje*. And, if Madame Tussaud modeled wax figures from the heads of guillotine victims, so Casado painted the heads of Ramiro II's victims "live" from the decapitated heads of corpses he had delivered to his studio from one of Rome's hospitals. According to a rumour that no doubt enhanced the painting's mass appeal, when the messenger emptied the sack of heads onto the ground, Casado nearly fainted – but took up his brush the following day (Díez 356–7).

Sandberg (92–5) notes how the new wax tableaux of the 1880s created a "reality effect" by giving some of the figures the ability to look, mirroring the gaze of the spectator. This produced audience identification – indeed these diegetic spectators figured the emotional response that the non-diegetic spectator was expected to adopt. Pantorba (111) notes that the "miradas de horror" in the canvas were echoed by those on the faces of the crowds who flocked to see Casado's *Leyenda del rey monje*. What, one has to ask, might have been the function of that horror for the nation-formation project? Spectators would have known of Cánovas del Castillo's 1854 historical novel *La campana de Huesca: Una crónica del siglo XII*, published in his youth the same year as his *Historia de la decadencia de España*. The novel's illustrations included the Gothic scene of the king displaying his rebellious subjects' decapitated heads, fashioned into a bell clapper (the *campana* of the title), to the nobles who form the diegetic audience. Cánovas's text ends with the king absolved and spending the rest of his life in prayer; but one wonders what attracted the future architect of the Restoration's centralizing project to this gruesome subject matter, which he chose to foreground in his novel's title. The play of gazes within Casado's canvas ensures that one identifies with the horror of the nobles contemplating the massacre from the steps on the right, encouraging a reading of this painting as a condemnation of monarchical tyranny. Or does it? An eyewitness recounted hearing Casado, *incognito*, ask a bystander at the 1881 National Art Exhibition what he thought of the painting. Casado was appalled when the viewer replied that, in his view, the king ought also to kill the nobles in the picture for protesting at his dispensation of justice. Misreading was clearly possible (Díez 358–60). Indeed, the catalogue description of the painting explained the event as Ramiro II's revenge on "los soberbios varones del Reino" for disregarding "la autoridad rural y los fueros del pueblo" (Díez 352) – which makes Ramiro the champion of popular rights. I would suggest that the function of the painting was precisely to stir up debate about political rights and justice, and, at a more basic level, to trigger an emotional response of horror that filled spectators with a sense of the importance of responding to injustice, no matter how that injustice was defined. The painting could thus function as a training in citizenship, using horror to open – rather than close – debate.

It is even harder to determine how spectators might have responded to Pradilla's *Doña Juana la Loca*, except for the fact that we know from eye-witness reports that they were transfixed by it – that is, reduced to the same immobile staring that is enacted in Juana's figure. For these paintings are not so much historical representations as – like the contemporaneous wax tableaux – historical enactments. Like a wax tableau, Pradilla's painting gives the spectator the sensation of being an interloper contemplating a scene that is poised between life and death: wax being associated with embalming and yet producing a "living image" (all the writers on waxworks comment on this uncanny quality of the medium). What this means is that the spectator internalizes Juana's own inability to determine whether Felipe I is really dead. This is not a "mad" question for what is at stake is the status of the past as "living dead": gone but still with us in its effects. This question, dramatized explicitly in Pradilla's painting, is effectively raised by all these historical paintings, whose status as "living pictures" figures the past as hovering equivocally between life and death. It is an especially important question for nations on Europe's periphery anxious about their relation to modernity; that is, anxious about the pull of the past but also about the consequences of breaking free from it. Sandberg suggests that this explains the vogue for wax museums in 1880s Scandinavia. Tamayo y Baus's famous 1855 theatrical melodrama *Locura de amor* had picked up on this same anxiety: it ends with Juana asking her courtiers for silence so as not to wake Felipe's "sleeping" corpse; this scene was reproduced in an 1866 panting by Lorenzo Vallés, whose simple grouping of figures and plain backcloth represents a stage in the history of the visual image prior to the development of the sophisticated wax tableaux of the 1880s. One may note here the popularity in wax museums of comatose figures – e.g. Sleeping Beauty – whose apparent death is belied by a mechnically propelled heaving bosom.

I am not here arguing that Spanish historical paintings were influenced by the new wax tableaux: Pradilla's painting predates the 1880s, and we have very little information about waxworks in nineteenth-century Spain, where they remained an itinerant, ephemeral art form. What I wish to suggest is that these contemporaneous cultural phenomena correspond to similar visual developments, which in both cases express anxieties about whether the past is dead or alive, and use frozen dramatic re-enactments to train spectators in shared habits of looking that define them as national citizens. I would also suggest that, while these paintings produced certain inescapable emotional responses, they allowed these to be applied to a range of alternative readings of the visual configuration. In the case of Pradilla's painting, the spectator cannot help reproducing – that is, identifying with – the emotional response of Juana la Loca to the sight of Felipe's coffin. But how exactly does the spectator interpret this emotional response that he or she is forced to internalize? Juana's vacant look evokes an unspeakable trauma – and we may recall here Peter Brooks' observations on the melodramatic genre's ability to "speak the unspeakable," frequently through the dramatization of muteness. On the one hand, Juana's madness – her fixation on her Habsburg husband – may have been read as an emblem of the "disturbance" caused to Spain's historical destiny by the Habsburg dynasty, Felipe becoming king (with Juana's father Fernando el Católico's connivance) after having Juana declared mentally unfit to rule. Alternatively, female spectators especially may have interpreted Juana's traumatized figure as a mute protest against her husband's and father's unjust treatment of her (and they would surely have picked up the pathos of her clearly delineated advanced pregnancy). If Casado's painting reproduces a single emotion of horror in the spectators within his canvas, the onlookers in Pradilla's painting represent a range of emotional responses, from sympathy to dismissal. I suggest that the strength of Pradilla's painting is that, while binding spectators emotionally to its central figure (Juana), it forces them to try out a range of possible interpretations of the emotion they see dramatized in her figure, and which they internalize, without being able to articulate its contours. The painting thus provides a schooling in the need to think twice before claiming to understand the motivations of other people; that is, in responsible social relations. It is also a schooling in the need to reflect before coming to hasty conclusions about one's reading of the national past.

In her book *Democracy and the Foreigner* (2001), Honig has suggested that the nation is perhaps figured better not through the genre of romance, with its happy end, but through that of the Gothic (Honig 107–22).[6] Honig has in mind the female Gothic, which invites us to reflect on helplessness and our habit of invoking saviors which perpetuate the problem. Pradilla's painting can be read as an example of the female Gothic, but I wish to argue here for a reading of Spanish historical painting in general, with its emphasis on spectacles of horror, in the light of the Gothic genre in its broadest sense. For horror requires us to react empathetically, and its extremeness forces us to confront issues of injustice, while requiring us to reflect on what the nature of the injustice might be. Horror, which does not tell us what to think but requires us to feel, can thus be seen as a democratic genre: a schooling in responsible civic participation. I started this chapter by wondering how Spanish spectators interpreted these gruesome representations of their national past. I end it by suggesting that the only thing we can know with any certainty is what they felt, and that was an intense involvement: this was a history that "grabbed" you and made you part of it, like it or not. And, as Honig (2001) observes, democracy requires us to find ways of cohabiting with those we would rather not live with. As far as Spanish spectators' intellectual interpretations of these paintings are concerned, the point, I would argue, is that the paintings forced them to work these out for themselves; that is, they functioned as a schooling in democratic public debate.

Notes

1. Gruesome subjects are too many to detail. Some fall into the *carpe diem* formula; most are scenes of unjust execution or slaughter. Particularly popular were the collective suicides of Sagunto and Numancia, which paralleled contemporaneous archaeological excavations designed to provide a myth of origins for a "Spanish" spirit of independence, going back to the third and second centuries BC respectively (Álvarez Junco 267).
2. For the many paintings of Juana la Loca, see Reyero (1989: 326–33); Díez (250–3, 306–17); Salvá Herán (66). Pradilla's painting won first prize at the 1878 National Art Exhibition, and was the only painting to be awarded the *medalla de honor* between 1856 and 1895 (Pantorba 19). It won *medallas de honor* also at the 1878 Paris and 1882 Vienna World Exhibitions. Casado's painting won prizes at the World Exhibitions of Vienna, Munich and Düsseldorf in 1882 and 1883. See Díez (316, 360). For Pradilla's and Casado's careers, see García Loranca and García-Rama; Portela Sandoval.
3. I thank Rebecca Haidt for introducing me to Sandberg's and Schwartz's work on wax museums.
4. This information about lower-class responses to the Prado was given in Eugenia Afinoguénova's paper "The Prado Museum and the Birth of the Spanish School" at the 2002 Modern Language Association conference, New York.
5. For a description of the Anatomical Museum of Madrid's Facultad de Medicina, see Gil and Romea's 1881 guidebook, which also notes the anatomical collection of the Anthropological Museum (opened 1875). For waxworks and popular entertainments in Spain, see Gil and Romea; Sánchez Vidal (19–132); and the sources used by the latter: Varey; Baroja; Gutiérrez Solana (1918, 1961, 1991). The current Madrid Museo de Cera was not created till 1972. Despite the tackiness of its displays (especially those where a jumble of historical figures line the walls, as in the early wax cabinets), those of its displays which are organized in tableaux form conform exactly to its late-nineteenth-century Parisian and Scandinavian counterparts, including the reconstructions of paintings and self-reflexive games (see the illustrations in Schwartz; Sandberg).
6. My thanks to Doris Sommer for mentioning Honig's book.

Works Cited and Consulted

Álvarez Junco, José. *Mater Dolorosa: La idea de España en el siglo XIX*. Madrid: Taurus, 2001.

Arias Anglés, E., W. Rincón García and A. Navarro Granell, eds. *Exposiciones nacionales del siglo XIX: Premios de Pintura*. Madrid: Centro Cultural del Conde Duque, 1988.

Avilés y Merino, Ángel. *Catálogo de las obras de arte existentes en el Palacio del Senado*. Madrid: Est. Tip. Hijos de J.A. García, 1903.

Baroja, Pío. *Las figuras de cera*. Madrid: Caro Raggio, 1979/1924.

Bourdieu, Pierre. *Distinction: A Social Critique of the Judgement of Taste*. London: Routledge, 1996/1979.

Boyd, Carolyn P. *Historia Patria: Politics and National Identity in Spain, 1875–1975*. Princeton, NJ: Princeton University Press, 1997.

Brooks, Peter. *The Melodramatic Imagination. Balzac, Henry James, Melodrama, and the Mode of Excess*. New York: Columbia University Press, 1985.

Cánovas del Castillo, Antonio. *La campana de Huesca: Crónica del siglo XII*. Málaga: Instituto Cánovas del Castillo, Exma Diputación de Málaga, 1997/1854.

Charney, Leo and Vanessa R. Schwartz, eds. *Cinema and the Invention of Modern Life*. Berkeley: University of California Press, 1995.

Díez, José Luis, ed. *La pintura de historia en el siglo XIX en España*. Madrid: Museo del Prado, 1992.

Fernández de los Ríos, Ángel. *Guía de Madrid: Manual del madrileño y del forastero* (facsimile of 1876 first edition). Madrid: La Librería, 2002.

García Loranca, Ana and Ramón García-Rama. *Vida y obra del pintor Francisco Pradilla y Ortiz*. Zaragoza: Caja de Ahorros de Zaragoza, Aragón y Rioja, 1987.

Gil, R. and T. Romea. *Guía de Madrid*. Madrid: Imprenta de Fortanet, 1881.

Gutiérrez Burón, Jesús. *Exposiciones nacionales de pintura en España en el siglo XIX*. Madrid: Universidad Complutense, 1987. 2 Vols.

Gutiérrez Solana, José. *Madrid, escenas y costumbres* (2nd series). Madrid: Imprenta Mesón de Paños 8 bajo, 1918.

—— *Madrid, escenas y costumbres* (1st series). In *Obra literaria*. Madrid: Taurus, 1961/1913.

—— *Madrid callejero*. Madrid: Castalia, 1995/1923.

Habermas, Jürgen. *The Structural Transformation of the Public Sphere: An Inquiry into a Category of Bourgeois Society*. Cambridge: Polity Press, 1989.

Hernández Ruiz, José. "Historia y escenografía en el cine español: Una aproximación." In *Ficciones históricas: El cine histórico español,* monographic issue of *Cuadernos de la Academia* 6 (1999): 151–65.

Honig, Bonnie. *Democracy and the Foreigner*. Princeton, NJ, Princeton University Press, 2001.

Labanyi, Jo. *Gender and Modernization in the Spanish Realist Novel*. Oxford: Oxford University Press, 2000.

Miguel Egea, Pilar de, ed. *El arte en el Senado*. Madrid: Senado, 1999.

Pantorba, Bernardino de. *Historia y crítica de las Exposiciones Nacionales de Bellas Artes celebradas en España*. Madrid: Alcor, 1948.

Pilbeam, Pamela M. *Madame Tussaud and the History of Waxworks*. London: Hambledon, London, 2003.

Portela Sandoval, Francisco. *Casado del Alisal 1831–1886*. Palencia: Excma Diputación Provincial de Palencia, 1986.

Reyero, Carlos. *Imagen histórica de España (1850–1900)*. Madrid: Espasa Calpe, 1987.

—— *La pintura de historia en España: esplendor de un género en el siglo XIX*. Madrid: Cátedra, 1989.

Salvá Herán, A. *Colecciones artísticas del Congreso de los Diputados*. Madrid: Fundación Argentaria and Congreso de los Diputados, 1997.

Sánchez Vidal, Agustín. *Los Gimeno y los orígenes del cine en Zaragoza*. Zaragoza: Patronato Municipal de las Artes Escénicas y de la Imagen (Archivo de la Filmoteca de Zaragoza), Área de Cultura y Educación del Exmo Ayuntamiento de Zaragoza, 1994.

Sandberg, Mark B. *Living Pictures, Missing Persons: Mannequins, Museums, and Modernity*. Princeton, NJ: Princeton University Press, 2003.

Schwartz, Vanessa R. *Spectacular Realities: Early Mass Culture in Fin-de-siècle Paris*. Berkeley: University of California Press, 1999.

Singer, Ben. *Melodrama and Modernity: Early Sensational Cinema and its Contents*. New York: Columbia University Press, 2001.

Varey, J.E. *Títeres, marionetas y otras diversiones populares de 1758 a 1859*. Madrid: Instituto de Estudios Madrileños, 1959.

–5–

Isidora in the Museum

Luis Fernández Cifuentes

Properly and predictably, Isidora, the protagonist of Benito Pérez Galdós's *La desheredada*, starts her reconnaissance of the city and of her place in the city with a visit to the Art Museum "cinco días después de su llegada a Madrid" (Galdós 1970: 1006). Her wanderings about the place during the previous four days had not included any tour of the city proper. First, in an episode that bears the title "Final de otra novela," she had made one sad call to nearby Leganés, "tristísimo pueblo" (997), and to its insane asylum, itself a separate "limbo enmascarado de mundo" (989), material for a self-contained "ciudad teórica" – a sort of inverted utopia (987). Then, she had gone for an unwittingly disastrous inspection of a closer yet still "excentric" zone (997) defined as "la caricatura de una ciudad" and characterized as "los bordes rotos y desportillados de la zona urbana [...]. Aquello no era aldea ni tampoco ciudad; era una piltrafa de limpieza para que no corrompiera el centro" (997–8). Both territories represent, if nothing else, all that is alien to the urban contour of Isidora's presumed identity.

The more clear-cut city center is defined by an entirely different set of views for the discriminating eye of the native just returned: "las cosas bonitas de Madrid, el Museo, el Retiro, la Castellana" (1006). Unlike the segments of Madrid's periphery, spaces recognized as repulsive, marked, sooner or later, by death,[1] and hence charged with an expelling force ("lo primero es que usted salga de esta casa": 997), these icons of Madrid's center appear endowed from the start with a centripetal, revitalizing force. Such a center comprises all that is worth seeing, everything her gaze may desire. Later in the novel – at the crucial turning point that closes Part I and is paradoxically titled "Suicidio de Isidora" – such irresistible, centripetal force will be restated as follows: "A medida que se acercaba a la zona interior de Madrid y recibía su calor central, se iba robusteciendo en ella la idea del vivir, del probar y del ver y del gustar" (1077). In the meantime, Isidora is distinguished primarily by a voracious gaze: "devoraba con sus ojos las infinitas variedades y formas del lujo y de la moda"; "mirar todo como cosa propia"; "mirarlo todo" (1032). Such is the gaze that finds both its inaugural impulse and one of its favorite objects in that center crowned by the museum.

Isidora's visit to the Prado amounts to a very brief scene in a very long novel.[2] However, placed as it is at the start of Isidora's urban life and rich in resonances throughout her story, the scene encapsulates the visual and spatial paradigms that govern the novel's urban action. To be sure, the powers that brought about the nineteenth-century urban revolution conceived the Art Museum as the ultimate visual offering of the city's center, a temple for the modern cult of the visual arts (Sedlmayr 30), the place where people's eyes were guaranteed to fulfill their greatest expectations as well as acquire true notions and standards of definitive visual values – what Ripley calls "a literacy of the eye" (13). Thus, on the one hand, the museum's offerings – its grand architecture as much as its collections – were meant to improve the life of all citizens, their aesthetic sensibility, the quality of their mental life. A nineteenth-century curator of Marseille's Art Museum declares it "an instrument of civilization intended to shape and to purify the public's taste through the presentation of masterpieces" (Sherman 211–12). Bennett quotes one Thomas Greenwood who wrote in 1888: "A Museum and Free Library are as necessary for the mental and moral health of the citizens as good sanitary arrangements, water supply and street lighting are for their physical health and comfort" (18). Enlightened travelers who visited the Prado at about the time of Isidora's urban initiation, did comply: "El día que se entra por la vez primera en un museo como el de Madrid, constituye una fecha histórica en la vida del hombre" (Amicis 118). On the other hand, Sedlmayr (3–8) has shown how the museum's building became, for at least two decades – earlier or later, depending on the country – the city's master building, an Apolinean proposition whose concept and style were to be reflected, however modestly, in most other buildings, particularly private ones.[3] Galdós remembered some time after 1883: "La creación de los museos, enteramente moderna, ha traído, sin duda, el gusto por los museítos particulares, ya sean de sellos, ya de cajas de cerillas, ya de botones" (*Fisonomías* 197). Gold has traced throughout Galdós's *Novelas Contemporáneas* the proliferation of "characters driven by an overwhelming impulse to reenact within the confines of their own four walls the same kind of operations carried out by public museums and academies on a much grander scale: acquisition, assemblage, exhibition" (320). Isidora is one such character. For one thing, the interiors she inhabits – which the narrator never fails to describe in great detail – constantly (and unsuccessfully) strive to abide by such fundamental urban law: "¡su gran ideal de rodearse de hermosos cuadritos al óleo, de los primeros pintores!" (Galdós 1970: 1085). For another, Isidora shows a superior (and unforgiving) eye to observe other people's sluggish compliance with museum standards of taste and order: "aún puedo yo dar lecciones a esta gente" (1059), she declares, for example, after registering the incoherent juxtaposition of "magníficas estampas de mujeres bellas" and Velázquez's dead Christ, in Saldeoro's museum-like walls.

These trends are conflated in the episode of Isidora's initial visit to the Prado Museum. Her reaction to what she sees in Villanueva's majestic building – reported in quasi-religious terms – appears to underscore precisely the sacred "superiority" of the institution and the precious awakening it affords her: "Sin haber adquirido por lecturas noción alguna del verdadero arte, ni haber visto jamás sino mamarrachos, comprendía la superioridad de lo que a su vista se presentaba; y con admiración silenciosa, su vista iba de cuadro en cuadro, hallándolos todos, o casi todos, tan acabados y perfectos, que se prometió ir con frecuencia al edificio del Prado para saborear más aquel goce inefable que hasta entonces le fuera desconocido" (1007).

Moreover, the museum experience will then govern her assessment of all other visual experiences within that first journey of urban initiation: the Retiro Gardens are reduced to "una ingeniosa adaptación de la Naturaleza a la cultura," with a dress code akin to the museum's; the public zoo becomes a sort of dastardly Museum, dismissed as a spectacle for the mob ("el Pueblo");[4] the admired parade of aristocrats along the Castellana Avenue is qualified in museum terms, when Isidora observes there, with the eyes of an artist, "un magnífico fresco de apoteosis, donde hay ninfas, pegasos, nubes, carros triunfales y flotantes paños"; the street becomes then "una sala de árboles" in a museum-like urban setting (1013–14). Miquis himself partakes of this notion of the museum as a yardstick of emblematic urban spaces when he describes his academic environment: "El hospital es un museo de síntomas, un riquísimo atlas de casos, todo palpitante, todo vivo" (1012). Thus, in subtle and not so subtle ways, the museum appears to be both the core and the benchmark of an urban perimeter about which Isidora will immediately claim proprietary rights.

The novel, however, does not allow such pure superiority to go unchallenged, not even at this inaugural point of the story. The aesthetic as well as the ideological hegemony of the museum is elaborately undermined by the narrative itself – without major interferences from the narrator – in at least two different moments of this chapter, bracketing Isidora's presumably uncontaminated contemplation of the works of art and their palatial lodgings. During the first moment, the narrative completes the configuration of Madrid's center with a reference to another object of great interest to Isidora's gaze: store windows. Isidora and Miquis walk towards the museum; "y avanzaban poco en su paseo, porque Isidora se detenía ante los escaparates para ver y admirar lo mucho y vario que en ellos hay siempre" (1007). Immediately, the first characterization of the impact of the museum tour on Isidora's senses involves a significant opposition, even a confrontation, between museum and display windows: "En el Museo, las impresiones de aquella singular joven fueron muy distintas, y sus ideas, levantando el vuelo, llegaron a zonas mucho más altas que aquella por donde andaban al rastrear en los muestrarios llenos de chucherías" (1007). Throughout the novel, though, as the attractions of the city's center are reinstated ever more emphatically – sometimes with the complicity of the narrator's own voice – the narrative offers a more one-sided approach to display windows, so that the regal galleries of the museum appear to fade into the urban background, displaced (and not only at that late hour) by city streets lined with modern shops and their seductively exhibited merchandise: "Madrid, a las ocho y media de la noche es un encanto, abierto bazar, exposición de alegrías y amenidades sin cuento [...]. Las tiendas atraen con el charlatanismo de sus escaparates" (1078).[5]

Within and without the novel, museum showrooms and shop windows were lending themselves to significant interactions at the time of Isidora's inaugural walk through Madrid's center. First, both museum and shop windows, in their modern formats, were products of the same era. Isidora's visit to the Prado can be calculated to have taken place in the early spring of 1871. Educated readers of *La desheredada* must have been aware of the fact that the museum had been in existence, however precariously, since 1818, but it was only on September 29, 1868, that "el Museo dejó de ser El Real Museo de Pinturas para llamarse Museo Nacional del Prado"; two years earlier, it had become the full-fledged democratic institution any modern museum was created to be (Madrazo 236). As for display windows, *La desheredada*'s narrator offers the reader this relevant piece of information: "empezaba a desarrolarse el gusto por presentar los objetos mercantiles con primor, halagando los ojos del que compra" (1099). Isidora's voracious eyes, forever divided between the sublime exhibitions of the museum and the "primor" exhibited in shop windows, are quintessential targets of such "desarrollo del gusto."

Second, the museum, as a new form of display of beautiful artifacts, was far from alien to the interaction of aesthetics and economics in the marketing of ordinary commodities. The museum's visual impact did awaken in Isidora two kinds of mercantile impulses that, in one form or another, will surface repeatedly throughout the novel. One is a purchasing impulse: "compraré cuadros de los grandes maestros, y tapices y antigüedades" (1142). Another, a manufacturing impulse, reflected in her choice of a job for her brother Mariano: "vino en determinar que sería grabador, es decir, fabricante de esas preciosas estampas que adornan las publicaciones ilustradas y de las magníficas reproducciones de los Museos ... Para que la industria pueda hacerse pasar por noble, necesita fingir parentescos con el arte" (1098). The text appears to imply that the museum had succeeded in generating visual standards which shop windows were rising to, to the point that shop displays could be spoken of in the same terms as museum exhibits. The long, heterogeneous list of merchandise exhibited in Madrid's shop windows to Isidora's visual satisfaction is summarized as "prodigios sin número que parecen soñados, según son de raros y curiosos" (1032).

Third, this elaborate urbanization of Isidora's ambitious but ambivalent eye anticipates a complex critique of the museum which would be fully articulated only in the second half of the twentieth century. Originally, it had been understood that the museum would function "as the institutional counterpart to the critical discourse of the 'autonomy of art', which [...] served as a 'compensatory ideology' to insulate artistic production from the taint of the marketplace" (Sherman 193). However, Walter Benjamin would soon perceive the museum "as simply one of many dream spaces, experienced and traversed by an observer no differently from arcades, botanical gardens, wax museums, casinos, railway stations, and department stores" (Crary 23). Later on, two different but complementary discourses endorse this kind of assessment, thus validating Isidora's complex "circulation" between museum and store windows, art and merchandise, aesthetics and economics. On the one hand, critics conclude that "Museums were also responding to a tremendous new local interest in art, both a consequence of and a continuing impetus to the dramatic expansion of exhibitions and the art market at mid-century" (Sherman 130–1).[6] On the other, Crary's analysis of the structure of vision in the nineteenth century – "there is never a pure access to a single object; vision is always multiple, adjacent to and overlapping with other objects, desires and vectors" – leads to the following verdict about museums: "Even the congealed space of the museum cannot transcend a world where everything is in circulation. [...] The observer of paintings in the nineteenth century was always also an observer who simultaneously consumed a proliferating range of optical and sensory experiences. In other words, paintings were produced and assumed meaning not in some impossible kind of aesthetic isolation, or in a continuous tradition of painterly codes, but as one of many consumable and fleeting elements within an expanding chaos of images, commodities and stimulation" (Crary 20).

The second moment closes the scene. Isidora's tour of the museum prompts her to ask a question which represents yet another way of undermining the ideal purity, indeed the "sublimity" of the museum's alleged function within the modern city: "Preguntó a Miquis si en aquel sitio destinado a albergar lo sublime dejaban entrar al Pueblo, y como el estudiante le contestara que sí, se asombró mucho de ello" (Galdós 1970: 1007). On the one hand, Miquis's answer – so much in consonance with his modern liberalism ("reina la igualdad" [1015]), and with his unabashed recognition of both himself and Isidora as "pueblo" – is nevertheless pre-empted by Isidora's very question: if she had to ask, the reader may assume that in the museum Isidora had seen no one from Madrid's "Pueblo," a striking fact, particularly on a Sunday morning when visits were free of charge.[7] On the other hand, Miquis's answer reflects the official "theory" on museums without registering its failure "in fact": "The theory, of course, of this new age of liberal thought was that the former private collections were now to be open to all for public education and enlightenment. But in fact the collections continued to be admired as if they were private. [...] The tradition of grandeur persisted. Marble, vast vistas, high, pedimented ceilings, gilding and decoration assumed that these were indeed noblemen's palaces only just vacated, and that the public was admitted on sufferance, as it were" (Ripley 38).[8]

Thus, Isidora's question was exposing an unacknowledged but enduring practice which made the comprehensive notion of "public instruction" not quite applicable to the allegedly democratic institution of the museum. At the same time, this practice easily accommodated Isidora's own radical views of the world, the city, the center, urban society, and herself with regard to each. There is only one other direct reference to the museum in the novel, many pages later, and it openly reveals – in Isidora's own voice – – the institution's combined provision of sublime views and a restricted sense of belonging that favored only the upper classes: "Tres o cuatro veces nada más he estado en el Museo [...]. Aquello sí es grande. Con el talento que hay colgado de aquellas paredes había para hacer un mundo nuevo, si éste se acabase. Yo me figuraba que había pasado a otro mundo, a Venecia, a Roma, a la Corte del Buen Retiro. Unas veces creía que estaba cubierta de brocados y otras que andaba a la ligera, como se anda por el Olimpo. Aquella es belleza, chico, aquella es gracia. Yo decía: eso lo siento yo, esto es cosa mía, esto me pertenece" (1143). Joaquín Pez's response to such *exaltado vuelo* is predictable: "¡Eres noble, eres noble!" (1143). This way, the institution of the museum unwittingly provides from the start an equivocal (if not altogether perverse) guiding paradigm for Isidora's expedient categorization of city spaces – as proper or alien, inclusive or exclusive – throughout the novel.

Such categorization begins not so much with the museum as with the aristocratic palace. As Ripley would have it, the mystifying nineteenth-century museums appeared to be but "noblemen's palaces only just vacated." Indeed, a "nobleman's palace," not quite vacated, starts occupying considerable space in Isidora's urban horizon shortly after her visit to the Prado. The Palacio de Aransis will both underscore the museum's guiding prerogative in the city and undermine its presumed democratic functions, for, among other privileges, the private palace will loom much larger than the public museum in the unraveling of *La desheredada*. First, a number of evident if, at times, caricaturesque similarities appear to confirm not only the place of such palaces in the museum's lineage, but also, and more emphatically, the fact that the palace is now seen mostly through "la óptica del museo," as Ernest Junger once put it (Sedlmayr 33). Miquis will lead the visit to the palace as he led the visit to the museum. Two of the modest visitors, admitted clearly "on sufferance" – the palace's concierge "era complaciente" (Galdós 1970: 1048) – are introduced by Miquis's mocking parlance as cultivated aristocrats worthy of such surroundings.[9] As in a museum, "de las paredes colgaban cuadros modernos de dudoso mérito y algunos retratos de señores de antaño" (1043). All three visitors "pasaron de sala en sala, cada vez más admirados" (1049). Miquis's liberal disposition is then reflected in a characteristic indictment: "Es un insulto a la Humanidad que haya estos palacios tan ricos" (1049). In a latter visit to the same

"Palacio" (1125), Isidora will be accompanied by Bou, whose mockery will underline and critique again the fact that the palace is but "a private collection," not quite yet "open to all for public education and enlightenment."

In both visits, one apparently minor detail will emphatically tighten the connection between palace and museum: the best painting in the house is "un hermoso cuadro colocado sobre la chimenea. [...] Era la pintura, como de Madrazo, tan fina, tan conforme con la distinción, elegancia y gracia del original!" (1045). Madrazo, of course, had been and would be again the director of the Prado Museum, where his paintings were exhibited alongside the masterpieces of the past. Madrazo's painting "era un retrato de mujer": as it turns out, Isidora not only contemplates the portrait but also contemplates herself in the portrait thus adding another nuance to the museum connection. In her next visit to the palace, Isidora will make her claim to aristocratic heritage precisely on the grounds of her resemblance to the subject of the painting; namely her identification with the portrait both as a matter of likeness and as a matter of aesthetic value: "soy el retrato vivo de mi madre" (1075); "ahora que la veo [declares the Marquesa] no puedo negarle que me interesa un poco [...], es usted muy hermosa" (1074). Thus, for Isidora the purpose of that second, crucial visit to the palace is not so much to see as to be seen, to be recognized ("Anagnórisis" is the title of the chapter) and approved as an object worthy of contemplation, and so entitled to a space in the palace as well as in the museum: "soy mi propio testigo y mi cara proclama un derecho" (1075).

Sociologists and cultural historians have pointed out time and again that the museum was created not only as a place for the general public to contemplate art but also as a "space of emulation": "Going to a museum, then as now, is not merely a matter of looking and learning; it is also – and precisely because museums are as much places for being seen as for seeing – an exercise in civics" (Bennett 102). The museum public was inevitably divided in two: the upper classes that were welcome to display there, as in a stage, their exemplary deportment amid works of art with which they had historical and formal affinities (Sherman 190), and the lower classes that were invited into the Museum in order to contemplate the upper classes as models to emulate, while educating their eyes with works of art hitherto alienated from them (Bennett 47, 100). The language of *La desheredada* will often remind the reader of both Isidora's affinity with the works of art and Isidora's qualifications as a model to be "emulated." On the one hand, she is declared of "pura escuela veneciana" (Galdós 1970: 1110); "religiosa o mitológica visión" (1116); "Joya digna de un rey"; "pareces una Diosa ... Vengan las duquesas a tomarte por modelo" (1106). On the other, such "superioridad" allows her to proclaim about the lower classes (ironically represented here by her own cousins): "Estas pobres cursis se despepitan por imitarme y no pueden conseguirlo." The narrator concurs: "Con ella nació, como nace con el poeta la inspiración, aquella facultad de sus ojos para ver siempre lo más bello, sorprender lo armonioso y elegir siempre de un modo magistral [...], que comúnmente no se halla en las zonas medias de la sociedad" (1039). It is only consistent for Isidora's voracious gaze to find in herself another favorite object of contemplation: "luego que se vio totalmente ataviada y pudo contemplarse entera en el gran espejo del armario de luna, quedó prendada de sí misma, se miró absorta y se embebeció mirándose, ¡tan atrozmente guapa estaba!" (1112–13).

And yet such an apparently coherent paradigm is destabilized during Isidora's second and most important visit to the palace in search of definitive approval. Placed approximately at the center of the novel, the encounter becomes a turning point when Isidora's gaze, in fact her entire viewpoint, is challenged by the commanding authority of the Marquesa's gaze, which oscillates from appreciative contemplation to reproving surveillance, from calculation to disregard: "Isidora vio que la Marquesa sacó unos lentes de oro, y aplicándolos a sus ojos, la miraba, la observaba detenidamente, callada, fría, como si examinara un objeto raro, pero no tan raro como para despertar admiración [...]. 'En cuanto al parecido, nada tengo que decir, porque si alguno hay, es puramente casual ... Me hará usted el favor de retirarse' " (1073–5).

From that instant on, while Isidora becomes revitalized by the sight of shop windows (1077) and eventually sells herself to the highest bidder, the narrative makes increasingly clear that she will never be accommodated among the upper classes either as a figure of museum quality or as a museum authority, for she is certainly not the *genuine* noble product she claimed herself to be. At the same time, though, the narrator as much as the protagonist and most of the characters that surround her will continue to propound an equivocal but recognizable distance between Isidora and the *pueblo* that the elites all but excluded from the museum (Sherman 191, 211). Neither elite nor *pueblo*, what was she then? ("¿Qué era?" inquires the text itself: 1106). If she did not belong in the museum or the palace, where then? *La desheredada* does not answer such questions. Instead, it keeps on moving Isidora within the perimeter of the city to other spaces directly or indirectly related to the museum, where the same questions are asked again, forever relocating the protagonist but never quite locking her out of some translation of the museum.

The popular San Isidro Fair is one such space, and it does constitute yet another turning point in Isidora's closeness to and estrangement from the museum paradigm. It represents Isidora's highest triumph as an exhibition piece and a major step in her downfall towards final invisibility. The connection of all types of fairs, including the popular Fair, to the museum has been traced by Bennett and others, mostly with reference to the visiting public: the "mob" or the *pueblo* that was expected to gather at the Fair was the same that conservatives feared to let into the museum for it might cause "the destruction and desecration of art" (Bennett 55–8). Galdós takes the connection somewhat farther: he underlines not so much the features that Madrid's Feria de San Isidro evidently shares with the museum concept, but rather the degeneration contributed by the Fair to those common features. For example, distinctive of the Fair's exhibitions are "las innobles instalaciones donde se encierran fenómenos para asombro de los paletos." Isidora does not miss a single one: "vio la mujer con barbas, la giganta, la enana, el cordero con seis patas, las serpientes, *las ratas tigres provenientes do Japao*, y otras mil rarezas y prodigios." More significantly, Isidora chooses to dress herself as a "mujer del pueblo" in order to both fit in and shine at the Pradera. The novel will then resort to the language of museums and high culture in order to characterize Isidora's warped success at the Fair: "En medio de Madrid surgía, como un esfuerzo de la Naturaleza que a muchos parecería *aberración* del arte de la forma, la Venus flamenca [...]. Por donde quiera que pasaba, recibía una ovación. *Preguntaban todos quién era*" (1112–13, emphasis mine). All throughout, though, the Fair turns out to be as much a bazar as it is a museum ("Nunca como entonces le saltó el dinero en el bolsillo": 1113). As a consequence, Isidora's public exhibition represents not only an arguable case of formal degeneration but a also grave transgression of the mercantile principles of the upper (male) bourgeoisie. A few pages earlier, Isidora had reiterated in no uncertain terms her condition of object purchased for her master's eyes only: "me compra cuanto apetezco con tal de que no lo luzca, con tal de que nadie me vea. Quiere que me ponga guapa para él solo. Basta que cualquier persona me mire para que él se enfade, porque cree que con los ojos se le roba algo de lo que tiene por suyo [...]. Quiere absorber mis miradas todas" (1110). As a punishment, Isidora will now be forced to move, in one single evening, from the display cases of the Fair (and popular acclaim) to crushing obscurity and ever more degrading sales of herself in eccentric neighborhoods: "la repugnancia de la zona del Sur [...] en que su mala suerte la había traído a vivir" (1121).

The question so pertinently repeated at the fair – "quién era" – will surface again in the city prison, the last of Isidora's public stages within the museum's sphere of influence. The answers appear again significantly divided between high aristocracy and ignoble populace, work of art and merchandise, museum and shop window: "Quién aseguraba que era una duquesa perseguida por su marido; quién la tenía por *una cualquiera* de esas *calles* de Dios" (1148; emphasis mine). Even more so than the popular Fair, the prison and the museum have been repeatedly connected. Bennett (59), following Foucault, links them as "institutions of confinement [...] within the power-knowledge relations of nineteenth-century societies." First, both present similar architectural problems, concerning the visibility of the subjects, either for their surveillance or for their exhibition (Bennett 68). Second, both share "mechanisms for the transformation of the crowd into an ordered and, ideally, self-regulating public": prisons, by rendering "the populace visible to power and, hence, to regulation"; museums, by rendering power – the orderly ruling classes amid ordered art objects – visible to the populace (98–9).

Once again, *La desheredada* appears to take such connections one step further. Isidora's presence in Madrid's "Cárcel Modelo" conflates prison and museum, the display of power and the power to display, on a single urban space. On the one hand, upon installation in the "Sala primera," Isidora chooses to present herself "como una reina" (Galdós 1970: 1150); i.e. not a subject under surveillance but a "figure" for contemplation. Residents and visitors alike appear to comply, with full support from the language of the narrative: "[las presas] se agolpaban a la puerta de la sala para verla pasar" (1148); Miquis, the quintessential museum-goer, "sintió viva emoción cuando vió aparecer detrás de las dobles rejas del locutorio aquella figura hermosa, aquel rostro pálido, con expresión de noble conformidad" (1149); Relimpio visits the prison while under the influence and declares: "creí que entraba en encantado y hermosísimo palacio" (1169).

On the other hand, of course, the new stage, like the vigilant presence of the law, cannot remain permanently masked to Isidora's discriminating eye: "qué desmantelado cuarto [...], qué desnudas paredes" (1148). At that point, the prison becomes the counterpart of the museum. Isidora's performance in prison turns out to be but a re-enactment of the transgression that brought her there in the first place: "falsificación" (1147–9). In a sardonic article, Galdós relates the blooming of the "art of fakes" to the creation of museums: "Se ha desarrollado de un modo alarmante el arte de las falsificaciones" (*Fisonomías* 203). Isidora is a fake and thus belongs in prison, but only to make prison not only a live Museum of Fakes but also a kind of Fake Shop. The surveillance of authenticity is, to be sure, a primary task within the museum, and a thorny issue since the inception of museums. *Et pour cause*: fakes not only defy authenticity and aesthetic value, but also they do it both in the market and in the museum, thus exposing the mercantile side of art exhibits. The "question" of fakes is sharply brought to the fore in the Marquesa's dismissal of Isidora from the palace, but returns at the close of the prison scene only to exhibit its mercantile facet – a thinly disguised purchase of Isidora but only for her value as a fake: "La señora Marquesa me ha autorizado para ofrecer a usted un auxilio, siempre que se preste a dar a esta enojosa cuestión un corte rápido y decisivo" (1162).

In a little known essay on museums, Goodman suggests an even more comprehensive set of relationships: "a museum functions much like such other institutions as a house of detention, a house of rehabilitation, or a house of pleasure; or in the vernacular, a jail house, a madhouse, or – a teahouse" (140). *La desheredada* starts in a madhouse; it moves through museum and prison; its last chapter intimates that its *Venus's* final display case will be some "house of pleasure." The reader might be tempted to follow Goodman and complete the museum circuit of projections with connections to the protagonist's ultimate destination. Galdós's novel, however, opts for a different kind of closure: "quizá no nos veremos más ... Adiós [...]. Cayó ella despeñada en el voraginoso laberinto de las calles. La presa fue devorada, y poco después, en la superficie social, todo estaba tranquilo" (1180). While visibility, exhibition and the primacy of the gaze (Isidora's as well as the gazes of her admirers) mark the intense presence of Isidora in museum, palace, Fair and prison, the end of the novel places the emphasis on the opposite urban contingency: loss, disappearance, invisibility, forms of final severance of the protagonist's original ties to the museum. The reader, so far such a privileged spectator, will never be allowed to contemplate Isidora's exhibition at a "house of pleasure" – here more of a plebeian, *excentric* shop than a presentable translation of the museum.

Notes

1. Deaths closely related to both her past and her future: her father's at the madhouse; Zarrapicos's at her brother's hand. Such family ties to the lowest ends of the urban periphery, at the start of the novel, may be interpreted as a forewarning of Isidora's doom. After all, the "family romance" that Isidora will hold on to as authentic family document – the key to *La desheredada*'s plot – was her father's design, a symptom of the insanity that brought him to Leganés.
2. The "much more detailed account" offered in the original manuscript can be found in Schnepf (322).
3. What would eventually be called Museo del Prado was designed in 1795 by Juan de Villanueva (1739–1811) as a Science Museum (including already the *peristilo de columnas*, inspired by the Pantheon, that Sedlmayr, following Karl Friedrich Schinkel, acknowledges as emblematic of museum architecture). The Villanueva building was turned into an Art Museum around 1818 somewhat against the grain, since "the greatest development during the nineteenth century of the true spirit of museums came in the area of the sciences" (Ripley 44).
4. In *Madrid por dentro y por fuera*, Eusebio Blasco does not make a single reference to the museum but, instead, has this to say about the zoo: "El Patio grande del Parque zoológico, es el centro de reunión de todo lo más escogido de la sociedad; la estación de término en el viaje de circunvalación por el Retiro, y un espectáculo barato y permanente [...]. Allí están reunidos y compactos [...] el matrimonio modelo y el famélico cesante, la robusta nodriza y el chistoso soldado, los juguetones chiquillos y el alegre estudiante, el encopetado personaje y la graciosa modistilla" (Blasco 288, italics in original).
5. For another take on this sequence of *La desheredada*, see Mercer (10).
6. Moreover, towards the end of the nineteenth century, "Museums were meant to redeem the fortunes spent creating them by raising the level of the public taste," which suggests that a museum-goer was expected to become a better consumer, and not only of art (Harris 141).

7. "It is open Sundays without charge, from 10 to 3 in winter, and 8 to 1 in summer" (Ford 45). Tuesday through Saturday, the visitor's fee was half a peseta, the cost of a most ordinary meal in a modest tavern (as reported, for example, in Galdós's *Misericordia*). The situation had been quite different before the 1868 democratization of the museum. Mesonero Romanos wrote in 1831: "Este museo está abierto al público todos los miércoles y sábados por las mañanas desde las nueve en invierno, y desde las ocho en verano, hasta las dos de la tarde. A los señores viajeros se les franquea la entrada en los demás días, presentando sus pasaportes" (226). Galdós himself had reported in the fall of 1865: "Los domingos por la mañana se reúne una gran concurrencia en el Museo de Pinturas" (Shoemaker 134).
8. Other versions of this almost obsessive critique are in Bennett (8, 28) and in Sherman (211).
9. In the same vein, Miquis, a true democratic museum-goer, will soon mock Isidora's aristocratic pretensions as unbecoming to her less than humble lodgings: "Cuadros de Fortuny, tapices de los Gobelinos, porcelanas de Sèvres y de Bernardo Palissy … Muy bien. Bronces, acuarelas … Bien se conoce en esta rica instalación el buen gusto del marqués viudo de Saldeoro. Adiós, marquesa […]. Ceno en el palacio de Relimpio" (Galdós 1970: 1066).

Works Cited

Amicis, Edmondo de. *España. Impresiones de un viaje hecho durante el reinado de Don Amadeo I.* Trans. Cátulo Arroita. Barcelona: Maucci, 1899.

Bennett, Tony. *The Birth of the Museum. History, Theory, Politics*. London and New York: Routledge, 1995.

Blasco, Eusebio. *Madrid por dentro y por fuera. Guía de forasteros incautos*. Madrid: San Martín y Jubera, 1873.

Crary, Jonathan. *Techniques of the Observer. On Vision and Modernity in the Nineteenth Century*. Cambridge, MA: MIT Press, 1990.

Ford, Richard. *Handbook for Travelers in Spain*. "Fifth edition, revised on the spot." London: Murray, 1878.

Gold, Hazel. "A Tomb with a View: The Museum in Galdós's *Novelas contemporáneas*." *Modern Language Notes* 103(2) (1988): 312–34.

Goodman, Nelson. "The End of the Museum?" In *The Idea of the Museum*. Ed. Aagaard-Morgensen, Lars. Lewiston, PA: Edwin Mellen Press, 1988.

Harris, N. "Museums, Merchandising, and Popular Taste: The Struggle for Influence." In *Material Culture and the Study of American Life*. Ed. Quimby, Ian. New York: Norton, 1978. 149–74.

Madrazo, Mariano de. *Historia del Museo del Prado, 1818–1868*. Madrid: C. Bermejo, 1945.

Mercer, Leigh. "Appreciating Women: Art and Bourgeois Legitimization in the Nineteenth-Century Spanish Novel." Unpublished manuscript.

Mesonero Romanos, Ramón de. *Manual de Madrid*, Madrid: Graficum, 1990.

Pérez Galdós, Benito. *La desheredada*. In *Obras Completas, Novelas*, Vol. I. Madrid: Aguilar, 1970.

—— *Fisonomías sociales (Obras inéditas)*. Madrid: Renacimiento, 1923.

Ripley, Sydney Dillon. *The Sacred Grove. Museums and their Evolution*. London: Victor Gollancz, 1970.

Schnepf, Michael. "Galdós's *La desheredada* Manuscript: Isidora in the Prado Museum." *Romance Quarterly* 37(3) (1990): 321–30.

Sedlmayr, Hans. *El arte descentrado. Las artes plásticas de los siglos XIX y XX como síntoma y símbolo de la época*. Trans. Gabriel Ferraté. Barcelona: Labor, 1959.

Sherman, Daniel J. *Worthy Monuments. Art Museums and the Politics of Culture in Nineteenth-Century France*. Cambridge, MA: Harvard University Press, 1989.

Shoemaker, William H. *Los artículos de Galdós en* La Nación *(1865–1866, 1868)*. Madrid: Insula, 1972.

–6–

Thresholds of Visibility at the Borders of Madrid: Benjamin, Gómez de la Serna, Mesonero

Andrew Bush

For I see that when one man casts, the other gathers.
Seamus Heaney

Camera Obscura

Walter Benjamin peers through a doorway on Ibiza in the spring of 1932 and observes a shadowy room, dazzling whitewashed walls, and four chairs, meticulously arranged in a symmetrical order ("Ibizan Sequence," 588–9). It is an emblematic moment, if less familiar than that of Benjamin's urban *flâneur*, window-shopping in the Parisian arcade. He stands at a threshold of visibility.[1]

A first approach to this threshold might look to the darkened room as an optical device, a camera obscura, so as to draw certain distinctions with respect to the predominant, Cartesian mode of visualization and the corresponding representation of the visible in Italian Renaissance art. I follow Svetlana Alpers in underlining two aspects of the alternative Dutch "art of describing," for which the mechanical reproduction of nature by the camera obscura served as a theoretical analogue.[2] First, asserting a fundamental seventeenth-century assumption "that finding and making, our discovery of the world and our crafting of it, are presumed to be one," she notes that in Dutch painting, such as the work of Ter Borch, "it is as if visual phenomena are captured and made present without the intervention of a human maker" (Alpers 29, 30). Second, this elision of the painter is doubled by the effect on the viewer, who, Alpers argues, is "neither located nor characterized, perceiving all with an attentive eye but leaving no trace of his presence" (27) in contrast to the perspectival illusion of Italian painting, which "begins not with the world seen, but with a viewer who is actively looking out at objects – preferably human figures – in space, figures whose appearance is a function of their distance from the viewer" (41). Thus, the unseen seer of the paradigm of the camera obscura needs be distinguished from the active egocentrism that represents the world on the preconceived geometric grid of its own projection, and its correlate, the voyeuristic eye at the keyhole that tropes desire, usually masculine desire, as that center.[3] Yet, as Teresa Brennan has argued, "Human beings did not and do not always see out of self-centered eyes. There is another receptive vision, whose very existence disrupts the subject-centered standpoint" (Brennan 228).

Brennan's historicizing of optics and her theory of "receptive vision" enable a more nuanced approach to Benjamin at the threshold. "When the notion of the active eye," the eye irradiating rays, the vision that touches its objects according to the Aristotelian tradition, "went underground it was replaced, in the seventeenth and eighteenth centuries, by the eye as passive receiver," writes Brennan (224). She continues:

> Eventually, we arrived at a position where we could recognize once more that vision was constructed, but the construction was now an inward-turning one as well as a projected gaze. This position was an advance, but its cost was the rejection of any notion of *constructed* physicality. Together with this rejection, I will suggest, goes a loss of the other reality, the alternative receptiveness manifest in another way of seeing. These things go together because the power of the constructed fantasy, the projected gaze, becomes stronger and covers over that other reality. (Brennan 224)

Hence, I return to Benjamin before his camera obscura to suggest that what he emblematizes is a receptive vision, another way of seeing, neither egocentric nor passive.[4]

In this regard, I note that more than the finely crafted wickerwork of the chairs, it is the symmetry that seems to have struck Benjamin as the mark of deliberate display: "No collector could hang rugs from Isphahan or pictures by Van Dyck on his vestibule walls with greater pride than the farmer who puts out such chairs in the otherwise bare hallway" (Benjamin, "Ibizan Sequence," 588). In the constructed physicality of the symmetry, Benjamin finds and makes a "central axis" upon which, he notes, there "rests an invisible pair of scales in which Welcome and Rejection are equally balanced" (588). Pausing at the threshold to have a look, neither hurrying on nor, it seems, daring to enter, Benjamin occupies that very point of balance. And at that point he is receptive to what he designates as the "preciousness" of objects that he initially represents as the pride of the collector:

> Moreover, they are not just chairs. They change their function instantly when a sombrero is hung on the back of one of them. And in this new arrangement the straw hat appears no less precious than the simple chair. In this way fishermen's nets and copper kettles, rudders and clay jars, come together and are ready, as the need arises, to change places and form new combinations a hundred times a day. They are all more or less precious. ("Ibizan Sequence," 588–9)

The hanging hat is the metaphor of a metaphor: a figure for the balance of Welcome and Rejection, now the balance upon which the preciousness of objects – more or less – will be weighed. This value, I stress, is not intrinsic to a given object, nor even to a display of like objects typical of the collection, but rather resides in the arrest of mutability in the combination of disparate articles. And here it is well to remember that unlike the fixed image of the photograph or the series of stills in film, the camera obscura provides a space in which images – or here in Benjamin's emblem, the objects themselves – can indeed "change places" within the frame.[5] Eschewing the more startling juxtapositions of surrealism, Benjamin nevertheless discovers and reconstructs the preciousness of objects in their poise, in the "standstill" of the balance. What appears to Benjamin's eye, aided by the optical device of this darkened room, is the constellation of a hat and chairs, the instant outside "homogenous, empty time."[6]

Benjamin emblematizes the moment when objects are blasted out of homogenous time by the art of collecting, and their preciousness – distinct from use-value or even exchange-value – rises to the threshold of visibility for a receptive eye.[7] But the point of the balance is delicate, and in the pages that follow I will look to the axis of Welcome and Rejection as it is represented at the borders of Madrid, where, ultimately, I seek to catch a glimpse of a reciprocal moment when preciousness – the collection-value – dips below the threshold of visibility.[8] This is, therefore, a chapter about loss, and in its own historicizing gesture, moves backward from the modernity of Benjamin's contemporary, Ramón Gómez de la Serna, which has proven welcome to the critical account of Spanish letters, to a moment of rejection in and of Ramón de Mesonero Romanos, in and of Spanish Romanticism. Though other optical technologies will be invoked along the way – microscope, eyeglasses, telescope, in sum, varieties of "the strictly modern invention" of the use of lenses (Alpers 10) – the threshold between appearance and disappearance remarked here is primarily a function of the art of collecting and receptive vision.[9]

Microscope, Glasses

Cities, too, have such boundaries, or their trace: "ese sitio ameno y dramático, irrisible y grave que hay en los suburbios de toda ciudad, y en el que se aglomeran los trastos viejos e inservibles, pues si no son comparables las ciudades por sus monumentos, por sus torres o por su riqueza, lo son por estos trastos filiales," declares Ramón Gómez de la Serna in the prologue to the first edition of *El Rastro* (1915).[10] He then adds: "Por eso donde he sentido más aclarado el misterio de la identidad del corazón a través de la tierra, ha sido en los Rastros de esas ciudades por que pasé, en los que he visto resuelto con una facilidad inefable el esquema del mapamundi del mundo natural" (Gómez de la Serna 57). The latter trope was a mainstay of the naturalism whose moment was coming to a close. Though in its fading light, it would be well to recall the biological research of Santiago Ramón y Cajal, "a man known for his vision," in the words of Laura Otis (64), who focuses upon the techniques of microscopy that led him to the Nobel Prize (and the associated metaphors she finds in his fiction). Ramón y Cajal's enduring contribution was to redraw the map of neurobiology, as it were, by demonstrating conclusively that neurons are not, as was thought, an undifferentiated reticular mesh, but rather discrete cells, each bounded by its own membrane.[11] I will not follow Otis farther than to underline her own governing trope of the membrane, and to suggest that on the map of the natural world, the Rastro might be situated just there, at the membrane of Madrid: a living boundary at which the city performs the vital functions not only of assimilating or welcoming, but also of excretion or rejection.[12]

Still, Gómez de la Serna will be among those who lead Hispanic letters from the modes of nineteenth-century realism to those of modernism, and his preferred trope, and that of the moment in formation, derives not from natural, but rather what Benjamin calls materialist history. One learns to read the secrets of modernity, as one reads fortunes from tea leaves, in *trastos*, whether Yeats' "foul rag and bone shop of the heart," Joyce's "Throwaway" in *Ulysses*, or Gómez de la Serna's (206) own image of as "la menuda basura reunida en pequeños montoncitos" and Carmen Martín Gaite's *cuarto atrás*, a trope magnified recently in A.R. Ammons' ecological epic, *Garbage* (1993).

Michael Ugarte (108) captures the epochal shift from naturalism to modernism when he writes, "For Ramón, junk is more worthy of urban description than poverty."[13] The lucid pages that Ugarte dedicates to *El Rastro* are an important point of departure for any study of the text, and I extract three observations from them. First, Ugarte remarks that already in the prologue Gómez de la Serna "uses the phrase 'las cosas del Rastro' as a refrain" (109). Ugarte extends that observation when he further asserts, "There seems to be no humanistic hierarchy; every object, including human objects, has its particular worth" (110) – more or less precious to the receptive eye, I add. Finally, registering his own surprise as Gómez de la Serna's irony, Ugarte points out, "Ironically, the activities of exchange, barter, and the market do not seem to take precedence in Ramón's reading of the Rastro, even though these activities are after all the flea market's raison d'être" (110). More surprising than ironic, however, Gómez de la Serna contests the point. Even functionally, given the negligible use- and exchange-value of the objects, the early-twentieth-century Rastro may have served more as a site of disposal at which rejected items could be removed from circulation. Or, to speak in the terms of a different refrain from the text at large, objects in the Rastro are not so much bought and sold or bartered, as they disappear: "Las cosas del Rastro desparecen de aquí algún día. Un día cualquiera, en una callada sucesión. Es lo grande. Es su misión" (Gómez de la Serna 198). From an economic point of view, the Rastro is primarily the space where unsightly objects slip definitively from view. The Rastro, in this sense, is a boundary of the visible, but it is also a limit case for an alternative vision, a threshold from which the receptive eye sees precious objects.

In *El Rastro*, Gómez de la Serna presents a collection, and above all in its microcosm, the section entitled "Montón de cosas" (78–90). The space of that display differs from the text as a whole. The 1915 version of the text culminates in a set of sections that give Gómez de la Serna's art of describing a definite itinerary, otherwise by no means evident. He reports on the sudden arrival of dusk in the Rastro (203–5); followed by a section dedicated to the "Plazoleta final" (205–8); and he concludes with the return journey back through the Rastro to "la vida de la ciudad" (211), from which he now feels a certain rebellious alienation, and the final resting place of "nuestra casa" (212) as the text's asymptote. So, it appears, retrospectively at least, that time has been passing all along and that Gómez de la Serna has followed a definite and progressive path, that is a trajectory organized by the street plan. Not so in "Montón de cosas": in this section the objects themselves organize the exposition: a series of separate paragraphs devoted to collections, that is things of a kind (fans, pipes, kitchen utensils, inter alia). The relation between one paragraph, one display case, and another seems wholly arbitrary. In that regard, the organization of the section (and, generally, *El Rastro* at large) belies the heterogeneous distribution of objects exhibited by any individual vendor, if the Rastro of today is any indication, which is to say that the presentation of *las cosas del Rastro* in "Montón de cosas" does not follow the plan of a realistic itinerary. It corresponds, rather, to the more sober space of later insight.

The text is framed nonetheless, though its framing device, too, represents the logic of the *cosas del Rastro* themselves, rather than the subject-centered perspective of the magisterial modern gaze. In the first display and the last, Gómez de la Serna offers erstwhile containers, tropes for the "space of precious objects," a *mise-en-abîme* of the Rastro itself: "un cofre-fort, feo, pesado, de pie como un oso, con las dos pezoneras de sus registros relucientes en el pecho blindado e incomovible" (78); and *baúles*, which he describes once again in terms of natural history: "A todas estas cosas [i.e. los baúles] les nace un galápago en el alma, un animal así como un galápago. Porque ¿qué animal puede haber más duro y más *cosa* que un galápago, todo él caparazón, pues la cabecita y los pequeños muñones de sus patas son sólo algo accidental en el que es verdaderamente la *cosa* que se mueve y vive?" (90). The giant turtle may well be a living *thing*, but so too the things of the Rastro are *living*, though it be the life, or afterlife, of the torso, blasted violently from its context in the *vida de la ciudad* and *nuestra casa*. For what animal, I might well ask, could be more torso than the *galápago* with the "pequeños muñones de sus patas"?[14]

I would examine more closely at least some of this heap of living things. First, to confirm Ugarte's observation concerning commerce, already in the initial display of the *cofre-fort*, Gómez de la Serna asks, "¿Qué ladrones lo transportaron aquí o qué quiebra supone?" (78). The objects on view appear in the Rastro as they disappear, which is to say that Gómez de la Serna introduces them outside the space of commercial transaction. (The French loan-word, *cofre-fort*, increases the sense of contraband.) But not entirely. Gómez de la Serna can neither keep the art of collecting free of commerce, nor the art of describing free of narrativity. On the one hand, the very undermining of the Rastro as a marketplace, gives rise to suspicions that are narratives in potential: if not by legitimate transaction, then perhaps a robbery, a bankruptcy, a human drama.[15] On the other, even the simulacrum of commerce – the idle question, how much do you want for that …? – can transform the receptive eye of the collector into the aggressive eye of the vendor:

> "Esto que no sé para lo que sirve lo doy por lo que me den," pero como nadie lo ha querido, allí ha quedado para su satisfacción de propietarios de riquezas incalculables y raras, la más pintoresca e interesante satisfacción que puede dar la propiedad, hasta que llega un hombre extraño que se acerca y pregunta: "¿Cuánto vale esto?" Y entonces, como tasadores idóneos y versados, sospechando de pronto un valor desconocido y una admirable aplicación en ese objeto tratado hasta ese momento con menosprecio, responden con picardía: "¿Cuál? ¿Eso? Por eso quiero mucho dinero …" (89–90)

Though Gómez de la Serna speaks of "menosprecio" toward the close, I would argue that this note arises as a consequence of the vision the passive/aggressive modern eye, figured here rhetorically posed as a calculating question. It is only in terms of the exchange-value articulated as "¿Cuánto vale?" that pride of possession, like that of the Ibizan farmer or fisherman and his chairs, is transcribed as deprecation (or even depreciation) for the object of the collection now viewed as unsold merchandise. Previously, unmoored from use-value ("no sé para lo que sirve") and reduced to a negligible exchange-value at best ("lo doy por lo que me den"), the objects had been precious ("riquezas incalculables y raras") to the receptive eye.

The primary *transaction* in the Rastro – when transactions do occur – is the extraction of objects from the space of their preciousness, and their reinsertion into the world of utility, and with it, of exchange value. But it must be recalled that such transactions have as an alternative the simple disappearance of objects. The Rastro, then, may be conceived as a vast field of vision, bounded by disappearance on the one hand and the appearance of usefulness on the other. The receptive eye, operating between those two extremes, may now be further qualified as that which sees the *cosas del Rastro* and perceives them as torsos, fragments, ruins, ghosts. The receptive eye, in its moment of later insight, glimpses the incomplete object in the present and, at the same time, the past that continues to cling to it. A hallucination, perhaps. But the Rastro, from the point of view of the receptive eye is a place for *seeing things*.[16]

This second sight of the receptive eye is made more accessible through a specific technology of vision – again, an older technology: eyeglasses. Few are the moments in "Montón de cosas" when Gómez de la Serna allows the reader to witness the fall of objects from the space of their collectibility, their preciousness, into the world of utility. But in the display case of "Lentes y gafas en profusión" (87–8) he offers a hypothetical narrative:

> Algún hombre rudo, casi siempre con facha de campesino, de carromatero u obrero de azadón más que de obrero de fábrica, se acerca, las coge con timidez por las antenas, se las pone con calladas y dulces maneras, mira las otras cosas del puesto para ver cómo se ve, se extasia ante unos clavos, abre ese libro desperdigado que hay siempre en los puestos, lee un párrafo como un filósofo una máxima, mira con toda su alma y su buena fe par ver mejor de lo que ve su vista cansada, pero el ensayo no le satisface, coge otros anteojos, vuelve a la experiencia, vuelve a dejar ésos y vuelve a coger otros, hasta que por fin cree encontrar los que necesitaba y los compra. (88)

A pre-modern client ("de azadón más que de obrero de fábrica"), this shopper reenacts the meeting of faith and scientific method (functional equivalent of that opthamologist flipping lenses and asking us, patiently, "which is better now, number one or number two?" as we sit, bewildered by the choices). Still more precisely, it is the scene in which early modern scientific method, deeply committed to taking account of the visible, absorbs good faith. Gómez de la Serna's viewpoint is later, though they are contemporaries, and he is more skeptical. "¿No le arrancarán los ojos porque su cristal sea excesivo?" asks Gómez de la Serna; "¿No serán simples cristales de ventana, que en su cándido deseo, en su ilusión de ver, le han hecho ver mejor?" (88). That is, Gómez de la Serna can ask whether technological advances are not illusory, for he defines *ver mejor* in other terms to which the customer, committed to a modern, instrumentalist vision, despite his apparent rusticity, is unreceptive.

Before Gómez de la Serna had narrated the rustic experimentalist into the scene, he had asked other questions: "¿No influirán estas gafas y estos lentes en la visión del que se las ponga después del *otro*? … Esta sospecha se tiene, pero no se cree. Se dice como una buena intención de que en la vida todo debiera ser menos ingrato, y por lo tanto los lentes del otro debían revelar al nuevo dueño algo de lo que el otro amaba recorder" (87–8, Gómez de la Serna's emphasis). Lacking the requisite *buena fe* ("se tiene pero no se cree"), Gómez de la Serna hastens to add, "Pero no; esos lentes y estas gafas tienen la mirada en blanco, indiferente, perdida y vidriosa de la muerte" (88). But to impute a deathly gaze to the glasses is to admit that they had a life, the very animation that a technologized vision is meant to deny. So Gómez de la Serna reduces the death – and the afterlife, troped as a continuing influence – still further. "¿De la muerte?" he asks rhetorically, "Quizás no tanto; tienen sólo la mirada del aire en que todo se condensa" (88). The apparent opacity is not a ghost, a layer of vision irradiated onto the lenses from the eye of extramission of the previous wearer, but the *sfumato* of Italian Renaissance painting, whose mode of representation subordinated objects to the self-centered subject.

Yet the closing skepticism concerning a technologically enhanced, and in that sense a better vision, inverts the rhetorical inflection of Gómez de la Serna's questions. Indeed, the better vision is just that which, putting on another's glasses, allows the subject to become decentered, to see as another saw. Removed from the question of their use-value, the glasses are a privileged object among the "Montón de cosas" in that they make receptivity itself visible.[17] Privileged, but not unique: Gómez de la Serna also tropes the living influence of that which is lost to the past in terms of a "soplo fino" retained by the heaps of smoking pipes, a *soplo* that Gómez de la Serna relates to the breath of life with which God inspired "la estatua de barro de que salió el hombre" (80). Benjamin calls that *soplo* "aura," but recalling his delight in "the sensuality of street names" and the related naming of "little squares" and whole quartiers, would lead me to propose "rastro" as that which becomes available to the specific mode of visualization of this place.[18]

Telescope

The *rastro* of death, or rather of the dead, that adheres to objects that have been touched by a prior vision, and especially visible in the glassy look of *gafas*, brings Poe to Gómez de la Serna's mind when he notes the reddish rust on straight edge razors in the "Montón de cosas" (80). But one might say more generally that the anti-technological vision in *El Rastro* evidences a patina of Romanticism, of which Poe would be a particular, but by no means anomalous avatar, and through which Gómez de la Serna would see his way clear to a more skeptical, a more corrosive modernism.

Though pointedly critical, Edward Baker is a sure guide to the persistence of Romanticism:

> This unhappy state of affairs [i.e. the predominance of a latter-day *costumbrismo*, passing as *casticismo* in mid-twentieth-century Spanish letters] was deeply rooted in romanticism, and that fact should make us mindful of something which, as historians of literature and culture, must command our attention. Romanticism, unlike all literary and artistic movements prior to the nineteenth century, cannot simply be the object of an archeological recuperation, for it is the only one which, long after it was emptied of aesthetic life, did not disappear. On the contrary, as the originary artistic movement of

> a bourgeois culture long ago turned in on itself, it remains with us in a static or involutive mode of existence as a zombie, the aesthetic and ideological undead lurking in our collective unconscious. (Baker 74)[19]

If this was true of the most recent mid-century and now our own turn-of-the-century, so much more so was it the case in the earlier twentieth century of Gómez de la Serna, who, as I have already observed, witnessed the disappearance of objects emptied of *commercial* life (a good post-romanticism?), but also privileged a certain vision of the undead (a bad post-romanticism?) lurking in eyeglasses, pipes, copper vessels and the signs of the smithy.

Baker specifies the failings of that bad post-romanticism:

> That [mid-twentieth-century] sensibility floated comfortably on the anecdotized trivialization of the city's history and it deployed a methodology which could function only by going unrecognized. The method entailed the reduction of the city's inhabitants and their culture, especially the working classes and popular culture, to a nature, and the further reduction of that nature to a collection of tics, so that with the aid of a complicit public, art imitated life, but only to the extent that life imitated the *género chico*. (Baker 74)

More commonly identified with a vanguard whose Romantic methods function by going unrecognized, Gómez de la Serna, too, would reduce the material culture of Madrid's lower class to a *mapamundi* of the natural world, as has been noted. Furthermore, he succumbs to the temptations of narrativity – anecdotizing – whenever he historicizes the transactions reconstituting a modicum of exchange value as a fall from the space of collections. I have argued, however, that in his mode of visualization, embodied in the eyeglasses as a technology for seeing things from the decentered outlook of an *other*, Gómez de la Serna offers an art of describing that brings into focus the preciousness of objects, not a mere collecting of tics. I recognize that this vision that sees the present as the torso of the past remains fundamentally Romantic,[20] but I would now urge that the Romantic roots of the receptive vision call for further thought.

Thus, Ugarte's remark that "The *Rastro* is not a work of local color and much less a nostalgic perusal" (108) is misleading, both in the assessment of Romanticism and of its relation to Gómez de la Serna. Nostalgia suggests a perspective in which the present, conceiving of itself as a site of ruins, views the past as a site of lost integrity. The Romantics, up to and including Gómez de la Serna, I would counter, have no access to a past that is not already fractured, ruined, or emptied, like Benjamin's chairs. Division is the constant preoccupation of Romanticism and its associated trope is the boundary line that separates an inside from an outside – not least the borders of the modern nation-states that arose with or even *as* the primary Romantic project. When Ugarte (109) asserts that

"Ramón's intention … could not be further from that of an urban critic demanding city sanitation, as did Larra and Mesonero," he is no doubt right, but only in signaling that the Enlightenment program presisting in nineteenth-century *costumbrismo* is both more triumphant in the science and technology of Gómez de la Serna's day, and, consequently, more thoroughly under attack in his late Romantic reaction. Larra and Mesonero, like Espronceda, Zorrilla or Gómez de Avellaneda, lived in a period of greater ambivalence, valuably historicized by José María Rodríguez García as an "avoidance of Romanticism" dating back to Jovellanos.[21] That ambivalence, a balance between Welcome and Rejection, promoted a vision of and at the threshold that provides a grounding for turn-of-the-century modes of seeing things.

To inspect that earlier mode of visualization and representation, I turn to an *artículo de costumbres* by Ramón de Mesonero Romanos, "La calle de Toledo" (1832), exemplary, for this purpose, in its thematization of vision, its metaphors, and its technologies. In addition, the text takes us to the same space of casting and gathering, the same border of Madrid, though at a different stratum of excavation.[22] The narrative may be summarized briefly: the narrator, identified explicitly in the closing words as the writer of the text, goes to the outskirts of Madrid to meet a cousin arriving by coach from Andalusia. They cross the Puerta de Toledo on foot and immediately enter "el cuartel más populoso y animado" of Madrid (39). "Desde luego," the narrator tells his cousin: "Debes suponer que no será el más elegante, sino aquel en que la Corte se manifiesta como madre común, en cuyo seno vienen a encontrarse los hijos, las producciones y los usos de las lejanas provincias; aquel, en fin, en que las pretensions de cada suelo, los dialectos, los trajes y las inclinaciones respectivas presentan al observador un cuadro de la *España en miniatura*" (39–40).

Madrid as *madre* is almost a folk etymology, glossed here not as the genealogical point of origin – quite the contrary – but rather, in this neighborhood *popular* at least, the site where all are welcome and none rejected. If not bedrock, this is nonetheless the deeper layer upon which *El Rastro* and indeed the Rastro itself, rest. I recall in this context the *pezoneras* in the *pecho blindado* of Gómez de la Serna's *cofre-fort*, which, viewed from this earlier stratum, can be seen as the persistent image of the receptive mother, though highly ironized. The receptivity of the Rastro, troped as the point of rejection or refuse heap, covers over Mesonero's Romanticized Madrid, as welcoming mother.

This emphasis on receptivity does not so tilt the balance toward welcome that Mesonero thereby forfeits a critical stance, as Ugarte's reference to nostalgia might imply. To recall Otis's metaphor, the Puerta de Toledo functions in his text as a permeable membrane, distinguishing inside from outside, permitting but controlling movement in both directions. As the narrator and his cousin move through the gate and up la calle de Toledo, the welcome consists in a concentrated display of regional differences – presented, it must be admitted, as a collection of tics, much as Baker suggests. But the tics are held up less to the fictitious new arrival than to a condescending *madrileño* readership, of course. And his verbal tic, as it were, is first recorded by the narrator's ear and reader's eye through the controlling gateway of Mesonero's orthography for the Andalusian cousin's accent:

> –Y bien, primo mío, ¿qué te parece del aspecto de Madrid?
> –Que ze pué desir dél lo que de Parmira, que es *la perla del dezierto*. (38–9)

The Andalusian cousin's opening salvo establishes a counterpoint for the theorization of vision in Mesonero's text. The allusion to Palmyra functions simultaneously as a mark of erudition and of irony, that is as an expression that this provincial, far from overwhelmed by the *aspecto* that first meets his eye, considers himself equal, if not superior to the metropolitan situation.[23] But the Andalusian's emphasis falls not on the analogy of Madrid to ruins so much as on its setting in the *dezierto*,[24] as he continues: "y oyez, y tuverion rasón zus fundadores en zituarle sobre Alturas, porque zinó, con ezte río, adónde vamo-a-paral" (39) – the commonplace *desprecio* of the Manzanares, a metonymic displacement of the baroque *desprecio de la corte* already expressed in Mesonero's epigraph, drawn from Bartolomé Leonardo de Argensola:

> Como aquí de provincias tan distantes
> concurren, o por gracia o por justicia,
> diversas lenguas, trajes y semblantes;
> necesidad, favor, celo, codicia,
> forman tumulto, confusión y prisa
> tal, que dirás que el orbe se desquicia.
> (quoted in Mesonero 38)

The topos had been revived in late-eighteenth-century Hispanic letters as a defensive response to an early phase of modernity that would prove decisive for the coming Spanish Romanticism and its vicissitudes. The Enlightenment strain in Larra and Mesonero, mentioned by Ugarte as critics of Madrid's sanitation, is an extension of that same impulse, but what is lacking for both of these urban writers is a counterbalancing *alabanza* of an updated rural utopia whose image had been the all but inevitable murmuring brook of the eighteenth-century locus amoenus, e.g., the "plácido arroyuelo bullicioso" in Meléndez's "Mi vuelta al campo" (Meléndez 260).

The *madrileño* narrator, apparently wounded in his civic pride, tries to divert discussion from the map of nature to the history of technology. "Ya te entiendo," he replies, "pero, en cambio, tienes aquí éste, que si no es un gran puente, por lo menos es un puente grande" (39). This self-deprecating irony of his own does not satisfy the aggressive vision of his cousin, however, which easily extends from the river to include the bridge, too: "la que haciéndose ojos toda/por ver su amante pigmeo," as he recites from the verses he had read in "un libraco viejo" (39).[25] The eroticizing of bridge and river, *corte* and courtier cousin, adds insult to injury.

"¿Acabarás con tu pintura?" (39), asks the *madrileño* narrator, impatiently interrupting the recitation. But his real defense will be a narrative counterattack, an anecdote in which he reduces his Andalusian cousin to the stereotyped, native tic of an aggressive eroticism. "Aquí la turbación de mi provincial," declares the narrator when he sees his cousin's head turned by the arrival of a different carriage, this time bearing a group of fashionably dressed women, languorously peeling oranges. The Andalusian cousin is nearly run over in the street where he stands and stares:

> "Oiga, señor vision," le dijo [una de las manolas], "déjenos el paso franco."
> "¿Adónde van las reinas?"
> "A perderle de vista."
> "Si nesesitazen un hombre al eztribo … "
> "¿Y son así los hombres en su tierra? ¡Jesús, qué miedo!" (44)

and, in a modern version of a medieval insult, "le dirigieron a las narices una cáscara de vara y media, con lo cual, y aguijando el caballejo, desaparecieron en medio de la risa general" (44).

Read simply as anecdote – and perhaps the writers of Franco's Spain at mid-century could see no more – the narrator has the last laugh. He turns the tables on his cousin transforming him from the active subject to passive object – in either case, of abuse. But the Romantic text is more than its anecdote and the *señor visión* a witness to the deficiency of that modern dichotomy. The text presents the issue, from the outset, as a problematic of magnification.

Mesonero responds to the burden of baroque *desprecio* in his epigraph with the following opening: "Pocos días ha tuve que salir a recibir a un pariente que viene a Madrid desde Mairena (reino de Sevilla), con el objeto de examinarse de escribano" (38). He will not receive his cousin like Madre Madrid, however. Instead, he relates: "Las diez eran de la mañana cuando me encaminé a la gran puente que presta paso y comunicación al camino real de Andalucía, y, ayudado de mi catalejo, tendí la vista por la dilatada superficie para ver si divisaba, no la rápida diligencia, no el brioso alazán, sino la compasada galera en que debía venir el cuasi-escribano" (38).

It appears to be, as Alpers might say, a southern view: Galileo and his telescope rather than Kepler and the camera obscura. The prior and prioritized eye, enhanced by an appropriate technology, views the world on a grid of measurable distances from the fixed subject. But the etymology of the *catalejo* (*catar*, that is *captar*, *lejos*) recalls an older and rejected theory of vision, articulated here in the language of *tender la vista por la superficie*. The critical elaboration awaits its Andalusian accent. As long as the centralizing perspective controls the text – and the nation – through its technologies of power (telescope, professional examinations, city gates), the text remains divided along the lines of the inside–outside dichotomy. But Mesonero allows himself a moment when he collects, rather, objects of a kind, human objects, Andalusians:

> "A un lao, zeñores," exclamó mi primo, levantándose; "a un laíto, por amor de Dioz, que viene aquí la gente." Y decíalo por una sarta de machos engalandos que entraban por la puerta con sendos jinetes encima.
>
> "A la paz de Dios, caballeroz," saludó con voz aguardentosa un Viejo que al parecer hacía de amo de los demás.

The text continues to record its distance by means of the alienating orthography, but the Andalusians have recognized each other, and in the place of the *vista tendida*, offer an extended hand as the sign of proximate relation:

> "Toque esos sinco, paizano," dijo mi primo sin poderse contener. "¿De qué parte del paraízo?" (41)

Having learned that the stranger hails from Jaen, the two Andalusians further establish their shared identity – two insiders in on a joke – as a matter of proximity: "Buena tierra zi no estuviera tan serca de Castiya"; "Más serca eztá del sielo" (41).

But now they are in the very heart of Castilla, and these two of a kind engage the madrileño mode of visualization. The rider from Jaen asks, "¿no me dirá zu mersé,' dirigiéndose a mí," writes the narrator, "de dónde han traído ezta puelta?, Porque, o me engañan miz vizualez, o no eztaba años atraz cuando yo eztuve en ezte lugar."[26] The conversation continues:

> "Así es la verdad," le contesté; "porque hace pocos años que se sustituyó este monumento a las mezquinas tapias que antes daban entrada por esta parte a la capital."
>
> "Ahora," repuso el escribano, "la entrada parece mesquina al lado de la puerta." (41–2)

Monumental magnification – the Puente de Toledo with its *ojos*, the new Puerta de Toledo, the view through telescopes and microscopes – aggrandizes the eye of the self-centered subject, but at the cost of diminishing its objects. At stake in Mesonero's text for his post-Romantic heirs is, if not the recovery of the preciousness of objects, then a mode of visualization that acknowledges their loss. It may be too late to save appearances – but not to save the disappearances. The last laugh may go to the *manolas*, the symbols of Madrid, and their narrator; but the

Andalusian cousin is the witness of their disappearance, and Gómez de la Serna will return to the scene to describe, in their wake, the collecting of the things of the Rastro on their way to extinction.

Notes

1. See also Benjamin, "Spain 1932," for a variant text.
2. Alpers speaks against the customary art historical argument that holds that the camera obscura was a common technological aid in the practice of Dutch art: "although many sixteenth- and seventeenth-century treatises that discuss the artistic use of the camera obscura recommend tracing its image," she writes, "we have no evidence of cases in which artists actually did this." Hence, she urges an argument "from analogy" over the argument "from use" (Alpers 1983: 30).
3. See Steven Melville's critical reading of Sartre and Lacan, beginning with Sartre's eye at the keyhole (Melville, esp. 104). I note, however, that Melville omits the crucial role of sound in that paradigmatic scene. In the context of the present volume, I too will restrict attention to vision, while recognizing that much remains to be said about the threshold of the audible.
4. My argument by analogy to the camera obscura, both as I find it in Alpers' (1983) account of Dutch art and, by extension, in Benjamin's emblem, runs counter to Brennan (1996). For Brennan the "key event" in the rejection of the theory of extramission and the consequent "passification" of the active eye "was Johannes Kepler's 1604 analogy between the eye and the camera obscura" (220). I draw upon Alpers, however, for whom the Keplerian model of vision analogous to the camera obscura is not the "passive receiver" of "nothing less than the virtual truth" against which Brennan would distinguish her "receptive vision," but rather a highly mediated mode of visualization (see Alpers 26–71).
5. See Mary Ann Doane's extensive meditation on time and the illusion of motion as enabled by the gap between frames (Doane 2002: esp. 176–205).
6. See Benjamin, "On the Concept of History," sections xiii and B (395, 397); as well as his remark in section xvii, "Where thinking suddenly comes to a stop in a constellation saturated with tensions, it give the constellation … a shock …" (396). Benjamin's concepts of homogenous, empty time and the constellation, as they are articulated in his "Theses on the Philosophy of History" (to allude to the more familiar title of this text as it appeared in *Illuminations* in 1969) are important cruxes in his work, much discussed in the secondary literature. See, for instance, Dipesh Chakrabarty (esp. 72–96) for an elaboration of Benjamin's critique of homogenous, empty time in the context of postcolonialism and also Fritz Breithaupt.

7. Benjamin situates his emblem within his larger project of historical materialism, when he remarks, "In the house, which has no bed," as he writes in his "Ibizan Sequence," "there is the rug with which the occupant covers himself at night" (589). In contrast, "In our well-appointed houses, however, there is no space for precious objects, because there is no scope for their services" (589). As capitalist industry alienates workers through the division of labor, so too, Benjamin suggests, the bourgeois home: the very definition of the "well-appointed" house will be one in which objects are likewise alienated by a strict division of labor – each object appointed its own task. The well-appointed home, then, is also well-lit: it does not allow for the mutability and the instantaneous "flashing up" (Benjamin, "On the Concept," 390) of Benjamin's emblematic camera obscura.
8. For Benjamin himself, the axis of Welcome and Rejection would ultimately run along the border of Spain, where, turned back to France whence he had hoped to flee the Nazis, he committed suicide at Port Bou. For the account of his guide to the border, see Lisa Fittko.
9. For Benjamin's reflections on collecting, see "Eduard Fuchs" and "Unpacking My Library." Note as well of course that the whole of Benjamin's *The Arcades Project* constitutes an essay on and in collecting (see esp. 203–11), to which my own chapter is deeply indebted. Among the rich critical literature on the *Arcades Project*, the ground-breaking work of Susan Buck-Morss remains essential; see also Burgin, Gilloch and McLaughlin for discussions of Benjamin's contributions to urban studies.
10. I cite from the second edition of 1931 as it appears in Gómez de la Serna's *Obras completas*, here, 57.
11. One cannot but remark on the tropological inversion – and yet the continuing influence of biology as a source of the imaginary – in the privileging of the reticular in the trope of the rhizome in Deleuze and Guattari (9–37).
12. I note that Gómez de la Serna (84) makes the explicit connection, all but self-evident in Castillian, between excretion and vision, *culo* and *ojo* (see also the opening pages of Paz), in his materialist history through the image of a chamberpot.
13. Although see the section of *El Rastro* dedicated to "Los mendigos"(176–9), and note 18 below.
14. See, in this regard, the collection of walking sticks among the "Montón de cosas": "Parecen inútiles y mancos todos estos bastones … " (80).
15. A regular feature of the text: see, for instance, the humanizing perspective assumed in the question "¿Quién las trajo aquí?" that Gómez de la Serna asks of some miners' lamps, and the narrativizing sequels, "¿Un minero a salvo? ¿La viuda de un minero asesinado en la mina?" (81).
16. I am indebted to the title of Seamus Heaney's collection of poems, *Seeing*

Things, for reinvigorating the ambiguities of the phrase; the same debt is acknowledged in the epigraph.

17. I use Brennan's "receptivity" here, rather than a Benjaminian locution, "collectibility," which, unfortunately, would echo with "collectible," a term now used precisely for what I have called "transaction," or the fall of objects from the space of their preciousness to the space of commerce.
18. On the concept of "aura," see Benjamin, "The Work of Art in the Age of Its Technological Reproducibility." On the "peculiar voluptuousness of naming streets" and other urban entities, see Konvolut P of Benjamin's *The Arcades Project* (516–26; quotations here and above are, in order of citation, 517, 516, 517).
19. I register a minor objection: the persistence of aesthetic forms is, I believe, a typical feature of literary history when considered with regard to the *longue durée*. Romanticism is distinctive, then, only in that it persists into the present. Hence, where Baker remarks "did not disappear," I would emend, "has not yet disappeared."
20. I have discussed a theoretical model for the visualization of the past as torso through the trope of the amputee in *The Routes of Modernity* (Bush 36–40).
21. See also my discussion of the "hesitant step" in Meléndez, Bello and Heredia (Bush, esp. 250–1. For an overview of the *costumbrista* narrative, see Charnon-Deutsch 13–53).
22. I hasten where Benjamin's sound principle urges "cautious probing with the spade in the dark loam" ("Excavation," 576), in an unending task of recovery. Most regrettably, I skip the stratum that Galdós occupied on these same grounds, when he set his blind beggar Mordecai Almudena "en un vertedero de escorias, cascote y basuras" in *Misericordia* (Galdós 1998: 235), balanced there precariously between rejection and welcome. All references to Mesonero's "La calle de Toledo" will refer to Mesonero Romanos 1984, and will be cited parenthetically by page number only.
23. No longer a cultural commonplace in our times, Palmyra's ancient ruins were an important reference point for Enlightenment philosophers and their Romantic heirs (see esp. Volney).
24. Compare María Zambrano's (114) description of the Madrid of *Misericordia*: "una ciudad plantada en el desierto [...] rodeada de vertederos y escombreros, de tétricos estaciones de ferrocarril."
25. Arriving in Madrid many years ago, Paco Vidal el Bueno, *que en paz descanse*, received my family with a *refrán* that gave evidence of the persistence of the same baroque wit: "tantos ojos por tan poca lágrima," said don Paco of the Manzanares and its bridges.
26. For a brief history of the Puerta de Toledo, see Gómez de la Serna's contemporary Pedro de Répide (550–1), whose articles on *Calles de Madrid* first appeared in 1921–25.

Works Cited

Alpers, Svetlana. *The Art of Describing: Dutch Art in the Seventeenth Century.* Chicago: University of Chicago Press, 1983.

Ammons, A. R. *Garbage*. New York: W. W. Norton, 1993.

Baker, Edward. "Introduction" to "Madrid Writing/Reading Madrid," special section of *Arizona Journal of Hispanic Cultural Studies* 3 (1999): 73–83.

Benjamin, Walter. *The Arcades Project*. Ed. Rolf Tiedemann. Trans. Howard Eiland and Kevin McLaughlin. Cambridge, MA: Belknap Press of Harvard University Press, 1999.

—— "Eduard Fuchs, Collector and Historian." Trans. Howard Eiland and Michael W. Jennings. *Selected Writings* 3.260–302.

—— "Excavation and Memory." Trans. Rodney Livingston. *Selected Writings* 2.576.

—— "Ibizan Sequence." Trans. Rodney Livingston. *Selected Writings* 2.587–94.

—— "On the Concept of History." Trans. Harry Zohn. *Selected Writings* 4.389–40.

—— "Spain 1932." Trans. Rodney Livingston. *Selected Writings* 2.638–52.

—— "Theses on the Philosophy of History." *Illuminations*. Ed. Hannah Arendt. Trans. Harry Zohn. New York: Schocken, 1969. 253–64.

—— "Unpacking My Library: A Talk about Collecting." Trans. Harry Zohn. *Selected Writings* 2.486–93.

—— *Selected Writings*. Gen. Ed. Michael W. Jennings, *Volume 1: 1913–1926*. Eds. Marcus Bullock and Jennings. *Volume 2: 1927–1934*. Eds. Jennings, Howard Eiland and Gary Smith. Trans. Rodney Livingston et al. *Volume 3: 1936–1938*. Eds. Eiland and Jennings. Trans. Edmond Jephcott, Eiland et al. Cambridge, MA: Belknap Press of Harvard University Press, 1996–2002.

—— "The Work of Art in the Age of its Reproducibility: Second Version." Trans. Edmond Jephcott and Harry Zohn. *Selected Writings* 3.101–33.

Breithaupt, Fritz. "History as the Delayed Disintegration of Phenomena." In *Benjamin's Ghosts*. Ed. G. Richter. 191–203.

Brennan, Teresa. "The Contexts of Vision from a Specific Standpoint." In *Vision in Context*. Eds. Brennan and Jay. 217–30.

—— and Martin Jay, eds. *Vision in Context: Historical and Contemporary Perspectives on Sight*. New York: Routledge, 1996.

Buck-Morss, Susan. *The Dialectics of Seeing: Walter Benjamin and the Arcades Project.* Cambridge, MA: MIT, 1989.

Burgin, Victor. "The City in Pieces." In *The Actuality of Walter Benjamin*. Eds. Laura Marcus and Lynda Nead. London: Lawrence and Wishart, 1998. 55–71.

Bush, Andrew. *The Routes of Modernity: Spanish American Poetry from the early Eighteenth to the Mid-Nineteenth Century*. Bucknell Studies in Latin American

Literature and Theory. Lewisburg, PA: Bucknell University Press, 2002.

Chakrabarty, Dipesh. *Provincializing Europe: Postcolonial Thought and Historical Difference*. Princeton, NJ: Princeton University Press, 2000.

Charnon-Deutsch, Lou. *The Nineteenth-Century Spanish Story: Textual Strategies of a Genre in Transition*. London: Tamesis, 1985.

Deleuze, Gilles and Félix Guattari. *Milles plateaux. Capitalisme et schizophrénie*. Vol. 2. Paris: Minuit, 1980.

Doane, Mary Ann. *The Emergence of Cinematic Time: Modernity, Contingency, the Archive*. Cambridge, MA: Harvard University Press, 2002.

Fittko, Lisa. "The Story of Old Benjamin." In Benjamin, *The Arcades Project*. 946–54.

Gilloch, Graeme. *Myth and Metropolis: Walter Benjamin and the City*. Cambridge: Polity Press, 1996.

Gómez de la Serna, Ramón. *El Rastro*. *Obras completas*. Vol. 1. Barcelona: Editorial AHR, 1956. 49–255.

Heaney, Seamus. *Seeing Things*. New York: Farrar Straus Giroux, 1991.

McLaughlin, Kevin. "Virtual Paris: Benjamin's *Arcades Project*. In *Benjamin's Ghosts*. Ed. G. Richter. 204–33.

Meléndez Valdés, Juan. *Poesías selectas: La liva de marfil.* Eds. J.H.R. Polt and Georges Demerson. Clásicos Castalia 108. Madrid: Clásicos Castalia, 1981.

Melville, Stephen. "Division of the Gaze, or, Remarks on the Color and Tenor of Contemporary 'Theory.'" In *Vision in Context*. Eds. Brennan and Jay. 101–16.

Mesonero Romanos, Ramón de. *Escenas maitritenses*. Ed. Marcos Sanz Agüero. Madrid: BUSMA, 1984.

Otis, Laura. *Membranes: Metaphors of Invasion in Nineteenth-Century Literature, Science, and Politics*. Baltimore, MD: Johns Hopkins University Press, 1999.

Paz, Octavio. *Conjunciones y disyunciones*. Mexico: Joaquín Mortiz, 1969.

Pérez Galdós, Benito. *Misericordia*. Ed. Luciano García Lorenzo. Letras Hispánicas. Madrid: Catedra, 1998.

Répide, Pedro de. *Las calles de Madrid*. Ed. Federico Romero. Madrid: Afrodisio Aguado, 1981.

Richter, Gerhard, ed. *Benjamin's Ghosts: Interventions in Contemporary Literary and Cultural Theory*. Stanford, CA: Stanford University Press, 2002.

Rodríguez García, José María. "The Avoidance of Romanticism in Jovellanos's 'Epístola del Paular." *Crítica Hispánica* 25(1–2) (2002): 93–110.

Ugarte, Michael. *Madrid 1900: The Capital as Cradle of Literature and Culture*. University Park, PA: Pennsylvania State University Press, 1996.

Volney, Constantin-François. *Les Ruines, ou, Méditation sur les révolutions des empires*. *Oeuvres complètes*. Vol. 1. Paris: Parmantier, 1826.

Zambrano, María. "*Misericordia*." *La España de Galdós*. Barcelona: La Gaya Ciencia, 1982.

–7–

Seeing the Dead: Manual and Mechanical Specters in Modern Spain (1893–1939)

Brad Epps

Facing the Image

"He is dead and he is going to die." So writes Roland Barthes with regard to a photograph of Lewis Payne by Alexander Gardner. Taken in 1865, the photograph depicts a young man – strong, beautiful, and shackled – who is to be executed for the attempted assassination of the Secretary of State of the United States of America. The photograph, like all old photographs, ostensibly "captures" a person long dead, but unlike many photographs it presumably captures something else: the expectant knowledge of death, its imminence. For Barthes, the upshot is a "defeat of Time" by way of a double recognition: "*that* is dead and *that* is going to die" (96, emphasis original). *He* slips into *that*, and as such he becomes a thing, an object of contemplation, *our* contemplation, we the living, here we the reading. Photography, with its lure of objectivity (it is not for anything that *objectif*, *objectiu*, and *objetivo* also mean "lens" in French, Catalan, and Spanish), does indeed give the *impression* of capturing the dead and the dying, of suspending Cronus and his voracity even as it pays homage to them. But photography and other mechanical modes of reproduction are obviously not the only ways of depicting the dead, the condemned to death, and the dying – the dying who are also the living – and of offering them up to our ever so fragile contemplation. Long before photography was even a dream, painting, sketching, etching, carving, sculpting, and other more manual modes of reproduction took on the dead, the condemned to death, and the dying, and did so in ways that could not quite so easily dispense with the trace of the hand that, studiously or not, attempted to capture something passing or passed. In the modern age, however, both modes of reproduction coexist, one inflecting the other in ways that ensure that the representation of death is perpetually torn between the realities of perceptual subjectivity and the illusions of evidential objectivity.[1]

In what follows, I will be considering some of the ties and tensions between manual and mechanical representations of death, and more specifically of the dead and the condemned to death, in late-nineteenth- and early-twentieth-century Spain.[2] More specifically still, I will be focusing on two quite different works: a group of twenty-eight drawings by Santiago Rusiñol from circa 1894 of detained and possibly condemned Anarchists (Figures 7.1 and 7.2), and a 1936 photograph by Agustí Centelles of two victims of street fighting at the outbreak of the Spanish Civil War (Figure 7.3). The works, known as *Caps d'anarquistes* and *Morts a la plaça [de] Catalunya* respectively, are obviously only two of countless works that deal with death. Neither of the two works that I have chosen to study can thus account for the subject matter in its entirety, nor, moreover, is there any *necessary* relation between them. That said, both works share a common locale, to wit, Barcelona; both tackle violent events of momentous social impact that are historically interrelated (police and military repression, direct action, revolution, and war); both refrain from providing captions that name their subjects (perhaps because, for whatever reason, they cannot name them); both are dogged by factual uncertainties; and both have an iconic status that remains relatively marginal: neither work, that is, enjoys widespread recognition – whether it be within each artist's *oeuvre* or within the larger field of the drawing and the photograph. What the two works share is moderated, nevertheless, by what separates them. Not only is one a group of drawings and the other a photograph, but also, more pointedly, the drawings are produced within a highly select and self-conscious climate of modernist art and artistry, buffeted by positivism and such pseudo-scientific ventures as phrenology, while the photograph is produced within a hard-nosed, hands-on climate of journalistic truth and passionate political engagement in which artistry is saddled with suspicion.

Beyond such generic and contextual differences, however, one work centers on figures arrested, most likely subjected to torture, and perhaps even condemned to death (or facing that possibility), while the other centers on figures already dead; one offers up to view faces, and almost only faces, while the other offers up no face at all. In an important way, Centelles's photograph of the faceless dead, of the dead face down or covered up, has little in common, beyond the technology of its production, with Gardner's photograph of Lewis Payne, whose beauty so fires Barthes's imagination.[3] In fact (and the status of facts, their tendency to be taken at "face value," is a key concern of this chapter), Rusiñol's drawings may have just as much in common with Gardner's photograph as Centelles's photograph does; though from a somewhat different perspective, it may also be the case that Rusiñol's drawings have little in common, beyond portraiture and penalization, with Gardner's photograph. However formulated, the relations between media, genre, subject matter, national context, and so on are anything but straightforward and consistent. I say this in order to resist the sensation that my move from Rusiñol to Centelles supports, by way of historical chronology, a kind of technological teleology in which the manual is superseded by the mechanical and by which subjectivity is stabilized

Figure 7.1 Santiago Rusiñol (1861–1931), *Caps d'anarquistes I and II* 1894. Charcoal and ink on paper. 19.8 × 27 cm; 19.9 × 26.8 cm (MCFS 30.777–30.778). © Consorci del Patrimoni de Sitges. © 2004 Artists Rights Society (ARS), New York/VEGAP, Madrid.

and enigma depleted. If I pay less attention to Centelles in what follows it is all too simply because of the limits of space and, less crucially, because of a relative dearth of prior, published studies on *Morts a la plaça [de] Catalunya* with which to engage. If anything, in Centelles's photograph subjectivity is destabilized and enigma paradoxically reinvigorated, and to such a degree that, at present, I can offer only a sketchy approximation to the mechanically produced image. Lest my word plays appear coy, I want to make it clear that I do not see photographs as reducible always and only to the photograph and drawings as reducible always and only to the drawing; nor do I see the material divisions between the photograph and the drawing, the mechanical and the manual, as always and everywhere more important

Figure 7.2 Santiago Rusiñol (1861–1931), *Caps d'anarquistes III and IV* 1894. Charcoal and ink on paper. 19.9 × 26.9 cm each (MCFS 30.779–30.780). © Consorci del Patrimoni de Sitges. © 2004 Artists Rights Society (ARS), New York/VEGAP, Madrid.

than the subjective negotiations between them (which include, for instance, the varying, subjectively charged meanings of the face and the faceless, however produced). That said, the differences between the two works, tempered and tensed by the aforementioned similarities, may also allow for a fractured picture of a fractured place – say, Catalonia or, for that matter, sovereign Spain – that at once reaffirms *and* calls into question the viability of "seeing" (a) culture, its objective and subjective turns, its necessities and accidents, its facts, fantasies, and fictions. Having introduced the specific objects of my inquiry, it is to the issue of culture and, within it, of national culture, particularly as it is touched by the faces and defacements of death, that I will, however, turn first.

Figure 7.3 Agustí Centelles (1909–85), *Morts a la plaça [de] Catalunya* July 19, 1936. Black and white photograph. © 2004 Artists Rights Society (ARS), New York/VEGAP, Madrid.

Facing the Nation: Seeing, Spain and Death

If death, as Sarah Webster Goodwin and Elisabeth Bronfen contend, is constructed by culture, by *a* culture, it is also that which "grounds the many ways a culture stabilizes and represents itself" (Goodwin and Bronfen 4). Then again, such mortally inflected grounds of cultural representation are not always, or ever, truly stable, for death, even as it spurs representation, remains radically resistant to representation and functions as "a signifier with an incessantly receding, ungraspable signified, always pointing to other signifiers, other means of representing what finally is just absent" (Goodwin and Bronfen 1993: 4). The slippage of death, its fissured reiterability, always and everywhere different, is inseparable, then, from the stability of death, its fissureless finality, always and everywhere the same. Fundamental as it may be, death is also, of course, disruptive and destructive of culture, a culture. "Culture itself," Goodwin and Bronfen (4) go on to argue, "would then be an attempt both to represent death and to contain it, to make it comprehensible and thereby to diffuse some of its power." But if this is so for culture writ large, its seems particularly so for *national* culture, whose very meaning may well be measured, as Benedict Anderson (1991) has remarked, in the willingness to die and to kill (7). In Anderson's formulation, national and nationalist imaginings, suffused with religious imaginings, at once issue from and lead to death, "as the last of a whole gamut of fatalities" (10). War memorials and monuments, among which Anderson singles out the tomb of the Unknown Soldier, provide concrete form to the nation and its debt to death. Anderson's general theoretical take nonetheless bears nuancing. For Spanish national culture, itself a far from undisputedly coherent construction, appears to be caught in the general play of death and representation in especially incisive and insistent ways.

Over and again Spain is seen – perhaps most acutely from the outside but also from the inside – as obsessed and/or at peace with death. And the saints, martyrs, and mystics; the relics and rituals; the alternately hyped and diminished legacy of the Inquisition and the *auto de fe*; the panoply of torture devices and practices; the age-old rhetoric of austerity, resignation, and fatalism; the protracted history of internecine violence, absolutism, and totalitarianism; the nationally charged practice of bullfighting; the once seemingly endemic poverty, scarcity, and economic backwardness, all contribute to such a (mis)perception. The *leyenda negra*, or dark legend, is perhaps the most enduring sign of a specifically Spanish mode of death, one that experienced a curious revival – curious as a revival because so laden with fatality – in the modern period. José Gutiérrez Solana, Emile Verhaeren and Darío de Regoyos, Pío Baroja, and other uneasy heirs to Goya turned their sights to what they variously presented as a nation mired in misery, violence, and death. Andrés Trapiello (10), in his introduction to Gutiérrez Solana's *La España negra* (1920), asserts that such sights and spectacles, however borne out by external reality, are deeply subjective in nature: "*España negra* always begins in one's self, by simply looking behind what everyone else sees."[4] Yet the look behind, a sort of critical double take, is by no means invariable; the centrality of the self that Trapiello invokes spins sights, spectacles, and subjects into so many particularities and particularisms. The general sweep of particularities is such that the very notion of Spain comes into crisis, not by way of an unlimited individualism (each one seeing what he or she wants to see) but by way of more delimited or particular generalizations that give voice and visibility to *other* nations and nationalisms within the Spanish state. The deadly specters of the black legend contribute, in turn, to the symbolic reconfiguration, even the projected dissolution, of Spain – as if a nation so bound to death were bound to die. But the symbolic power of legends, rituals, and received ideas typically requires a material basis – or at least the idea of a material basis. By the late nineteenth century, uneven economic development and modernization had splintered the idea of Spain so profoundly that Joan Maragall, the premier poet of Catalan modernism, dubbed the country "una cosa morta" (Maragall 1988: 33), a dead thing, from which Catalonia, if it were to live and prosper, should free itself. *Una cosa morta*: if Lewis Payne, a real individual (executed for a crime against the state), becomes a dead thing for Roland Barthes, Spain, a figurative collectivity, also becomes a dead thing for many of its citizens – most notably, many Catalans who would prefer to live as citizens in, and of, another country, one they might call their own.

So vexed is the state of the Spanish nation in the modern period that the very notion of "seeing Spain" is dubitable; at the very least, it is fraught with blind spots, omissions, and partialities that cast the designated object – Spain – into an impossibly ideal position and that make it as elusive a sight, *toutes proportions gardées*, as death itself. And yet, for all the difficulties, some mortally flecked part of Spain does appear to come into view amid a welter of works in which death, disease, and suffering figure prominently. Publications that contain illustrations of the dead and the dying (Bécquer, Verdaguer, Darío, and a long etcetera) exist alongside such artworks as Darío de Regoyos's *Por los muertos* (1886), Santiago Rusiñol's *La morfina* (1894), Ramon Casas's *Garrot vil* (1894), Isidre Nonell's *Capella ardent* (1897), and Pablo Picasso's *Cabeza de mujer muerta* (1902–3), all of which confront death in a modern age. Deploying a variety of pictorial devices and depicting an array of social scenes that range from the isolated anguish of drug addiction (from which Rusiñol himself suffered) to the spectacular coldness of capital punishment, these works participate in the restless fascination with death – restless because increasingly deprived of the redemptive support of religion – that marks a great deal of *fin-de-siècle* art. Given the transnational contacts and cosmopolitan cravings of many of the above-mentioned artists, among them Rusiñol, it is perilous, however, to fixate on national or local origins. For the desire for an artistic community beyond the limits of the land and language; the often impatient dismissal of anything that smacked of folklore and local color; and the at times overweening investment in the idea of Europe (a veritable pleonasm for modernity) served to put the brakes on a more discernibly local, regional, or even national art. As Rusiñol expressed in a speech delivered on November 4, 1894 at the Third Modernist Festival in Sitges: "we value Leonardo da Vinci or Dante more than a province or a people" (154). This is not to say, however, that local, regional, or national factors did not signify, for they most certainly did, but rather that the referential power of place was often little match for the more autonomous and interpictorial turns of the work of art.

The force of reference is obviously different for photography: different, because so insistent as to seem all but ineluctable. As Susan Sontag (1977) remarks, "[w]hile a painting or a prose description can never be other than a narrowly selective interpretation, a photograph can be treated as a narrowly selective transparency" (6). It *can* be treated so, usually is treated so, but Sontag knows that "the work that photographers do is no generic exception to the usually shady commerce between art and truth" (6). Such shady commerce shades into the political, is itself political, and is perhaps never more so than when what is depicted is war, that practice by which nations clash and/or tear themselves apart. As terrible as the acts of direct action or terrorism may have been (so terrible that Barcelona, at the height of modernist creativity, became known as the city of bombs), and as startled into some form of artistic response as Rusiñol and other self-proclaimed esthetes may have found themselves, it is not until later, when photography goes mobile with the Leica camera (which Centelles acquired early on and with which he distinguished himself from his compatriots), that Spain as a particular national place – shot through with other national places – rises once again to international prominence. Its rise is here shadowed by its fall: the Spanish Civil War constitutes, without question, the event by which Spain becomes the center of Western-dominated international concern, reflection, and perception. Interestingly, the images that give force to the centrality of war-torn Spain are largely by photographers and filmmakers from outside Spain, notably among them Robert Capa, Gerda Taro, David Seymour, Joris Ivens, and Henri Cartier-Bresson. The names are not incidental, for the photograph, which was often reproduced and disseminated without authorial attribution (there are, of course, exceptions), increasingly appeared to give way to the photographer – named, photographed in turn, and even promoted as "great," as was the case with Capa. In the process, the much-touted objectivity of the photograph, its mechanical and chemical ability to arrest and preserve reality *as it is* (or *as it was*: the photograph, however instantaneous, is always retrospective), came under the shadow of doubt the more its truth was tethered to the photographer, to a subjective presence behind the camera. Or to put it a bit differently, the force of reference spiders out to the individual photographer and further confounds the differences between the manual and the mechanical, art and truth.

But if the names of some photographers became famous, their nationality was often forgotten, ignored, or disavowed. As Sontag notes: "[t]he photographer's nationality and national journalistic affiliation were, in principle, irrelevant. The photographer could be from anywhere. And his or her beat was 'the world.' The photographer was a rover, with wars of unusual interest (for there were many wars) a favorite destination" (*Regarding* 2003: 35). If Rusiñol and his modernist pals – even as they contributed to the revitalization of Catalan culture – celebrated a borderless cosmopolitanism populated by vagabonds, Wandering Jews, traveling minstrels, and melodious grasshoppers in opposition to industrious ants, many of the best known photographers of the Spanish Civil War fostered a politically engaged internationalism that similarly threw national coordinates into question – even as a specific nation was at the ostensible center of their attention. And yet, as already noted with respect to Rusiñol, although international or cosmopolitan dynamics may throw national coordinates into question, they do not and cannot entirely dispense with them. All too briefly styled, while the name of Goya has dominated the history of the representation of the Napoleonic invasion of Spain, monumentalized as a time when Spaniards came together to resist foreign invaders, the names of such native Spanish photographers as Centelles were often lost in a swirl of foreign names, names of people presumably better equipped to report, and to do so objectively, the events of the Civil War. The recuperation of Centelles after the death of Francisco Franco has involved, that is, the recuperation of a modern mode of cultural production – photography – within a wider Spanish *national* framework. Centelles's photographs seem to refer – at least as Chema Conesa, Marie-Loup Sougez, and others have presented them – to Spain's ability, thanks to a native son, to represent itself, to see itself, and to take a place of pride in modernity and, in so doing, to overcome the very death that the photographs illustrate.

The referential plays of Centelles's photographs and of Rusiñol's drawings bear, in short, on Centelles and Rusiñol themselves; on their audience and, more conspicuously, on their critics; on aesthetic, intellectual, and political movements, trends, tendencies, schools, and whatnot that pass or purport to pass borders; and on historical events of varying international importance. They also bear on the nation, that imagined, bounded community that is here, amid all the differences between Rusiñol and Centelles (the former a major force in cultural Catalanism; the latter a Valencian settled in Barcelona), far from stable or self-evident. And finally, or perhaps primarily, the referential plays bear on the finality of death, a presumptive finality inasmuch as representation, whether manual or mechanical, serves partly to gainsay the absence, loss, and disappearance that death entails. Indeed, the mortal charge of nationality, the every-ready sense of patriotic sacrifice, casts national culture in an elegiac mode in which memory is vital. The point is important. Photography may well be, as Sontag asserts, "an elegiac art, a twilight art," which "promote[s] nostalgia" and whose subjects are, "just by virtue of being photographed, touched with pathos" (*On Photography* 1977: 15), but it clearly does not have a monopoly on death and loss, on elegy, nostalgia, and pathos. A variety of practices and products, among which the *memento mori* and the death mask, no less than the *camera obscura*, mirrors, perspective boxes, and other contraptions, gave historical depth to newer photographic technologies. And vice versa: photographic technologies, dependent as much on chemical reactions as on human interventions, provided a new "take" on the iconographic tradition and, furthermore, on the very act of seeing. Of course, neither photography nor painting and drawing, neither the mechanical nor the manual (and if drawing can be mechanistic, photography can be manual), can realize the dream – or nightmare – of what Norman Bryson has theorized as the essential copy (13), the referentially secure representation, *beyond* history, of the living and the dead. What both photography and drawing can realize, however, and what I will attempt to draw out and develop by way of factual data and speculative propositions, is something like a record of the history of the dreams and nightmares of the essential copy and the representation of the "real thing" – that is to say, a partial sight and seeing of Spain.

Facing Violence: Necessity, Chance and the Terror of Bourgeois Life

Santiago Rusiñol's *Caps d'anarquistes* (Heads of Anarchists, *c.* 1894) – a set of twenty-eight charcoal sketches of men and women whose heads, distributed more or less evenly on four sheets of vellum, seem to float, as if decapitated, against a washed-out background – presents a motley crew of (presumed) Anarchists, all now dead and some, if not all, marked by death at the time of the sketches.[5] The Anarchists in question, each one accompanied not by a name but a number and all rendered in a manner more or less consistent with phrenological protocols, are explicitly associated with the bombing of the Gran Teatre del Liceu on November 7, 1893, one of the most spectacularly violent events to shake the "good families" of Barcelona in the last decade of the nineteenth century. As the center of Catalan operatic culture, itself pivotal to the staging of the Catalan bourgeoisie, the Liceu was an obvious site for direct action. Of the two bombs thrown by Santiago Salvador Franch during the première in Barcelona of Gioacchino Rossini's *Guillaume Tell*, only one exploded, but it killed over twenty people and wounded many others. The carnage was terrible. Although discrepancies about the death toll – Laplana (175) writes of twenty-eight,[6] Lahuerta (41) and Bookchin (120) of twenty-two, and Jardí (26) and Coll (120) of twenty – mar the factual neatness of the recorded history of the event and push at longstanding positivist assumptions,[7] on a more symbolic level, the explosion constituted an irruption into, and interruption of, the putatively smooth unfolding of a powerful project of civic and national progress. Against this backdrop, the sketches that Rusiñol produces might be seen as an attempt on the part of a champion of aestheticism, elsewhere so critical of an empirical, "prosaic" understanding of order, to make sense of a disorder that far exceeded the disorderly postures of a group of bourgeois Bohemians who railed against their own class. Or they might be seen as the manifestation of an ambivalent fascination with the forces of a *different order*, one adumbrated in the violent disordering of the bourgeoisie.

However the sketches are "seen," the tensions between the empirical and the symbolic were unquestionably charged in the late nineteenth century, when naturalism and positivism were buckled by supernaturalism and neo-mystical spiritualism. Of course, the personal was also at issue, and in ways that set the previously noted phrenological protocols on edge. Insofar as Rusiñol is concerned, more than his general social class was assaulted in the bombing of the Liceu: his wife, Lluïsa, and his brother, Albert, were reportedly among the injured (Laplana, 175–6; Panyella, *Epistolari*, 49). Whatever the exact nature of Rusiñol's relations with his family members (he was estranged from his wife for many years), it is still "reasonable" to suppose that the drawings are shot through with a personal interest that renders them ambiguous testimonies of a time of heightened class conflict in which the artist himself was necessarily implicated. The great narrative of collective history is riven, in other words, with smaller, less retrievable narratives of personal history. To be sure, subjective motives and intentions are perhaps always irretrievable, but even the so-called objective circumstances in which Rusiñol produced the sketches remain unclear (hence the "*c.* 1894"). Isabel Coll, in what may well be the most detailed account of the drawings, gives November 21, 1894 as the date of the verdict – the same date that Enric Jardí and others rightly give as that of Salvador's execution by garrote (27) – and says that "Rusiñol *must have been* present" in the courtroom (121, emphasis added). Tellingly, Coll is more tentative about factual details than she is about Rusiñol's feelings. Like Laplana,[8] she refers to some form of "attraction," but she locates it in the personality of the Anarchists themselves (Coll 121). Calling the drawings "true psychological studies," Coll claims that they evince Rusiñol's "*desire* to convey to us diverse reactions" of each of the detained (121, emphasis added). For other viewers, however, the *personality* of the Anarchists may be less self-evident in the sketches than that of the artist, which is also far from self-evident.

Leaving aside what Rusiñol actually "felt" and "desired," and exactly when and where he made his sketches (which is admittedly to leave aside quite a bit), it seems likely, historically speaking, that his feelings, desires, and sense of the Anarchists were shaped, at least in part, by the widely diffused theories of Cesare Lombroso, a major force in criminology and criminal anthropology. Lombroso builds on the theories of Austrian physician Franz Joseph Gall, who is credited – or discredited – with founding phrenology, according to which bumps, depressions, and other external features of the skull correspond to internal cerebral functions. Although Gall's theory, first articulated in the late eighteenth century, was already in trouble by the early nineteenth century, Lombroso adapted it to the purposes of criminal investigation, which was (and in many ways still is) linked to moral inquiry. Lombroso's emphasis on characters and types entailed the relative suppression of individuality as anything other than the aggregate of otherwise classifiable parts and features. Under the spell of characterology, individuals characterized as criminal, delinquent, and degenerate were virtually interchangeable (Galera Gómez 109). The lack of precise information regarding Rusiñol's subjects – even the *Cau Ferrat*, Rusiñol's museum-house where the sketches now hang, has no record of their names – is thus overdetermined. It is not just that such information may have been lost or discarded, but also that characterological determinism, supported as it was by a loosely processed Darwinianism, may have made such information seem unnecessary: a type was a type, and proper names and individual biographical data were, in some sense, inessential. The virtual interchangeability of people deemed to be criminal (another sort of "nation" within a nation) was not merely theoretical; it was brutally operant in the aftermath of the attack on the Liceu. Gerald Brenan notes that the police, unable to locate the material author of the bombing, "arrested five Anarchist leaders *at hazard* and, although it was clear that they had no connection with the terrorists, the judges found them guilty" (Brenan 164, emphasis added). Hazard is here circumscribed by determinism, for the other Anarchists were judged the same as Santiago Salvador and were tried, convicted, and executed with him. In the repressive atmosphere that attended the attacks,[9] but that also gave rise to them (a number of civil liberties were suspended just a few months *before* the attack on the Liceu, and torture and execution were omnipresent, as Álvarez Junco (486) notes), an Anarchist was an Anarchist; a criminal, a criminal.

According to Juan José Lahuerta, who sees in the face of one of the arrested Anarchists of Rusiñol's drawings the face of one of the beggars that occupy the lower left foreground of Joaquim Mir's *La catedral dels pobres* (a large canvas from 1898 in which Gaudí's Sagrada Família fills the background), Rusiñol sees only what is necessary in his models: the delinquent, the criminal, the dangerous, antisocial type (Lahuerta 35). Such "necessary" seeing is part and parcel of a socially structured blindness, Lahuerta suggests, for the type, as we have seen, overwhelms the individual to the point of erasure, subjugating the "natural" or "live" model to a phenotype (35). As Lahuerta presents him, Rusiñol may believe that he is seeing the real thing, human nature itself, and that he is seeing it by way of real human beings, but he is dazzled by a delusion, a mightily general one, in which the details, quirks, and idiosyncrasies of the individual are no match for typological paradigms, for the discrete and discernible categories of science. And yet, if this is so, why draw so many figures when drawing one would seem to suffice? One answer, which comes so quickly as to raise yet more questions, might be that the twenty-eight figures are variations on a theme or a type; another answer, closer to Coll's, might be that the obsessive pull of the event behind the figures, its sheer magnitude, is such that Rusiñol compulsively tries to give as full an account of it as possible; still another might be that *necessity itself is necessarily prone to hazard*, to chance, to accident, and that the only way to convey necessity might be to draw out some of its hazardous details.

The problem with the preceding conjectures – and conjectures they certainly are – is that Rusiñol painted many more gardens than Anarchists, and the gardens, while typically viewed as variations on a theme, are *not* typically viewed as so ideologically burdened, as if some traumatic event lay behind *their* production, as if hazard, chance, and accident could be overlooked there too in favor of the necessary realization of necessity. Then again, the garden paintings partake of landscape while the heads of the Anarchists partake of portraiture, a genre closer to the limited purview of phrenology and, beyond that, more attached to the ethics – if not the science – of the face. It is the face, the face as traced by the hand, that constitutes the work here under consideration, a face taken to be criminal, a face multiplied, perhaps pluralized, as so many faces, numbered and ordered. Or rather, it is from the very beginning a number of faces, faces in the plural, that constitutes the work here under consideration. Phenotypes or not, Rusiñol's sketches, his studies, are traces of faces that would otherwise be lost entirely. To say, then, that Rusiñol sees only what is necessary and to see, after him, only what is said to be necessary is to deprive the sketches of their sketchiness, the studies of their ongoing studiousness (they are *not* presented as definitive), and, furthermore, to deprive the spectator of a sight which is not saturated by Lombrosian models, themselves prone to ambiguity, as Galera Gómez (110) notes.

Coll, in contrast to Lahuerta, signals the differences amid the similarities, and she does so by attending to the eyes on the faces of the heads designated as Anarchist. Focusing first on the four female figures, Coll professes to see in one ignorance, in another surprise, and in the two remaining ones conscious desire and determination. But even as Coll points out the differences in the configuration of the faces, she appeals repeatedly to fairly standard notions of personality, desire, and perceptible motivation – or the lack thereof. When Coll comes to the eyes and faces of the male figures she makes explicit what she had merely intimated in her overview of the female figures: a division between those who do not know (ignorance, surprise) and those who do know (calculation, determination). The former are scarcely better than idiots, bloody lambs involved in a wolfish slaughter; the latter, in contrast, are fanatics, calculating and determined, yet also ignorant – not of the ramifications of their actions but, it seems, of social reality itself (Coll 122). Accordingly, Coll also seems to see only what is necessary, but in a decidedly different light than Lahuerta: the *necessary wrong* of the Anarchists, the utter meaninglessness and immorality of their actions, and, just in case there were any doubt, the absolute objectivity of the artist himself (222). For Coll, Rusiñol is commandingly objective (talented, discerning, and exactingly capable of rendering life in all its variety) and, as such, necessarily captures and conveys the truth of those he draws; for Lahuerta, Rusiñol is slavishly objective (enthralled to Lombrosian ideas, blind to everything but the same) and, as such, necessarily misses the truth of those he cannot "truly" draw. And yet, "necessary" as Rusiñol's sketches may be, they are arguably no more so than other documents, including written ones, in which a significant imbalance in power at once links and separates the viewer from those viewed, the writer (and reader) from those written about, the scientist from those studied. The subalternist notion of reading in reverse, in which the subordinate of times past is only legible *through* dominant discourse, might thus be recast as a seeing in reverse, an interpretative act in which a presumably phrenological sight *and* a presumably moral insight might be seen otherwise, as partly accidental and blind.

After all, had Rusiñol's wife and brother been sitting in rows twelve or thirteen of the Liceu they might have died; had the other bomb exploded, the carnage might have been much worse and might have generated an even stronger response; had

Salvador been immediately apprehended, other Anarchists might have been spared; had proletariat artists had the same access to the prisoners as Rusiñol (whatever or indeed whenever that access actually was) the sense of necessity and the (im)moral charge of the figures drawn might have been brought more glaringly into question. Of all of these possibilities rendered impossible by history (which converts them into fruitless, speculative games), the one that arguably contains the most material force is the unexploded bomb. Interestingly, it is the unexploded bomb that captures Lahuerta's attention, firing his imagination even more than the face of one of the Anarchists. A shiny, prickly ball, the bomb is, for Lahuerta (42), more significantly a sacred image, a fetish, a little idol, a necromancer's stone, and a relic from outer space. It is all of these things, as Lahuerta knows, only insofar as it is seen as *other* than an artifact of violent social protest, as *other* than a material remainder – and apparently a not entirely direct reminder – of class conflict. If the unexploded bomb endures as an artifact housed in Barcelona's Museu d'Història de la Ciutat (though the authenticity of the bomb has been questioned), the exploded bombs endures largely as a memorable measure of the unexploded bomb's potential; both, together, endure as so much "proof" of the accidental nature of even the most determined acts.

Although the literature on the attack on the Liceu provides scant information about Santiago Salvador,[10] whom Coll (222) identifies as figure number 10 in the sketches (one of the most symmetrical and, as Barthes might put it, handsome of the figures), it does tend to specify, if only in passing, the *type* of bomb that Salvador used: "Orsini." The Orsini bomb, a spherical contrivance replete with a timing mechanism and dotted with protruding metallic pins, could fit uncomfortably in the hand and could be put together with relative facility. Named after an Italian nationalist of aristocratic extraction, Felice Orsini, who attempted to assassinate Napoleon III in 1858, the bomb became, as Lahuerta signals, a quasi-fetishistic object, feared and celebrated – depending on one's politics – for its destructively mobile force. According to Brenan, a text titled *Indicador anarquista* circulated throughout parts of Spain in the last decade of the nineteenth century and provided instructions on how to build explosive devices such as the Orsini that Salvador used to wreak his wrath on the class that he hated (Brenan 164). "Wrath" is indeed the word, for Salvador's assault on an unsuspecting bourgeoisie at play in the house of culture was apparently an act of revenge for the execution of Paulí Pallàs, who had killed a guard in a frustrated attack on General Martínez Campos on September 24, 1893. Less than a month and a half later, amid the chaos that followed the attack on the Liceu, Salvador was on the run from the law – for him, surely a self-interested tool of the dominant class. Arrested in Zaragoza and imprisoned in Barcelona, Salvador was executed, as mentioned, a year after the bombing, on November 21, 1894. Within the mimetic, circular logic of revenge and retribution, Salvador replays Pallàs's act all the way to the end, where the justice accorded by law asserts itself in the guise of capital punishment. The cycle of violence, flight, arrest, and execution, in which one person stands in for and gives a sort of extended communitarian afterlife to another, outstrips, however, the personal, whose importance I have here been stressing. For if Salvador remits to Pallàs, and if one of Rusiñol's figures can remit to one of Mir's, the Orsini bomb can remit, far beyond the play of individuals, to the biblical apple of good and evil.

As Lahuerta perceptively reminds us, none other than Antoni Gaudí, in a sculpted scene on the Chapel of the Rosary of the Sagrada Família, depicts a devil handing an Orsini bomb to a crouched male figure in working-class attire. A modern mechanical apple, as Lahuerta calls it (40), the Orsini bomb finds a place amid the Christian imagery that Gaudí, increasingly messianic in his creativity, produces. The bomb is not, however, the only thing from the attack on the Liceu to have a cultural afterlife of its own. Gutiérrez Solana, in the aforementioned *La España negra*, describes a showcase in a wax museum in Santander in which the victims of the exploded bomb are offered up to the viewing public:

> In one showcase you see the explosion of a bomb in the Liceo Theater, in Barcelona, during the performance of the opera *William Tell*. The people, dressed in formal attire, trample one another as they flee; a woman in a low-cut dress, a pearl necklace around her neck, and a feather fan in her hand, with a disjointed face and her eyes closed as if she were sleeping, has her head resting on the shoulder of a gentleman whose head hangs down from the back of his seat and whose shirt is covered with blood; her legs have been torn away and the hem and petticoat drip blood. (Gutiérrez Solana 65)

The life size figures of wax seem to be placidly slumbering, but they are in fact terribly mutilated. More intriguingly, their lifelikeness is so great that they do not merely appear to be asleep; *they appear to be dead* (63). That the appearance of death should bolster the appearance of life surely strengthens the "impression of mystery" (63) that, according to Gutiérrez Solana, the unnamed wax artist attempts to convey, but it also reinforces a sense of the grotesque that is crucial to the legend of *la España negra*. For Gutiérrez Solana luridly verbalizes a still show, lurid itself, that has moved beyond the original site of destruction. Offered up as entertainment along with other incidents of murder and mayhem, the scene of the ravaged bodies of elegant opera goers becomes yet another installment in an ongoing saga of death and destruction that does not stay in one place. Whatever historical value the unexploded Orsini bomb may have, the destructive effects of the exploded bomb had already become the stuff of a nationally marked culture industry by 1920, the date of Gutiérrez Solana's text.

It is as if the horrendous dismemberment that Joan Maragall (1984) expressed in "Paternal," a poem that he wrote upon returning home from the Liceu on the very night of the attack, were given sensationally visible form in the wax museum that Gutiérrez Solana visits. Maragall's (179) "colltorçades testes" (twisted heads) that "regalen sang" (drip blood) are here supplemented, so to speak, with "bloody imprints of open hands and spattered brains" (Gutiérrez Solana 66). And the blood, spattered everywhere, finds nearly perfect passage from the real to the represented in the stickiness of paste and the suppleness of wax: the figures, speckled with rivulets of glue and exposed to the heat of the museum, go soft, drip, melt: "the wax has dripped into the ears and they seem as if they were full of honey" (Gutiérrez Solana 66). Blood is sweeter than honey, as Salvador Dalí was fond of saying, but here the wax that continues to melt after it has been formed in the image of the dead offers an oozing counterpart to the metallic solidity of the bomb, that "very strange growth" that Lahuerta (41) locates in the psychic body of the bourgeoisie. An oozing bodily figure, so lifelike as to seem at first glance to be sleeping in death, brings to mind a putrescent cadaver, a body that becomes a messy mass of liquefaction. What both Gutiérrez Solana and, to a lesser degree, Maragall (1984) present is consistent with what Philippe Ariès (568) calls the "dirty death," a modern passing in which the realities of corporeal destruction, in tense concert with the bourgeois penchant for discretion and cleanliness, are exposed to the glaring light of day. Ariès does not deny that earlier ages, most famously the Baroque, are rife with images of suppurating sores, rotting flesh, and mangled corpses, but what he signals is the expansion of death in an age so obsessed with decadence and degeneration that it resorted to phrenology and other "sciences" in order to uphold some semblance of order, some stable social division.

The twenty-eight faces – twenty-seven of which are designated by a number,[11] as in the phrenological studies that Gutiérrez Solana (89) describes elsewhere – convey a sense of fractured community, as if they at once pertained to companions in political protest and revolutionary change *and* to accomplices in a crime in which they did not necessarily have a hand. Impressed by phrenological protocols as they may be, the sketches or studies are not forever fixed by that impression: the necessary does not eradicate the accidental; or in Barthesian terms, the studiousness of the *studium* does not vanquish the poignancy of the *punctum*: the sense that the detained and depicted are destined to die, and to die, quite possibly, at the hands of the state. By invoking the *punctum* I am not saying that some subjective accident "rescues" Rusiñol's images of the Anarchists or that it endows them with the same poignancy that Barthes finds in the photograph of Payne. After all, the poignancy that Barthes designates by way of a *punctum*, a pricking of the viewer, appears to be largely an accidental effect of mechanical reproduction, a subjective rift in an ostensibly objective medium, but also a "horrible" recognition that the image bears "an anterior future of which death is the stake" (Barthes 96). A drawing simply cannot pretend to the same degree of objectivity and hence to the same accidental puncture of the machine's (by now much contested) capacity to capture reality as it really is. And whatever beauty it holds and conveys cannot be so matter-of-factly ascribed to the being represented. Beauty and poignancy are not, however, what most insists in Rusiñol's sketches, laden as they are with the terror, violence, and repressive justice that attends the event from which they issue and to which they refer. They lack not only color (other than that conferred by the passing of time, the browning of the paper), but also iconographic accoutrements that would stabilize their meaning. Faces without bodies or background, they look out – they seem to look out – from their serialized isolation at a spectator that they can never see and that can never see them.

And yet, all representations of the face are similarly structured, and their structure is one of radical non-reciprocity, a face-to-face that can never truly take place – but that does take place, in spite of it all, again and again. The *illusion* of an ocular exchange or inter-viewing is crucial to a compassionate attitude in and towards art, to a sense of shared suffering (*com-*, together + *pati*, to suffer). In Laplana's (176) account, Rusiñol *pities* the Anarchists: "those poor people – thought some of Rusiñol's friends, and Rusiñol himself – do nothing but blindly follow their own destinies." He pities them, furthermore, because they, presumably unlike him, *cannot see* themselves for what they are: human beasts who *blindly* follow their destiny. The formulation is involutely naturalist because the subjects of Rusiñol's sight cannot see that they cannot see, remain blind to their blindness. But it is also uncannily romantic because the clinical detachment that, say, Zola advances and that makes of the artist a forensic surgeon is undercut by the compassion, however pitifully condescending, that the artist reportedly feels. Feeling for the unfeeling (so unfeeling that they, or someone *like* them, can throw a bomb into an "innocent" crowd), seeing the blind (so blind that they do not know that they are blind), Rusiñol executes his drawings which also are, or would be, the Anarchists' drawings. But blind to their blindness, the Anarchists look out, blankly it would appear, and in so doing convey a suffering and rage that is beyond their comprehension and, for that very reason, all the more painful to the subject who supposedly can see, to Rusiñol and people like him: ambivalent bourgeois beings, disturbed by the stultifying power of their class yet unable or unwilling to turn against it entirely, to see it, in short, with the eyes of the Anarchists.

The preceding view is inevitably partial, for the compassionate attitude is by no means prominent in the bourgeoisie's perception of the Anarchists – as Joan Maragall's fruitless appeal to spare the lives of those sentenced to death in relation to the cataclysmic events of July, 1909 known as the *Setmana Tràgica* makes abundantly clear. The refusal to die "for Spain" in yet another colonial war, this time in Morocco, issued in death too: in skirmishes with the authorities, in subsequent capital trials, and in the iron-fisted repression of anti-bourgeois movements, most notably Anarchism. Barcelona did not become the "ciutat del perdó" or "city of forgiveness" in 1909, nor had it become so in 1893, despite the efforts of "aristocratic ladies," as Brenan (164, n. 1) rather paternalistically styles it, to spare a falsely repentant Salvador, who reportedly shouted "*Viva el anarquismo!*" at the moment of his death. Compassion, forgiveness, and pity, wrapped up in the garb of Christian piety, were no match for a system of justice still enthralled, under capitalism, to retribution and revenge, and given to Christian platitudes of its own. At the other extreme of an exchange of sights there is, then, that sight which is so searing and searching as to be of the order of inquisition. Its hallmarks are fear and repulsion instead of pity and compassion, disgust and defiance instead of sorrow and suffering. The Aristotelian resonances notwithstanding, the division that I am here articulating might be recast, via Derrida, in terms of biocularity (or even polyocularity) and monocularity. The compassionate attitude, with all the power plays and imbalances that it entails, relies, as indicated, on a biocular exchange of sights, an inter-viewing, that is also a complex crossing. In the words of Derrida (1–2), the "two [points of view] will cross paths, but without ever confirming each other, without the least bit of certainty, in a conjecture that is at once singular and general, the hypothesis of sight." The repulsive attitude, in contrast, is monocular, not because it does not involve an exchange with another person, but because it sets the other – and the sight of the other, the other's sight – at naught, spurns the crossing as anything but a crossing out. Far from being chiastic, it is straightforward; far from living with non-reciprocity, it takes it, at its most extreme, as a license to kill. Gutiérrez Solana, referring to the glass-eyed mannequins in the wax museum, sums up the monocular view: "they look at us with their cruel, fixed, and impassive eyes" (63). These eyes are those of the criminals who supposedly see only death and who seek, moreover, to see it reflected in the panicked eyes of their victims. But the cruel and impassive eyes of the policeman, the civil guard, the judge, or the executioner, indeed the cruel and impassive eyes of the "good citizens" of Barcelona, furious at the fury launched at them by a man named Salvador and a bomb named Orsini, are also at work and must be considered, amid all the skepticism of speculation, too.[12]

What exactly Rusiñol saw in the Anarchists that he drew, whether he felt pity or fear, compassion or repulsion, or a confusing mixture of both, will always be a subject of speculation and hence will always be fraught with skepticism. What is less subject to skepticism is that the drawings, although designated as *studies of heads*, are more properly sketches of faces. They do not purport to give a full account of the skull; they do not fan out into a perspectivism that aims at three-dimensionality; they are not crisscrossed or overlain with the circles, lines, and spheres that mark manuals of anatomy. Accordingly, the asymmetries that Lahuerta adduces, the tiny wide-spaced eyes, curved foreheads, and protruding jaws that he takes to be proof of the phrenological status of the images, are *also*, in some measure, of the viewer's making. For instance, while the eyes of many of the figures indeed appear cocked and bulging (especially figures 2, 4, 11, 12, 20, 25, 27), the eyes of some of the figures (1, 6, 13, 18, 21) are not – at least as I see them. What thus distinguishes Rusiñol's sketches – and, mind you, I am not making a case for greatness – is that they *waver* between the phrenological study, forerunner of the police sketch, and the portrait, which was not, according to a number of critics, Rusiñol's forte, but which he nonetheless cultivated with success (Doñate and Mendoza, 20). What also distinguishes them is that the faces are aligned in a manner that suggests both order – in general, the four folios consist of two rows of between three and five figures each – and a *stilting* of order: in one of the folios two figures appear to be "squeezed" into the upper right corner, one (number 17) so much that the top of his head is slightly cropped off, as if subjected to a craniotomy. But no brain is here drawn into the light; rather, it remains resolutely out of sight, ob-scene. Bodies and busts are absent as well, though collars, scarves, and the beginnings of shoulders, expressed by faint lines that seem to curve downward into emptiness, suggest a more substantive materiality. The faces are presented, in general, frontally, though a few are in three-quarters profile or slightly cocked to one side. The faces are overwhelmingly male, bearded in a manner that indicates age as well: longer, more sparsely lined for the elderly and shorter, more darkly lined for the younger adults. Taken together, they suggest a (de)generational line that stretches back into the past and forward into the future.

Numerically dominant as the men are, there are also four women, one on each of the four folios and each one occupying a position in the center of the upper row of figures, as if to reinforce their importance (and the semblance of orderly repetition from one folio to another). Although the women also appear to be of varying age, the cheeks of all four are so densely shaded as to seem slightly bearded too. As Lahuerta (35) notes, Lombroso held that excessive body hair distinguished the degenerate from the non-degenerate woman. The non-degenerate woman is likely to be part of the well-heeled public targeted in the bombing of the Liceu, members of the class that is ever so figuratively shadowed in the shaded faces and shady looks of the Anarchists. To be sure, in Rusiñol's Anarchists, the members of the bourgeoisie can be "seen" only in reverse, against the grain of the sketches, as the "good, law-abiding types" against which the criminal acquires perceptible meaning. The sketches of the Anarchists are thus *also* sketches of the bourgeoisie, their *negative image*, an incomplete, would-be catalogue of their fears – spectacularly manifested in the contorted figures of the wax museum. Within the context of class conflict, the "bearded woman" is especially significant, for, as Lahuerta remarks, she is "doubly threatening" as a woman and a criminal who "looks at us" supposedly upright spectators with a "challenge" (35). The challenge goes to the heart of an entrenched gender division according to which men kill and women succor and implies that class here trumps gender, that women cannot be lumped into a group with children as so many "innocents." The challenge is indeed great.

So many years since the death of all those alive in 1893, the challenge is also one of interpretation, of an historically oriented act of seeing whose historicity is such that the interpreter cannot abstract him or herself entirely from the present and from the accidental interference of other times and places. If Eliseu Oriol Pages, the commissioner of a symposium on Gaudí in Washington in 2002, can relate the Orsini bomb of Gaudí's Chapel to the attacks on the United States in September 11, 2001, it bears asking who is the "we" that is ostensibly the object of the Anarchist woman's challengingly double vision, who is the "we" that sees, and reads, and cares about such sights in the present. For the slanted eyes and views askance that Lahuerta, Coll, I, and others see, *to different effect*, in Rusiñol's sketches do not perforce lead us inward, to the mental and moral functions of the brains, or personalities, of those depicted; they also lead us outward, towards Rusiñol as artist-viewer and, perhaps no less importantly, towards ourselves as viewers, here and now, each with his or her own complex, irretrievable history. Whether "we" see the figures with a sense of compassion or with a sense of trepidation, with sympathy for a frustrated revolution (so frustrated that it resorts to terrorism) or anxiety at the persistence, renewal, and displacement of revolution and of terrorism, whether "we" view them monocularly (they look at "us," "we" at them, but only as a threat) or biocularly (their vision and "ours" crisscrosses), the hand of the artist is present in its very absence, in the traces of the faces. How to "read" the invisible hand of the artist becomes, then, yet another problem for speculation.

"A draftsman cannot but be attentive to the finger and the eye," Derrida (6) writes, "especially to anything that touches upon the eye, to anything that lays a finger on it in order to let it finally see or let it be seen." For Derrida, in drawing, the eye and the hand are endowed, or perhaps burdened, with especially enigmatic significance. They produce, together, a tracing into view that is in the same stroke a tracing out of view, a perspective overcast with a loss of perspective, a seeing touched with blindness. In *Memoirs of the Blind*, the text from which I have been quoting, Derrida sets his sights on pictures of the blind, *literally* the blind, repeatedly depicted with outstretched, groping hands. In Rusiñol's drawings, the blindness is figurative, and the artist's hand is likewise figurative, out of sight on the surface of the drawings and evoked, at best, in the half-open, half-closed hand of one of the figures (number 4) but adumbrated, more subtly, in every charcoal trace. Amid so many much skepticism and speculation there is no question that Santiago Rusiñol has had a hand, a major one, in what and how we see the nameless, numbered Anarchists. Rusiñol's hand, the trace of his hand and of the charcoal that it once held, is at times looser and lighter, at times heavier, and the eyes that *seem* to look out at us are similarly lighter and heavier.

But what is the look or *mirada*, the sight or *vista*, here at stake? If Derrida draws attention to the hand and the eye and distinguishes between the monocular and the biocular, Norman Bryson, influenced by French musings on the *regard* and the *coup d'oeil*, distinguishes between the gaze and the glance (in Catalan, the *esguard* and the *cop d'ull*) in ways that are germane to the status of the seeing subject in Rusiñol's drawing. For Bryson, the gaze and the glance are related by way of a slightly different division than the one that Derrida proffers, a division that "separates the activity of the *gaze*, prolonged, contemplative, yet regarding the field of vision with a certain aloofness and disengagement, across a tranquil interval, from that of the *glance*, a furtive or sideways look whose attention is always elsewhere, which shifts to conceal its own existence, and which is capable of carrying unofficial, *sub rosa* messages of hostility, collusion, rebellion, and lust" (Bryson 94, emphasis original). The gaze and the glance, so defined, designate not so much different visual attitudes (more or less compassionate, repulsive, or challenging) as different seeing subjects. Lest force of habit lead to equivocation, I want to make it clear that the seeing subject is not merely the artist and/or the viewer of the work of art; it is also the subject that is ostensibly objectified in and as the work of art: that is to say, the Anarchists whose eyes – and, beyond that, whose attitudes of seeing and looking, of gazing and glancing – issue *at once* from the artist's eyes and hand as well as from the Anarchists themselves, from some perceived, interpreted trace of them.

The division between the gaze and the glance that Bryson advances brings to mind the division between the bourgeois artist and spectator (however critical of the bourgeoisie) and the Anarchists themselves. After all, the artist, especially if in any way under the influence of phrenology, contemplates his subjects – here arrested – with a certain aloofness and disengagement, *at least in theory*; and the subjects at which the artist gazes "look back," if they look back, by looking askance, awry, or away, by glancing in a shifting, shifty, manner that may conceal anything and everything but "unofficial, *sub rosa* messages of hostility, collusion, rebellion, and lust," the very messages that the artist, if so inclined, *expects* to see, *draws* into the field of vision. But Rusiñol's expectations remain far from clear, his views of Anarchism – repeatedly if equivocally linked to Catalan *modernisme*, as Castellanos (9) has noted – and of subversive politics in general, far from simple and straightforward, even though, as Josep Pla (224) states, Rusiñol was a satirist of the bourgeoisie, but never a subversive. The very lack of clarity, however, might open up some unexpected possibilities, some accident, beyond the quasi-legislative, quasi-policing power of the phrenological gaze. One of these possibilities or accidents might just be materialized in the waver of the hand, its now heavier, now lighter, touch on the paper and on the eye. For however sideways, downcast, or furtive the Anarchists's glances, or however defiant their gazes, they are the effects of a hand that draws and that, in drawing, cannot, as Bryson contends, quite cover its tracks with the same surety that the hand that paints does. The suppression of historical human time, the time of process, accident, and contingency that Bryson ascribes, generally and a bit tendentiously, to oil painting does not hold for the drawing, the sketch, or the study (a study that is more of the order of the essay than the inquiry) where the wavering trace of the hand impresses still. What it impresses, how it impresses, and what its impression means remain, however, other matters, which I do not pretend to elucidate, now, except by displacement to another impressive medium: the photograph, where the trace of the hand is even less recoverable than in painting. Having gazed, as it were, at Rusiñol's sketches, I will cast now an all too sketchy glance at one of Centelles's photographs.

Defacing Violence: War, Emotion and the Banality of Death

Unlike Rusiñol, Agustí Centelles was not ambivalent about the bourgeoisie. A man of working-class origins and working-class loyalties, Centelles was neither the darling of a disaffected, embattled Bohemia nor an uneasy outsider to a substantively democratic or revolutionary project. He did not face the opposition of a family of industrialists for whom art was a useless pastime or a sign of decadence, nor did he fret about who would purchase the marble for the artwork that he planned to create, as Rusiñol puts it at the end of his most famous work, *L'auca del senyor Esteve*. Centelles was less concerned about art than life – if that tired and not quite true binary still has any significance. He did not present himself, at any rate, as a man beyond politics or as a cosmopolitan citizen whose true country was art and whose guiding lights were Dante and da Vinci. He did, however, struggle to find a way to make a living out of photography, to convert his passion for pictures into a job, and then later to document a struggle which he unabashedly understood as one for social justice. For a while he worked in established studios, but when he acquired his Leica, he achieved an autonomy, mobility, and spontaneity that was rare for a photographer in the Spain of his time. His subjects included sporting events (runners and cyclists), festivals (the *Festa Major de Gràcia*, *Caramelles* in the Plaça de Sant Jaume), and portraits of famous Catalans (Pau Casals, Pompeu Fabra, Francesc Macià), but it is his photography of political demonstrations, rallies, street disturbances, and outright war for which he is best known.

Some of Centelles's photographs of the devastation wrought by war in Barcelona, Lleida, Belchite, Teruel, and elsewhere were reproduced in *Visions de Guerra i Reraguarda* and other governmentally sponsored propaganda venues, although many were printed without attribution. Whether Centelles's name was attached to them or not, his photographs circulated and contributed to popular perceptions of death, resistance, and defeat during the war. But other photographs that he took did not circulate until much later: in the vertiginous final days of the Republic, Centelles stashed many of his materials in a suitcase, secreted them out of Spain, managed to hold on to them while in a concentration camp in Bram, France (where he took more photographs), and finally stored them away in a farm in Carcassonne. There they remained until after the death of Franco, when

Centelles returned to retrieve them and, finally, to make them public. The belated publication of the photographs generated considerable interest in Centelles, who, late in his life, experienced a sort of cultural rebirth: after having been forced to abandon journalistic photography under Franco, Centelles received a number of awards, among them, in 1984, the *Premio Nacional de Artes Plásticas*. He died, in 1985, feted by a new democratic establishment, but his pictures continue to provide a riveting sense of the Republic's last years. Centelles's trajectory, for obvious historical reasons, is markedly different from Rusiñol's, whose works did not circulate without attribution and as part of a larger effort at securing support for the Spanish Republic. However this statement may ring in ethical and political terms, it is first and foremost a "fact" of history.

The magnitude of the Spanish Civil War – the first to be extensively covered by a new breed of reporters, namely, photojournalists, willing, even eager, to move with the action – casts its shadow over Centelles's work with a decisiveness that makes aesthetic reflection, along with its trappings of technique and virtuosity, a pale, somewhat spoiled cousin of ethico-political seriousness. As Chema Conesa writes, "the conscious photographer displaces the photographer who shields himself behind the image's technical excellence, attempting an informative, angelic asepsia" (3). And yet, the photographs that were then largely perceived as slices of the reality of a war whose outcome had yet to be decided and in which photographs might actually make a difference, have acquired over time, and from the distance of a democratic return, a second order aesthetic value: that of works whose *horrific* emotional freshness is in the preterit. Centelles's photograph of a woman wailing beside the body of a man killed in the bombing of Lleida (November 2, 1937); of members of the Assault Guard, loyal to the Republic, using the carcasses of horses as a barricade from behind which they continue to fight (July 19, 1936);[13] and of a man and woman, baby in arms, walking amid a throng of fellow anti-Fascist militia fighters (July 28, 1936), all stand out for their emotional charge. Conesa, like Sougez (444), underscores the emotionality of Centelles's images and takes it as evidence of political engagement, of the surpassing of documentary distance into the passion of communal belonging. For Conesa, Centelles's status as a Spaniard (not a Valencian or a Catalan, but a Spaniard) appears to exempt him from the suspicion of detachment and careerist self-interest that attended foreign photojournalists, especially those who rambled from war to war. Discounting the dubious assumptions that Conesa makes about foreigners and Spaniards, it is the assumption about emotion – touched on briefly in my view of Rusiñol – with which I would like to tarry.

Centelles's *Morts a la plaça [de] Catalunya*, taken on July 19, 1936, at the very outbreak of the Civil War, is a case in point: a photograph, precisely dated (unlike Rusiñol's drawings), in which death is presented flatly and without a face.[14] It depicts two dead men and two dead or injured horses stretched out in the emptiness of the Plaça de Catalunya, a grand square – not far from the Liceu – that connects the old city and the rationalized, grid-patterned nineteenth-century expansion of the new city. There exists another shot of the same scene from the opposite angle, likewise reproduced in the previously cited *Visions de guerra i de reraguarda*, which gives a closer view of the two bodies, one of whose head is covered with a kerchief or towel. In both photographs, and certainly the one that I reproduce here, the lifeless human bodies occupy the center of the foreground, their centrality slightly skewed, in the photograph on which I am focusing, by the presence of a gleaming, dark automobile that fills the far left side. The bodies are stretched out, one's head to the other's feet, one's feet to the other's head. Neither face is visible, but one is turned to the side, while the other is covered with a white cloth, which serves as a kind of preliminary, miniature shroud: clearly, someone has initiated the rites of respect for the dead, the veiling of a lifeless face and eyes. What appears to be either a belt or a riding crop lies on the ground nearby, spectrally retracing a hand that once held it and that now rests on the dusty hardness of the square. The hands of the figure closest to the automobile seem to be clutched in the throes of the last of life. There is little still vital activity visible except in the far background, where a few men loiter and, a little in front of them, a flock of pigeons patters about. The presence of these living creatures, barely distinguishable except as general forms, accentuates, by contrast, the desolation of the scene. It is a curiously *calm* desolation, for the photograph is neither blurred nor out of kilter (though five or six imperfections dot, or puncture, its surface) and clearly appears to have been taken in the wake of, or in a lull in, the fighting. No emotion is visible on the invisible faces, no compassionate or challenging exchange of looks is possible: the death of war has taken place in the great square of Catalonia – and life goes on.

The banality of such a statement – "life goes on" – is inescapable. Barthes claims that "[w]ith the Photograph, we enter into *flat Death*," by which he means not just that photography "freezes" or "arrests" death as it is happening but also that the "horror of Death" is "precisely its platitude" (92). Barthes writes of flatness in reference to that most emotional of events, "the death of one whom I love most" (93), which is for him the death of his mother, and in so doing he renders flatter the death of the many whom he does not know, whom we do not know: the nameless, faceless masses of the dead that the two dead bodies in *Morts a la plaça [de] Catalunya* invoke. It is, after all, the outbreak of the conflict, and we know now of the thousands, if not millions, of dead to follow, who followed. The photograph thus functions, *now*, as a *retrospective prelude* to a devastating war, typically understood as a prelude to another more devastating war, World War II. Albert Balcells (37) writes of bloody skirmishes in the Plaça de Catalunya, but he does not indicate whether the two dead men, both dressed in civilian clothing, were supporters of Franco's rebellion "shot" by people still loyal to the Republic – many of them Anarchists – or Republican militia fighters. Joan Fontcuberta (in a private communication) reports that the dead may be functionaries of a building near the square who defended the Republic. *Visions de guerra i de reraguarda* presents the dead more confidently as two anti-Fascist combatants, two "brave freedom fighters of the people." There is, however, nothing easily apparent about the political affiliation, let alone identity, of the victims. The outcome and aftermath of the war are also not apparent, nor is even the outbreak of the war, nor for that matter is war itself. Without extrapictorial information (caption, date, Centelles's name, details about the fighting), the dead might be taken for anything from gangsters to the victims of a random shooting or an act of terrorism. Then again, without extrapictorial information, the figures that Rusiñol draws might be taken as other than Anarchists detained and possibly condemned to death. What *is* apparent in Centelles's photograph, and what separates it most powerfully from Rusiñol's drawings, is the very appearance of death, an *appearance* that, as the word implies, is not perforce true or real and may suggest mere show, pretense, or propaganda. A few well-placed or misplaced words – or bodies – could alter the appearance of anything, death included. Skepticism suffuses spectatorship, speculation, and sight itself, but still not to the point that it eradicates historical reality, the truth, however manipulable and reproducible, of death. Seeing Centelles's photographs nowadays, when Spain is a constitutional monarchy, the death therein depicted acquires another dimension. Turning Barthes around, we might say that Centelles "captures" the struggle and figurative agony and death of the Republic: *that* is dead, and *that* is going to die – and remains "dead" despite the efforts, most notably in Catalonia, of a Republican left still today.

Another death haunts Rusiñol's drawings as well, a death beyond that of the individual Anarchists and the artist. This other "death" would appear to be that of Anarchism itself as a viable world-historical formation and, beyond that, of an array of alternative social formations, economic systems, and configurations of humanity, communism – Anarchism's uneasy adversary – chief among them. The much touted "death" of these political formations, replaced by the "rebirth" of religious formations, constitutes one of the greatest differences between both Rusiñol's *and* Centelles's time and "ours." From Rusiñol to Centelles, an upper-class esthete and a working-class reporter, a painter-poet and a photojournalist; from an Anarchist attack to a full-fledged civil war in which Anarchism figured prominently; and, finally, from a climate of art for art's sake to one of media in the service of society,[15] much, of course, differed as well. But one of the things that does not differ, or not so dramatically, from Rusiñol's time to Centelles's to "ours" is the paradoxical fragility of the nation, paradoxical because so resistant, so durable, so prompt (still) to grand gestures of patriotic duty and death. The Anarchists that Rusiñol draws, no less than the Nationalists and Republicans that Centelles photographs, all constitute fractured testimonies to the violence that (still) attends national sites and sights. The attacks in Madrid of March 11, 2004, immediately sensationalized by the media and manipulated by certain politicians and public intellectuals as the worst terrorist violence in the history of Spain – worse than the 1987 Hipercor bombing (also in Barcelona), worse than the bombing of the Liceu – have produced their own images, from trains torn apart like tin cans to bloody, shocked survivors on cell phones to hunks of human flesh scattered about the rails. The images include photographs and hand-drawn sketches, but are also videotaped, digitalized, and electronically disseminated in a matter of seconds across the world. What sense of artistry and of truth; what emotional charge and ethico-political meaning; what interplay of chance and necessity or of body and machine; what sight of Spain is herein illuminated and obliterated will be something on which those not yet born will, perhaps, reflect as well. Then again, that may be as flat as saying that life goes on.

Dedication

This chapter is for Jordana Mendelson and Juan José Lahuerta.

Notes

1. I am deliberately pushing at the assumption that reality is tied to evidential objectivity and illusion to perceptual subjectivity. However valid such an assumption may be, it is not ironclad: evidential objectivity is shot through with illusion and perceptual subjectivity with reality.
2. I thank Elisenda Casanova of the Consorci del Patrimoni de Sitges for allowing me to reproduce Rusiñol's drawings and for helping me ferret out more information; Maria Fernanda Meza of the Artists Rights Society for permission to reproduce the photograph by Centelles and Joan Fontcuberta for locating it; Juan José Lahuerta, Jordi Castellanos, Luis Fernández Cifuentes, Josep Sobrer, and, most especially, Jordana Mendelson for their generous and illuminating help and advice; and Joan Matabosch for granting me access to his wonderful collection of documents related to the Liceu.
3. Barthes's view of the photograph seems to be modulated by libidinal projection: "the photograph is handsome, as is the boy" (1981: 96). The French original is more delicious: "La photo est belle, le garçon aussi" (1980: 148). *Le garçon est beau, bien sûr,* and yet *belle* is the word that is used, the point of comparison, the proper if ever so slippery grammatical ground for *aussi*, "also."
4. All translations, unless otherwise indicated, are mine.
5. In the catalogue of the *Junta de Museo* of 1942, the work's title is "Retratos de anarquistas presos con motivo de las bombas del teatro del Liceo." The

Consorci del Patrimoni de Sitges uses the shorter title, "Caps dels anarquistes" or "Caps d'anarquistes," and provides additional information: Data: c. 1894; Tècnica: Carbonet i tinta (a la signatura) sobre paper al·lissat (vitel·la); Mides: 19.8 × 27 cm; 19.9 × 26.8 cm; 19.9 × 26.9 cm; 19.9 × 26.9 cm; Signatura: "S. Rusiñol" (angle inferior dret, d'un dels quatre folis); Número d'Inventari: MCFS 30.777–30.780.

6. An article titled "L'atentat del Liceo," which appeared a few days after the attack in *La Esquella de la Torratxa*, gives the death toll as twenty-eight.
7. Positivism, with its penchant for calculations and calibrations, is saddled with all sorts of difficulties. If the precise number of victims of the attack on the Liceu remains unclear, or at least a matter of some discrepancy, the precise number of victims of the Spanish Civil War is an even more dubious and politically charged matter. As Josep Fontana notes in his prologue to *Visions de guerra i de reraguarda* (1977), the journal in which Centelles published a number of his photographs, the Francoist efforts to fix the exact number of the dead at 296,793 (considerably fewer than the "millions of dead" which was bandied about) are absurd: "Ridícola [sic] pretensió de comptar els difunts amb precisió en un país que mai no ha estat capaç de comptar els vius, ja que és sabut que el cens del 1940 té un marge d'error molt superior a aquesta xifra 'exacta' dels morta de la guerra civil" (Fontana 5). Positivist criticism, which is far from depleted in Spain, is non-theoretical or, worse yet, anti-theoretical at its peril. My own attempt, as I hope will be clear, is to bring a theoretical gaze to bear on positivism and its protocols – hence my interest in the number, names, and faces of the dead, for the not so simple reason that numbers, names, and faces are, it seems, never sufficient in and of themselves. *Visions de guerra* was, by the way, a propagandistic journal published during the Spanish Civil War. In 1977, shortly after the death of Franco, the various issues of the journal were compiled and reprinted; it is from this reprinted collection that I here quote.
8. According to Laplana (176), Rusiñol "felt drawn [*atret*] to witness the hearing of those implicated in the attack, and took … notes on the faces of the twenty-eight Anarchists." Laplana places Rusiñol at a hearing related to Anarchist activities in Barcelona, but he also places him in Paris, a few days after if not indeed *before* the attack (Laplana 176), a possibility that Vinyet Panyella seems to support (*Santiago Rusiñol*, 203). In a note, Laplana specifies that the hearing did not take place until July 11, 1894 and that Rusiñol could have attended a war tribunal on a previous attack – for there were quite a few. Roca Pou (4), in a fascinating unpublished memoir that I was able to read thanks to Joan Matabosch, gives July 11 as the date of the death sentence.
9. Juan Buscón, in an article that appeared in *Barcelona Cómica* just a week after the attack, calls for vengeance and ridicules attempts on the part of

members of the liberal party to resist enacting "exceptional measures" ("medidas excecpionales") against the Anarchists (Buscón 2).

10. Roca Pou (see note 8) provides some interesting details about Salvador's imprisonment and his relationship with his wife and young daughter.
11. The *Gran Enciclopedia Catalana*, in an entry on Santiago Salvador, refers to twenty-seven other people implicated in the attack and gives July 11, 1894 as the date of sentencing and November 21, 1894 as the date of execution of Salvador and six of the twenty-seven others.
12. "Before doubt ever becomes a system, *skepsis* has to do with the eyes," writes Derrida. "The word refers to a visual perception, to the observation, vigilance, and attention of the gaze [*regard*] during an examination" (1).
13. Fontana (1977) thanks J. Milicua for pointing out to him that the photograph in question is the result of a cropping, that is to say, an editorial decision – and hence not an untouched testimony to reality. Fontana then refers to "una versió 'completa' on es veu un home dret darrera dels guàrdies parapetats, amb una pistola a la mà. La mateixa gosadia, tal vegada irresponsable, d'aquest home fa minvar la tensió del conjunt" (Fontana 1977: 2, n. 1).
14. According to Joan Fontcuberta (in a private communication), the title of the photograph is also *Milicians a la plaça Catalunya, Barcelona, 19 de juliol de 1936*.
15. If art in the service of society at times entails a questioning, even a repudiation, of art, it is obviously not of the same order as the anti-art of such avant-gardists as Salvador Dalí, Sebastià Gasch, and Lluís Montanyà in their *Manifest groc* or of Joan Miró in his collages in defiance of painting.

Works Cited

Álvarez Junco, José. *La ideología política del anarquismo español (1868–1910)*. Madrid: Siglo XXI, 1976.

Anderson, Benedict. *Imagined Communities: Reflections on the Origin and Spread of Nationmaking*, 2nd edn. London: Verso, 1991.

Ariès, Philippe. *The Hour of our Death*. Trans. Helen Weaver. New York: Oxford University Press, 1981.

Balcells, Albert. "Agustí Centelles i el seu temps: Els orígens d'un reporter gràfic." In *Agustí Centelles (1909–1985): Fotoperiodista*. Barcelona: Fundació Caixa de Catalunya, 1988. 29–42.

Barthes, Roland. *Camera Lucida: Reflections on Photography*. Trans. Richard Howard. New York: Farrar, Straus and Giroux, 1981. *La Chambre claire*. Paris: Seuil, 1980.

Bookchin, Murray. *The Spanish Anarchists: The Heroic Years 1868–1936*. New York: Free Life, 1977.

Brenan, Gerald. *The Spanish Labyrinth: An Account of the Social and Political Background of the Spanish Civil War*. Cambridge: Cambridge University Press, 1974.

Bryson, Norman. *Vision and Painting: The Logic of the Gaze*. New Haven, CT: Yale University Press, 1983.

Buscón, Juan. "De lunes a lunes." *Barcelona Cómica* 6 (46) November 14, 1893: 2–3.

Castellanos, Jordi. "Aspectes de les relacions entre intel·lectuals i anarquistes a Catalunya al segle XIX. (A propòsit de Pere Coromines)." *Els Marges* 6 (1976): 7–28.

Coll, Isabel. *Santiago Rusiñol*. Sabadell: Ausa, 1992.

Conesa, Chema. *Agustí Centelles: La lucidez de la mejor fotografía de guerra*. Madrid: La Fábrica-Tf. Editores, 1999.

Derrida, Jacques. *Memoirs of the Blind: The Self-Portrait and Other Ruins*. Trans. Pascale-Anne Brault and Michael Naas. Chicago: University of Chicago Press, 1993.

Doñate, Mercè and Cristina Mendoza. "Rusiñol, pintor." In *Santiago Rusiñol: 1861–1931*. Barcelona: Museu d'Art Modern, MNAC/Madrid: Fundación Cultural Mapfre Vida, 1997. 17–31.

Fontana, Josep, ed. *Visions de guerra i de reraguarda*. Barcelona/Palma de Mallorca: José J. de Olañeta Editor, 1977.

Fontcuberta, Joan. "Agustí Centelles com a model." In *Agustí Centelles (1909–1985): Fotoperiodista*. Barcelona: Fundació Caixa de Catalunya, 1988. 7–14.

Galera Gómez, Andrés. "La antropología criminal frente al anarquismo español." In *El anarquismo español y sus tradiciones culturales*. Eds. Bert Hofmann, Pere Joan i Tous and Manfred Tietz. Frankfurt am Main: Vervuert Verlag; Madrid: Iberoamericana, 1995. 109–20.

Goodwin, Sarah Webster and Elisabeth Bronfen, eds. *Death and Representation*. Baltimore, MD: The Johns Hopkins University Press, 1993.

Gutiérrez Solana, José. *La España negra*. Ed. Andrés Trapiello. Granada: La Vuelta, 1998.

Jardí, Enric. *La ciutat de les bombes: El terrorisme anarquista a Barcelona*. Barcelona: Rafael Dalmau Editor, 1964.

Lahuerta, Juan José. "La tentación del hombre: Notas sobre una escultura de Gaudí." In *¿Qué es la escultura moderna? Del objeto a la arquitectura*. Eds. Javier Arnaldo et al. Madrid: Fundación Cultural Mapfre Vida, 2003. 33–44.

Laplana, Josep de C. *Santiago Rusiñol: El pintor, l'home*. Barcelona: Publicacions de l'Abadia de Montserrat, 1995.

"L'atentat [sic] del Liceo." *La Esquella de la Torratxa* 774. November 10, 1893: 706.

Maragall, Joan. "La ciutat del perdó." In *Elogi de la paraula i altres assaigs*. Barcelona: Edicions 62, 1978. 191–3.

—— "La independència de Catalunya." In *Articles polítics*. Ed. Joan-Lluís Marfany. Barcelona: Magrana/Diputació de Barcelona, 1988. 33–5.

—— "Paternal." In *Obra poética*: Versión bilingüe. Ed. Antoni Comas. Madrid: Clásicos Castalia, 1984. 178–9.

Oriol Pages, Eliseu. "Gaudí, las nuevas tecnologías, América y el 11 de septiembre." *El Tiempo Latino* (2002): 5.

Panyella, Vinyet. *Epistolari del Cau Ferrat: 1889–1930*. Sitges: Grup d'Estudis Sitgetans, 1981.

—— *Santiago Rusiñol, el caminant de la terra*. Barcelona: Edicions 62, 2003.

Pla, Josep. *Santiago Rusiñol i el seu temps*. Barcelona: Destino, 1981.

Roca Pou, Pere. "D'aquella nit del Liceu." Unpublished article.

Rusiñol, Santiago. "Discurs en la Tercera Festa Modernista." In *Els modernistes i el nacionalisme cultural (1881–1906)*. Barcelona: Magrana/Diputació de Barcelona, 1984. 151–4.

Sontag, Susan. *On Photography*. New York: Farrar, Straus and Giroux, 1977.

—— *Regarding the Pain of Others*. New York: Farrar, Straus and Giroux, 2003.

Sougez, Marie-Loup. *Historia de la fotografía*. Madrid: Cátedra, 2001.

Trapiello, Andrés. 'Introduction." In José Gutiérrez Solana, La España negra. Granada: La Vuelta, 1998.

–8–

Santiago Rusiñol's *Impresiones de arte* in the Age of Tourism: Seeing Andalusia after Seeing Paris

Elena Cueto Asín

It has been said that Santiago Rusiñol enjoyed writing about the places he painted because in the description and narration of experiences he found the "complemento necesario" to the images he captured on canvas (Casacuberta 26). Casacuberta, author of the most thorough study of Rusiñol's literary career to date, observes that in writing he found "[u]n altre llenguatge a través del qual explorar noves maneres d'arcar-se i d'aprehendre la realitat" (26). She also notes the crucial role that journalism played in the professionalization of the amateur writer. When Rusiñol traveled to Granada in October of 1895 his main purpose was to further develop his career as a painter. The truth, however, is that he was also commissioned to write a series of articles entitled *Cartas de Andalucía* (*Letters from Andalusia*) that he sent regularly to the Barcelona daily *La Vanguardia*. Given its dual quality as literature and as cultural testimonial, the writing done about and from Granada is as worthy of critical attention as his paintings, perhaps for more than merely "un interès biogràfic i un interès de època," as claimed by one of the Rusiñol's biographers, Josep Pla, for whom Rusiñol's early writings were nothing more than exercises lacking in literary refinement (*Rusiñol* 161).

A year after the initial appearance of *Cartas de Andalucía*, all nine installments (including illustrations by Miguel Utrillo, Macari Oller, and Arcadi Mas i Fontdevila) were published as part of a gift book for subscribers of *La Vanguardia* entitled *Impresiones de arte*. The volume sets the articles written from Granada in 1895 alongside another collection called *Desde otra isla*, sent from Paris between 1893 and 1894.[1] In the earlier series, Rusiñol records impressions of his stay in Paris and a trip he made to Italy, which are also accompanied by drawings by both the author and Ignacio Zuloaga. Prior to the appearance of *Impresiones*, the Barcelona newspaper had published *Desde el molino* with a similar format and purpose, including illustrations by Ramón Casas, in which he chronicles his 1890–1 visit to the French capital.[2] For various reasons the collection has received significantly more attention from both critics and publishers than *Impresiones de arte*. It is possible that the first series had a greater public impact at the time of its publication. Nevertheless, the two collections included in the second volume also enjoyed a good deal of popularity among readers of the Barcelona paper. Indeed, they received so much attention that the canvases that resulted from his stay in Granada were shown in Paris the following year and marked the beginning of Rusiñol's success as a painter outside of Spain.

The multifaceted creativity of Rusiñol makes it necessary to keep in mind two disciplines – literary criticism and art history – when approaching any aspect of his work. Critics writing on the period during which the author wrote for the press in Castilian as well as when his first works in Catalan began to appear, coincide in noting a parallel aesthetic evolution in both his literary and pictorial styles. With respect to Rusiñol's artistic production in Granada, this can be observed in the transition from Impressionism to Symbolism that initiates his period as a painter of gardens, and from the journalistic chronicle to the cultivation of poetic prose that culminates his career as a writer (Panyella, *Paisatges* 94). In light of the latter transition, the composition of the book *Oracions*, written at the same time as *Cartas de Andalucia*, has received a good deal of critical attention since it is considered representative of the concretization of a new poetic style of communicative expression with nature that marks a definitive change in Catalan literature (Sánchez Rodrigo 15). In the paintings produced during the artist's stay in Granada, art historians draw attention to the appearance of a new language of light used to achieve dramatic and symbolic effects that demonstrate that for Rusiñol "la pintura es un medio de expresión literaria" (Coll Mirabent 105). More than a parallel evolution, however, such estimations point to a fusion between the two arts, and invite Rusiñol's literature to be seen as more than merely supplementary. Even so, *Impresiones de arte* has most often been seen as background or secondary materials that, along with his correspondence, serve as a diary that facilitates the comprehension of his vision of art across different media.

Impresiones de arte merits attention beyond its possible function as a useful set of notes or sketches; it is an example of travel literature that appeared and was consumed at a crucial moment in the development of the genre and of the context of turn-of-the-century Barcelona. Within this frame, I am interested in analyzing the position of Rusiñol as observer and transmitter of impressions, and the changes in identity that are reflected in the natural and human landscape that inspired him as a writer and a painter. To do so it is necessary to turn to social histories of travel and its development as a key aspect of modernity, and to studies by scholars such as Buzard, who examines the different cultural manifestations born of the tourist industry that forever transformed the experience of travel. It is also imperative to consider the new figure of the tourist as a significant element of modern culture, "a rhetorical instrument that is determined by and in turn helps to determine the way nations represent culture and acculturation to themselves" (Buzard 4). Even though the study of travel and tourism has focused almost exclusively on Anglo-Saxon world experiences, as a line of investigation it offers a new means of appraising the narrative forms practiced by Rusiñol. It allows his journalism to be observed within the broader context of other types of literature influenced by or in dialogue with a leisure activity that had become generalized among the growing European bourgeoisie as a result of the Industrial Revolution's impetus towards democratization and modernization and new technologies of diversion and transportation.

The fact that the visit to southern Spain appears in the same volume as Rusiñol's travels to Paris and Italy makes his exercises as a chronicler abroad a key point of reference for critics to observe how his skills at travel writing develop, and how the use of different settings modify his perspective as a commentator. The collection opens with the foreigner's experience in the center of the cultural capital of Europe (to paraphrase Walter Benjamin), then moves on to Italy, the birthplace of Western artistic traditions, and ends in the local environment of his home country where marginality in dialogue with external forces of modernity is uncovered as cultural identity. In his journalistic chronicles, Rusiñol adopts the model of the international travel writer whose intellectual activity distances him from the figure of the conventional tourist.

The connection to an international phenomenon is not incompatible with an appreciation of *Impresiones de arte* in the intellectual context of *fin-de-siècle* Spain, and in the emergence of a generation of intellectuals, who along with the earlier generation of Realists, acquire a critical view of the national reality through the experience of travel. Their vision is one of an authentic, not folkloric Spain, and is recorded in recurring references to landscape found in both literary texts and visual representations. "Paisaje y figure humana," write Calvo Serraller and Martínez Novillo (20), are "productos ambos del pasado, vistos por los ojos de la modernidad" and are repositories of concern about the essence of the Nation and its internal situation. *Cartas de Andalucia* connects Rusiñol to the contemporary spirit of 1898 in as much as the letters reflect the ethnic and historical realities of Spain. The contemplation of the natural and human landscape of Andalusia by a Catalan is effected from a somewhat ambiguous position of identity – perhaps shared by the readers of *La Vanguardia* – in which the cultural affinity within the limits of the national is made compatible with the distance propitiated by an exotic and colorful image – the same distance that would contribute to the appreciation of Rusiñol's paintings abroad.

During two extended stays in Paris, Rusiñol learns to use his assignment as a foreign correspondent to shape an individual point of view while working in such widely admired surroundings. By the 1890s Paris is already an indisputable mecca of international tourism, attracting the curious masses with its monumentality, its fashion, spectacles, and grand exhibitions. In the same way, it also draws an intellectual public eager to submerge themselves in the epicenter of the European artistic establishment and vanguard. Like other young Spanish artists, among them many upper-middle-class Catalans, in Paris Rusiñol seeks the means to complete his education and to absorb the rich atmosphere of innovation offered by the city. The column in *La Vanguardia* presents a way for him to disseminate and share his experiences in a literary project of another scale than that of the earlier reportages of his excursions around Catalonia he wrote for the paper.[3] In Paris, Rusiñol also initiates a series of outings or excursions that have similar objectives of amplifying his knowledge while enjoying famous sights of historical and artistic interests beyond the city's limits that would appeal to a general public. The artist and writer, conscious of the mass experience that joins together intellectuals and non-intellectuals by converging on the same places, will seek a means to distinguish himself from the crowd. With an anti-tourist attitude, he will aspire to be identified as a "real" traveler, an explorer and expert on new spaces, and not as a mere tourist. By then the classification "tourist" had come to describe the member of an organized group and had lost its air of distinction: travel was no longer a privilege reserved for the few. The term could no longer be associated with the Grand Tour and the prototype of the young aristocrats who, with their mentors, had been visiting the main sights of Europe (particularly Rome) as part of their elite education (Buzard 6). It is not long before the popularization of the once exclusive activity causes it to be rejected from positions of distinction like that occupied by Rusiñol.

Once in Paris, Rusiñol begins to disassociate himself from the ignorant tourist by integrating himself into the life of the city and by establishing ties linked to quotidian experience as well as to a familiarity with a concrete field of study: art. The author presents himself in *Desde el molino* and *Desde otra isla* in the company of friends and shares with his readers the group's day-to-day activities and experiences. First they settle into the permanent quarters where they will reside for several months. These living arrangements have an important function in the articles: they serve as singular backdrops that mark the character of the experiences recounted and that determine the very titles of the collections. The titles of both collections refer to the places Rusiñol resided during his two stays in Paris: first overlooking the famous Moulin de la Galette in Montmartre and later in the residential Quai de Bourbon on the Île de Saint Louis. The apartments – one humble and cold, the other luxurious – are described in detail in the first installment of each series. Both are situated in parts of the capital rarely frequented by tourists, and they provide a setting befitting the attitudes of the bohemian artist or the elegant dandy with which the group of friends chooses to identify.

A set of unconventional attitudes contribute to the distinction of the author as a "real" traveler by aligning him with the Romantic characterization of the rebellious individual who disobeys the norms of sociability crystallized by an increasingly industrial and bourgeois society. The dissolute and bohemian life in the context of Montmartre is supposedly attenuated by the change of locations in the second series. In *Impresiones de arte*, the foursome of Rusiñol, Josep María Jordá and the Basques Ignacio Zuluoaga and Pablo Uranga is described in the second installment entitled "El personal," as "los cuatro mosqueteros de la isla," "cuatro personas distintas y cuatro naturalezas [...] reunidas por los vínculos del arte" in the carefree environment of camaraderie and freedom that they created around themselves (Rusiñol 717, 728). An example of this is found in the episode "El Greco en casa" when several authentic paintings by El Greco are acquired from an art dealer. Their elation following the cheap acquisition soon degenerates into vandalism as they proceed to tear up their rented luxury apartment: "El grito que lanzamos, al quedar solos con ellos, fue de los que saltan diapasones, y no pueden describirse, de los que dan patente merecida de locura a los ojos del prudente vecindario. Bailamos, rompimos, para hacer broma, dos jarrones de la China, braceamos y caímos en brazos de los demás, en un viva entusiasta" (Rusiñol 738).

While reproachable as an act of rebellion, the raucous behavior of Rusiñol and his friends is justified, and is even entertaining, in the exceptional context reproduced in the text. The bohemian stance more proper to Montmartre than to the Île de St. Louis, determines the originality of the artist's character, and is already familiar to the Barcelona public. Casacuberta observes that Rusiñol's reputation as an extravagant bohemian is established in Barcelona before he parts for Paris and anecdotes about him appear in newspapers of the time (17). She also notes an "ambivalence" in the public image that the artist projects of himself that seeks the recognition of the pragmatic bourgeoisie who sees the work of the artist as lacking in seriousness (19). In a biography, Panyella reiterates this when she observes in Rusiñol a lifelong tendency to publicly hide his true personality behind the mask of an artistic persona, "a no deixar transcendir altra cosa que la imatge d'artista que volia donar de si mateix" (*Rusiñol* 11). It is Panyella's opinion that the first-person chronicles written in Paris before he was famous were the perfect instrument to project such an image and to validate his activities there: "No era només un article, sino tota una afirmació d'estatus" (*Rusiñol* 118).

Ultimately, the very role of foreign correspondent concedes the aura of distinction and reaffirms the writer's status as a traveler. By the beginning of the twentieth century, as Moura observes, only through the act of writing can the traveler gain recognition as explorer without traveling to unknown lands beyond the limits of the civilized world: "Les guides ou journaux de voyages rédigés par nos auteurs dessinent en réalité le périple d'un touriste idéal, assez parfait pour mériter de ne plus appartenir a l'engeance touristique" (Moura 275). The independent, distinguished, and cultured tourist achieves a position of superiority the moment his written and published reflections about his visits demonstrate a sensibility that is not commonplace, even if the place described is already extensively explored and accepted as a tourist destination (Moura 275). From the middle of the nineteenth century, this sensibility will gain importance in the midst of the proliferation of narratives of travel and the differences in style, tone, and structure that increasingly separate these two types of writing: "the objective, informative 'guidebook' on the one hand, and the impressionistic 'travel book' (or the more tentative 'travel sketch') on the other" (Buzard 67). By cultivating the second formula, exemplified by the work of John Ruskin, Rusiñol will successfully achieve the importance that, according to Porter, lies behind all travel narrative: namely to serve as a vehicle of cultural mediation for exploring that which is foreign. The writer who cultivates this genre "brings into sharp focus that illuminating moment when two cultures are brought to sudden proximity," and adds interest to the narration when he is able to combine the exploration of spaces with the internal exploration of the self and share both of these with his readers (Porter 3–5).

In Barcelona, a city constantly expanding on every level, developments in other parts of Europe, especially Paris, are followed with great interest. The press is the principal source of information from abroad, and *La Vanguardia* (under the direction of Modesto Sánchez Ortiz after 1888) plays a central role as the voice of a liberal and dynamic bourgeoisie. Apart from attention given to issues of economy and international politics, the Catalan daily keeps its readers up to date on the latest cultural trends through the regular collaboration of intellectuals and artists. As Gaziel, the historian and former director of paper, points out, "plomes catalanes reputades, que feient entrar en castellà per les pàgines del diari originalment caciquista, els aires d'Europa i els batecs mes vius o mes innovadors del nostre propi esperit" (34). Among the types of culture disseminated by the paper, the culture of tourism is actively propagated through the constant presence of information about the possibilities for leisure and travel around Spain and abroad. Rusiñol's reporting can be seen to contribute to this promotion of leisure travel at same time that it attempts to distance itself from direct association with the practices of tourism. The written episodes offer the attraction of a style that mixes information about famous places that one might visit with individual commentary and perceptions about these locales based on the experiences of the author as protagonist. The formula is effective for the average newspaper reader with the means to travel, more likely to be a conventional tourist than an explorer, but who at the same time finds pleasure and entertainment in the illusion of participating in the latter category by way of reading. Josep Pla, writing as a correspondent in Paris in the 1920s, gives testimony to the contemporary impact of the articles when he pays homage to them on a walk through Montmartre, "el de Rossinyol i Ramon Casas que tanta influencia tingué a casa nostra" (*Rusiñol* 52). The dissemination of Rusiñol's first chronicles from Paris would be key in the rise of Paris as a destination for study that was initiated by he and his cohorts and would continue through the next generation of students from the Barcelona Academy of *Bellas Artes*.[4]

Clearly, *Desde otra isla* is a product of the desire to repeat the success of *Desde el molino*. The two works are significantly different in content, despite the repetition of the basic format. While the first series recreates a marginal, and often sordid, Parisian universe, the second presents a stroll through the monumental center of the city during which the author pauses to provide detailed explanations of points of architectural interest, masterpieces housed in the Louvre, activities at the art schools where they take lessons, *Société de la palette*, etc. The informative content and commentary about artistic patrimony is befitting of the title the collection would eventually have in book form: *Impresiones de arte*. In both series of articles, but especially in the second, the presence of tourism is consciously omitted. If by the 1890s Montmartre no longer represents an obstacle for tourists (in spite of the bohemian aura and its marginal location with which it is described in *Desde el Molino*) then the omission of tourists at the sights dealt with in *Desde otra isla* is much more problematic. The writer chooses not to allude to those other groups of admirers which cross the same streets and squares of the French capital, and with whom the protagonists of the series inevitably must cross paths. Such exclusion undoubtedly gives his experiences a certain charm that would otherwise be overshadowed if they were recognized as widely shared. The absence of other groups of visitors contributes to surround Rusiñol's daily routine in Paris with a refinement only possible with the luxury permitted by leisure time, something that every tourist is conscious of sacrificing for the sake of rapid and organized travel. Repeated allusions to the peace and tranquility of the places that the writer has the privilege of visiting at a slow pace correspond to the position that Urry associates with what he calls anti-tourism: "a 'romantic' form of tourist gaze in which emphasis is upon solitude, privacy, and a personal, semi-spiritual relationship with the object of the gaze" (45). For example, "Al salir a la calle ¿Cuántas veces el aroma de sus flores nos atrae y nos sentamos en sus pórticos respirando arte en su sombra antes de ir hacia ese París inquieto? ¡Cuántas veces, pasando, nos detenemos delante de un detalle indescifrable, de una flor que no habíamos observado, de un grifo que parece observarnos con los ojos vacíos, de una lápida sepulcral misteriosa!" (Rusiñol 734). Contact with the city's inhabitants and knowledge of the day-to-day rhythm of the metropolis are gathered in a manner found in less intimate mode of description employed by the *flâneur*, for example: "En el interior del ómnibus se puede observar que todo el mundo tiene aires de persona reflexiva. Será el aburrimiento o lo que sea, pero es el caso que las naturalezas más ligeras, las mujeres de esas llamadas airadas, las cabezas de pájaro, todas tienen una seriedad que solo dura mientras van en el glorioso vehículo" (Rusiñol 728).

The impression of total adaptation to the Parisian environment entertains readers who, while not entirely fooled, recognize Rusiñol's capacity to adjust to a great urban center, "té gràcia, sap descriure les coses per aquests topants com si es trobés al passeig de Gracia" (Pla *Obra completa* 27). It also suggests that the explanation for his easy acclimation lies in the fact that he hails from another great city. The parallelism most certainly contributes to the aspiration of Barcelona to see itself in the process of becoming a great city, and to discover in themselves the necessary measure of cosmopolitanism.[5] The act of seeing oneself integrated and of disguising one's condition as visitor is transformed upon leaving the adopted city of Paris and traveling to other points in Europe where, along with his readers, he will inevitably have to confront the tourist reality. This first happens in *Desde el molino*, in the narration of an excursion to the city of Rouen, and later in *Impresiones de arte*, on a more extensive journey through Italy. There the author combines the appreciation of monuments and visits to exceptional collections of art with criticism of the highly developed structure of the organized tour groups with which he and his companion, Ignacio Zuloaga, are forced to share time and space. Many of the elements that come into play in the pursuit of a distancing vision will be used again in *Cartas de Andalucia*. Here, attention centers primarily on criticizing technological advances like the trains that have transformed the landscape, and the urban development in the old quarters of the cities they visit. Also targeted with irony is the objectification of the scenery invented by the tourism industry: the guide and guidebook and the souvenir in the form of commercialized objects, as well as diaries and photographs.

For the most part, during the nineteenth century the critics of tourism are closely tied to those who criticize the expansion of its machinery, in a relationship of cause and effect. The train which revolutionized the world of transport is the first to be accused of destroying the spontaneity and leisurely pace of travel (Buzard 32). Rusiñol (804–5) describes it as "ese armatoste que precipita los hechos en el saco del recuerdo antes de tiento, y convierte en algo lejano lo visto momentos antes" that "deja en el ánimo un vacío, la sensación de haberse olvidado de algo moral en el pueblo que se aleja detrás de las ventanillas." In his reports about his excursions in Catalonia he praises the choice of a rustic *tartana* or a bicycle as the ideal means of transportation if one desires to thoroughly see the region. Rusiñol's position is not that different from the one Miguel de Unamuno takes in *En torno al casticismo* (1895) in which the philosopher rejects (even though he makes use of them himself) all of the advances and gadgets of mechanized travel in his physical and spiritual discovery of the Iberian Peninsula. Both examples make apparent the contradiction that is inherent in the adoption and rejection of modernity. It is well known that the construction of the railroad in Spain facilitated the discovery of its landscape by Spaniards as well as foreigners. The train afforded writers and artists along with other transitory visitors the means to become familiar with the diverse setting of the land. The comfort and ease with which certain trajectories could be made, thanks to this mode of transportation, give rise to a more realistic vision of the territory and its inhabitants and puts into check the excessively anecdotal commentary of earlier travelers (Calvo Serraller and Martínez Novillo 77–8). Even though this superficial vision corresponds to the earlier Romantic travelers, intellectuals like Unamuno and Rusiñol begin to associate it with the contemporary tourist who threatens to steal from them the privileged position of being the only legitimate observers. These intellectuals take advantage of the possibilities for travel brought about by technological advances at the same time that they lament their use. In the case of the Catalan author, he does this through the press as a venue that in many ways promotes new technologies in advertisements and news items. The first line of the initial installment of *Cartas de Andalucia*, in which Rusiñol describes his journey to Granada, stresses a sensation of geographical distance: "Nunca España, al consultar las hazañas de su gloriosa historia, nos pareciera tan grande como vista y recorrida en el tren de la clase de los rápidos. Tan cortés era el que montábamos, cabalgando por esas Manchas de Dios, que no halló pueblo ni villorrio en su largísimo curso, al cual no saludara con frases muy bien silbadas, deteniéndose un momento en todas partes para no ofender a nadie" (Rusiñol 774).

Previously, Rusiñol had described the ability to cross expanses of territory with great speed when he returned from Italy to Paris, passing through Switzerland and its wondrous natural landscape. Upon leaving Granada for other Andalusian cities, the mechanics of the train are revealed to be an accomplice to the urban renovations that are, for the artist, the lamentable outcome of modern technology: "Dejábamos Granada y un doloroso presentimiento nos decía que esa artística ciudad, que huía tras de nosotros, iría desapareciendo del mapa pintoresco de los pueblos; que iría dejando su suntuoso traje antiguo para vestirse de prendas nuevas; que sus cármenes de verde y descuidada y espléndida cabellera, se trocarían en jardincitos a la inglesa o en solares ruinosos; que sus calles misteriosas morirían deslumbradas por la luz de anchas e inspiradas reformas" (Rusiñol 805).

Technology is represented, for example in the case of Malaga, as a foreign influence and "no tiene ni un asomo del carácter de la hermosa Andalucía, ni un destello de inventiva, ni un rayo de novedad" (Rusiñol 806). Casacuberta (48–9) points out that Rusiñol's disapproval of projects of renovation constitutes one of the pillars of his aesthetic discourse: professing a respect for the past, he uses the opposition between past and present to criticize the prosaic and unifying materialism of modern bourgeois society. Implied here is a further attack on modernity that is paradoxically absent in the author's vision of Paris, in which the rapid modern pace of life is an inherent part of the charm and attractiveness of the city, and that causes his reflections on the south of Spain to take on a tone of orientalism. Notwithstanding the connection between historical conservation and an attitude of anti-materialism, the rational geometric planning of new streets and avenues in Andalusia, with their corresponding commercial enterprises, is perceived as the product of an industry of international exchange that is also somehow related to the presence of groups of foreigners, who are superficial and disinterested in the place's true character. Practicality and rationalism are associated with the use of the tourist guide with its referential character. Rusiñol dissociates his narrative from "esa riqueza de detalles, datos y fechas que tan del agrado son de los ingleses viajeros, amantes de saber por el sistema decimal la medida, objeto y proporción de toda obra de arte" (857). It so happens that the tourists in these texts, with few exceptions, are British and repeatedly demonstrate a visible lack of appreciation of southern European cultures. The characterization is already present in Rusiñol's earlier description of a trip to Florence: "Esa manada de ingleses que viajan de turistas. Triste de la tristeza gris del norte, se les ve saliendo de las calles acompañados de sus sempiterno guía, paseando el spleen por las ruinas, siempre serios, como viajando por fuerza, severos siempre, gozando de la belleza por obligación y apuntando los datos y fechas de entradas y salidas, de goces y sensaciones en sus libritos de memorias, para rumiar lo visto bajo su cielo de plomo" (Rusiñol 744).

Following the presentation of this perception, the author assures the reader that he and his traveling companions are very different from this other group, in spite of finding themselves in the same places and engaged in the same activity of admiring the artistic patrimony of another country. Once again, there is an insistence on the personalized gaze defined by Urry, and on silence and reflection as distinctive forms of assimilation: "largos ratos sin decir una palabra, trabajando con furor, absortos y creyéndonos en el desierto, ensimismados con los cuadros e intentando penetrar en el vago pensamiento del artista (Rusiñol 759). The romantic observer, in the center of a space that is inexorably tourist, needs a multitude deserving of his gibes in order to rescue his own identity based on difference, and to eliminate the obvious coincidences and similarities he has with them (Urry 45). An example of this is found in a comic episode in which Zuloaga, busy copying one of the masterpieces of the Uffizi Gallery in Florence, falls from his scaffolding and lands on top of one of the many English women that crowd the space below him. Unlike Rusiñol and his buddies who are there to do serious and sensitive work, the women tourists at the Uffizi are described spending their time "recorriendo salas de manera sistemática" and "pintando como quien hace calceta" (Rusiñol 758).

In the face of the pose that the writer maintains (that of a man adapted to the Parisian environment) the irritating encounters with the tourists that invade Italy and Spain can also be seen to encapsulate a progressive affirmation of the same southern European identity that is misunderstood by visitors from the north; moreover, as a Catalan he feels somehow more capable of understanding this reality. The identification with Mediterranean culture that Rusiñol stresses in various instances is perfectly compatible with a cosmopolitan attitude. The combination of the regional and the cosmopolitan is one of the defining characteristics of the spirit Catalan of *modernisme* of which the author participated. The compatibility between the two might offer an explanation for the ambiguous position that Rusiñol adopts in *Cartas de Andalucia*, which is already announced in the very choice of Granada as his next destination.

According to Pla, who echoes Utrillo's memoir, upon his returning to Barcelona from Paris (and Italy), Rusiñol proposed to make a trip to Mecca, or to Timbuktu. However, the plan was soon abandoned due to the length of the journey and the failure to communicate with several key contacts, which would have greatly facilitated such an adventure. The author, however, did not desist on his idea to travel to a Muslim country, and, as his biographer explains, decided to go to Andalusia instead (Pla, *Rusiñol* 147). In the end, the choice did not suppose a great sacrifice since the author had a certain esteem for Granada, and there he would have the chance to observe Arab art and architecture, and to experience the sensation of being far away but in a space in which he had linguistic and cultural competence.

On the one hand, the desire to go to distant continents reveals Rusiñol's will to act the part of the authentic traveler and perhaps to make up for the efforts he made to maintain this stance in nearby places and tourist destinations. On the other, the resignation to travel to Andalusia as a substitute reveals that at the beginning of the twentieth century the south of Spain continued to be considered "distant." The way in which Utrillo recalls and comments on the final decision on the trip's destination, makes this point clear: "Deciderent sortir tot seguit cap a Andalusia, que tant si es vol com si no es vol continua essent una terra islàmica com en temps dels Hixems, alahaquems i Abderramans. Si fos possible una nova transmigració islàmica, una gran part d'Andalusia s'identificaria amb el nou regisme en poc temps" (Utrillo 43).

Since the end of the eighteenth century, Andalusia had occupied a special place in notions of the exotic fostered in the imaginary of travelers from northern Europe, who, in the Romantic spirit, sought out inspiration in the Middle Ages and in far-off lands beyond the limits of Western civilization. Southern Spain with its medieval Arab past satisfied the fantasies of British, French, and North American travelers, and came to be included in the broader processes of Orientalization experienced in the Asia and African colonies of France and Great Britain, described by Said (11–12). For him, the vision of the exotic is based on the necessity of the bourgeoisie to establish itself as a social class and as the main protagonist in the push towards modernity and progress, and this is achieved by identifying the absence of these markers in the Other. Or perhaps, from the more positive position suggested by Litvak, this tendency might simply be a response to the opening of new fields like ethnology and a certain questioning of Enlightenment rationality, that in either case gave rise to a literature of escape and contributed to an amplification of ethnocentric perceptions of the world, in particular of the complex history of the Iberian peninsula (Litvak 17–20, 250). What is certain is that from the middle of the nineteenth century on, an image of a peripheral Andalusia is propagated as a setting for the development of the tourism industry as a "región exótica – aunque relativamente domesticada" that offers the possibility of becoming "un 'oriente' lo suficientemente 'próximo' para poder ser accesible por un número considerable de viajeros, que en última instancia acudían allí para apreciar una 'diferencia' identitaria" (Egea 150). The focal point of Andalusia's exoticism is Granada's Alhambra and the veneration of this place gives rise to a cult referred to as "Maurophilia" or "Alhambraism." Hoffmeister studies the phenomenon's literary manifestations that had many predecessors from the baroque to early Romanticism (114). Indeed, such an imaginary recreation of the territory is accompanied by a body of literature, originating inside and outside of Andalusia, for a growing market of books aimed at middle-class consumers (Egea 150–1).

Rusiñol's impressions of Paris had been read by Barcelona readers with an enthusiasm that made them feel closer to the model city, but would they follow the author to Andalusia with the same impetus of identification? Would Andalusia be a third chapter in the author's tour through foreign artistic and architectural scenery? Would the charm of approaching the modern north be broken in a description of the south, trapped in tradition but also undeniably part of a shared national territory, Spain? For reasons beyond an evolution in his style, the new series of articles would decidedly not reproduce the bucolic sense of belonging and pride which permeate Rusiñol's descriptions of his travels around Catalonia that he published before parting for France. In Granada, he and his group of Catalan friends were viewed by locals with a mix of regard and astonishment, and, as Pla notes, this was not unintentional: "procuraren adaptar-se, tot i que sempre fossin tinguts per estrangers" (*Rusiñol* 150). The success Rusiñol enjoyed in artistic circles and the long-lasting friendship that emerged during the period of his stay are well documented. It seems that the group from Barcelona "eren vistos, de vegades, com a exòtics turistes amb vestits de Terrassa i de Sabadell, a qui calia entendre per mitjà d'algun intèrpret" (Sánchez Rodrigo 15). The Granadans' dual assessment of the Catalan visitors at once highlights the juxtaposition of cultural similitude and difference, and corresponds to the persona that Rusiñol adopts upon his arrival in the south, and is reproduced in *Cartas de Andalucia*. In a playful manner, he not only observes the phenomenon of tourism in the Andalusian city from a distance, but also reserves the pleasure and the privilege of occasionally undoing this distance and engaging in tourist activities.

The first installment of the series contains an episode that illustrates perfectly this play of identities. In it he recounts how, on the day after the group's arrival, it finds itself hounded by guides offering their services in various languages, including Catalan. They end up hiring the Catalan interpreter until they realize that they no longer need him, following a meal at a typical *mesón*, when they felt that "ya el país entraba y corría por nuestra sangre, rompimos a hablar por lo andaluz con tal brío y desenfado, que nuestras pobres gargantas quedaron entumecidas. El guía continuaba hablándonos en catalán, pero nosotros despreciábamos y suprimíamos todas las eses finales, retorcíamos los labios a modo de asistente de comedia, y dale que te dale dirigíamos a la noble concurrencia párrafos tan audazmente andaluces, que comíamos más palabras que alimentos" (Rusiñol 777).

The anecdote, while humorous, is also disrespectful of regional peculiarities.[6] Even though the incorrectness might be unintentional here, it also reproduces the unconventional and somewhat rakish attitude of the Parisian dandy or bohemian. Moreover, the episode showcases the understanding of the Andalusian milieu that the author and his pals possess, which distinguishes them from the crowd of visitors. Later in the series, the group hires another guide, this time a "Gypsy Prince" who once served as a model for the painter Mariano Fortuny, "vestido con los deshechos de taller arreglados a sus hechuras y gustos, para encanto del extranjero que va a la zaga de lo típico y característico" (Rusiñol 788). On this occasion the services of the gypsy are contracted ironically, as he is familiar with and anticipates the stereotypical modalities of his ethnic group. His speech is transcribed in the text with all of its dialectic features reproduced for the reader.

Critical commentary alluding to the presence of tourists in Granada is less prevalent here than in the essays on Italy, in part because there is, in fact, less tourism, but also perhaps in accordance with the tendency registered in Paris of simply ignoring those activities with which he did not want to be associated or take part. Rusiñol never hides the fact that he is an outsider. Even so, he constantly displays a degree of authority and insight that is not typical of average visitors from outside of Spain. He reiterates this position, for example, by underscoring his ability to discern the "authentic" from the false items that are offered for sale to tourists:

> Cornucopias de todas edades y formas, clavos y aldabas con más hollín que antigüedad, tapices de las Alpujarras conservando la tradición del tejido hispano-moro, velones con más mecheros que latón, platos de reflejos metalizados por medios artificiales y curiosos específicos, y otros deshechos salidos de los desvanes o envejecidos por el mal uso del ingenio, colocados en la semioscuridad, y entre ella el anticuario dentro del nido, esperando que distraído y con el librito en la mano, pase el inglés para venderle los despojos de esta tierra. (Rusiñol 776)

As he did in Paris, Rusiñol rents a house with his friends, "despreciando los hoteles como bienes terrenales" (Rusiñol 777) and seeing them as "un establiment per a anglesos" (Pla, *Obra completa* 148). In subsequent episodes he records his strolls through the city, providing informative details and impressions of its artistic monumentality – the Alhambra and the Generalife palaces, and other hidden corners and streets which he roams with pleasure – just as he had done during his stay in Paris. Among the places that he most admires are the *cármenes* or gardens, which also begin to appear in his paintings, "y rincones sin fin, al parecer encantados y mágicamente silenciosos" (Rusiñol 778). The chapter titled "Los cármenes de Granada" is the most richly illustrated episodes in the collection as all of the artists involved in the project contributed an image. The attraction exercised by these figureless spaces has to do with the modernist sense of the sublime found in the unobstructed detail of such banal things as doors, windows, steps, and fountains surrounded by flowers (Figure 8.1). Similarly, Rusiñol also wanders into the marginal areas of the city where tourists seldom stray, like the gypsy neighborhood of Sacromonte, where he observes a poverty that recalls the Montmartre of *Desde el molino*. Panyella suggests that his earlier experiences in France could have served as a point of reference for the later encounter: "Les vivències del maquis montmartrès havien otorgat a Rusiñol i Utrillo una mena de capacitate d'adaptació a tota circumstància que voregés la marginalitat urbana" (*Rusiñol* 252).

Various scholars have seen in the prose Rusiñol uses to present the beauty, magic, and charm of the city evidence of a modernist style not present in his earlier travel writing (see Sánchez Rodrigo; Panyella, *Paisatges*). Among the expressions of this aesthetic exaltation there is a note of yearning to identify with the landscape that, at the same time, is not exclusive of a vision projected from

Figure 8.1 Miguel Utrillo (1862–1934), "Los cármenes de Granada," date unknown. Illustration from the chapter of the same title in *Impresiones de arte*. Charcoal and pencil on paper. 24.4 × 15.6 cm. © Museo Cau Ferrat de Sitges. © 2004 Artists Rights Society (ARS), New York/VEGAP, Madrid.

outside that situates the author within an angle of Orientalist perception. "La Alhambra lo es por dicha nuestra, y no se concibe Granada sin la Alhambra, como España no se concibe, vista desde el extranjero, sin este gran monumento, ya que sin ella habríamos perdido en la geografía artística mucho más que perdiendo una provincia" (Rusiñol 782). Although this passage demonstrates the pride derived from the admiration of an architectural treasure unique in all of Europe, it can also be interpreted as shaded by colonialist overtones: in the same way that the appreciation of the land or the *provincia* transmits a sense of distant ownership, the riches of a colony are a source of geopolitical pride for the metropolis. What is more, the author feels comfortable in his role as the traveler from an industrial and modern north that, despite being part of the same national territory, is separated by a long journey by rail. Rusiñol adopts a proximate vision of an object that had previously been depicted in painting and in writing by foreign travelers. His luminous descriptions of Granada are not free of stereotypes and associations that connect the present to its medieval past; with nostalgia for the period prior to the Christian Reconquest (in fact, an entire chapter is dedicated to the reenactment of the historical siege of the city by a group of itinerant actors). His allusions to this legendary past, "en quien me gusta creer más que en la historia," in which he evokes images of Moors and odalisques, contain many imaginative elements that are also found in Washington Irving's *Tales of the Alhambra* (1829) (Rusiñol 781).

Rusiñol's obsession on the legendary extends beyond Romantic nostalgia and contains a genuine concern for the present state of Granada's artistic patrimony, which he somehow feels is his own. He is conscious of the crucial role the palace plays in foreign imaginings of Spain. The passage cited above continues with a positive evaluation of efforts to save the Alhambra from the neglect and vandalism that resulted from the building being left open and unprotected until well into the twentieth century. He laments: "¡Pobre Alhambra! ¡Lo que debía de padecer aquellos días, al sentirse herida de muerte por el puñal de la torpeza! ¡Que dolor debieron sufrir sus paredes enfermizas, rasgadas por uñas innobles! ¡Qué amargura en su alma de edificio de sentirse incomprendida y despreciada!" (Rusiñol 783). The dilapidation, "¡avergüenza decirlo!," of what the country had to offer in terms of historical and architectural uniqueness reflects negatively on Spain in comparison with other European countries that had preserved their patrimony as a sign of wealth and civic-mindedness. A year before, Rusiñol had put forth to his readers the model of France and the state of that country's cultural treasures, and now he points out the poverty of the region as a sign of the overall decadence into which Peninsular culture had sunk: "la alberca de los arrayanes donde se bañaban sultanas y donde se bañan las columnas y la torre de los Embajadores reflejadas, servía de lavadero a carne de bestia humana" (Rusiñol 783). What is not mentioned in his indignation is that the recuperation of such monuments can only come about through an awakening of local identity, fed by the arrival of tourists whose numbers would multiply in the decades that followed, converting what was once a Romantic extravagance into a common destination among the bourgeoisie.

The metaphorical pain provoked by the Alhambra, so closely linked to the anguish Unamuno felt for the nation as if it were an organic part of the individual ("Me duele España"), is repeated in another installment, in which the author observes the human conditions in the neighborhood of Sacromonte. Conscious of the greatness of times past, the decadence and isolation of Spain appear reflected in the backwardness and hardship in which the area's gypsy population lives: "descendientes quizá de raza de árabes como despatriados en la que fue su gran patria" (Rusiñol 778). Rusiñol's words are transformed into the brush strokes of an expressionist painter as he describes in detail the situation in the neighborhood:

> Allí chiquillos desgreñados, revuelto el pelo de color indefinible, rubio de ocre, castaño gris, negro usado y desteñido, cayéndoles por los ojos como cascada de estopa, llevando retazos de ropa sucia por medio traje y dejando las piernas al descubierto, como brazos de esqueleto, de un moreno ceniciento manchado por el polvo del camino; allí mujeres con harapos de los colores más subidos, con telas pintarrajadas de cadmiun y bermellón en gritería de tonos brutales y escandaloso, bruñido el cabello, el rostro mate y una flor en la cabeza, como nota delicada en un muro ruinoso. (790)

This description, along with others, brings the text into contact with the aesthetic employed by Darío Regoyos and Émile Verhaeren in their *España negra* (*Black Spain*) that recounts a trip the two made through the north of Spain in 1888.[7] Rusiñol's depiction is not that different from those created by other artists associated with the so-called Generation of 1898 such as Ignacio Zuloaga, who upon returning from France sets up a studio in Seville, or José Gutierrez Solana, well known for his gloomy and carnavalesque images. An example of this is found at the end of the above passage in which the artist completes the scene of decrepitude and misery by mentioning "apariciones de brujas, de fantasmas y de duendes, horrores de fealdad, momias gitanas disecadas en su cueva" (Rusiñol 790). All the while he is unable to avoid speaking from the perspective of the casual visitor which he constantly assimilates and rejects: "y allí todos, esperando que pase algún forastero, para echárseles encima en frenética gritería como manada de avechuchos, para seguir corriendo detrás del coche convirtiendo la carretera en fantástico pandemónium" (790). Some of the illustrations by Utrillo, like "Carrer de la miseria"for the chapter "Córdoba," recall those street scenes by Regoyos and Pablo Uranga in which anonymous figures, rendered in dark colors, are dwarfed by the imposing magnificence of a built environment that represents Spain's regal and ecclesiastic past (Figure 8.2).

Throughout his career Rusiñol shares many of the tendencies that characterized the group of artists based in Castile, even though his name, and that of his Catalan friends who join him in Granada, is not usually associated with the movement and is more often considered alongside those associated with a so-called *España*

Figure 8.2 Miguel Utrillo, "Carrer de la miseria," date unknown. Illustration from the chapter "Cordoba" in *Impresiones de arte*. Ink on paper. 28.1 × 21.4 cm. © Museo Cau Ferrat de Sitges. © 2004 Artists Rights Society (ARS), New York/VEGAP, Madrid.

blanca (*White Spain*). Such divisions disappear when distanced from the complexities of turn-of-the-century Spain, and a preoccupation with Spanish themes can be seen as common to the work of the entire generation of artists (Calvo Serraller and Martínez Novillo 235). With regard to literary associations, the economic and social conditions of the gypsies are commented in *Cartas de Andalucia* through the prism of 1898. Although tinted with reformism, and accompanied by a brief history of the community and its establishment in Sacromonte, the portrait includes references to the lack of industriousness typically attributed to the group: "Los laboriosos (que son pocos) se dedican a la noble profesión de forjar clavos y herraduras, y los demás, no trabajan. Esperan a los extranjeros, se entretienen, cantan flamenco, viven de miseria y libertad, comercian con ropa vieja por pasatiempo, y como principal tarea cambian borriquillos viejos por otros más reviejos, barnizándolos y haciéndoles pasar, si no por jóvenes, por burros de mediana edad, como luego comprobamos" (Rusiñol 791).

Again his perspective moves towards the Orientalist vision of authors like Théophile Gautier who, in his *Voyage en Espagne*, saw the indolence of the gypsy as an expression of the south's idiosyncrasy. Rusiñol's similar view can be looked upon as an acceptance of foreign representations of the gypsy minority as part of the process of constructing a national "other" of the dominant culture. Spanish literature abounds with depictions of the gypsies, especially in connection with the Spain's folkloric culture, and stereotypes them as lazy, nomadic, and untrustworthy. As Charnon-Deutsch and Labanyi have pointed out, this is carried over into graphic art, in the use of images of gypsy (mostly women) in the Spanish press which is heavily influenced by the popular press of northern Europe (264–5). Gypsies are not unique to the Andalusian landscape, yet French and English travelers come to equate the south, and what they see or imagine there, with the rest of Spain. The chapter "El barrio de los gitanos" includes an illustration by Rusiñol of a young woman originally titled "Noia de Consuegra," which must have been executed on an earlier trip to La Mancha or perhaps on his way to Granada (Figure 8.3).

Figure 8.3 Santiago Rusiñol, "Noia de Consuegra," date unknown. Illustration from the chapter "Barrio de los gitanos" in *Impresiones de arte*. Ink and charcoal on paper. 23 × 18 cm. © Museo Cau Ferrat de Sitges. © 2004 Artists Rights Society (ARS), New York/ VEGAP, Madrid.

Gautier and other French travelers who visited Spain in the nineteenth century (such as Victor Hugo, Gustave Doré, and Alexandre Dumas) were responsible for the popularization of Spanish themes and Spanish art in France. In large part they contributed to the rediscovery of the Spanish masters Velázquez and Zurburán and the appreciation of Goya. At the same time, however, these intellectuals also alimented the taste for the *españolada* (things Spanish) based on the proliferation of images of *bandoleros*, *majas*, Gypsies, flamenco dancers, bullrings, convents, Moorish ruins, and castles that were highly profitable for art dealers (González and Martí 33).[8] The success of painter Mariano Fortuny in Paris served as the primary inspiration for the expansion of this highly lucrative tendency among aspiring Spanish artists residing in the French capital, and curiously, it is an admiration of the work of Fortuny that leads Rusiñol to make an earlier trip to Granada. It is noteworthy that the author's encounter with the Gypsy guide, who had once served as a model for the famous painter, gives way to a commentary on the exploitation of the *españolada* aesthetic, since the man also "[s]irvió mucho a los ingleses para apuntar en el librito la típica indumentaria de sus ropas; las guías le mencionaban en sus entretenidas páginas," and "[d]esde entonces no había pasado por Granada pintor cursi, sin que le hubiese retratado más o menos" (Rusiñol 789).

Rusiñol takes part, although somewhat laterally, in the movement aimed at the demystification of "Spanishness" initiated by members of the generation of painters in Catalonia and in other parts of Spain: Zuloaga, Isidro Nonell, and Regoyos. In 1896, he exhibits his paintings from Granada at the Champ de Mars in Paris where he receives immediate recognition. Especially popular are his canvases depicting gardens – so popular in fact that one of them, "Jardín de Granada," is acquired by the French government. Following this triumph he receives various commissions, including one from the Casa Groupil and the Museum of Philadelphia, and goes on to be the first Spanish painter to show at the Musée Luxembourg, an institution dedicated to the work of living artists. From this series of events, the following conclusion can be drawn: the success and renown of Rusiñol's images of Granada in Paris returns him to the point of his departure, to the place where his journey began only a few years before. In the same way that the publication of *Impresiones de arte* brought together his experiences of the two cities, the two would also serve as points of reference and destination, based on their proximity and distance from Barcelona, in the continued evolution of Rusiñol's career as a writer and an artist.

Notes

1. The use of the word "other" in the title *Desde otra isla* refers to the fact that this series was preceded by another group of articles written in Majorca called *Desde una isla*.

2. The original illustrations belong to the Museo del Cau Ferrat (Rusiñol's residence in Sitges) and were the subject of a public exhibition for the first time in February 2001.
3. Of note are the series *Por Cataluña: Desde mi carro* (1889) and the article "De Vic a Barcelona en bicicleta" (1890).
4. For a further discussion of Rusiñol's work in Paris see Cueto Asín.
5. At the same time, Rusiñol also began to publish in *L'avenç*, a regionalist Catalan cultural journal. Casacuberta (40) comments on how the magazine sees the author's residence in Paris as a source of regional pride: "De fet, no hi podia haver ningú millor que Rusiñol – un artista català més o menys instal·lat a París en contacte amb la més candent actualitat artística, literària, musical, dramàtica – per mostrar cap a on portava la vitalitat de la cultura catalana, en contrast amb l'esmorteïda activitat cultural i la manca d'ambició i de curiositat intel·lectual que distingia la resta de Espanya."
6. Such attitudes did not seem to interfere with the friendships that the group and, in particular, Rusiñol had established in Granada. Rusiñol's presence and writings were highly appreciated by the locals, and an episode of his *Cartas de Andalucia* was reproduced in the Granadan newspaper *El Popular*. See Panyella (*Rusiñol* 160–1).
7. Like *Impresiones de arte*, their essays and images were first published in the newspaper and later appeared in book form in 1899. See Verhaeren and Regoyos.
8. The fashionableness of the *españolada* in France, accentuated by the fact that Eugenia de Montijo, Empress of France and wife of Napoleon III (1852–70), was Spanish, is registered in descriptions of Spanish themed parties and dances, and Goyesque costumes at court. It can also be seen in Act III of Giuseppe Verdi's *La traviata* (1853) and inspired Georges Bizet's *Carmen* (1875).

Works Cited

Buzard, James. *The Beaten Track: European Tourism, Literature, and the Ways to Culture. 1800–1918*. Oxford: Clarendon Press, 1993.

Calvo Serraller, Francisco and Álvaro Martínez Novillo. *Paisaje y figura del 98*. Madrid: Fundación Central Hispano, 1997.

Casacuberta, Magarida. *Santiago Rusiñol: Vida, literatura i mite*. Barcelona: Curial, 1997.

Charnon-Deutsch, Lou and Jo Labanyi. *Culture and Gender in Nineteenth-Century Spain*. Oxford: Clarendon Press, 1995.

Coll Mirabent, Isabel. *Santiago Rusiñol*. Sabadell: AUSA, 1992.

Cucto Asín, Elena. "Santiago Rusiñol in Paris: The Tourist/Travel Writer." *Catalan Review* 16 (2002): 89–102.

Egea Fernández-Montesinos, Alberto. *García Lorca, Blas Infante y Antonio Gala: Un nacionalismo alternativo en la literatura andaluza*. Seville: Fundación Blas Infante, 2001.

Gaziel. *Història de "La Vanguardia" (1881–1936) i nou articles sobre peridisme*. Barcelona: Empùries, 1994.

Gónzalez, Carlos and Montse Martí. *Pintores españoles en Paris (1850–1900)*. Barcelona: Tusquets, 1996.

Hoffmeister, Gerhart. *European Romanticism: Literary Cross-Currents, Modes, and Models*. Detroit, MI: Wayne State University Press, 1990.

Litvak, Lily. *Erotismo y fin de siglo*. Barcelona: Antoni Bosch, 1978.

Moura, J.M. "Mémoire culturelle et voyage touristique. Réflections sur les figurations líttéraires du voyageurs et du touristes." In *Travel Writing and Cultural Memory*. Ed. Maria Alzira Seixo. Amsterdam: Rodopi, 2000. 265–80.

Panyella, Vinyet. *Paisatges i escenaris de Santiago Rusiñol (Paris, Sitges, Granada)*. Barcelona: Curial, 2000.

—— *Santiago Rusiñol, el caminant de la terra*. Barcelona: Edicions 62, 2002.

Pla, Josep. *Obra completa*. Vol. 4, Barcelona: Destino, 1971.

—— *Santiago Rusiñol i el seu temps*. Barcelona: Destino, 2002.

Porter, Dennis. *Haunted Journeys: Desire and Transgression in European travel Writing*. Princeton, NJ: Princeton University Press, 1991.

Rusiñol, Santiago. *Obres completes*. Vol. 2. Barcelona: Selecta, 1976.

Said, Edward. *Orientalism*. New York: Pantheon, 1988.

Sánchez Rodrigo, Lourdes. *Oracions a la natura: La prosa poètica de Santiago Rusiñol*. Sitges: Grup d'estudis sitgetans, 1992.

Urry, John. *The Tourist Gaze: Leisure and Travel in Contemporary Societies*. London: Sage, 1990.

Utrillo, Miguel. *Història anecdòtica del Cau Ferrat*. Sitges: Grup d'estudis sitgetans, 1989

Verhaeren, Emile and Dario de Regoyos. *España negra*. Palma de Mallorca: José J. de Olañeta, 1999/1963.

–9–

Landscape in the Photography of Spain

Lee Fontanella

Landscape in photography corresponds almost exactly with the discovery of photography, and especially with non-daguerreotype photography; that is, with photography as we usually think of it, a positive/negative process with a repeatable visual product, always more or less the same. Although for many photography is still, after 170 years, a realist phenomenon, landscape is invention, even in the photographic medium. The "invention" of landscape has at least two possible interpretations. One is that one "comes upon" a given scene in reality – falls into it, in the way that the early 1840s adventurer, John L. Stephens, experienced his "incidents" of travel in the Yucatan, as he called them; he "fell upon" scenes (and a couple times, he actually did fall into them).[1] Another possible interpretation is that "invention" is subjectively artistic. As an historian of photography, I find the first meaning – that connoting "coming upon" something – more descriptive of what occurred in the case of nineteenth-century tourist photographers in lands strange to them. But the second interpretation – that involving subjective artistry – is, in fact, what photography moves toward as it develops over the past century and a half, and as indigenous photography grows increasingly accomplished and less amateurish. This differentiation is what I want to underscore. It is what is significant. It is, to a degree, a product of the way in which the photographic medium came to be used and of the styles that resulted from those applications.

Three centuries prior to my own jumping-off point of 1850, Anton van den Wyngaerde (Antonio de las Viñas), a Flemish artist, was employed by Felipe II first to depict the sites the king had seen in England when he married Mary Tudor (1554), then to depict sites in Spain, beginning in 1561.[2] He is said to have painted stage scenery and palace murals with cityscapes, such as one of Guadalajara when it had a population of 12,000. He painted five of Tarragona two years before that of Guadalajara, at least one of which was in sharp contrast to the one of Guadalajara since it had significantly more detail. In this regard, we should remember one basic premise of the representation of anything, as pointed out to us by Ernst Gombrich in the course of what he called his "meditations on a hobby horse":[3] when what is depicted *matters* to us, when it acquires deep-seated value, abstraction and minimalism do not suffice, and we tend to require progressively heightened representational detail. Maps – and Gombrich was intensely interested in maps as visual representation, as we know from his essay "Mirror and Map" – became increasingly filled in (Gombrich 1982). Similiarly, Wyngaerde's fundamental scapes become progressively more detailed as kingdom and empire grew in significance for Felipe II – and as it grew correspondingly important to Wyngaerde to connote that importance in his drawings.

Can we apply the same representational notion to early-nineteenth-century depictions of Spanish views? I would answer a resounding "yes," for multiple reasons. Psychologically, the aspect of Romanticism that has people in concert with nature, especially with vast and sublime nature, enhanced the *value* of landscape. I venture that in general terms that phenomenon is actually lessened (however unduly) in the context of tourism, especially when the landscape is considered exotic – i.e., not one's own. More subtly, representational detail mattered more and more, as visual mediation allowed it to be depicted in an ever more facile way: faster, more repetitiously, and in greater detail. Lithographic methods and fine-line engraving since the start of the nineteenth century tended to displace the woodcut that nowadays we find an appealing throwback to visual primitivism.[4] In so doing, they allowed for speed-up in visual mediation and lengthier repetition of the image, even while they permitted greater detail. If this was so for four decades prior to photography, i.e., beginning in 1795 with the cultivation of the lithograph, what then could be said of the repeatable, still more rapid, less manual photographic image from 1839 on? After all, by the mid-nineteenth century, in Spain, a certain Romantic involvement with the land meant that greater value had accrued to the land as representational subject. Although this would never in Spain reach levels of Wordsworthian profundity and significance (levels reached by some British writers as early as the invention of lithography) it nevertheless was considerable by mid-century.

When the discoverer of negative/positive photography, William Henry Fox Talbot, went on his photographic excursion to Loch Katrine, he made several views of that site. Apparently, he documented the lake. Yet in another sense, this was to make the scene his – more vitally interpreted, to appropriate Loch Katrine. Probably the most masterful of photographic peripatetic excursions that I have ever seen was carried out by a photographer who had just shortly before (1851) photographed Sevilla for the most important nobleman of that city, the Duque de Montpensier, brother-in-law to the Spanish Queen:[5] namely, the Vicomte de Vigier, another nobleman, photographed Sevilla with a very modern eye. In his "Étude d'aloès" (Aloes Study), he eschews the perspective of tempting landscape and focuses instead on exotic details. The so-called "Caños de Carmona" are the background, for instance, but are of secondary interest. At least 75 percent of the photography consists of a cactus. That image is rivaled only by the impressive noria (water wheel) image, whose photographic subject is not the titular one (the water wheel), but rather the reeds that make up the majority of the photograph. About two years later, in July and August of 1853, the Vicomte de Vigier made a trek between the Aragonese Pyrenees and Pau.[6] His "Vue de la partie de la Maladetta et des montagnes d'Aragon du haut du port de Vénasque" (View of a Portion of the Maladetta and Aragonese Mountains from a High Point on the Vénasque Pass) represents the presumed goal of that trek. Twenty-four views are presented so that it appears that the objective of the peripatetic tour is to look out over Aragon as final achievement, while it is possible that the starting point was probably a departure from Spain with an initial retrospective into Aragón, and a continuation on through French villages, toward Pau then Paris. More often than not, these are wonderful scapes, such as the "Vue du lac d'Oo, ou Seculejo, près Bagnères" (View of Lake Oo, or Seculejo, near Bagnères), but sometimes they seem anthropological in purpose, such as the one of "Le Village de Montauban près Luchon" (Montauban Village near Luchon), depicting humble homes and the laundry that is hung out to dry. At their most brilliant and modern, they are scapes with an implicit brief narrative, e.g., "Bloc dans le Chaos St. Sauveur" (Boulders in Chaos St. Saveur). Here, a specific, personalized incident is made more the subject than the scape of the *sentier* (path) toward St. Sauveur. In this way, we have implied the narration of an incident (a rockslide) personal enough to have interrupted not only the path – in other words, the photographer in the course of his journey – but also his photographic result. Personal fate, or accident, rather than scopic permanence, becomes the chief subject. This unforgettable view by Vigier signals early on in photography the personalism that will lie at the root of the invention of landscape in photography; falling upon an unexpected wonder of nature; coming across a scape as if by accident; an incident of travel that is affective.

Almost coincidentally, another photographer, R.P. Napper, from South Wales, attempted in a letter to sell his "Andalusian views" to the Duque de Montpensier. Napper had been an envoy photographer working for Francis Frith, possibly since 1857, who right away got into a business argument with that photographic magnate, Frith of Reigate, and so solicited the patronage of Montpensier.[7] Right after making his Andalusian views, Napper returned to South Wales, in order to carry out his peripatetic excursion, unwittingly (I must suppose) after the fashion of Talbot and Vigier. Tracing the River Neath, he personalized his trip with milestone observations, such as the mining of Dimas Rock, which he lamented expressly and significantly, because it signified unwarranted intrusion, a despoiling of the land. Napper finally concludes with his photograph of "Napper's Glen," thus appropriating, as Talbot did, one of the photographic sites along the way. The photographing was simultaneous with the labeling with one's own name, which went well beyond Talbot, insofar as it seemed to make more permanent the implicit personal narration. (Hypothetically, "I fell upon this glen, and, by virtue of the photographic image, I have made it mine, and be it so called henceforth".) Although these photographs – with the exception of the view of the Aragonese pass – are not strictly of Spain, they were made by Hispanophiles who sojourned in Sevilla and photographed that city and, in the case of Napper, were photographers of Andalusian types. This more "anthropological" sort of photography seems to me to be vaguely related to landscape, but not intimately involved in it, probably because it is so much a part of the activity of the transient "outsider."

As photography grew artistic – and it did so with clear intent rapidly, in its second decade – the photographic subject, human or otherwise, took a bit of a back seat to effect and message (whether moral or more simply narrative). Similarly, when landscape became interrupted, it often yielded to subjectivism, such as in the case of "les Blocs" in Vigier's "sentier" in the Pyrenees. Even at a very early point, landscape was sometimes not the primary photographic subject; rather, the subject became the very *contemplation* of scapes, so that the viewer might relate to the human experience depicted in the photographic image, rather than to the landscape presumably observed, and, by extension, the viewer would appreciate the land. The very best example I can think of is a pre-1855 image by an unknown photographer, possibly Flemish, in which a young man contemplates a field through a rail fence (a "scrim" of subjective illusion?) (reproduced in Bernard 32). It is important to point out these possibilities, because they all hint at a subjectivist direction in the photographing of landscape.

This was, of course, done in early lithographs of Spain, such as in an 1824 view of Montserrat, drawn by Edward Hawke Locker, for *Views in Spain*, in which human subjects look out over a river valley. Similarly, in 1839, the same year that the discovery of photography was announced to the public in many corners of the world, J.J. Williams published his "Vue du ravin de Badajos, prise de la Gorge du Cabouco" (View of the Badajos Ravine from Cabouco Gorge), in which a figure, his back to us, contemplates a natural scene of otherwise almost incomprehensible sublimity. This view of the Canaries was published in the *Histoire Naturelle des Isles Canaries* (Natural History of the Canary Islands), by Sabin Berthelot and Philip Baker Webb.[8] We identify here with a peripatetic traveler venturing into the Garden Primeval or into the Valley of Death, and the possibility of identification with the human experience is thrilling. More so, perhaps, than in the case of the comparably passive folk at the "Desfiladero de Pancorvo" (The Narrow Pass at Pancorvo), drawn by the eminent Genaro Pérez de Villa Amil for the ambitious publication *España artística y monumental* (Artistic and Monumental Spain), printed by the famous Lemercier for A. Hauser, in Paris (1842–50); here, folk are in the scape, but they do not contemplate it as if it held the special interest that indeed this locale has always held for viewers. And doubtless even more so than in the work by famed traveler in Spain, David Roberts, who used witless pastoral animals in his "The Escurial", for his *Picturesque Sketches in Spain: Taken During the Years 1832–1833* (1837), because Roberts does not apply the visual trope of looking *at* by seeing *through* our surrogate in the visual image.[9]

The apex of scapes were drawn and lithographed by Alfred Guesdon (1808–76), as evident in his view of Córdoba, "Vista tomada desde encima del Guadalquivir" (View Taken from above the Guadalquivir River, 1860), for his serial publications of "L'Espagne a vol d'oiseau" (Spain from a Bird's-Eye View).[10] But these were almost always cityscapes, where the city mattered more than the land. (The city had mattered ostensibly more than the land in Wyngaerde's sixteenth-century depictions, more aimed at information than at fulfilling artistic inspiration.) How was this possible before there were airplanes, and when so much precise detail was necessary in order to be able to make the "vue a vol d'oiseau"? By aerostatic balloon, and with a tripod and camera, no less. Three hundred years before, Wyngaerde had no recourse to the late-eighteenth-century invention by Montgolfier, the aerostatic balloon, let alone photographic equipment, so he would have to climb to a high vantage point. Still in 1871, that is what the Barcelona photographers Manuel Moliné and Rafael Albareda were doing when they photographed *la plana*, the plains of Lleida (Lérida) across the River Segre, from the vantage point of the citadel, in anticipation of the royal visit in September by King Amadeo de Saboya.[11] Wonderful as these ten large-format images are, as technically capable as Moliné and Albareda were, their purpose is still fundamentally informational, as a matter of fact. Moliné and Albareda are offering a visual memento to the king (while they are promoting themselves in the act of announcing, *de facto*, their photographic capability). They may have been artistically inspired (the quality strongly hints as much, and Moliné had been a painter in his youth), but that was not the ostensible purpose of these views.

In Madrid, Guesdon's assistants were none other than the British photographer Charles Clifford and Jane Clifford, his wife, who maintained Clifford's studio after his unexpected, premature death. Clifford came to be Spain's greatest photographer of the nineteenth century.[12] However, one could not justifiably dwell on Clifford in respect to landscape, because he was not given, except in a small percentage of his images, to photographing scapes. Rather, as in the case of the huge majority of photographers, he photographed significant monuments, historically symbolic sites, and (to him) exotic items, such as the "Nopales y pitas" (Prickly Pear and Agave) of Málaga, with its hint of scape, but not landscape as primary motif. When there is an appearance of landscape in Clifford's photographs – as there was, for example, in several images pertaining to the Extremadura excursion in the company of the Duque de Frías, landscape is incidental to monument or architectural structure, ruins (with their moral-symbolic charge), etc. I make an issue of this purposely to reiterate a point I speculatively made earlier on: the more that a land was thought of as exotic – i.e., out of one's customary sphere of experience – the less one tended to identify with scape and to photograph instead monuments, cultural symbols, and exotic items. Napper's work (contemporaneous with Clifford's) proves the case: in Andalusia, he photographed, almost exclusively, the human types of Andalusia; back in the Vale of the Neath, South Wales, he photographed the land to the point of becoming one with it and even labeling it his – a step beyond the more respectful Wordsworthian manner. In Clifford's work, as in the case of Vigier's landslide across the path to St. Sauveur, scopic vision is often blocked by the startling, significant object. For example, the high end of the aqueduct of Segovia startles the photographer as he rounds a corner of the city. Although he made several views of the aqueduct, which would become more conventional, seen in retrospect, of course, photographs of the sort of the "startling" high end of the aqueduct are consummately anti-scopic, however majestic. Take this view as a metaphor for photography realized in the exotic land. The photographer is ever surprised as he comes upon significant sites that merit the patient attention of his lens – and, of course, it is not the land in sympathy with an indigenous photographer that we ultimately find represented in such circumstances, rather the structure full of meaning: symbolic, historical, or, more simply personal, as in the case of one of the properties of the Duque de Frías, his massive "hunting lodge" called El Rosario, as it sits on a rise.

It grows clearer that landscape is culturally rooted, insofar as it represents a marriage between the culture of the artist vis-à-vis the object represented. For example, William Henry Jackson's pioneering photographs of the American West, or those of Carleton Watkins, are sometimes views that look from foreground darkness toward the hope of a beyond, but a beyond that drifts off into mysterious (gray) ambiguity. Thus, they symbolize the entire mystique of pioneering and exploration, aspiration toward a sublime, wondrous unknown. But this is not Clifford, stunned by the looming presence of the meaningful monument. When Clifford does photograph landscape, such as in the case of his September 30, 1860 view of the Cueva de la Virgen (Cave of the Virgin), in Montserrat, it is often still to mark a symbolic and/or historic purpose. This Cueva view, then, is a view of the seemingly impossible path that the royal party took on its way to this mountain shrine, more than it is a landscape, and, as such, it is the job of the photographer (an adjunct to chronicle in this instance) to photograph in such a way that the image signifies that difficulty. So, landscape appears to give way to obscurity and confusion here; precisely what the chronicle of the royal journey underscores for this difficult trek. (Truth be told, Montserrat is one of the few sites in which topography itself so fascinated Clifford that he broke from his customary mode and made a number of views of the land.) This confusion between land and what land embraces is not characteristic solely of Clifford. I venture that it is the norm in a land such as Spain, which was then fundamentally touristic (generally speaking, still, "romantique Espagne" from the French viewpoint and Imperial Spain extended, for the British, who would see Isabel II as the Catholic Queen revived and heir to the Emperor Carlos V). Even when the non-outsider is not the photographer (not a French or British person, as was so very often the case for Spain), the confusion can still exist between scape and the object it embraces, as is evident in an unpresupposing but marvelous 1864 view (by F. de Marcos and J. María Saavedra) of the "Abadía de San Frutos tomada desde S.E." (The San Frutos Abbey, From the Southeast), near Segovia (reproduced in González 113). It is the same question we will eventually be obliged to pose, in mid-twentieth century, when we find Spanish photographers making views of ruined Spanish castles in their scopic settings.

If we heed those "meditations" of Ernst Gombrich, in order to have landscape, land has to *matter*; it has to have acquired a personal value for the image-maker and be in some grade of sympathy with the image-maker. I have been suggesting that one reason why, in Spain, photographic scapes may not have appeared until later is that so many of the most noteworthy early photographers in Spain were sojourners in the land; less of the land (that is, pertaining to it, indigenously) than tourists wandering through it. In 1892, J.H.T. Ellerbeck wrote his "Guide to the Canary Islands, Calling at Madeira," and he sold, from hotels in both La Laguna (Tenerife) and Liverpool, from the stock of 525 views he made of the islands (see Vega de la Rosa 2000, 2002; Teixidor Cadenas). Ellerbeck was still the exoticist, as we can see by his fascination with the details of landscape (just as Clifford had been in his Málaga image of "nopales y pitas"); but he was also the adventurous explorer, as he photographed the remnant volcanic "Caldera de la Palma" (Volcanic Crater, La Palma). (The imagistic *modus operandi* is the same as that used by William Henry Jackson and so many other Far West surveyors in the United States.)

Maybe we should not find it hard to comprehend that landscape begins to be cultivated in full by Spaniards in areas where land meant so much; in the Balearic Islands, for example, where it vies with the sea. Gaspar Rul-lan Garcias (*c.* 1930) made a view of s'Estaca (Valldemossa), in which sea is quantitatively more than land, and it appears, besides, that land struggles to stave off a sea that may have the upper hand (Mulet 246). Similarly, in the Canaries, Adalberto Benítez Tugores (also *c.* 1930) made his "Paisaje" (we can tell from the titles that the motives are land, as opposed to sea; these are not maritime views). Antoni Mulet Gomila (*c.* 1920) made a view of the land surrounding Galilea, in Baleares (Mulet 250). And I would like to think that when Francesc Martorell made his great view of the "Molíns" (Windmills) (*c.* 1925), he did so assuming that the mills were, like castles, part and parcel of the lay of the land (Mulet 261). (We know from literature that "molins" have the capacity to abet enchantment.) What becomes evident is that under the enormous influence of the so-called pictorialist style, effect became at least as important as the representational content. And so, even where land did have a marked value, the effect might outweigh the landscape, as it does, I think, in an image (*c.* 1930) of the "Sombra del Pico y Cráter Viejo, Puerto

Orotava" (Shadow of the Peak and the Old Crater in Puerto Orotava, Canaries), by Hanns Zinsel. The virtual peak, suggested by its shadow, becomes more focal than the fascinating landscape of the Old Crater – we know by the title, if not by the image itself.[13]

The exception to the axiomatic rule that landscape photography in Spain is cultivated first by Spaniards (or acculturated foreigners), especially in places where land really mattered, would be pictorialism, which carried the implication of something I would call a manual slow-down of the photographic medium. Pictorialism, a stylistic term which we associate with undertakings in image-making as early as around 1860 in Britain, connoted many, many things, but one essential factor was the implicit license to manipulate the image, in order to achieve a desired effect; perhaps even to make the image "painterly" through the use of brush strokes with pigment in the making of the positive. The style caught on in Spain toward end-century, it became standard on Spanish soil at least by 1920, and the most truly Spanish thing about pictorialism is that as a valid technique and consequent style, it endured so very long a time – much longer than it endured in most countries. So when, for example, Ernesto Baena, in the Canaries, creates his "Puesta del sol" (Sunset) (*c.* 1930), in which effect is primary, he wanted to photograph the effect of a sunset, more than the landscape it affected (Vega de la Rosa 2002: 106). This is substantiated by the title.

In pictorialism, detail often grew purposely less distinct – even less in quantity – in the interest of mood and atmosphere. In part, especially initially, this was a (leftover) impressionistic means of imitating the way the human eye saw: not with uniform distinctness in all areas scoped, and not with evenly distributed interest or clarity in all portions of what was in scope. This was the theoretical hook used by one of the most crucial figures in the history of photography: P.H. Emerson.[14] A perfectly logical extension of painterly impressionists, Emerson cultivated East Anglia's Norfolk Broads as photographic subject, because representationally, the Broads – at least, as Emerson recorded them – lent themselves by nature to the visually diffuse, atmospherically brooding achievement that was often the aim of photographic pictorialists. Devoted followers, such as George Davison, famous for his landmark "The Onion Field" (1889), even resorted, as in this case, to the pinhole camera, in order to achieve the effect of the human eye.

Thus, pictorial photographic result is perfectly married to realism, rather than to the idealist Francoist fancy to which some would connect it in an attempt to define it. López Mondéjar cultivates the idea of an intimate link between Franco's regime and Spanish photographic pictorialism. He denigrates the style largely on the basis of that presumed link, calling the stylistic manifestations in its late years "Tardopictorialismo." This theory, in which I put no stock, is echoed in several of his writings (López Mondéjar 30). In fact, Spanish pictorialism – reflecting a genuine, indigenous intent to honor one's land – is arguably Spain's most autochthonous photographic style. And it was, for most of the reasons just explained, the medium *par excellence* for the communication of landscape.

Paradoxically, the pictorialist cultivation of effect in Spanish photography yields (and not always so incidentally) views of the land that, as time goes on, make us wonder if effect is persistently the primary interest, or if the land returns as primary concern, although the titles of the views might lead us to believe that we are still rooted in effect. It is immensely tempting for me as an historian to use a 1932 photograph by Joaquín Gil Marraco (Zaragoza) as an example of such a claim. It is an image after effect: the effect that fog – a frequent motif in pictorialism – would produce. But the title is, conveniently, "Se levanta la niebla (en la Arboleda de Macanaz)" (The Mist is Lifting in the Macanaz Grove). It is tempting to take this particular title as a death-knell to the style, but it was far too early (1932) to do that for the case of Spain. The "Crepúsculo" (Twilight) (1927; a bromoil), by Vicente Martínez Sanz (Valencia), represents another trope of pictorialism, in which effect outweighs the landscape that is the vehicle by which effect is achieved (see Vicent Monzó and Pep Benlloch). It is not surprising that Galicia yielded a good number of landscapes, and that it was the area in which the painterly style reigned supreme perhaps longer than in any other single region. (It might be argued that it even dominated Galician photographic societies, almost as a shibboleth, through the 1940s.) The 1934 "Boirineo", by Andreu Mir Escudé is just one example. One of the pictorial photograpers who persisted longest in that style – another Galician – and who was surely one of the best to cultivate the style, was Inocencio Schmidt de las Heras (see King). As late as the late 1940s, he would make Galician views of this sort. In 1947, he made "Valle de Bens," an extraordinarily modern view for a pictorialist, for its having defied customary framing and for having made of scape a vertical, not horizontal phenomenon. (Such examples had been in evidence in Great Britain as early as the turn of the century; witness, for example, Clarence White's "Early Morning.")

Among landscape photographers in Spain, it is a Spanish pictorialist who stands out: José Ortiz Echagüe.[15] Brilliant technician, master of the painterly medium called Fresson pigment, Ortiz Echagüe was also one of Spain's very first airplane pilots and, eventually head of SEAT cars. As early as 1909, he used the airplane to his advantage, in order to achieve aerial scapes; a modern-day Guesdon, but with focus now on the land – his own land – as opposed to the cityscape, which had had its practical, as well as esthetic and sympathetic purposes, as Felipe II well knew when he commissioned Wyngaerde. In 1905, with his "Paisaje en el Río" (River and Countryside), Ortiz Echagüe anticipated the equally wonderful work of Schmidt de las Heras four decades later (Figure 9.1). "El Duero por Soria" (The Duero River Near Soria) (1910) convinces us of Ortiz Echagüe's sympathy with the land (Figure 9.2). In a facile, unthinking way, he is often evaluated as a Francoist toady (López Mondéjar 33). Thereby his pictorialist style (as opposed hypothetically to, say, a journalistic style, which presumes to be truer, but is not necessarily so) is seen as a brand of closet-rightism. I do not see it that way at all. Three views from 1935, when he was photographing for the second volume of his tetralogy, called *España, pueblos y paisajes* (Spain, Towns and Countryside Scenes) (1938) – "Montserrat," "Guadalest," and "Sierra de Grazalema" – are images by an artist working to discover, through photography, the essence of his own land. The title of another 1935 view gives away the motive: "Castilla, cerros y nubes" (Castile, Hills and Clouds), by which we might infer a search for the essence of Spain through the land. While photographing for the third volume of the tetralogy, *España mística* (Mystic Spain) (1943), landscape becomes incidental to "mystical" event, but perhaps no less thrilling ("Penitentes en Cuenca" (Penitents in Cuena)). By the time of his fourth volume, *España, castillos y alcázares* (Spain, Castles and Fortresses) (1956), land returns as subject, but only insofar as it is part of the fortress that is titular subject ("Huesa del Común"). Ortiz Echagüe set out to highlight his own world through the photograph, in order to lend order and essential definition to a Spain that was chaotic, both historically and in terms of current politics. Ortiz Echagüe had respectable followers (in another, later photographic style), such as Reinhart Wolf, who expressly acknowledged his debt to Ortiz Echagüe (*De*

Figure 9.1 José Ortiz Echagüe (1886–1980), "Paisaje en el río" 1905. © 2004 Artists Rights Society (ARS), New York/VEGAP, Madrid.

Figure 9.2 José Ortiz Echagüe (1886–1980), "El Duero por Soria" 1910. © 2004 Artists Rights Society (ARS), New York/VEGAP, Madrid.

España). Wolf's images of castles, from about the mid-1980s, are remarkable, but they are not quite the indigenous work of Ortiz Echagüe, who struggled through the camera to comprehend the Self. The protracted photographic activity of Ortiz Echagüe to classify, distinguish regionally, order visually, points to an undertaking rooted in existential need. It was more than a profession or an occupation, and it was certainly not tourism. It was even more than a response to a calling, more than an avocation. In photographing his own country in a systematic way, and focusing on different categories of subjects – castles, towns, regional garb, and ritual customs – he grew in his "Spanishness," while he interpreted, in his particular way, a Spain that was in a chaos difficult to comprehend otherwise.

True, during the Spanish Civil War, the pastoral landscape so common to pictorialism underwent the intrusion of elements of journalistic realism, as we can see in "Frente de Aragón" (The Aragonese Front) (1937) by Agustí Centelles, in which armed soldiers, goats, and a flock of sheep take over the countryside (reproduced in Fontcuberta 172). I would mention, also of the same era, the prodigious Nicolás de Lekuona.[16] Born in Guipúzcoa in 1913 and killed in the Civil War at age 23, he would have been one of Spain's most brilliant of twentieth-century artists. Painter and photographer, he ideated his own landscapes in photomontages-collages on rag-paper, as early as 1935. True landscapes of the mind, his inventions seemed to have little purpose beyond their consummate personalism, apart from their stunning grace and beauty. Lekuona's work signals that we do not have to wait until the 1970s and 1980s – a period in which a number of Spanish photographers cultivated depictions of their own fantasies – in order to find invented landscapes. Lekuona's images often amounted to remakings of a world so imperfect that the highly personal refashioning of that world would serve as artistic consolation for daily pain.

We should not feel uncomfortable in having to wait until the late nineteenth century or early twentieth in order to detect the indigenous cultivation of landscape photography in Spain. After all, it was part and parcel of the sensibility of the Institución Libre de Enseñanza and the Generación del '98, as we can so easily tell in the writings of "Azorín," for example. Similarly, we should not feel ill at ease with the fact that landscape photography in Spain – that landscape photography that was something more than touristic – should have been most and best cultivated in the pictorialist style. I have implied here that it is the critical miscomprehension of the sincere, existential aspect of Spanish pictorialism that could be at the root of the hesitation to admit pictorialism as the true seat of Spanish photographic landscapes. And, in Spain, that was a stylistic trend of the first half of the twentieth century, primarily.

Notes

1. Accompanied by Frederick Catherwood, a daguerreotypist and likely the first photographer of the Yucatan, John Lloyd Stephens wrote his incomparable *Incidents of Travel in Yucatan*, first published in 1843 and accompanied by engravings based on the daguerreotypes.
2. The deluxe edition, with fold-outs of some of the drawings, and with text by Richard L. Kagan, was published by Ediciones El Viso in 1986. Except for Galicia, Asturias, Cantabria, País Vasco, the Pyrenees and southern Levante, Wyngaerde depicted numerous cities and towns all over Spain.
3. "It needed two conditions, then, to turn a stick into our hobby horse: first, that its form made it just possible to ride on it; secondly – and perhaps decisively – that riding mattered" (Gombrich 7).

4. Many writings of William M. Ivins, Jr. imply this, but particularly to the point is his Chapter 6 ("Pictorial Statement without Syntax, the Nineteenth Century").
5. The Seville views by Vigier were printed under the title *Sevilla, 1851.*
6. This superb album is in the Gilman Collection (Metropolitan Museum, New York).
7. See Fontanella, "A Quiet Nook for these Practical Days." The information on this important photographer, who announced the availability of "seventy-one Andalusian views" is, sadly, scant, although the letter mentioned leaves no room for doubt that he had a falling-out with Frith of Reigate.
8. Berthelot and Webb get considerable attention in Vega de la Rosa, *Derroteros.* This excellent volume accompanied a photographic exhibit, and it is an eye-opener in respect to the present subject of landscape in the photography of Spain. Similarly, the work by Mulet concerning Mallorca is very suggestive for this particular subject.
9. The Locker, VillaAmil, and Roberts works referred to here are reproduced in Cabra Loredo, 94, 64 and 38, respectively).
10. Guesdon published views in *L'Illustration, Journal Universel.*
11. I describe the royal journey of Saboya in the facsimile publication of the Moliné and Albareda photographs, *Lleida 1871* (Gõni Gracenea).
12. My conclusion is not hasty, rather drawn after years of having studied Clifford and having written two books on him, the first with an essay by Gerardo F. Kurtz, in which the Guesdon relation is treated (Fontanella 1996, 1997).
13. The specific images by Zinsel, Benítez Tugores, and Ellerbeck were part of the aforementioned "Derroteros ... " exhibit (December 2002), but do not appear reproduced in the Vega de la Rosa book of that title. The Ellerbeck image can be found in Vega de la Rosa *Catalogar Islas* (33).
14. See the model study by Nancy Newhall. Nancy was Beaumont Newhall's first wife and died a premature and accidental death. The book on Emerson was her work.
15. For visual purposes, there is no modern edition comparable to the large-format volume published (in four different languages) by T.F. Editores which accompanied the comprehensive exhibition of Ortiz Echagüe photographs that opened in July 1998 in Barcelona. See my contribution to the volume, "Realzar el mundo" (Fontanella 1998). For a comprehensive view of Ortiz Echagüe, his work and methods, see Domeño Martínez de Morentin.
16. The great book on this photographer remains to be written. One overview is by Moya.

Works Cited

Bernard, Bruce. *Photodiscovery: Masterworks of Photography, 1840–1940*. New York: Harry N. Abrams, 1980.

Cabra Loredo, María Dolores. *Una puerta abierta al mundo: España en la litografía romántica*. Madrid: Museo Romántico, 1994.

Domeño Martínez de Morentín, Asunción. *La fotografía de José Ortiz-Echagüe: técnica, estética y temática*. Pamplona: Gobierno de Navarra and Universidad de Navarra, 2000.

Fontanella, Lee. "A Quiet Nook for these Practical Days." In *Shadow and Substance*. Ed. Kathleen Collins. Bloomfield Hills, MI: Amorphous Institute Press, 1990. 209–19.

—— *Charles Clifford: Fotógrafo de la España de Isabel II*. Madrid: El Viso, 1996.

—— *Charles Clifford: Fotógrafo en la corte de Isabel II*. Madrid: El Viso, 1997.

—— "Realzar el mundo." *Ortiz Echagüe*. Eds. Valentín Vallhonrat and Rafa Levenfeld. Madrid: T.F. Editores, 1998.

Fontcuberta, Joan, ed. *Idas y caos: Aspectos de las vanguardias fotográficas en España*. Madrid: Ministerio de Cultura, 1984.

Gombrich, Ernst. *Meditations on a Hobby Horse and Other Essays on the Theory of Art*. 2nd ed. London: Phaidon, 1965.

—— "Mirror and Map: Theories of Pictorial Representation." In *The Image and the Eye: Further Studies in The Psychology of Pictorial Representation*. Ithaca, N.Y.: Cornell/Phaidon, 1982. 172–214.

Goñi Gracenea, Xavier, ed. *Lleida 1871: La visita del rei Amadeu I de Savoia*. Lleida: Universidad de Lleida, 2000.

González, Ricardo. *Segovia en la fotografía del siglo XIX*. Segovia: Doblón, 1997.

Ivins, William M., Jr. "Pictorial Statement without Syntax, the Nineteenth Century." In *Prints and Visual Communication*. Cambridge: MIT Press, 1953. 113–134.

Kagan, Richard L. *Cuidades del siglo de oro: Las vistas españolas de Anton Van Den Wyngaerde*. Madrid: El Viso, 1986.

King, S. Carl. *Schmidt de las Heras: Fotografías 1944–1960*. A Coruña: Centro Galego de Artes da Imaxe, 1999.

López Mondéjar, Publio. *Las fuentes de la memoria, II: Fotografía y sociedad en España, 1900–1939*. Barcelona and Madrid: Lunwerg, 1992.

Moya, Adelina. *Nicolás de Lekuona: Obra fotográfica*. Bilbao: Museo de Bellas Artes, 1982.

Mulet, María Josep. *Fotografía a Mallorca, 1839–1936*. Barcelona and Madrid: Lunwerg, 2001.

Murray, J. *Murray's Views in Spain*. London: 1824.

Newhall, Nancy. P.H. *Emerson: The Fight for Photography as a Fine Art*. New York: Aperture, 1975.

Pérez de Villa Amil, Genaro. *España artística y monumental*. Paris: Lemercier, 1842–50.

Roberts, David. *Picturesque Sketches in Spain: Taken during the Years 1832–1833*. London: Hodgson and Graves, 1837.

Stephens, John L. *Incidents of Travel in Yucatan*. New York: Dover, 1963/1843. 2 Vols.

Teixidor Cadenas, Carlos. *La fotografía en Canarias y Madeira*. Madrid: Carlos Teixidor Cadenas, 1999.

Vega de la Rosa, Carmelo. *Derroteros de la fotografía en Canarias, 1839–2000*. Santa Cruz de Tenerife: Caja Canarias, 2002.

—— *Catalogar Islas: Canarias según Ellerbeck*. Tenerife: Centro de Fotografía, 2000.

Vicent Monzó, Josep and Pep Benlloch, eds. *Vicente Martínez Sanz, 1894–1945*. Valencia: Generalitat Valenciana, 1985.

Vigier, Joseph. *Sevilla, 1851*. Sevilla: Sociedad de Bibliófilos Andaluces, 1977.

Wolf, Reinhart. *De España*. Madrid: El Viso, 1982.

–10–

From Engraving to Photo: Cross-cut Technologies in the Spanish Illustrated Press

Lou Charnon-Deutsch

The introduction of photography and later of photomechanical technologies in late-nineteenth-century illustrated magazines was transformative, easing the transition from limited run productions catering largely to the monied classes to mass produced periodicals targeting a middle-class readership. This chapter examines this transformation in two of Madrid's most popular periodicals during the thirty-year period from 1880 to 1910, widely considered the heyday of Spanish illustrated weeklies.[1] Launched in 1857, *El Museo Universal* ran until 1869 when it folded into Abelardo de Carlos' *La Ilustración Española y Americana* (*IEA*), the most lavish and prestigious Spanish illustrated magazine of the nineteenth century that published its last issue in 1921. The more affordable and widely read *Blanco y Negro* (*ByN*) debuted in 1891 and ran until 1936, outlasting in its first series the *Ilustración Española* by fifteen years.[2] Issues that arise in comparing these two publications include: the date of the first images influenced by photography and the technology used to reproduce them; the impact of photography on the engraving workforce prior to and following the invention of photomechanical reproduction; the thematic and political content of the first photographs; the novel compositional techniques that distinguished photographs from engravings; the printed quality of the first photomechanically reproduced images vis-à-vis those of the engravings that continued to be published alongside of them for several decades; editorial comments about new photo technologies; the explosion of photographic reportage in the 1890s; and the reasons for the eclipse of the large format illustrated weeklies.

The first successful photographs, in the form of direct-positive daguerreotypes on metal plates, were produced in Spain in 1839 (Fontanella 7).[3] Because of the time it took to expose the plates (up to ninety minutes), the first images typically were of buildings and other stationary objects, executed by scientists and other intellectuals who regarded themselves as experimenters and did not conceive of becoming professional photographers. Their concern was with fidelity to the original, technological advances in photography emulsions, and the new media's scientific and social applications rather than its aesthetic properties. Coming several decades later, the first professional photographers were foreigners such as R.P. Napper who traveled about Spain selling cameras and training purchasers in their use. In the early decades of photography, development processes were cumbersome and therefore impractical outside the studio. Field photography only became feasible once daguerreotypes were substituted by wet collodion emulsifiers in the 1850s, which permitted shorter exposure times (López Mondéjar 79) and inaugurated the age of modern photojournalism. The first field photographers lacked an extensive market for their product, since photoengraving had not yet been refined and it was impossible to produce mass quantities of their photographs for use in the printing press. Nevertheless, they represented the earliest vanguard of press reporters who scoured the world to produce exotic scenes which they sold to magazines whose sketchers and engravers then copied and reproduced them using one of the traditional engraving techniques outlined below.

When improved technology reduced exposure times from minutes to seconds, photographic portraiture became the rage in Spain as it did elsewhere in Europe. By the 1860s, in addition to individual portraits, well-to-do clients could purchase albums of household scenes, fine art, buildings, monuments, and provincial types produced by photo studios that sprang up in the major urban centers of Madrid, Barcelona and Sevilla. Although their number cannot compare with those in France and England, by 1863 there were thirty-nine photography studios in Spain. The most popular product of these establishments were miniatures, album-sized portraits, and especially *cartes de visites*, calling cards with a visual reminder of the caller's identity fixed on a cardboard surface.[4] While the market for these cards was not vast owing to the relatively small class of Spaniards as yet able to afford this luxury, calling cards were the first mass produced photo images prior to the use of photography in newspapers and magazines. The early photographers working in studio settings emulated portrait art, producing unique images of subjects posed according to the conventions of portrait painting and engraving. Eventually people flocked to studios not only to have their own photographs taken but also to purchase images of famous actors, bullfighters, and royalty. Others without the means to purchase these relatively expensive items could gape at the windows where the albums and portraits were on rotating display.

Ever since photography was invented, magazine editors and book publishers dreamed of being able to apply it to the mass printing of images, but the two technologies – photography and mechanical reproduction – were not initially compatible. Despite the fact that by the 1860s the photograph was becoming a much more widely distributed product, its use in the press was still limited by technical obstacles. There are hundreds of different methods for the serial printing of images, but until the late 1800s they fell into three basic types depending on the method for getting ink to paper: relief printing or xylography (usually woodblocks), grooved printing or intaglio (incisions made on stone or metal plates), and planography or lithography (printing from a flat surface). All three methods predated photography – the hurdle was to adapt photographic processes in order to imprint images on printing blocks or plates, thereby bypassing several labor-intensive steps. This accomplished, the role of the sketcher could be eliminated from the reproductive process as well as that of the hand engraver who in the past would have manually rendered the sketcher's creation on blocks using various tools, for example the burin (the engraver's wedge-shaped cutting tool) or other elements (usually acid) to cut into the material and create the necessary printing matrix or plate. It was not until the last decade of the nineteenth century that photomechanical reproduction achieved through heliogravure, or the combining of intaglio printing and photography, made this possible. Yet, as this chapter will show, the impact of photography was felt in the illustrated press long before technical advances and procedures of photoengraving completely replaced other engraving techniques in the printed press.[5]

When the highly specialized enterprise of mechanical engraving and the equally complex new field of photography began to merge, it was in order to share images not technologies. That is, magazine artists often copied photographs when producing their engravings for the press. Magazine engravings often listed as "taken from photographs" became an important draw of the illustrated press beginning in mid-century. It is no accident that around the same time that field photography became professionalized, in the1850s and 1860s, the first mass distributed illustrated magazines began to appear in Europe and the United States: in Great Britain, the *Illustrated London News* (1842), in France *L'Illustration* (1843), and in the United States *Harpers Weekly* (1857). The instant success of these magazines was owed largely to improved engraving techniques and machinery that facilitated mass produced images, and not to the process of photoengraving (that is, the production of etched plates by photographic means). And yet the photograph was from the start an important element in their production since it inspired engravers to achieve more realistic images. The use of photographs, even in this indirect way, lent the magazines a contemporary appeal and it also made the job of engravers and sketchers easier, thus saving the publishers time and money. Photography became in a sense a shortcut to art. Original artwork no longer had to be delivered to the workshop to be sketched: a photo of an original would do just as well. Sketch artists no longer had to go to a museum, an artist's studio, or the field to capture an image, they could sit at a desk and copy from a photograph that was startling in its detail. Artists' knowledge of perspective and composition could be scant as long as they were skilled artisans.

The intermediate photo was a time- and money-saving device even though photographic technology at this point in Spain was in no position to interface with lithographic, xylographic or intaglio reproductive engraving. The method of choice for producing print and image together from 1850 to 1890 was either xylographic (an engraved woodblock that was combined with moveable type and inserted in a large frame and pressed together) or intaglio (which used a metal plate whose grooves had been produced through an electrolysis process). With their limited resources, however, Spanish printing houses could not produce enough printing plates and blocks to satisfy an apparently insatiable taste for large format line engravings. As a result, many of the fine arts plates used to produce images in the pages of the *Ilustración Española y Americana* and other similar illustrated magazines were imported form abroad, signed by engravers such as Stéfane Pannemaker of Paris, or Richard Bong of Berlin, among many others.[6] By importing hundreds of plates from France and Germany *Ilustración Española* could keep its workforce at a minimum and its pages filled with high quality engravings at a price that was relatively inexpensive (Fontbona 75). However, this limited the number of prints engraved after Spanish painters or sketch artists and consequently lent the magazine an international rather than national character.[7]

Even though in the early years of the *Ilustración Española y Americana* (from 1857 to 1869 when it was called *Museo Universal*) the use of photography was with rare exceptions limited to this secondary role, its editors took an avid interest in the new photo techniques, quickly understanding their potential utility.[8] In August of 1858 (Volume 2: 115) Felipe Picatoste y Rodríguez offered readers of *Ilustración Española y Americana* a biography of Daguerre, praising his 1822 diorama in Paris'[9] and summarizing the scientific and medical uses of the new technology: "Pocos descrubrimientos han hecho en el público impresión tan viva como la del daguerreotipo. Los amantes de las ciencias y de lo maravilloso no han experimentado nunca ansiedad mayor que la que causó el admirable invento por medio del cual pueden reproducirse cuantos objetos se presentan a nuestra vista con su más minuciosos pormenores" (115). Picatoste marveled at the fact that images collected recently in Egypt and Palestine could be projected on a stereoscope creating the impression of three dimensionality which was one of the most exciting photographic applications of all time in part because it could be owned by private individuals. With a note of envy Picatoste reported that in Paris and London magazines were already offering these "fotografías estereoscópicas" as a bonus to their readers.[10] Although Picatoste understood photography's enormous potential, ("¿Quién sabe hasta dónde se llegará todavía?" he asked) he did not conjecture at that time that it would invade the world of mechanical reproduction as well as that of print journalism. Printing and photography were in separate domains, the former that of ideas and the latter that of the senses: "La imprenta vino a fijar las ideas: el daguerreotipo dará permanencia a todo lo que caiga bajo la inspección del más importante de los sentidos."

Already as Picatoste was writing about the future of the technology, the photo was making its first visual appearance in magazines, not, as pointed out above, as an actual photo but as an engraving based on or taken from a photographic image. In the same year as his article, 1858, *El Museo Universal* announced the collaboration of Charles Clifford, one of Queen Isabel's favorite photographers, who, along with other professional photographers like Jean Laurent and graphic chroniclers like Juan Comba later in the 1860s and 1870s after the death of Clifford, would supply the magazine with hundreds of photographs that had been shot all over Spain, part of the vogue of photo albums of local types, typography and constructions.[11] From 1860 to 1880 many engravings listed in the magazine captions as taken from a photograph did not differ radically from other engravings taken from original sketches. For example, a well-executed 1858 image in *El Museo* (2 (August 15 1858): 117) of the "Patio de las Muñecas" in the Seville Alcázar, according to the caption, was taken after a photo by Pizarro. Since at the time the only light source was available light, the engraver added detail to the inner rooms of the patio that would likely have been obscured in the original photograph. A sketch of a human subject demonstrates this practice more clearly. Figure 10.1 shows a very heroic General Prim taken from a photograph that appeared in 1860 (*El Museo* 4 (February 5, 1860): 18). The engraver unmistakably took liberties with the original both in the foreground and background renderings and shadings, as well as the figure of the horse and Prim himself. In these cases sketcher-engravers were simply using the photograph as a subject that in their hands could be transformed into a more artistic, and often more heroic, composition.

It is also clear, however, that by the 1870s the photo original was beginning to have an impact on engraving technique not just on the subject matter of engravings. By then some sketchers, in an implied acknowledgment of the popularity of a technology that would eventually cost them their livelihood, were striving to make their sketches appear more like the original photograph which resulted in a radical departure in the use of shadow. A comparison between an original photograph entitled "Bohémiens ou *gitanos*" by Jean Laurent from his 1872 collection shot *in situ* entitled *Coustumes et Coutumes d'Espagne. Etudes d'après Nature* (*La Andalucía del siglo XIX*, p. 220) and an engraved sketch entitled "Habitantes de la provincia de Segovia" produced after a photo by the Laurent Studios that appeared in the *Ilustración Española* in 1880 (24 (January 22, 1880): 48) demonstrates this influence. Compared with the photo, a composition that in Laurent's case typically sought to imitate the fine line sketch (Fontanella 22), the sketch is highly stylized. However, the engraver has conscientiously reproduced the subjects' squinting eyes and the deep shadows on both the man and the woman's face. He has also included background shadows that a sketcher working from an oil painting or in a studio would not likely have included since they have no recognizable referent. The aim, then, was to lend the engraving the same feeling of *d'après nature,* a practice of which Laurent was understandably proud.

Figure 10.1 "General Prim, jefe del cuarto cuerpo del ejército de África." *El Museo Universal* 4 (February 5, 1860): 18.

If the engraver was very skilled, the angle of lighting, copied exactly, would produce a very compelling image such as the engraving of "Unas segadoras en la campiña de Córdoba" (Figure 10.2) (*IEA* 20 (July 15, 1876): 24), after a photo also produced by the Laurent Studios. It seems that some engravers were attempting to emulate photography even when they reproduced sketches not taken from photographs. For example, Figure 10.3, a detail from an engraving taken from a pencil sketch by Alfonse Legros, entitled "La pequeña María" (*IEA* 21 (January 30, 1877): 69), is a combination of lines and dots evoking a rather haunting immediacy when compared with the more common portrait engravings of fictional characters whose soft lines and shadows were the norm in most images published that same year. This is before the use of half-tone photoengraving; the stippled effect of María's face was achieved with a drypoint stylus or some other incision tool or chemical biting into the plate, and it is even posssible that no phottography at all was involved in the entire process.

Numerically speaking, the most ubiquitous images of the *Museo Universal* magazine were engravings of large-scale, man-made objects such as bridges, ships, aqueducts, dams, ruins, and railroads, following the convention of printed papers prior to the second half of the nineteenth century. Altogether Volume 2, 1858, of *El*

Figure 10.2 "Unas segadoras en la campiña de Córdoba." *Ilustración Española y Americana* 20 (July 15, 1876): 24.

Figure 10.3 Alfonse Legros, "La pequeña María." *Ilustración Española y Americana* 21 (January 30, 1877): 69.

Museo contained forty such images, surpassing all other categories.[12] Photography helped to prolong this convention because at first moving objects, especially action scenes, were difficult to shoot owing to the long exposure periods required. Beginning in the 1870s, however, the fine line engraving that had been used for centuries to picture monuments and buildings bore the mark of the photograph in terms of perspective and shadow. Depending on how much the sketcher decided to tamper with the photograph in his line rendering, the effects are especially visible in the use of shadow. For example, in Figure 10.4, an 1878 engraving of the "Iglesia de Santa María del Mar" (*IEA* 22 (April 22, 1878): 257) taken from a photo by Jean Laurent, clearly emulated the photograph from which it was drawn. In the foreground can be seen the deep shadows of other buildings that engulf the upper portion of the atrium and arched windows, which would have been an unconventional effect at the turn of the century. The effect is especially dramatic when viewed alongside the idealized image of Segovia's Alcázar (Figure 10.5), printed in that same year (*IEA* 22 August 8, 1878): 76). Here the artist-engraver has enhanced the most "virile" portions of the castle to accentuate its upper thrust and guide the eyes to its rounded towers and away from its foreground.

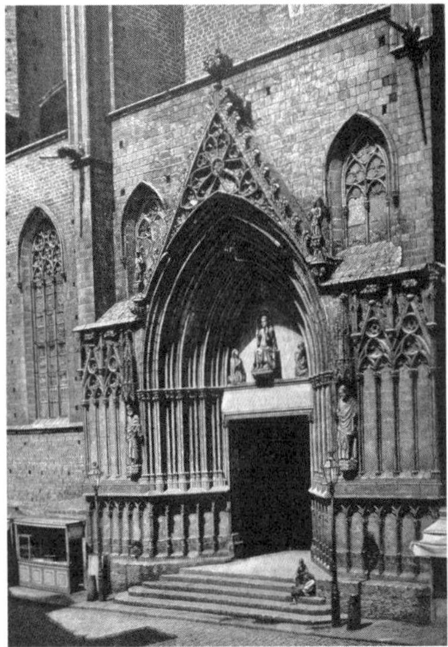

Figure 10.4 "Iglesia de Santa María del Mar." *Ilustración Española y Americana* 22 (April 22, 1878): 257.

Figure 10.5 "Segovia, Estado actual del Alcázar." *Ilustración Española y Americana* 22 (August 8, 1878): 76.

Comparing the Church of Santa María del Mar with Segovia's Alcázar, it is clear that the photograph helped put into evidence the mythologizing effects of the engraving: side by side with the engraving, the photograph cloaked itself in objectivity and immediacy. It would not have escaped viewers of photographs such as Figure 10.6 shot around 1863 by R.P. Napper (López Mondéjar 42) that "real" Gypsies radically diverged from conventional artistic images. For example Jules Lefebre's painting of the famed "Mignon" (*IEA* 22 (October 15, 1878): n.p.) engraved by Adolphe Pannemaker (Figure 10.7) contained many conventional Orientalist touches such as the open blouse, musical instruments, and the wistful look. From the 1870s to the turn of the century most illustrated magazines helped readers to interpret the countenance of such figures as "Mignon" in the section called "Nuestros grabados." For example, in his comments the editor of *La Ilustración Española y Americana* makes us privy to Mignon's most secret thoughts, praising her for being the perfect expression of her literary version. In other words, as a visual she is parasitical on the text *Mignon* while the editor's interpretation is parasitical on her engraved image. This represents a key moment in the use of images in serial publications: the image was still often seen as accessory to a text, but at the same time a second text offered compensatory connotations that were not always obvious in the graphic itself. The interplay between text and image was at this juncture very complex, especially in the case of interpretive engraving such as this.

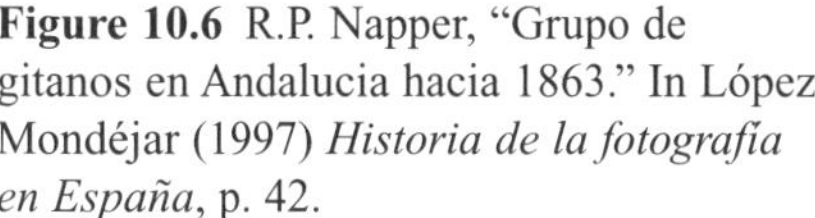

Figure 10.6 R.P. Napper, "Grupo de gitanos en Andalucia hacia 1863." In López Mondéjar (1997) *Historia de la fotografía en España*, p. 42.

Figure 10.7 Jules Lefebre, "Mignon." *Ilustración Española y Americana* 22 (October 15, 1878): n.p.

The photograph, in contrast, invariably carried a caption but was judged not in need of interpretation because it aimed to produce what Roland Barthes called a "continuous message" (17), by which he meant an image that professed to be a mechanical analogue of reality. Co-existing with the engraving, the truth claims of photography seemed at the time entirely irrefutable; their very juxtaposition within the same media helped to foster the notion of photographic realism. For instance 10.8, a 1905 photomontage of the Sultan of Morocco (*IEA* 49 (July 8, 1905): 12) is subtitled "Fantasía y realidad." The caption clarifies that we are to understand the photograph on the right, a continuous tone image photomechanically reproduced, as real, and the image to the left, an artist's rendering that also has been photomechanically reproduced but that started off as a sketch, as a *fantasía*. In the engraving the Sultan's horse lunges forward in a heroic leap while the rider thrusts his lance skyward. The real Sultan in contrast is huddled in a cloak up to his shoulders; his grey beard and squinting eyes add to the perception of his advanced age. In comparison with the gravity-defying steed of the engraving, his nearly stationary horse looks singularly unheroic as well. Thus the photograph has the humanizing effect of demystifying Arab prowress, but it simultaneously casts the Arab Sultan as a pathetic figure, with connotations about the diminished importance of Arab leaders. Significantly, in that same year *Ilustración Española y*

Americana eliminated altogether its "Nuestros grabados" section, in part because by that time line engravings were becoming more sparse but also because photographs were increasingly embedded in the features that they illustrated, and apparently comments either on the photograph's creator, or the image's verism or artistic merit, were deemed superfluous. The photograph, whether photomechanically produced or used as a model by a sketch artist or engraver, had come of age.

One of the most obvious advantages of the photograph was its ability to capture large groups of people who previously would not have been sketched together owing to the difficulty of gathering large groups of people in one place for the time required to sketch them. With fast-paced improvement in photo processes, especially of dry plate processes that quickly replaced the more cumbersome wet plates, it was suddenly possible to "see" what groups of colonizers, adventurers, or indigenous peoples in Europe's far flung foreign empires looked like, and the fascination for group shots grew in the 1880s and 1890s. Figure 10.9, a typical group image published in 1880 (*IEA* 24 (February 22, 1880): 117) is of Lesseps' Commission that presided over the building of the Panama canal, photographed on location by Alfred Orillac. This is still a hand-touched engraving, not a photoengraving, but it demonstrates that the magazine's engravers were becoming very adept at emulating photographs. Nevertheless, they have been careful to insure that each man's face is clearly visible and have thus enhanced the portraiture status of the image. On the other hand, if a shot were of an anonymous group of individuals

Figure 10.8 "Vista de un campamento marroquí – El sultán en marcha – Fantasía – Realidad." *Ilustración Española y Americana* 49 (July 8, 1905):12.

whose identity mattered less than their collective role, engravers might feel more comfortable keeping the shadows that the sun would have produced in the photo, in order to achieve a more natural or photo-like image. Figure 10.10, for instance, shows an engraving after a photo of a group of soldiers being honored for military valor in Cuba in 1895 (*IEA* 39 (May 30, 1895): 329). By grouping the soldiers in the noonday sun wearing their hats, the photographer has obscured their faces but accentuated their shoulders, whereas in the shot of the Lessep commission the men's heads (and therefore individual identities) are emphasized. Not needing to individualize the visages of the soldiers, the magazine's engraver has conscientiously translated the shadows of the original, and consequently the effect of on-location photography is very pronounced in the engraving.

In the 1890s magazine editors were increasingly eager to have readers appreciate the difference between photo and engraving. Still, in the case of images taken "from" a photograph it is not always possible to tell what information was contained in the original and what enhancements were subsequently introduced by the sketch artist and the engraver working from photographs. No written information regarding the sketch artist's tampering is available, so conclusions about this common practice remain speculative. For example, the two images of Figure 10.11, both shot at the same time on the same ship, were juxtaposed on

Figure 10.9 Alfredo Orillac, "Panamá. Individuos qaue componen la comisión de estudios, presidida por Mr. de Lesseps." *Ilustración Española y Americana* 24 (February 22, 1880): 117.

Figure 10.10 Victoriano Otero, "Cuba. Grupo de soldados que defendieron valerosamente el poblado de 'Dos Caminos' premiados con la Cruz del Mérito Militar." *Ilustración Española y Americana* 39 (May 30, 1895): 329.

the same page in the October 22, 1895 issue of *Ilustración Española y Americana* (228). Both images started as photographs and both were photomechanically reproduced, but the image on the left has been touched up while that on the right is a photomechanically reproduced photo showing no evidence of an engraver's intervention. The mood of the men is considerably more jubilant in the engraving than in the photograph and one could speculate that the sketcher-engraver was aiming for a more patriotic appeal that the photographer could not as readily stage. The two images accompanied a news article on the Montevideo, written by a spirited patriot who was perhaps contemplating the engraving rather than the photograph when he exulted: "Va aquella gente a la guerra como a una fiesta, cantando unos, bromeando otros, contentos todos" (226). Although it is logical to conclude from these two images that a hand-worked engraving was ideologically more suited to furthering national interests since the engraver could subtly emphasize certain portions of a photograph he was reproducing, it should be remembered that the untouched photograph could serve the same ends. The two technologies were cooperative in producing war reportage such as this that helped the government to galvanize support for the nation's war efforts. Either way the photograph brought home the realities of Spain's imperial struggles even when it served only as an intermediary image that was translated by sketch artists.

By the late nineteenth century the classic verticality of line engravings of structures and typography, often devoid of human subjects, was yielding place to

Figure 10.11 Chute and Brook, "Antes de la salida." "Adiós al Río de la Plata. Montevideo. Embarco de voluntarios españoles para la guerra de Cuba, en el vapor "San Francisco" de la Compañía transatlántica." *Ilustración Española y Americana* (October 22, 1895): 228.

an expansive photographic horizontality. Already in the 1870s multiple negatives and wide angle lenses popularized large panoramas of Spanish rural and town scenography. In the case of *Ilustración Española,* such vistas increasingly included crowds of anonymous subjects shot with a camera in the field but still rendered by a sketch artist. Figure 10.12 (*IEA* 37 November 15, 1893): 300) is typical of 1890s group shots, in this instance giving witness to an "entusiasta despedida" of troops from Vitoria to Melilla. At the same time more intimate group shots began taking on an unposed informality that would have been inconceivable a few decades earlier. Figure 10.13, "La salida. Madrid banquete de las armas (del natural)" (*IEA* 38 (March 15, 1894): 144) is significant because of its compositional unstructuredness and because it represents a technically complex stage between photo and engraving. This image is clearly in the realm of photojournalism, capturing an important, unstaged action shot with a camera, something that the *Ilustración Española y Americana* was not noted for and which may have contributed to its demise. The image started out as a photograph which was then photomechanically reproduced, rendering continuous tones instead of lines in some areas of the image. However, the engraver has not entirely disappeared from the picture: he has taken the heliograph, or photomechanically produced plate, and touched up the architectural detail and some of the clothing to provide a more pleasing composition because the photomechanical process at this point was still in its infant stages and did not always render wide tonal swaths very well. The qualitative difference between photograph and hand-worked engraving is especially evident when similar objects are printed using two different methods. For example, in its May 22, 1905 issue dedicated to Zurbarán, *Ilustración Española* offered a sampling of both, indirectly making a statement regarding its stubborn use of traditional engraving techniques, when other magazines were relying increasingly on untouched photomechanical reproduction. When the photograph of Zurbarán's "Aparición de San Pedro Apóstol a San Pedro Nolasco" (308) is compared with the engraving of his "Santa Catalina" the differences are striking: the image resembling a sketch is far superior to the untouched photoengraving both in clarity and the reproduction of dark and grey areas which appear muddy in the photo. In other words, photographic processes could not always live up to the ideal of total transparency and magazine editors, by juxtaposing technologies, could make a case for the aesthetic as well as the realistic appeal of the line engraving.

Figure 10.12 Vicente Echavarri, Gonzalo Arregui. "Entusiasta despedida hecha por el pueblo y las autoridades a las tropas del Segundo Regimiento de Artillería de Montaña a su partida para Melilla, el 3 del Actual." *Ilustración Española y Americana* 37 (November 15, 1893): 300.

Capturing rapid action had long been one of early photographers' most important desiderata. As dry emulsion methods were refined permitting the use of less cumbersome field equipment, and as exposure times consequently decreased from minutes to seconds, activities shot in the field became more varied because photographers could now venture into more precarious locales – notably, war zones in Cuba and the Philippines in the 1890s. Even with improved technologies, however, engraving convention continued to influence photography: posing and composition were very much on the mind of the photographer even in what counted as spontaneous action shots. A comparison of three war shots demonstrates the levels of photographic composing that were commonplace during this period. Figure 10.14 is an engraving taken from a photo shot in the jungle in Cuba in 1895 (*IEA* 39 (December 15, 1895): 353). It could have been the engraver who tampered with the original to produce the pleasing circle of faces surrounded by lush greenery, although the photographer might also have had a hand in it by posing his subjects for heightened emotional effect. The result is an heroic portrait more than a battle scene. In the war photo taken in Santiago de Cuba (Figure 10.15) in 1897 (*IEA* 41 (December 22, 1897): 392), the photographer and probably

Figure 10.13 "La salida. Madrid. Banquete de las armas de infantería (del natural)." *Ilustración Española y Americana* 38 (March 15, 1894): 144.

not the engraver likely composed his shot by posing subjects in what seem implausible positions if this were an authentic battle scene. In contrast the third war image (Figure 10.16), a photomechanically reproduced photograph (*IEA* 39 (November 22, 1895): 293), also shot in Cuba, shows a more likely battle scenario whose composition is controlled by events, not, or at least not entirely, by the photographer.

Although its highly refined graphics continued to demonstrate that photomechanical engraving was still no match for the engraver's manual expertise, after the turn of the century the *Ilustración Española y Americana* went into decline, ceasing publication in 1921. According to Jean-Michel Desvois (343) this was because it lacked the capital of competitors like *Blanco y Negro*, which had purchased the newest German presses and hired operators from Germany to man them. *Blanco y Negro*, for the most part, used almost exclusively photomechanically reproduced images, while the *Ilustración* stuck stubbornly to the more traditional xylographic techniques.[13] In 1907 its editors justified their preference for the older techniques by claiming that xylography "eternamente preconizará, entre todas las evoluciones del siglo, su eterna y reconocida superioridad" (quoted in 150 años de fotografia 84). Another reason cited by Desvois is the competitors' lavish use of color compared with *Ilustración Española y Americana*'s "ausencia de color y su didactismo, frente a la ligereza de sus competidores" (347). Desvois

Figure 10.14 "La guerra en Cuba – guerrilla de tropas españolas en manigua." *Ilustración Española y Americana* 39 (December 15, 1895): 353.

Figure 10.15 "La guerra en Cuba – Guerrilla defendiendo el paso de un convoy en Santiago de Cuba" *Ilustración Española y Americana* 41 (December 22, 1897): 392.

Figure 10.16 "Campamento de Alto Songo (Santiago de Cuba) – Una guerrilla de descanso." *Ilustración Española y Americana* 43 (November 22, 1895): 293.

is correct about the editorial content but not about the use of color, a mistaken notion also perpetuated by Gómez Aparicio who claimed that *Blanco y Negro* was the first weekly to produce color graphics in 1897 (613). In its first years of publication, *Blanco y Negro* produced no color images, while *Ilustración* that same year offered its readers a half-dozen delicately colored "chromotypogravures," full-page bichromatographic reproductions of works by foreign artists such as that of Figure 10.17 which was produced from plates imported from France.[14] Because these images were either inserted as unnumbered pages or printed on high quality paper that blocked the print on the reverse of the page from bleeding into the

Figure 10.17 Corcos, "Fiel mensajera" *Ilustración Española y Americana* 35 (July 30, 1891): n.p.

image, they were suitable for framing, and editors often invited readers to extract them from the magazine for decorative purposes.

Color represented an extravagant expense but it added beauty and exoticism to the magazine. In accordance with convention, it was therefore coded as something high tone, frivolous and feminine. From 1890 to 1900, all of the chromo-typogravures of the *Ilustración Española y Americana* were of aristocratic women stepping out, well-dressed children, or charming and elegant domestic scenes. By contrast *Blanco y Negro* did not fully develop its chromatic photoengraving skills until later. Its first timid use of color in 1898 was in monochrome photoengravings (Carrete Parrondo et al. 458), and even when at the turn of the century it expanded its use of color (bichromotography in 1897, trichromatic images in 1899 and shortly after cuadrichromal images) (Desvois 347), the hues were often separated, the red inks casting an unnatural hue over many subjects, and the greens faded and unnatural. Yet *Blanco y Negro* enjoyed a huge success long before it refined its use of color printing. Consequently the answer to the riddle of its popularity and the demise of its competitor *La Ilustración Española y Americana* has to lie mainly in content and reader taste, rather than format and technical refinement. For one thing, although at first women also predominated in *Blanco y Negro*'s color engravings, its many and varied images of working- and middle-class women appealed to a wider readership. Even though *Blanco y Negro* followed the lead of other illustrated magazines in reserving color for the supposedly more "colorful" sex its populist appeal and inexpensive subscription allowed it to expand its local market at a time when the costly *Ilustración* was losing readers.

It is also not the case that the *Ilustración Española y Americana* was not using advertisements to help defray printing costs, as Desvois suggests. Advertising appeared in its very earliest numbers. By the late 1890s it began using photography to advertise products such as imitation pearl necklaces sold by Kepta, or Racahout de los Arabes Delangrenier, a children's breakfast drink imported from Paris. But by 1907, evidently to reduce costs, its two to four page advertisement supplement was printed on cheaper paper either appended to the end or unglamorously inserted as a protective sheath around the issue. By contrast, *Blanco y Negro*'s advertisements were much more "nuts and bolts" (false teeth, stoves, baby carriages, etc.) and considerably more numerous, leading some to suggest that the magazine had been created simply to sell goods.[15] By the turn of the century it also included a section called "Anuncios telegráficos," brief and inexpensive ads that included real estate listings charging one peseta for ads of between one and ten words, and ten céntimos for every word beyond that. *Blanco y Negro* was also one of the first magazines to offer photographs of dress models. In contrast, the more staid *Ilustración Española* relegated dress ads to its sister publication *La Moda Ilustrada*. Its more dignified pages appealed especially to a clientele interested in world events, fine art, scientific discoveries, and famous men. In fact, portraits of distinguished men, only a minor presence in the early years of *El Museo Universal*, became the dominant graphic feature of *Ilustración Española y Americana* in its last years, surpassing the number of images of man-made constructions and second only in number to line engravings of works of art. As Claude Le Bigot (145), speaking about the editorial content, put it, "el panteón de celebridades es ante todo un universo de varones." Women figured heavily in fine art engravings, but the number of photographs, sketches or art portraits of real women was nil.

Desvois is correct in pointing out that the much cheaper *Blanco y Negro* (twenty céntimos in 1891 compared with the expensive one peseta for *La Ilustración*) was a great draw for readers, but what he does not emphasize and which is fundamental in explaining the eclipse of the *Ilustración* in favor of *Blanco y Negro* (*ByN*) was its reader appeal in other ways. Significantly the magazine appealed more to families with an emphasis on modern life and its vicissitudes which were often depicted with cartoon figures. Beginning in the mid-1890s its "Sección Recreativa" offered a pot-pourri of word puzzles, charades, chess moves, and jokes that appealed to customers of all ages and lasted for many years. Instead of serialized novels it offered what it called *novelas telegráficas*, short stories that could be read in a sitting. It had a much more contemporary feel, with occasional features on living conditions such as the photo in Figure 10.18, captioned "La miseria en Andalucía" (*ByN* 4 (June 9, 1894) cover). Yet scenes of poverty were rare, far outnumbered by catastrophe scenes which were becoming a mainstay in magazines devoted to photo journalism.

Unlike many Spanish periodicals, including the vast majority of women's magazines, *Blanco y Negro* occasionally took a pro-feminist stance, for example in its article "El feminismo" (540 (September 7, 1901): n.p.), which attributed women's intellectual advancement to the feminist movement and indirectly called for equal rights reforms. This does not represent an editorial position on feminism, it should be noted, since just as many other articles were devoted to more conservative positions. While it stretched its artists to offer heroic sketches of those "Luchando por la patria,"[16] its wartime photography offered a greater naturalism and immediacy lacking in its competitors (*ByN* 5 (November 23, 1895): n.p) since it primarily used photomechanical processes. Even though technically its photographs were not as accomplished as its larger format competitors like *Ilustración Española*, it was from the beginning a much more inclusive magazine. For example, even in its wartime reportage the role of women was not forgotten as in Figure 10.19 (*ByN* 5 (November 30, 1895), n.p.), an image of the *cantinera* Dolores Cisnero. Nothing was better for the tired or wounded soldier according to the report accompanying article, than to hear "ese dulce eco de la voz femenina de la cantinera del bataillon."

Finally, *Blanco y Negro* fostered a star system through countless promotional images of actors and other performers often combining photographed heads with

Blanco y Negro
REVISTA ILUSTRADA

AÑO IV | MADRID, 9 DE JUNIO DE 1894 | NÚM. 162

LA MISERIA EN ANDALUCÍA

Figure 10.18 "La miseria en Andalucía" *Blanco y Negro* 4 (June 9, 1894) cover.

cartoon bodies. All turn-of-the-century illustrated magazines doted on the monarchy of England and Spain, and *Blanco y Negro*, with its numerous photographs of royalty, was no exception. But it also created other kinds of royalty, like the queens of the carnival or the kings of the bullring who were painted, sketched, engraved and photographed by Spanish artists and artisans instead of Germans or French, thus lending the magazine a much more local flavor and catering to the patriotic feelings whipped up at the end of the century. For dramatic effect, photographs were often cropped as in Figure 10.20 (ByN 4 (July 7, 1894): n.p.), eliminating distracting background and forcing viewers to zero in on the figure of interest, an uncommon montage in the more sedate large format illustrated magazines such as *Ilustración Artística* or *Ilustración Española y Americana* that practiced very little cropping. By the turn of the century, every article in *Blanco y Negro*, no matter how brief, was illustrated with a sketch or cropped photo. Although *Blanco y Negro*'s format remained half the size of the bulky *Ilustración Española*, its photographs became very professional looking and more numerous. This suited the evolving practices of new photojournalism with its obsession with catastrophic events that called for photographic validation.

Figure 10.19 Lebrón, "Dolores Cisnero, Cantinera del Bataillón de Pavía. *Blanco y Negro* 5 (November 30, 1895): n.p.

The *Ilustración Española y Americana*, meanwhile, had reached a level of refinement that surpassed that of its rivals, as can be seen in the train wreck photo in Figure 10.21 (51 (December 8, 1907): 336). It was therefore poised to become the twentieth-century Spanish magazine of great photographic achievement (the equivalent of *Look* or *Life* magazine in the United States, for example) but it chose a different path. Clinging to its traditional content, it continued to offer its readers images, now mostly photographs, of famous men or pretentious and retrievable art, like the two-page color supplement entitled "Nueva vida" after a water color by Sánchez Germona (Figure 10.22) that the editors invited readers to extract from the volume and frame on bristol board. Thus for the *Ilustración Española* and the other great illustrateds like *Ilustración Artística* and *Ilustración Ibérica* of Barcelona, there would be no "Nueva vida" after the first decade of the new millennium. The same can be said in general for the art of xylography that until the end of the century required sketchers and hand engravers to produce the quality engravings that were their mainstay visuals. Both were replaced by photoengraving specialists which helped cut production costs. As Fontbona concludes, xylography had finally lost its battle against the photoengraving. Bowing to the market, magazine editors

Figure 10.20 "El hombre del día. Rafael Guerra (Guerrita)." *Blanco y Negro* 4 (July 7, 1894): n.p.

> vieron claro que la ilustración ordinaria de sus revistas había que encomendarla a fotograbadores y no a xilógrafos. Era más rápido, más económico y más fiel, puesto que las imágenes se reproducían fotomecánicamente sin necesidad de traductores manuales. Los xilógrafos seguirían manteniéndose, por lo menos durante unos años, pero como artesanos creadores de estampas con carisma, destinadas a dotar a las revistas de unos complementos de calidad, con lo que el grueso de su actividad se vería seriamente mermado. (Fontbona 75)

The grand illustrateds with their foreign and high art engravings and arch conservatism were suddenly ceding to the new, smaller format and more locally produced

Figure 10.21 Untitled. *Ilustración Española y Americana* 51 (December 8, 1907): 336.

magazines like *Blanco y Negro*, "más aptas para rebasar los límites del consumo burgués y situarse en el ojo del huracán de las luchas por la modernización española" (Alonso 46). This definitive transformation from engraving to photograph propelled Spain if not into the very eye of modernization, at least into its swirling outer vortex, inviting readers to demand ever more immediate visual representations of a reality that seemed suddenly within humans' power to capture and reproduce.

Notes

1. See Botrel's statistical table of the Madrid Press from 1858–1909. What Botrel (30) terms the "climax" of the periodical industry occurred following the 1883 "ley de Prensa" which resulted in a definitive liberalization of the press and a resultant jump in the number of periodicals of all types. Francesc Fontbona lists the last two decades of the nineteenth century as the "gran época" (75) of the illustrated magazines.
2. To put into perspective the relative costs of the two weeklies, *Blanco y Negro*,

Figure 10.22 Sánchez Germona. "Nueva vida." *Ilustración Española y Americana* 49 (January 8, 1905): n.p.

which began charging five céntimos, doubled its price by the end of the century to ten. *La Ilustración Española y Americana* was priced at one peseta, a true luxury in a country where the medium daily salary at the turn of the century was three pesetas (López Mondéjar 85). After the Civil War *Blanco y Negro* was revived as a Sunday supplement to the newspaper ABC which still publishes it at the present time. For the sake of brevity, citations to *Ilustración Española y Americana* and *Blanco y Negro* will be abbreviated *IEA* and *ByN* respectively.

3. By this time Daguerreotype excursions to "exotic" countries such as Egypt, Israel, Greece and Spain were already popular in France. The Daguerreotype,

however, was never widely practiced in Spain. The invention of collotype (also called Talbotype after its inventor William Talbot) in the 1830s and later of the collodion process (using a wet method on glass plate negatives) in the 1850s quickly replaced the more cumbersome Daguerreotype procedures. According to Fontanella, the daguerreotype died out in Spain after the wet plate came into use in 1851 (7).

4. Photographic *cartes de visite* became instantly popular when they were introduced in Paris by André Adolphe-Eugéne Disdéri in 1854.
5. Heliographic techniques were refined in Spain beginning in 1875 with the creation of the Sociedad Heliográfica Española which, according to Carrente Parrondo et al. (434), resulted in "una rápida vulgarización del fotograbado en España, sobre todo a través de las 'ilustraciones'," or illustrated magazines. It also meant that fewer plates needed to be imported from abroad (*150 años de fotografíca* 82).
6. The invention of an electrolysis process (*galvanoplastia* in Spanish) that electrotyped an image on copper plates meant that multiple copies of intaglio plates could be issued. These plates, produced mostly in northern Europe until the turn of the century, were purchased by the hundreds by most of the large format Spanish magazine publishers. The important international firms that sold plates to Spain were (in addition to Pannemaker): Meisenbach, Yves & Barret, C. Angerer & Goschl Boussod et Valadon, and Héliogravure Dujardin (Carrete Parrondo et al. 439; *150 años de fotografíca* 77).
7. For more information on *La Ilustración*'s importation of foreign plates' see Carrete Parrondo et al. (156–7).
8. In 1863 *El Museo Universal* included a heliograph, that is, a photomechanically reproduced image, that it heralded as a great achievement. Later, in 1870, *La Ilustración Española y Americana* published several images using a similar procedure. However, neither the *Museo* nor its successor, *Ilustración Española Española y Americana*, capitalized on the new technology until the beginning of the twentieth century, preferring xylographic methods even when heliography became the norm.
9. The diorama was the first three-dimensional exhibit. The image was housed in a large, circular cubicle which, viewed through an aperture, gave viewers the impression of three-dimensionality.
10. The nineteenth-century stereoscope was a hand-held device with an arm holding a double photographic image extending outward from a viewing lens. The photographic images were shot using a twin lens camera at two slightly different angles. The resultant double image, when viewed with the stereoscopic lens, produced a three-dimensional effect. Present-day stereoscopic pictures are looked at through a View-Master, still available at some tourist spots and toy stores. Picatoste may also have been familiar with the British

astronomer and photographer Charles Piazzi Smyth's 1856 album of stereocopic images of Tenerife entitled *Tenerife: An Astronomer's Experiment' or Specialties of a Residence above the Clouds* that sold 2,000 copies, each one sold with a stereoscope (*150 años, de fotografica* 70).

11. Juan Comba, considered the father of graphic journalism in Spain (López Mondéjar 82) also collaborated with *Ilustración Española y Americana* beginning in 1880. For more on Comba see, *La prensa ilustrada en España* (100) and on Clifford and Laurent see Fontanella (16, 22–3). For information on Jean Laurent's photos of traditional Andalusian dress see Herranz Rodríguez. With their accomplished images of dams, triumphal arches, monuments, palaces and railroads photographers like James Clifford were important promoters of government and institutional projects (*150 años de fotografía* 70).
12. There were in addition ten sketches of smaller man-made artifacts. The next largest categories were local color types and cartoons (twenty), formal portraits (eighteen), fine arts engravings (nine), and renderings of political figures and royalty (five). Finally, in a testament to the journal's traditional venue, only two images depicted action and trauma scenes and two sketches illustrated scientific advances.
13. In 1901 *Blanco y Negro* boasted that it was the first periodical to introduce the Max Levi half-tone process "que tanto vigor y vida presta a los fotograbados" (*ByN* 523 (May 11, 1901): n.p.).
14. By the 1890s, the technologies for mechanical reproduction of images were expanding. For example, chromolithography, steel engraving and steel facing of copper plates, electrotyping of woodblocks, etc. were making speedy and cheap reproduction commonplace and finding more uses for photography. The first "chromotypogravures" produced by the *Ilustración Española y Americana* were color photoengravings produced by the firm C. Angerer & Groschl. Tricolor photoengravings first appeared in 1888 (Carrete Parrondo et al. 441). In 1890 the magazine switched to the firm of Boussod, Valadon & Cía (formerly Goupil) of Paris.
15. In its May 11, 1901 issue *Blanco y Negro* commemorated its ten-year anniversary in a lengthy article in which it railed against creators of the contention that it had been founded merely to publicize goods (523 (May 11, 1901): n.p.).
16. See "Un práctico en la Manigua" by Narciso Méndez Bringa (15 (November 16, 1895): n.p.), and "Luchando por la patria" by Estevan (5 (October 19, 1895): n.p.).

Works Cited

Alonso, Cecilio. "Difusión de las *Ilustraciones* en España." *La prensa ilustrada en España. Las* Ilustraciones. *1850–1920.* Montpellier: IRIS. Université Paul Valéry, 1996. 45–56.

La Andalucía del siglo XIX en las fotografís de J. Laurent y Cía. Almería: Consejería de Cultura, 1998.

150 años de fotografía en la Biblioteca Nacional. Eds. Gerardo F. Kurtz and, Isabel Ortega. Madrid: Ministerio de Cultura / Ediciones El Viso, 1989.

Barthes, Roland. *Image Music Text.* Trans. Stephen Heath. New York: Hill and Wang, 1977.

Botrel, Jean-François. "Estadística de la prensa madrileña de 1858–1909, según el Registro de Contribución Industrial." In Manuel Tuñon de Lara, Antonio Elorza and Manuel Pérez Ledesma, eds. *Prensa y sociedad en España (1820–1936).* Madrid: Editorial Cuadernos para el Diálogo, 1975. 25–45.

Carrete Parrondo, Juan, Jesusa Vega González, Francesc Fontbona and Valeriano Bozal. *El grabado en España. Siglos XIX y XX.* In *Summa Artis. Historia General del Arte.* Vol. 32. Madrid: Espasa-Calpe, 1988.

Desvois, Jean-Michel. "El fin de las *Ilustraciones*: El caso de Madrid." In *La prensa ilustrada en España. Las* Ilustraciones, *1850–1920.* Montpellier: Université Paul Valéry, 1996. 343–8.

Fontanella, Lee. *Photography in Spain in the Nineteenth Century.* Dallas, TX: Delahunty Gallery; San Francisco, CA: Fraenkel Galler, 1983.

Fontbona, Francesc. "*Las Ilustraciones* y la reproducción de sus imágenes." In *La prensa ilustrada en España. Las* Ilustraciones, *1850–1920.* Montpellier: Université Paul Valéry, 1996. 73–9.

Gómez Aparicio, Pedro. *Historia del periodismo español.* Vol. 2. *De la Revolución de Septiembre al desastre colonial.* Madrid: Editora Nacional, 1971.

Herranz Rodríguez, Concha. "Laurent y su visión de la indumentaria andaluza." In *La Andalucía del siglo XIX en las fotografías de J. Laurent y Cía.*" Almería: Consejería de Cultura, 1998. 219–35.

Le Bigot, "Claude."Los retratos en *La Ilustración Española y Americana*: Tretas y tramoyas de un género." In *La prensa ilustrada en España.* Las Ilustraciones, *1850–1920.* Montpellier: Université Paul Véry, 1996. 146–61.

López Mondéjar, Publio. *Historia de la fotografía en España.* Madrid: Lunwerg Editores, 1997.

La prensa ilustrada en España. Las Ilustraciones, 1850–1920. Montpellier: Université Paul Valéry, 1996.

Tuñon de Lara, Manuel, Antonio Elorza and Manuel Pérez Ledesma, eds. *Prensa y sociedad en España (1820–1936).* Madrid: Editorial Cuadernos para el Diálogo, 1975.

–11–

Spain's Image in Regional Dress: From Everyday Object to Museum Piece and Tourist Attraction

Jesusa Vega

The study of fashion is one of many ways of understanding modern Spain's visual construction. Indeed, the identification of certain forms of dress as representative of the Spanish people has fundamentally shaped perceptions of the nation, as much by foreigners as by natives of the country. With this in mind, this chapter seeks to understand the identification and assimilation of traditional dress in nineteenth- and twentieth-century Spain, beginning with an awareness of the gradual disappearance of traditional dress, its role in the formation of tradition, and the subsequent transformation of dress into a marker of collective identity through its exploitation as both a museum object and tourist attraction.[1] Confined to a brief historical period, the concept of regional attire originated in the last third of the eighteenth century and culminated with the celebration of the Madrid Regional Dress Exposition in 1925 and at Barcelona's International Exhibition in 1929. In scarcely a century and a half one finds a growing awareness of the need to conserve cultural heritage – that is, for dress to transcend the realm of art or history and to become ethnography, thereby preserving the memory of the nation's customs and collective practices. Simultaneously, this new awareness sought to construct an image of Spain that would lure tourists who would eventually become one of the nation's principle sources of wealth.

The arrival of the Bourbon dynasty to Spain in 1700 was not peaceful nor was social change gradual. In terms of fashion, Charles II's war of succession was seen as the struggle between the old style (as represented by Archduke Charles of Austria, who wore the traditional black Spanish suit and neckerchief) and the new, modern one (identified with the Duke of Anjou, nephew of Louis XIV, who wore a colorful French military suit and tie). After the Duke of Anjou's victory, the great challenge of the Bourbons was not only to modernize Spain, but also to erase its former image and to substitute it with one more in keeping with the era. Ultimately, the task was to articulate a new way of seeing the nation that would reflect the country's desire for progress and "civilization." In this context, the role of dress was fundamental. For along with the new clothing that the Spanish were ordered to wear by royal decree, their ways of relating to one another in society changed, as did their collective and individual identities.[2] In Spain's case in particular, the ascension of the new French dynasty, along with the cultural hegemony of France throughout Europe, accelerated the process of acculturation that took place among urbanites – primarily in Madrid, where the royal court was located – thereby guaranteeing the persistence of French influence. Indeed, according to travelers' opinions, by the end of the century the Spanish had become simulacras of the French.

Within this process of modernization, the contrast between those who succumbed to the innovations of fashion and those who did not was made increasingly obvious. As a result, the separation between the urban and rural populations – and the majority of the crown's subjects belonged to the latter – was emphasized. During the second half of the eighteenth century, real efforts were made to incorporate that large rural segment of the population into the project of progressive transformation, which was as fundamental for economic prosperity as for the change in Spain's image abroad. Indeed, these transformations attempted to inculcate the Enlightened ideal of the positive value of work while constructing a new vision: namely, the transformation from a ragged, backward common folk (one must keep in mind the impact of the *romances* and picaresque novels in constructing these negative characteristics) into a neat, industrious people, replete with signs of their own identity whose richness and diversity contributed to the splendor of the monarchy – an image that is, in which Spaniards might recognize themselves and in which foreigners could imagine a new Spain.

A true milestone in the construction of this image is found in Juan de la Cruz Cano y Olmedilla's extraordinarily famous prints, *Colección de Trajes de España tanto antiguos como modernos* (*Dresses from Spain, Both Old and New*) (1777–89), which were used as propaganda in the changes then taking place. Some prints, for example, adorned the offices of the Prime Minister, the Duke of Floridablanca, in 1778, and we know that they were commented upon by foreign ambassadors. This new image of the Spanish people acquires its full meaning, though, when juxtaposed with that of the urban sectors. If the latter were the expression of cosmopolitanism, the former personified the nation, adding an essential element to the patriotic sentiment of Enlightened citizens. In this way, the end of the eighteenth century visualized regional dress endowed with a greater respectability, albeit rather theatrically, emphasizing the distinct elements and ornaments that comprised and complemented the various rural populations.

At the beginning of the nineteenth century, representation through dress crystallized as the modern way of seeing the nation. The political crises of the time, namely, the gradual loss of influence in the American colonies and the clash against Napoleon, set in motion the mechanisms necessary to create a sense of patriotism in Spain. Characterization through clothing was utilized, for instance, in the prints published during the War of Independence. In José Coromina's "Levantamiento simultáneo de las provincias de España contra Napoleón en 1808" (The Simultaneous Uprising of the Spanish Provinces Against Napoleon in 1808), the provinces, represented by characters in their particular regional attire, try to hold up a royal bust that a French soldier attempts to knock down.[3]

This modern Spanish iconography would come to form part of the ideological construction of a tradition that would be forged during the nineteenth century, especially after 1833, the year of the death of the last absolute monarch, Fernando VII. Yet the nineteenth century's way of seeing Spain cannot be understood unless we keep in mind the substantial change in mentality that occurred throughout Europe with respect to Spain. This was especially the case among foreign travelers, who would prove to be essential agents in the construction of this image. Simply put, we can say that the backwardness of Spain greatly attracted the romantic traveler, whose desire was to live the adventure of traveling back in time. It was an experience that began with the descent from the Pyrenees. There the modern means of transportation disappeared and the traveler was put in contact with cultural forms that the Industrial Revolution had turned into mere antiquated traditions. For some travelers, like Hans Christian Andersen, Spain was much more than the scene of a remote period. Indeed, it was a place where the people still lived as if in a bygone era, and in this laid the country's prime attraction.

The enormous literary production of foreign authors writing about Spain was accompanied by a plethora of images in which one could envision the diverse characteristics of the various peasant types, as well as the customs in which their different costumes figured so prominently.[4] Yet to understand the success of such images one must know how they evolved from within, which in turn explains the rapidity and efficacy of their diffusion. The defense and representation of the native, to differentiate this vision from that of foreigners, nourished Spanish literature and visual production, and gave rise to what we know as *costumbrismo*, a literary term in which the writer, like the artist and even "social types," come to identify their own image with that presented to foreigners in stories and illustrations. Needless to say, as in the eighteenth century, this image was encouraged and disseminated from the highest cultural spheres, where its success was made absolute through the use of new means of reproduction; namely, printing, lithography, and photography. As an example we need only note Andersen's vivid experience at the Alhambra in Granada when he wanted to visit the "Patio de los leones" (Patio of the Lions) and the "Sala de las dos hermanas" (Room of the Two Sisters). By order of Queen Isabel II both areas had been closed so that they could be photographed by Charles Clifford, an Englishman. In fact, "para animar los retratos con personas vivas" (to animate the portraits with living people), an "entire gypsy tribe" had been sent to visit the Alhambra and were grouped on the patio. There, Andersen found

> un par de los críos más pequeños totalmente desnudos y dos muchachas jovencitas con dalias en el pelo posaban en la actitud de bailar; una gitana vieja, infinitamente fea, reclinada contra una esbelta columna de mármol, tocaba una zambomba, una especie de puchero de tocar, mientras que una mujer gorda, pero aún bastante guapa, vestida con falda de volantes y colorines, tocaba la pandereta.
>
> a pair of infants, completely nude, and two girls with dahlias in their hair posed like dancers; an old, horribly ugly gypsy woman rested against a slender marble column, playing a crude drum that resembled a kettle; while a fat, though rather beautiful woman, dressed in a flouncy and brightly colored skirt, played the tambourine. (Andersen 129)

Although foreigners paid more attention to the rural sector and Spanish observers looked more to the urban middle class, both segments of the population figured in this vision. People reacted to the increasing uniformity of customs and clothing by seeking out the distinct and the specific in Spanish culture, with a clear evocative sense among foreigners, and with an eagerness among Spaniards themselves to recapture what had been lost. The modernization of cities, the construction of the Isabel II Canal to supply Madrid with water, and the vigorous development of communications (principally the telegraph and railroad), brought to the Spanish a new awareness of the threat which progress posed to their traditional way of life, at the time concentrated in the rural regions. "No hay duda" (There is no doubt), wrote Gustavo Adolfo Bécquer in 1864,

> el prosaico rasero de la civilización va igualándolo todo. Un irresistible y misterioso impulso tiende a unificar los pueblos con los pueblos, las provincias con las provincias, las naciones con las naciones, y quien sabe si las razas con las razas. A medida que la palabra vuela por los hilos telegráficos, que el ferrocaril se extiende, la industria se acrecienta y el espíritu cosmopolita de la civilización invade nuestro país, van desapareciendo de él sus rasgos característicos, sus costumbres inmemoriales, sus trajes pintorescos y sus rancias ideas.
>
> that a prosaic measure of civilization is given equally to all. An irresistible and mysterious impulse tends to unite towns with towns, provinces with provinces, nations with nations, and maybe even races with races. While words fly through the telegraph wires, railroads extend, industry grows, and the cosmopolitan spirit of civilization invades our country, its characteristic features, timeless customs, painterly dress and ancient ideas disappear. (Bécquer, vol. 2: 407)

Bécquer lamented, moreover, that peasant dress had become a costume and the regional festivals and customs deemed ridiculous. He defended the need to conserve the memory of the old way of life as a means of resistance: maintaining diversity and, with it, the differential characteristics which figured prominently in the configuration of nationalities. This concept would lead him to search for a solution in which dress would have increasing prominence. Thus began his process of "salvation" and "recuperation" through different artistic media and in different contexts.

Bécquer emphasized painting's importance in leaving testimony to what had been lost: principally, the picturesque elements of society embodied in the organized, honest, and simple customs of the people, whose lives were led far from the speed of modern life and in harmony with the natural environment. Indeed, the importance of the picturesque must be emphasized when examining the invention of tradition and of Bécquer's own search for equilibrium between it and the modern world. In his opinion it was the last opportunity to collect and define a national tradition. According to Bécquer, to accomplish this task the state should patronize painters who, diverging from the beaten paths, would go in search of "los tipos originales" (original character types) and "las costumbres primitivas" (the primitive customs), traveling to "los rincones donde su oscuridad les sirve de salvaguardia, y de donde poco a poco los va desalojando la invasora corriente de la novedad y los adelantos de la civilización" (the far corners, where their very obscurity serves as their safeguard, and where, little by little, they are evicted by the invading current of modernity and the advancements of civilization) (Bécquer vol. 2:410). Ultimately, it was his brother Valeriano Bécquer who obtained a pension from the Ministry of Promotions to make "una colección, lo más completa posible, de cuadros que recuerden en lo futuro los actuales trajes característicos, usos y costumbres de nuestras provincias" (a collection, as complete as possible, of paintings that, in the future, will serve to remind us of the current characteristic attire, practices and customs of our provinces) (Puente), destined for the recently created Museo de la Trinidad (1868). Although Valeriano Bécquer painted various portraits of the peoples and customs of Aragón, Ávila, and Soria, it was his drawings published in *El Museo Universal* and *La Ilustración de Madrid* (for which Gustavo Adolfo Bécquer served as director: Cabra) that were most widely promoted. There, through text and image, the artist depicted the people who embodied the new values of a "traditional" Spain and who could be differentiated as much from those people who had been modernized as from those viewed by travelers. An illustrative example is that of the Spanish woman: the proposed model of femininity did not reference classical perfection, nor did she have any relation to "la mujer sílfide producto de la civilización" (the sylphic product of civilization) (Bécquer, vol 2: 985). Yet neither did this model correspond to the beauty of the Spanish woman, who quite frequently could be seen flowing in rivers of ink in the books of foreign travelers. Instead, modern Spain's feminine ideal was a "muchacha bonita de aldea, limpia, hacendosa y alegre, que huele a tomillo y mejorama" (a pretty village girl, clean, hardworking and happy, and smelling of thyme and sweet marjoram). Among the Bécquer brothers, there is an obvious exhaltation of the villagers as a repository of virtue, over and against the obviously urban "masses," the epitome of vice. This image, part of a long literary tradition, vindicated all those advocating the valoration and conservation of dress, and who irremediably searched for it both in rural and in modern fashions.

This first phase of the safeguarding of memory prioritized the visual collection of unknown riches. But it must be emphasized that such safeguarding neither affected the collective protagonist who contributed to that memory (and who, by realizing its importance and identifying with it, would ensure its survival), nor that object's original context (whose loss was considered irreparable). This is easily understood when one notes that at that time there were only traditional art museums in Spain (Géal). Because the construction of memory occurred through artistic blueprints, it was believed that painting, as opposed to dress, was preserved and privileged. Two important consequences can be derived from the consideration of painting over dress. Primarily, when finally deemed worthy of preservation, traditional dress would be considered valuable as an artistic prop, which would prove an obstacle to its transformation and incorporation into the new anthropological discourses of the second decade of the twentieth century in Spain. Second, there would be a complete absence in these images of any social problems, as the objective was to leave a testimony of the artistic through picturesque perseverance, and not a denunciation of the trying conditions of real life. With the activity of the Bécquer brothers there began a way of visualizing the Spain that had disappeared, with the aim of ensuring that the past would live in the present and that a continuity and heritage would be established among the generations – a tradition, which would guarantee this salvation. According to Gustavo Adolfo Bécquer, "la vida de una nación, a semejanza de la del hombre, parece como que se dilata con la memoria de las cosas que fueron, y a medida que es más viva y más completa su imagen, es más real esa segunda existencia del espíritu en el pasado" (the life of a nation, like that of man, seems to expand with the memory of what once was, to the effect that its image is more alive and complete, that this second existence of the spirit of the past is somehow more real) (vol. 2: 406).

From this moment on dress was followed more closely and became increasingly important in and of itself. If at first it was conceived in the same sense as were monuments or landscape paintings and in the same sphere as customs in general, in the end it was transformed into a point of reference. That is to say, folk types would come to be identified as such through the clothing they wore, as opposed to the way in which the Bécquer brothers saw it. According to them, it was unacceptable to distinguish the item of clothing from the human element and to transform dress into a museum piece. The picturesque character demanded a human presence (not that of a determined costume) as well as an understanding and interpretation of that human factor on the part of the artist. For the Bécquer brothers, humans were the only beings capable of awakening and interpreting these feelings, and of giving life to the past. Considering these assumptions, we can understand the Bécquers' complete rejection of photography, which according to them was a mechanical medium: the cold, objective mirror of reality. Instead, they considered the intervention of the artist's creative imagination – the "discernimento superior que guía el lápiz del dibujante" (the superior discernment that guides the draftsman's pencil) (vol. 2: 965), in the words of Gustavo Adolfo Bécquer – as necessary in constructing a reality stripped of all inadequacies, or at least in reconstructing those parts that had been lost. Nevertheless, this would also be made possible through the photographic medium, the plastic expression of progress and modernity that would prove the most effective and suitable for visualizing tradition.

Indeed, photography would become a fundamental agent in the creation of that double image of Spain which alluded to both progress and tradition. The most outstanding example is the work of the French photographer and Madrid resident, Juan Laurent, who was commissioned to document the great public works (iron bridges, railroad stations and installations, highways, ports, lighthouses, etc.) with which the government hoped to publicize Spain's conspicuous modernization throughout Europe.[5] Ironically, to satisfy international demand – Laurent had stores in Madrid, Stuttgart and Paris – he was ardently dedicated to traveling the country and photographing the people and monuments that had been threatened by this same progress. In this regard, the editor's note from the 1879 catalogue, *Guide de touriste en Espagne et en Portugal ou Itinéraire Artistique á travers ces pays, au point de vue artistique, monumental et pittoresque*, devoted to a collection of people and monuments, is noteworthy (*Madrid, Casa Laurent y Cia*, 1879). In it, the editor describes Laurent as an artist, which is to say that he remains in the realm of art, even though the catalogue consists of photography. Furthermore, it emphasizes the breadth of the work of an artist who, in the editor's own words, had been "consecrated" to travel Spain with the goal of leaving a document of the nation. The word "consecrate" infuses a sense of transcendent mission to the enterprise that would be in force until nearly the twentieth century. Indeed, to travel Spain in order to bear witness to it would become associated with the idea of abnegation and salvation. This was an attitude predisposed to a positive appreciation of the result and reinforced in the privations and the fatigue of the artist – sacrifices which lent even more valor to the enterprise and which emphasized the truth of the information. What is more, the result was a fusion of objective documentation and artistic creation. To a large degree, this ambiguity of photographs would condition both contemporaneous and future interpretations and readings.

In Laurent's catalogue there are numerous photographs dedicated to "escenas de usos y costumbres del país" (scenes of thc nation's practices and customs) that all figured under the epigraph "Tipos de razas, costumbres y trajes de España" (Racial

Types, Customs and Dresses of Spain). All are "estudios sacados del natural" (studies taken from nature).[6] That is to say, all are presented as images of reality. Yet this information, while not false, entails a nuanced analysis in order to understand the valoration of dress and the increasing disassociation from its point of origin and its wearers. Indeed, a good many of these photographs display the models attired in "typical" dress, paid for by the provinces, to participate in the popular festivities organized in Madrid on the occasion of King Alfonso XII's marriage to his cousin María de las Mercedes in 1878.

Besides showcasing the rich clothing that distinguished them, the models at these festivities danced and sang to the sound of their local music. All were objects of interest and sources of commentary for the Madrid papers, most notably *La Época*, *El Tiempo* and *La Correspondencia de España* (Gutiérrez). The following comment was made in this last on January 25, 1878:

> las gentes que residen en Madrid y son naturales de provincias, buscaban con ansia las comparsas de sus pueblos respectivos y se veía pintada en sus rostros la satisfacción de encontrarse con pasiones y el orgullo de creer que los trajes de esta o de la otra provincia eran mucho más airosos y ricos que los de los demás.
>
> the people who reside in Madrid and are natives of the provinces, eagerly seek out their fellow provincials, and we see on their faces the satisfaction of having found themselves with their countrymen and the pride in believing that the attire of their native province was much more graceful and sumptuous than that of the others.[7]

This indicates that during this period in the capital obvious examples could be found of personal or group identification through clothing, illustrating the importance of dress as a point of collective identification. Most likely this was a new phenomenon. In this way the methods applied by the Bécquer brothers had achieved definitive success, to the extent that in Madrid's stores one could purchase photographs of the models that had been exhibited in the shop windows. Yet to see these photographs is to understand that the next step had been taken in the process of the suit's decontextualization and its voyage to the museum. While the newspapers said that those attired in this clothing were the typical wearers of this dress (thus ensuring the clothing's picturesque character) the collection hung on the naked walls of the studios, eliminating the presence of the very person wearing it. Ultimately, they seemed less humans in their normal clothing than immobilized mannequins, whose movements had been frozen in the intense front and back lighting, giving them a timeless image through which the sentimental identification of Madrid's citizens had already been made possible, even though they would have never worn such clothing even had they lived in such places.

In reality, we cannot assess the veracity of these fashions. Indeed, we do not know to what extent those attired in these clothes were their typical wearers. But all evidence leads to the conclusion that, after this date, it would become increasingly difficult to believe that Spaniards from rural areas of the provinces were actually wearing these typical examples of folk dress. In fact, the relation that was established was the inverse: once this dress could be displayed as a museum piece, there arose the need to find the perfect person who could then be adjusted to fit the desire image. The next and last step on the road toward the museum would be to perfect the most authentic-looking cardboard and wax mannequin to substitute the human and display the clothing.

Paradigmatic of this is the testimony of an event that took place in 1908. In that year the City Hall of Madrid sent invitations to the capitals of the provinces to attend the centennial celebration of the Second of May, where they would be expected to don their traditional dress. Badajoz Town Hall's eloquent response that they would not attend is worth noting: "en esta población no hay persona alguna que vista el traje típico de los antiguos extremeños ni se conservan datos que pudieran servir para reconstituir con verdadera exactitud dicho traje" (among this population there is not one person who wears the typical dress of the old Extremeñans, nor is there a model that can serve to reconstruct said dress with exact truth).[8]

It is important to emphasize that the image we are left with does not correspond to reality. Rather, to the extent that the dress wearer vanished, more prominence was given to painting and other visual media. Just when it this dress ceases to exist is when it becomes more visible in photography and painting. Nevertheless, this way of seeing Spain, coinciding with the turn of the twentieth century, cannot be understood if we do not keep in mind the renovating perception of the Institución Libre de Enseñanza, the mournful vision of the Generation of '98, the crises of collective identity occurring in the country, and the new consciousness of the structural differences between the regions. All of this meant that artists and intellectuals, persuaded by a spirit of ethical and social regeneration, looked anew to the *pueblo* in all corners of the country. Remote from urban centers, the unchanging village was now a compendium of all of the positive national values, often defined through opposition to the negative attributes of the urban masses. They were also often seen as the repository of the particularities of the Spanish *raza* (race) in which the markers of national identity were left uncontaminated.[9]

With these historical and cultural contexts in mind, one can appreciate the definitive transformation of regional costume into an artistic piece in a museum. Note, for instance, the pictorial decoration of the library of Archer M. Huntington's museum which was built in New York and dedicated to Spanish culture, and on whose walls he wanted to see a living and true portrait of the *España actual* (the true Spain).[10] Huntington commissioned Joaquín Sorolla for the work in 1911. As an artist and painter Sorolla agreed that such an image of Spain could be found only far from the modern cities and had to be traveled to on foot or by mule – the only means of arriving at "sus tierras yermas, antaño cubiertas de frondosos bosques y hoy habitada por una población poco numerosa que conserva las tradiciones, que mantiene mejor que la de otros lugares la autenticidad de su carácter" (its waste lands, long ago covered with lush forests and today inhabited by a tiny population that preserves its traditions, that maintains the authenticity of its character better than the people of other places) (Codding 105). Only there could one find the Spanish people in whom the past lived, and where "los susurros del alma de los desaparecidos siguen vivos en los ojos y en la forma, en el ademán y el modo de pensar, en la fe y en la superstición, en la manera de vestirse y en los sueños" (the murmurs of the souls of those who have disappeared continue to live in their eyes and in their appearance, in their body language and in their thought, in their faith and in their superstition, in their way of dressing and in their dreams) (Codding 105). Spain's essence was assumed to be located in those villagers who struggled to eke out an existence, "hombres y mujeres de otros tiempos, pero hombres y mujeres de una pieza, altivos, que conservan una independencia y un sentido de la verdad y de la honradez tan auténtico que a uno se le llena el alma de aire fresco y de integridad" (men and women of other times, but proud men and women over all, who conserved an independence and a sense of truth and honor so authentic that they filled one's soul with a fresh air of integrity) (Codding 105). Sorolla's intention was "fijar, conforme a la verdad, claramente, sin simbolismos ni literaturas, la psicología de cada región" (to capture the psychology of each region, remaining loyal to the truth, and not resorting to the use of symbols or literary devices) and "dar siempre dentro del verismo de mi escuela, una respresentación de España; no buscando filosofía, sino lo pintoresco de cada región" (working always within the veracity of my school, to give a true representation of Spain; to not seek the philosophy, but rather the picturesque qualities of each region) (Muller 131). Huntington, for his part, hoped that painting would be capable of giving life to the multiplicity of objects comprising a testimony of Spanish cultures, including the many examples of regional dress that had been brought to New York to satisfy his desire for collecting.

As a painter, Sorolla sought to leave for posterity what he considered unchanging, that designated as true. He assumed the difficult and exhausting work of searching throughout Spain to find truthful documentation and to successfully communicate a certain sentiment in combination with the human presence – essentially, to depict the picturesque. But in Sorolla's case we do not perceive that same painful loss expressed by the Bécquer brothers. Indeed, it is enough to know how his work was executed to understand that from the beginning Sorolla knew that he was creating an artifice in the literal sense of the word. As if he were making a film, he fabricated elaborate productions in which to situate his models, who were made to fit in the space that Huntington had made available in the library. Consequently, it may be said that he had inverted the Bécquerian values:

dress had become the focus of regional iconography. In some cases, as in *La fiesta del pan de Castilla* (*Castille's Festival of Bread*), we might even speak of the exaltation and triumph of regional attire, treated with a monumentalism that dwarfs not only the figures wearing it, but also the landscape and its very artistic monuments.[11] The picturesque character relied on the selection of those themes in which groups were gathered, those which showed a happy (and in many cases jovial or festive) vision.

Through the many sketches and statements he made over the course of his journey, we know about the situation Sorolla encountered, as well as the changes that were introduced both in the form of his work and in its content. For instance, we know that the marketplace in Madrid had vendors from the Ansó valley dressed in their traditional attire as a tourist attraction; "gentes de Lagartera posaron para él en su improvisado taller de Talavera de la Reina porque para Sorolla representaban 'el antiguo Toledo'" (they had people from Lagartera come down to their makeshift Talavera de la Reina workshop so they could be made up to show that the "Old Toledo" was like (Muller134)); that models from Salamanca were contracted to be painted in the home of some friends who even gave Sorolla a man's entire regional outfit as a gift; that in Catalonia this picturesque element could not be found in any of the people; that Madrid was better at suppressing it, etc. To make up for these deficiencies, the artist employed historical documents. He utilized newspaper clippings or photographs, and in his journey through Spain he purchased objects and traditional regional clothing, some of which ended up in their own museum (opened to public on June 11, 1932) and others in the one in New York.

On June 29, 1919, Sorolla ended his work. Yet Spaniards could not enjoy it. A clause figuring into his contract stated that the paintings could not be shown in the country. This was considered a mistake, "porque poder admirarlos en España se había convertido en una 'aspiración nacional'" (because to be able to admire them in Spain had become a "national aspiration") and it seemed "una falta de patriotismo" (a lack of patriotism) to deprive Spain of the opportunity to feel proud of itself (Muller139). All of the negotiations to exhibit the work in the Museo del Prado failed – even those sponsored by King Alfonso XIII. The paintings were shipped to New York in the autumn of 1922 and the panels were completely installed in 1926. From this time on, only in the United States could one "see and know" Spain. Until very recently, this image would nourish the view of those who would have formerly traveled to the country.

In spite of everything, Sorolla's totalizing vision had significant consequences in Spain, aside from changing the national view of dress as something now worthy of being collected and shown by and for the Spanish people. Indeed, from this notion came the idea of having an exposition. On January 1, 1921, the organizing council of the *Exposición del Traje regional* (*Regional Dress Exhibit*) published the first circular, whose text began:

> Es un hecho indudable que España comienza a ser visitada con alguna frecuencia, por distinguidos extranjeros, deseosos de conocer nuestra copiosa y original riqueza artística […] siendo una de ellas, la que podríamos caificar de *tesoro escondido*, pues que, como a tal, es preciso buscar, conservarle cuidadosamente y ponerle a la luz para que todos lo conozcan y lo admiren, en sus variadas fases, de interés señaladísimo …; nos referimos *al traje regional*.
>
> It is an undeniable fact that Spain is beginning to be visited with some frequency by distinguished foreigners. For them the allure is our copious and original artistic wealth […] being one of what we might call *hidden treasures*. In this way, it is necessary to seek out, carefully conserve, and bring to light in order that everybody will know and admire it, in its various stages, of noted interest; … namely, *regional dress*.

The intention was "prestar un servicio al país" (to be of service to the nation) by bringing together "ejemplares de esos pintorescos trajes regionales, de tan extrañas hechuras y tan distintos de forma" (examples of those picturesque regional costumes, of such strange shape and such distinct form) that

> señalan con fuerza indestructible razas que vivieron aisladas en periodos de siglos, y que, al fundirse más tarde con las avencidadas en lugares cercanos – para dar como resultado nacimiento a un pueblo sentimental, artista, caballeresco, generoso y señoril – han conservado con cierta pureza el sedimento de sus tradiciones, no sólo en sus costumbres, sus ideología y sus sentimientos, sino también, en sus originales y curiosas vestiduras.
>
> powerfully point to the indomitable folk that lived in isolation for centuries, and who, upon participating in the advances that occur in nearby places – producing as a result the birth of a sentimental, artistic, noble, generous, and chivalrous people – have conserved with a certain purity the sediment of their traditions, not merely in their customs, their ideology, and their sentiments, but also in their original and curious vestment. (*Exposición* 6–7)

This appealed to the patriotic sentiment to encourage the safeguarding of the true memory of popular dress in its integrity:[12]

> desde el tocado, en los de mujer, y los distintos cubrecabezas en los hombres, hasta los diferentes calzados que se usaron y las variadas prendas que los complementaban, según las diversas ocasiones en que los vestían; las que utilizaban como abrigo y las legendarias y vistosas mantas; los diversos objetos accesorios; incluso las armas, adornos femeninos y joyas, entre las cuales seguramente habrá modelos interesantísimos que pregonen el arte de los maestros orfebres españoles, no desdeñando el mandar todo lo que haya pertenecido a aquellas vestimentas, por insiginificante que les parezca y por deteriorado que esté, teniendo gran cuidado en no suprimir nada ni hacer, en las prendas de vestir que remitan, la menor reforma, para que puedan estudiarse, tal

como fueron, con sus forros y sus detalles primitivos, evitando de este modo el que se susciten dudas sobre sus autenticidiad, requisito indispensable para su admisión.

from the women's headdresses and the men's distinct headcoverings, to the different footwear that they used and the various garments that accompanied them, according to the different occasions when they were worn; those which they used as overcoats and those legendary and colorful blankets; the diverse accessories; even the weapons, the women's accoutrement and jewels, among which surely there are interesting examples that testify to the great Spanish metalworkers, being uncritical of all that pertains to these vestments, as insignificant as they seem and as deteriorated as they may be, taking great care to not omit anything, nor to make the least reform in the garments they send, so that they may be studied as they were, with their primitive linings and details, avoiding in this way whatever might lead to doubts about these objects' authenticity, which is an indispensable requirement for their admission. (8–10)

Although an incipient anthropological and ethnographical interest can be seen, traditional dress continued to belong to the domain of the visual arts. The members of the Junta Organizadora (Organizing Council) were the Duke of Romanones (its president), the director of the Real Academia de San Fernando (who was put in charge of deciding the institution's location), and the artists Mariano Benlliure, Miguel Blay, Fernando Álvarez de Sotomayor, Juan Comba and the multifaceted Marqués de la Vega Inclán (Traver).[13]

The prizes and events surrounding the organization of the exposition meant that a number of newspaper reports and (more interestingly) true photographic indexes that dealt with regional dress would be published. An excellent example is the *Diario de Navarra*, where, during October of 1924, a good many of José Roldán Bidaburu's photographs were published, many of them from the Roncal valley. Another instance is *Compaire e Ildefonso San Agustín*, which was commissioned to take photographs of the people of Hecho (with the hope of earning the prize of the Office of Tourism), many of which were subsequently published in newspapers of the region, such as the *Heraldo de Aragón* and *El Noticiero*, where they illustrated articles by Ricardo del Arco and García Mercadal. In some provincial papers, such as *La Voz*, whole series of articles were dedicated to the patriotic enterprise of showing the "distintas regiones, villas y lugares dignos de ser conocidos y admirados por los demás españoles" ["distinct regions, villages, and places worthy of being known and admired by other Spaniards"] with the intention of "inyectar al pueblo español el afán de conocer su patrio solar, en la intensidad que otros países lo sienten" (injecting among the Spanish people the enthusiasm to know their fatherland with the same intensity as in other nations).[14]

Despite this policy of encouraging people to wear these dresses, the process of urbanization was irreversible – even in the villages where people were rewarded with the prizes. This situation was described by Domingo Miral in the article "La fiesta del traje aragonés en Hecho, Ansotanos y Chesos. ¿Son sus trajes algo pintoresco o son algo trascendental?" (The Festival of the Aragon Dress in Hecho, Ansotanos and Chesos. Is Their Clothing Picturesque or Transcendental?) (*El Noticiero*, February 14, 1924). Among other things, the article asserted: "Desde que la mujer va vestida de señora en Hecho, la emigración aumenta en proporciones alarmantes, las mujeres salen por docenas a servir en otras poblaciones y los matrimonios escasean en forma tal, que hoy es el problema más angustioso de cuantos reclaman pronta solución" (From the time that a woman dressed like a "lady" in Hecho, emigration has increased to alarming proportions. The women leave by the dozens to serve as maids among other populations and marriage has declined so much so that the most pressing issue of the day is how soon a solution to this problem will be found). For this author, the cause was natural: "desde que [las mujeres] llevan falda corta, zapato de charol y tacón alto y blusas, abrigos y trajes de cuerpo entero y batas, etc., etc., el campo les parece un tormento, los chesos toscos y ordinarios, el pueblo un destierro, la vida una cruz" (from the time that [women] have worn short dresses, patent leather high-heeled shoes, and blouses, overcoats, and full-length suits and dressing gowns, etc. etc., the countryside has seemed like torture to them, the people of Hecho uncouth and vulgar, the town a place of exile, life a cross).[15] Most definitively, modernization's giant strides overtook tradition and even managed to reach the most uncontaminated areas.

While all of the exhibit's expectations were not fulfilled, a good many were. Along with various regional dress, the exposition displayed samples of objects "típicos de cada región" (typical of each region). Many of them, as well, were of "gran interés artístico" (great artistic interest), as the exposition hoped that "el visitante pudiera apreciar debidamente las características y costumbres de cada una de las regiones de España" (the visitor could easily appreciate the characteristics and customs of each of the regions of Spain). With this objective, it was decided that the sculptor José Planes Peñalver would model the head of each mannequin (more than 400) to give them "una expresión adecuada a los distintos tipos regionales"(an expression suited to the distinct regional types). Set in different painted landscape scenes, the characters were portrayed in an active and realistic manner, and when possible, well-known painters and sculptors participated in their production. Many of the details regarding the production of the exposition have been lost (Berges Soriano 66–76). We do know that Mariano Fortuny Madrazo,[16] the person in charge of lighting it, came from Venice with the express purpose of participating in the project, in which he employed procedures and devices of his own invention that "aumentaban poderosamente la fuerza de la luz" (powerfully increased the force of the light).

Despite the exhibit's success (in its first month it brought in more than 70,000 pesetas), its anachronistic approach was evident. The era of the reconstruction of "España pintoresca" (picturesque Spain) had passed, and with it the era of the artist, making it possible to convey the picturesque sentiment through painting, wax, and cardboard, as reflected in some of the criticism of the exposition. We thus find an era of transition with regard to the appreciation of regional attire, presupposing deep contradictions which were made manifest when Juan Comba was replaced on the organizing committee by Luis de Hoyos Sainz, a member of the Sociedad Española de Antropología y Etnografía (Spanish Society of Anthropology and Ethnography), and the author of *Cuestionario y Bases para el estudio de los Trajes Regionales* (*Questionnaire and Basis for the Study of Regional Dress*). The moment had arrived when dress would be given scientific consideration, although there was still a long way to go. After all, the exposition also served to increase artists' zeal to travel Spain and to depict it in their paintings, sculptures, and photography through dress (Vega).

Although the Museo del Pueblo Español (Museum of the Spanish People) was not created until July 26, 1934, from the time of the exposition's organization there had been talk of the need for its formation. Indeed, the exhibit itself was considered the first step in the creation of the museum's collection (Quiñones; Berges Soriano). The hope was that in the Museo del Pueblo Español authenticity would be preserved but, once and for all, this attire would cease to be an artistic prop, and consequently, its picturesque quality would disappear. A number of truly interesting articles regarding this issue appeared in the press. Among these, the article published in *La Voz* on April 27th, 1925, and entitled "El alma, la vida y el traje" (The Soul, Life, and Dress), deserves brief mention. The author of this piece valorized the organizers' attempt to create "escenas de costumbres" (sketches of customs and manners), applying the "arte de presentación" (art of presentation) – its own type of shop window – to sound "la elegía de lo pintoresco" (the elegy of the picturesque). If the picturesque element in itself was not admissible, even less was that it tried to avoid regional dress' disappearance in real life: "El traje regional está bien en una exposición o un museo. No hay que dolerse de su decadencia, puesto que ella obedece a un estado económico y social más favorable que el aislamiento antiguo de las localidades" (Regional dress is an object which belongs in an exhibit or a museum. We need not be pained by its degradation, as it pertains to a more favorable socioeconomic state than the age-old isolation of the regions). It seemed logical to the author that, as the provincial Spanish citizen (*el provinciano*) became accustomed to going to the capital, and the villager to the nearest city, the spirit of imitation would spread. After all,

> se enteran de que el traje común es más cómodo y más barato y quieren vestirse como todo el mundo. "¿Por qué no se viste usted como un caballero del Greco cuando va a Toledo?," se podría preguntar al que lamenta la desaparición del traje regional. "¡Hombre – contestaría – , porque no tengo ganas de vestirme de máscara!" Este sentimiento es el que ha ido desterrando el traje regional.

> they understand that the common attire is more comfortable, and cheaper, and they want to dress like everyone else. "Why, Sir, do you not dress like one of El Greco's

> noblemen when you go to Toledo?," it might be asked of someone who laments the disappearance of regional attire. "Why Sir," he would answer, "because I don't like to dress in costumes!" This is the sentiment that is overtaking the presence of regional dress.

He admitted that the picturesque and its attraction to foreigners would be lost with this change in attire, but that hardly mattered to either the common person or to the popular aesthetic, as "una paletita garrida está mejor, probablemente, con una airosa falda moderna que cubierta con las siete campanas de sus sieta refajos" (a rustic street vendor is better off, probably, with an airy modern skirt than covered with the seven bell-like layers of her seven petticoats).

Of course, the massive dissemination of the picturesque regional dress did not disappear, thanks to its production in the new arena of film. On Hollywood film sets, actresses were often adorned in regional dress,[17] which had been, by that time, clearly transformed into traditional dress to represent the people.[18] Awards banquets and local events, occupying a cherished place among Spaniards, were mostly won by the "ladies" of influential families for whom the dresses were designed for that express purpose.[19] Governmental authorities also participated. For instance, the Republic's first anniversary, which was celebrated in the capital, featured a grand regional cavalcade that attempted to relive the celebration that took place in Madrid in 1789 on the occasion of Carlos IV's proclamation.[20] Above all, fashion's contribution to the increase in tourism and leisure was fundamental.

As regards tourism, the case of Lagartera is paradigmatic. There, where Sorolla was said to have found the ancient Toledo, Ortega y Gasset in 1933 saw a very different reality:

> Aunque he caminado bastante por los caminitos de España no conozco más que un rincón donde el traje *popular, tradicional*, en vez de retroceder se haya afirmado. Es el pueblo de Lagartera. ¿Quiere decir esto que, por un estrambótico destino, los vecinos de este lugar vivan hacia atrás y sufran lamentable involución? Todo lo contrario. Al decidir la repristinación de los viejos atavíos, este pueblo ejercita de la manera más curiosa su modernismo. Lo moderno es la industria y la explotación. Pues bien, los lagarteranos, que habían ya casi abandonado sus usos indumentarios, conservaron la tradición de sus bordados. Algunos finos aficionados pusieron de moda estas labores, tan propias, para el ornato de las casas, y el bordado lagarterano se convirtió en industria que explota sobre todo al turista. Pero la industria moderna necesita del reclamo. Y he aquí que, como anuncio de su industria tradicional, resuelve el pueblo entero de Lagartera rehabilitar sus antiguas ropas. Por las calles de Madrid se ve pasar a lagarteranas llevando la mercancía a domicilio: va con sus faldas huecas y sus colorines, con aire de faisanes.

> Although I have walked many of Spain's paths, I am not aware of more than a small corner where the wearing of *popular, traditional* dress has been affirmed instead of having disappeared. Such is the case in the village of Lagartera. Do I mean to say that, by some outlandish destiny, the inhabitants of this place live a backward life and suffer a lamentable regression? Quite the contrary. When they decided upon the revivification of the old attire, this town, in its own curious way, actually exercised its modernism. Modernity is industry and exploitation. Well then, Lagartera's inhabitants, who have almost abandoned their traditional clothing, conserve the tradition of its embroidery. Some refined enthusiasts made these labors fashionable and even so appropriate for decorating their houses that Lagartera embroidery became an industry which primarily exploited. But modern industry must be enticing, and therefore must advertise its traditional industry. Lagartera's entire population has resolved to resuscitate its ancient robes. Women of Lagartera can be seen walking Madrid's streets wearing household-goods, going about in their fluffy and colorful skirts, as if they were peasants.

Regarding leisure, the true milestone was Barcelona's Exposición Internacional in 1929. There a "Pueblo Español" was constructed, that, throughout the entire celebration, was inhabited by provincial types in typical attire. This was the official image that had been elected to represent the country, as much to the foreigner as to Spaniards themselves. Page-long announcements directed at Spaniards appeared in the papers, urging them to visit that stronghold of *arte, casticismo, espiritualidad* (art, social purity, spirituality) where they might find the *alma regional* (regional soul) with which the Spanish people were identified. This was how Spain was intended to be seen on the eve of the Civil War of 1936. It is easy, then, to understand the speed with which Franco's dictatorship appropriated this image, transforming it into a true simulacrum of the country – a simulacrum so effective that not even W. Eugene Smith's truthful documentation in *Deleitosa* could refute it (Brandes and Miguel 1998; Vega 2002).

Notes

1. Throughout this chapter the term "dress" describes clothing worn in everyday life, while "costume" denotes clothing worn in plays and forms of public pageantry. In Spanish the appropriate word – and the one employed in the original version of this text – is *traje*. Translator's note.
2. Álvaro Molina and Jesusa Vega researches this issue in *Construir la identidad, vestir la apariencia: la cuestión del traje en la España del siglo XVIII* (Madrid: Ayuntamiento de Madrid, 2004). The identification and evolution of the different elements of these suits directly relates to the administrative organization of the Spanish state – primarily the influence of the historic kingdoms, and later that of the provinces and regions.
3. AA. VV (1996), no. 53.

4. In Spanish the term for "costumes" is *atavíos*, implying elegance. Translator's note.
5. The photo albums were presented at the Paris International Exposition of 1867.
6. These quotes are taken from the unpaginated index.
7. For large format books, page numbers are often unavailable. Other quotes without page numbers in this chapter refer to press clippings from the Museo del Traje, or can be found in the information cited in note 14.
8. Badajoz Municipal Archives, Book of Minutes, April 11, 1908.
9. The process of the modernization of painting from the turn of the century emphasized regionalism, stressing Spain's diversity and resulting in the creation of the regional schools of painting. In all of these pictorial fields dress would be the protagonist, as much in local productions as in those that transcended regional borders. This was the case in the works of Darío de Regoyos and José Gutièrrez Solana's dramatic *España Negra*, to Joaquìn Sorolla's colorful *España Blanca*, and even to the Spain of Ignacio Zuloaga, which crystallized an international stereotype that was in many cases severe and in others erotic.
10. All references to these paintings and the essays by M.A. Codding and P.E. Muller are taken from the catalogue *Sorolla y la Hispanic Society: Una visión de España de entresiglos.* Madrid: Fundaciûn Thyssen-Bornemisza, 1999.
11. A detailed study of these suits can be found in Anderson. The synthesis and monumental ensemble were popular in the press: the editor of the *Ilustración Española y Americana* (*Spanish and American Illustration*) chose this course from the beginning.
12. In this artistic context, the popular has an exotic component that suggests a lack of the modern. However, as it makes no reference to the underprivileged, there is no implied social critique.
13. The latter's presence dress' role in the construction of Spain for the tourist industry. The first Royal Police Inspector of Tourism and Popular Artistic Culture, he established prizes for those inhabitants who most distinguished themselves by donning the traditional dress of their province.
14. This quotation is from J. Sánchez Rivers' article "Crónicas de Castilla: El típico y pintoresco pueblo de Candelarios" (Chronicles of Castile. The Typical and Picturesque People of Candelario). Although the date was not listed, it was most likely published in March, 1924; see the two collected volumes of news and articles that were assembled for the Commission and published throughout the Spanish press. Both refer to the organization and the development of the *Exposición del traje regional* (*Regional Dress Exhibit*) and were preserved in the Museo del Traje (Madrid).
15. Of course, among the detractors of modern fashion (embodied above all in the

women who participated in the transformation of their social roles) the discourse of recuperating dress was an excellent weapon, transcending its own borders. Articles were published with eloquent titles such as "Donde el cetro de la moda no alcanza: Trajes típicos de diversos países" (Where the Sceptre of Fashion Doesn't Reach: The Typical Dress of the Various Countries) *Estampa* 22, May 29, 1928. In this sense, one of the most recalcitrant authors is Ricardo del Arco, who took the opportunity to publish in a wide array of newspapers and magazines. That same year *Estampa* 38, September 18, 1928 published "Perfiles aragoneses: Trajes populares" (Profiles of Aragón: Popular Dress), where del Arco commented:

Tratar del traje popular es de actualidad. En Praga, organizado por la Comisión Internacional de Cooperación Intelectual de la Sociedad de Naciones, se reunirá en octubre del actual, un Congreso Internacional de las Artes Populares. Su objeto es científico y práctico […] evidenciar la originalidad de las diversas naciones, el fondo que las es común. El traje habrá de revelar concomitancias insospechadas. El modernismo (¡qué palabra hueca!) y la mal entendida renovación van echando cizaña en los surcos pueblerinos. Se huye del "ruralismo" como si incluyese en nuestro tiempo una nota de atraso y de vergüenza.

(The discussion of popular dress is a contemporary issue. In October of this year, Prague will be the site of an Internal Congress of the Popular Arts, organized by the Internal Commission of the Intellectual Cooperation of the Society of Nations. Its purpose is scientific and practical […] to evince the originality of the various nations, with one common aim. Through dress unexpected concomitances will be revealed to us. Modernism [what a hollow term!] and the poorly understood renovation have gone through the country, sowing discord in the fields. We flee from 'ruralism' as if in our time it had a note of backwardness and shame).

The accompanying photographs were taken by Mora and San Agustìn.

16. Regarding the activities of this multifaceted artist, see "Stage-Lighting and Theatre Design" (Osma 1980).
17. The article "El vestido de la mujer en la Escena Española" (Woman's Dress on the Spanish Stage), *Estampa* , 41, October 9 1928 referred to the acting of María Palou in Gorbea's play, *Los que no perdonan* (*Those Who Do Not Forgive*), which played at the Teatro Eslava, in admiring terms: "¡Traje de mujer castellana! Sucede con él lo que con el cielo y el suelo de Castilla: hasta en sus colores fuertes tiene dramatismo y austeridad" (The Castillian women's dress! The same thing happens to it as to heaven and Castillian land: even its strong colors there is a certain drama and austerity). Sometimes such articles could be ridiculous: (see Magda Donato's "Páginas de la mujer" (Woman's Pages) about fashion, in the same publication, some years later (no. 181, June 27, 1931).

18. L.G. Linares, "Lo pintorescos que somos los españoles vistos desde Hollywood" (Hollywood's Vision of Us Picturesque Spaniards), *Estampa*, 187, August 8, 1931. We might mention some of the films shot there in 1930: Gene Walsh's *Charros, gauchos y manolas*, Ramón Novarro's *Sevilla de mis amores*, and Robert Z. Leonard's *In Gay Madrid.*
19. Excellent examples can be found in the illustrated advertisements published in *Estampa* between 1928 and 1930.
20. T. Villalba, "Las fiestas de la República: artistas encargados en lo efímero" (The Festivals of the Republic: Artists in Charge of the Ephemeral) and "La fiesta de la República: la cabalgata de las Regiones. Reportaje fotográfico" (The Festival of the Republic: The Cavalcade of the Regions. Photographic Report), *Estampa*, 179 and 181, June 12 and 27, 1931 respectively. In the Republic's proclamation we can observe a clear tendency to give a more modern image to women – or, at least, a contemporary and true one. This study has been undertaken in the context of an investigative project entiled "Cultura visual: la construcción de la memoria y la identidad en la España contemporánea" (Visual Culture: The Construction of Memory and Identity in Spain) (BHA2001–0219).

Works Cited

AA.VV. *Estampas de la Guerra de la Independencia*. Madrid: Ayuntamiento de Madrid, 1996.

Andersen, H.C. *Viaje por España*. Madrid: Alianza, 1998. Anderson, R.M. *Sorolla Room: Costumes Painted by Sorolla in his Provinces of Spain*. New York: Hispanic Society of America, 1957.

Bécquer, G.A. *Obras completas*. Madrid: Turner, 1995, 2 vols.

Berges Soriano, P.M. "Museo del Pueblo Español." *Anales del Museo Nacional de Antropologia*. Vol. 3. Madrid, 1966.

Brandes, S. and J.M. de Miguel. "Fotoperiodismo y etnografia: el caso de W. Eugene Smith y su proyecto sobre Deleitosa." *Revista de dialectología y tradiciones populares* 43 (1998): 143–74.

Cabra, M.D., ed. *La Ilustración de Madrid*. Madrid: Ediciones del Museo Universal.

Codding, Mitchell. "Archer Milton Huntington, paladín de España en América." *In Sorolla y la Hispanic Society*. Madrid: Museo Thyssen-Bornemisza, 1999. 91–117.

Exposición. Exposición del traje regional. Guía. Madrid, 1925.

Géal, P. "La creación de los museos en España." *Anuario del Departamento de Historia y Teoría del Arte* 14 (2002): 289–98.

Gutiérrez, A. "Aportación para el estudio de la indumentaria española. Fotografías de J. Laurent, s. XIX." In *Conferencia Internacional de Colecciones y Museos de indumentaria, ICCOM*. Madrid: Ministerio de la Cultura, 1993. 143–57.

Muller, Priscilla E. "Sorolla y Huntington: pintor y patrono." Badajoz: Badajoz Municipal A Archives, Book of Minutes, 1908. 119–46.

Ortega y Gasset, J. "Prólogo." In J. Ortiz Echagüe. *Tipos y trajes*. Madrid, 1933.

Osma, Guillermo de. *Mariano Fortuny: His Life and Work*. London: Aurum Press, 1980.

Puente, Joaquín de la. *Museo del Prado. Casón del Buen Retiro. Pintura del siglo XIX*. Madrid: Museo del Prado, 1985. 30–2.

Quiñones, E.A. "El museo del traje español." *Estampa* 122 (1930): no pagination.

Traver, V. *El marqués de la Vega Inclán, 1º Comisario regio de turismo y cultura artísticapopular*. Madrid: Fundaciones Vega-Inclán, 1965.

Vega, Jesusa "El traje del pueblo, Ortiz Echagüe y el simulacro de España." In *José Ortiz Echagüe en las colecciones del Museo Nacional de Antropología*. Madrid: Ministerio de Educación, Cultura y Deporte, 2002.

–12–

Observing the City, Mediating the Mountain: *Mirador* and the 1929 International Exposition of Barcelona

Robert A. Davidson

Introduction: World Fairs, Tourism and Newspapers

The World Fairs of the nineteenth and early twentieth centuries were "Internationals" for commodities. Sizeable meetings, they drew together the latest products of ingenuity and labor and exposed them to the public gaze in vast modern pavilions on elaborately conceived precincts. Once the disparate components of a fair were in place, the exposition became a fantasy world of economic possibilities, reification and visual extravagance. Under a dictum of "look but don't touch," the ensuing phantasmagoria would effectively outweigh any real commerce whilst "the show" was in progress (Buck-Morss 85–6). In this manner, the optics of a fair took both symbolic and literal precedence over its economics.

Acknowledging the important visual components of the international exposition phenomenon is essential to a reading of fairs as cultural texts indicative of specific – and at times, contradictory – modern projects and shifting subjectivities in an increasingly mediated society such as that of early-twentieth-century Western Europe. In her book on collective memory and the city, Boyer perceptively expands on the visual possibilities of expositions when she posits them as stage-like spaces where spectators could easily compare "one image to another, contrasting the difference between nations and gauging the distance between the past and the present, the so-called developed and the backward" (Boyer 257). Far from negating the past in favor of a promising future, expositions relied surreptitiously on the temporal tension that Boyer identifies as part of their visual seduction and monumental appeal.

For more than 150 years, national and municipal governments in Europe and elsewhere risked massive debt in anticipation of attracting nations, vendors and especially crowds that they hoped would flock to witness the latest in modern achievements, thus solidifying the hosts' claim on a degree of propriety over the future (Gilbert 20). Gradual advances in transportation infrastructure combined with increases in leisure time and disposable income among the working and middle classes meant that the once exclusively elite activity of tourism could play a major role in the elaboration of these international events. Accordingly, advertising became more and more pervasive: rail stations were adorned with posters, whilst hoardings displayed iconic images of the host cities and promoted the glamour of sightseeing.

The press was another important factor in the relationship between an exposition and its spectators. Although the newspaper's role in the articulation of modern urban life and the elaboration of political processes has been well documented, its importance to the visibility and reception of expositions has been somewhat overlooked and underappreciated. Multiple editions of metropolitan papers could provide relatively instantaneous coverage of special events and hence duplicate the sense of topicality and immediacy that an exposition strove to epitomize. Dailies and weeklies contributed to the cultural mapping of the fairs by including pictures from the sites, reviewing the architecture, suggesting itineraries and supplying the all-important particulars of where, how much and for how long. Through the combination of these multiple roles, the press exercised its power as a mediator of the international exposition phenomenon, especially during the first half of the twentieth century.

A World's Fair was an immensely important event in the economic, political and social life of a modern city. It was an occasion before and during which questions of commerce and nationhood as well as collective experience and the nature of the modern spectacle intersected. How these convergences played out in the specific case of Barcelona and the Catalan capital's International Exposition of 1929 is the overarching theme of this chapter. As I hope to demonstrate, optics, politics and the competing national subjectivities of a modernizing country under a dictatorship combined to make the Barcelona Fair much more than a simple trade show or celebration of the future.

Catalan Cultural Modernity and Miguel Primo de Rivera

Literary journals and newspapers have played an important role in the consolidation of Catalan culture. As Resina has pointed out, when faced with an absence of "official" forums in the decades surrounding the turn of the twentieth century, *modernista* journals such as *L'Avenç* took on the ostensibly public role of modernizing culture (388). With the rise of a politically enabled Catalan bourgeoisie during this period, cultural modernity in Catalonia entailed a growing sense of nationhood and of difference in relation to the Spanish state. The Universal Exposition of Barcelona in 1888 was a watershed moment; it was the bourgeoisie's coming-out party, their chance to turn towards Europe and show off artistic and economic advances made during the *Renaixença*, a time of cultural recuperation in Catalonia. Although the 1888 event lost money and sparked both financial and political recriminations, its aftermath did not dampen the enthusiasm for greater European recognition and, importantly, equal cultural exchange – one of the tenets of *modernisme*, for which that year's gathering served as a foreword.

An increasingly enabled sense of Catalan specificity was a prominent feature also of *noucentisme*, a cultural movement begun in the early 1900s. *Noucentistas* such as Eugeni d'Ors and Enric Prat de la Riba sought to refine *modernista* excess and make cultural production an extension of (Catalan) state processes. Although the actual extent to which *noucentisme*'s goals matched its political means was open to debate, in 1923 this point was rendered moot when, reacting in part to the national problems of Catalonia and Euskadi, the then captain general of Barcelona, Miguel Primo de Rivera, seized control of Spain and established a dictatorship that would last until 1930.

Initially, the new dictator acted with the implicit support of the conservative, Catalanist *Lliga Regionalista* party, a group increasingly disturbed by labor strife and fearful of a possible class-based revolution. Even though Primo de Rivera supposedly gave guarantees regarding the preservation of Catalan culture, the general's subsequent actions belied his true intention: to maintain the territorial integrity of the Spanish state at the expense of linguistic and cultural plurality. At the heart of his campaign was the reinvigoration and strengthening of existing limitations on both public and private Catalan language education and usage. Put succinctly, the repressive dictatorship reimposed what may be considered a pre-modern cultural condition. Or, at the very least, by stifling the creation of links between the arts, language and statecraft, the seven years of Primo de Rivera's regime placed a modernizing Catalan culture in stasis.[1]

Mirador: A Vantage Point on the City

The successful recuperation and progressive consolidation of Catalan culture had hit a brick wall in Primo de Rivera. The 1888 Exposition had generated real momentum but hostilities during World War I scuttled plans for a sequel that city planners had envisioned for 1917. Once in power, the dictator did not revive preparations for this second fair until several years after the consolidation of his regime and the realization of his agenda for Spanish modernization, some tenets of which were at odds symbolically with Catalan conceptions of modernity and the metropolis. The cultural deep-freeze in Catalonia was not total, however, and by 1929, it had begun to thaw significantly as cracks appeared in Primo de Rivera's hold on power. The year of the Wall Street Crash saw the opening of the long-delayed International Exposition of Barcelona, the culminating spectacle of the city's *feliços vint*; 1929 was also the moment in which the important journal, *Mirador*, appeared on the cultural scene (Figure 12.1)

Figure 12.1 Artist unknown, *Mirador* banner, 1929.

In Catalan, *mirador* means "vantage point" and the journal to which the Catalanist lawyer and businessman Amadeu Hurtado applied this name was both figuratively and literally well positioned within the city it observed. Not only could the editors count on the active participation of Barcelona's cultural elite, but also the paper's office was strategically located at 62 Pelai Street, the corner where the city's famous Rambla emerged from the Gothic Quarter and met the Plaça de Catalunya. This square was Barcelona's newly forged center and axis between the rational, grid-like *Eixample* and the labyrinthine old city. Symbolically then, *Mirador* occupied the point of transition between Barcelona's past and future and ironically projected a new urban and cultural vision from one of the exact places where the restrictive medieval wall had held the city and its inhabitants captive until the 1850s.

Like the Madrid-based *La Gaceta Literaria* before it, the journal was expressly dedicated to literature, art and politics. Its first issue appeared on January 31, 1929 and it continued weekly until 1937. Arguably, the paper was at its most vibrant during the initial three years, when a Catalan Republic seemed possible given the slow dissolution of the dictatorship. A long time supporter of Catalanism, Hurtado was astute enough to recognize the growing importance of print media and mass culture to political organization and mobilization during the 1920s (Huertas and Geli: 14). For the bulk of that decade in Spain, however, state censors severely curtailed, if not completely suppressed, freedom of expression in the press, especially when it took the form of political dissent. As a result, Hurtado and his colleagues felt first hand the cultural stasis that the dictatorship had imposed and were effectively silenced within Catalonia for a period of several years.

Hurtado based *Mirador* on what he considered the French and English model of combining culture and politics (Huertas and Geli 26). Consequcntly, the journal strove from the outset to become decidedly European, albeit with a definite

Catalanist bent, as it struggled initially with censorship. *Mirador* endeavored to articulate alternative viewpoints whilst taking an intense interest in the local specificity of Barcelona. Thematic flexibility meant that the journal could be an important mediator as well of popular entertainment and the arts during its entire run, and it came to serve as an engaged voice of the past, present and future urban experience of Catalonia's political, economic and cultural capital.

Mirador and the International Exposition of 1929

Mirador's recurring interest in the built and natural environments of the city was a particularly integral part of its urban posture, a stance not at all incompatible with the more overtly political goals held by the editors. During the journal's inaugural year, the Expo had a tremendous cultural resonance in the city and even though the editors of *Mirador* did not favor Primo de Rivera's policies, the paper viewed the Fair as a means of drawing attention to the Catalan capital and it reveled in the energy that the event generated. As a space of performance and entertainment, the Exposition site held sway both in the metropolis and the journal's pages for roughly a year and a half.[2] It dominated civic coverage and served to underline the links between urbanism, architecture and politics in the journal's cultural commentary.

Geographically and historically speaking, the Fair's importance to Barcelona is even more significant when one considers that citizens and commentators alike had long associated Montjuïc – the mountain that overlooks Barcelona to the immediate south and home to a former military base – with urban control. A history of being subjected to the Spanish military's surveying gaze and of living in the sightlines of cannons that had fired on them in the nineteenth century had left indelible marks. It is easy to see, then, how the city's recuperation and reintegration of the military citadel (the Ciutadella) by means of the 1888 Universal Exposition established an important and symbolic precedent.[3] Although Puig i Cadafalch had proposed another Exposition as early as 1905, twelve years would pass until construction on the wild and undeveloped Montjuïc would finally begin. World War I halted the work, but nevertheless, the choice of the mountain for the next Fair made it clear that, having retaken the Ciutadella, the nascent metropolis was ready both to tackle another blatant reminder of centrist control and officially integrate a rural zone that sat on its doorstep. The subsequent "hijacking'' of the 1917–cum-1929 Exposition by the dictator and his functionaries thus converted both the contents of the fair and the geographical site it occupied into a politically and culturally contested space, one where competing visions of modernity came into contact.

Mirador's coverage of the Exposition and Barcelona's urban development dovetailed with consideration of the space's integration with the metropolis. Even though *Mirador*'s treatment and framing of the Expo and its effects on the city contributed to the urbanization and politicization of a Jazz Age metropolis very much living in the now, the Catalan capital's past as an arrested, walled city bubbled constantly beneath the surface of the journal's obsession with urban renewal. The paper made frequent references to the long civic imprisonment that Barcelona suffered from Madrid's refusal to permit the tearing down of the medieval walls until the middle of the nineteenth century. One later example that speaks to this point and demonstrates how *Mirador* literally reprinted historical memory as a reminder of past impediments to expansion is an article by editor Manuel Brunet that deals with the chaotic nature of the Old City and the establishment of a municipal body to oversee planning and development of a future Barcelona. In a case of some very curious optics, this story of the future went accompanied by a map from the past, namely, one of the captive, walled city from the early eighteenth century (Brunet 3). At no point in the article was this past mentioned; the totalizing, modernist depiction of the confined *urbs*, however, spoke volumes.

Montjuïc's role in that past was an unforgettable subtext. Even as a space of diversion and putting aside for a moment its own provocative components, the Expo was still charged with political importance through association. Its aesthetics resonated beyond the site's physical and temporal boundaries, making an acknowledgment of the political ramifications of the event crucial to a greater understanding of how the possible recuperation of the Montjuïc site may be read as a symbolic and literal attempt to transform the modern Catalan conception of their capital city and rewrite the spatial histories between mountain and metropolis, periphery and center.

Mirador's interest in one particularly contentious Exposition tourist attraction, the synthesized "typical" pre-industrial Spanish town or *Poble Espanyol*, is a useful touchstone in a discussion of the clash between modern subjectivities in the Spanish state of the time. I base my analysis on two factors: first, what I consider to be the *Poble*'s aesthetic and architectural effects vis-à-vis the socio-historical context and second, *Mirador*'s subsequent reception of the attraction. I propose reading the emblematic *Poble* as a highly politicized and monumental structure/spectacle representative of the dictator's desire to display and exhibit national unity through a valorization of the rural over the urban. More than any other aspect of the International Exposition, the *Poble* acted as an axis around which the political potential of the tourist spectacle inherent in the Exposition revolved. In the resulting tension between two contrasting national projects – the centrist Spanish one promoted (and enforced) by Primo de Rivera and the competing Catalan version championed by Barcelona's left-wing intelligentsia – *Mirador*'s unique brand of a historically sensitive, modern political urbanism becomes more clearly defined.

The *Poble Espanyol*

National and foreign tourists alike sought out the pastiche-like *Poble Espanyol*, one of the better known attractions on the Montjuïc site.[4] Aesthetically and architecturally it is of great importance – and not simply because of its popularity. Even though the Exposition of 1929 was dedicated to the modern values of industrial and artistic progress and vitality, the *Poble* was designed as a monument to (Spanish) national craftsmanship and design. In my reading of it, I contend that amidst the international trappings of the fair, it commandeered the local aspect of the Expo site's cosmopolitan mix of foreign and national. *Mirador*'s subsequent engagement with the site as a whole responds to the challenge to Catalan specificity inherent in this dynamic.

While it may be possible to argue that the Exposition's packaging as a touristic event should be interpreted as a depoliticizing action, a superficial covering of the space and, hence, of the past, with the surface appeal of mass spectacle, I would suggest that this same superficiality of form is at the root of the *Poble*'s aesthetic effect. It is reflected in the supposedly temporary, yet ostensibly permanent nature of the *Poble*'s trappings and encourages consideration of the specifically monumental nature of the *Poble Espanyol* within the politico-cultural context of the site. In his 1903 book, *The Modern Monument*, Riegl characterizes monuments in two broad camps: the intentional and the unintentional. The former describes deliberate attempts at designing memory and commemoration while the latter takes on its aura of value and importance as a result of the passage of time. In the case of the *Poble Espanyol*, one sees a curious mix of the two. I believe that the *Poble*'s role in the process of political inscription through monumentality needs to be emphasized, especially in light of its provocative spatial aesthetics.[5] Without a doubt, the *Poble* may be seen as a "homey construct beyond the home," one that binds Spain and its peoples in a pre-industrial village (Epps 172). Intriguingly, though, the artificial traces that contribute to a reading of the site as uncanny also permit its consideration as a political structure.

As Epps (172–3) observes, the "little homecomings" that the *Poble Espanyol* engenders among the Spanish tourists must be counterpoised with an international gaze that is potentially taking in a condensed Spain and Catalonia for the first time. Hence, visually, the *Poble* becomes both reminder and primary representative of the local. It is an intentional monument or sign that acts as a reminder of a totalizing, unified state as the arrangement of fine examples of Spanish architecture and the active presence of skilled artisans collapse the regional distinctions they ostensibly attempt to celebrate. Unity is achieved through dissolution, since the place of work, the living conditions and even the pace of daily life are harmonized to the artificial rhythms of the Exposition's opening and closing hours.

As is plainly evident from its name, the *Poble Espanyol* glorifies Spain's architectural history – not that of any one city or region. And while it is difficult to assume how individual visitors – Barcelona residents as well as those from elsewhere – personally reacted to the amalgam, it must be noted that the main entrance to the site is wholly Castilian in appearance. The imposing *Ávila* gate opens onto the *Plaza Castellana*, which in turn leads to a prototypical *plaza mayor* that does not include a single building modeled after one from Catalonia.[6] Consequently, from the outset of the visitor's foray into the town, there is a symbolic, yet explicitly visual architectural break with the true local, the Catalan national and geographic space.[7] This condition becomes even more relevant when one considers that, according to architect Francesc de P. Nebot, Ignasi Girona, president of the Institut Agrícola Català, proposed the original idea for an architectural "town" at the Exposition in 1915. Nebot himself drew up plans not for a Spanish town but rather, a *Catalan* one. In an interview conducted by *Mirador* at the end of August 1929, he states that it was to have been "compost amb elements d'arquitectura usats a Catalunya des de l'època romana fins a últims del segle divuit, a fi de donar a conèixer, a la vegada que la història de l'agricultura, la història de la casa catalana, al voltant de la qual s'és aquella desenrotllada" (Anon 1929b: 3). That this initiative was transformed into a project that reinforced the artistic and architectural unity of the state comes as no surprise considering Primo de Rivera's enmity towards the possibility of a pluralistic Spain. This fundamental change from a Catalan to a Spanish town also entailed a change in the perception of and engagement with the concept of rurality.

In keeping with Riegl's classification system, the *Poble* may be interpreted as well as an example of an unintentional monument. Paradoxically, this unintentionality had also been fabricated. In addition to their rural origins, the buildings chosen as models for the site were valued both for their artistry and for their antiquity, a historical value gained through the passage of time. This pre-industrial amalgam is only seemingly politically neutral in its guise as tourist attraction. By reconstructing an idealized past architecturally and giving symbolic importance to rural Spain, the site represents an erasure of the centrifugal national forces manifest in the rise of Barcelona and Bilbao as important economic and industrial centers in the country. The reminding aspect of the *Poble* is centripetal, an architectural fortifying of national unity and of a Spanish locality gained through force. Recreation through reminiscence becomes an agent of the past's imposition on the present as the turreted walls containing the *Poble* reinscribe the many years of Barcelona's own arrested development as a captive city.

Where exactly is the harm in a hokey, although formidably constructed and genuinely popular, tourist site such as the *Poble Espanyol* assuming the mantle of local in a cosmopolitan Fair that sought to trumpet Spain's modernity? One could say that the danger lies precisely in the spatial implications of this status as monument. If, as Gadamer (129) asserts, monuments hold what is represented "in a specific state of presentness," the modern creation of the unified state in the guise of the past transcends mere diversion. Worse still for the specifically Catalan subject, it enters fully into the sphere of entertainment and trivializes the real political and social consequences incurred by the process of forced unification. Complementing Gadamer's notion of presentness in this case is Lefebvre's view of the monument. He considers monumental space as offering those in society an "image of membership" (Lefebvre 220). This begs the question: what image is conveyed to the Catalan, Spanish, or foreign tourist who wanders the streets of the *Poble Espanyol*? As Epps (171) points out, Barcelona was virtually eclipsed in the *Poble*, yet, conversely, Seville took center-stage in the *Plaza de España* at the rival Exposición Iberoamericana.

The *Poble Espanyol* may have been the most spectacular example of a rural influence in the campaign to attract tourists to Spain and underline the country's unity but it was not the only one. A parallel exists between the *Poble*'s celebration of the non-industrial or pre-modern Spanish interior and the fledgling *Parador* system that Primo de Rivera's government instituted in the second half of the 1920s. The first *Parador*, or state hotel, appeared near Ávila in 1926. By 1928, the *Patronato Nacional de Turismo* had established a *Junta de Paradores y Hosterías del Reino* that sought to create a network of hotels in regions lacking such services (Read and Manjón 13). While the *Junta*'s first contribution was the cosmopolitan Hotel Atlántico in Cádiz, its main focus was on rehabilitating old castles, monasteries and palaces (13). By the end of 1932, there were six more sites operating in the provinces of Toledo, Madrid, Salamanca, Jaén and Ciudad Real (all outside Catalonia). Whether intentional or not, the *Poble*'s rustic packaging mirrors the official policy of attracting tourists to rural areas that had been recently opened up by the regime's massive public works and subsequently activated culturally by the *Parador* chain.

The reconstruction of buildings from all over the Spanish state was, then, modernity both disguised and denied. The *Poble* was and is a product of the twentieth century masquerading as something much older and more worn. And while during the Exposition the nearby *Palau de Projeccions* would show the latest in mass entertainment – films, large-scale music hall performances, etc. – the *Poble Espanyol* projected its audience/citizens backwards in time, defeating the modern Catalan metropolis through its compressed environs and the rustic façade it bestowed on the growing activity of international (and interurban) tourism.

The *Poble Espanyol*, *Mirador* and Montjuïc Reclaimed

If the *Poble Espanyol* may be read as both a reminder of Barcelona's walled captivity and as a literal, architectural image of a fortified Spanish unity, how did the

Catalanist and urban-minded *Mirador* mediate this potentially provocative space? The journal tackled the existence and symbolic implications of the *Poble Espanyol* in two different ways. First, the editors solicited reactions to the *Poble* in a survey conducted two weeks after the opening of the Fair. Then, the paper attempted to supplant the dictatorship's appropriation of the local, signified as it was by the castilianized Exposition and its main attraction, a Spanish Town originally slated to have been Catalan. *Mirador* accomplished this latter point by stressing the reclamation of Montjuïc. In addition to redressing the historical grief the mountain denoted, this move also marked a step in the modern dialogue between Catalonia and abroad as the journal looked to capitalize on the international cachet the Exposition had imbued on Barcelona as a whole. This last tactic carried over to the post-Primo de Rivera period but is important, nonetheless, for an examination of how the periodical engaged the challenge to Catalan modernity that the dictatorship set in motion and then how it tried to set the table, so to speak, for a possible Catalan Republic.

The Survey

The question of what to make of (and later do with) the *Poble* was broached quickly. Less than two weeks after the official opening, the journal's editors led with a front page survey in which they polled various artists and critics to learn what each of them would do with the town following the Exposition. If, on account of the censorship, the editors did not feel free to make their opinions known regarding the attraction, the space they accorded numerous critical voices was a statement in itself. While there were cries from Rafael Benet and Màrius Aguilar to destroy it, certain respondents, including the well-known J.V. Foix, offered that the *Poble* needed to be consolidated and vitalized. A not-so-forgiving Benet suggested donating it to the local fire brigade so that it might be used for training purposes. Aguilar was equally vehement in his belief that it should be torn down; in his words, it was "un pastitx. Una mena de mostruari. Com a atracció, ja està bé, però res més que com a atracció. Així és que, acabada l'Exposició, ja no té raó d'existir" (Anon 1929c: 1).

Meanwhile, in the other camp, a priest suggested holding a procession there for revitalization purposes. A group of musicians also submitted that, although far from the *Plaça Reial* (the Municipal Band's usual venue), by playing in the *Poble*, they could inject some needed energy. *Mirador* regular Joan Sacs saw the *Poble Espanyol* – so popular and renowned for its antiquated exteriors – as an ideal locale for a museum devoted to the modern *interior*. Sacs's views, in particular, reflected a strong nationalist sensibility regarding the notions of preservation and future utility. He believed that any museum should first and foremost be dedicated to Catalan furniture and design, with other Hispanic furnishings and articles from abroad being included only afterwards (Anon 1929c: 1). Although *Mirador* did take the interiors of the various pavilions very seriously, as evidenced by the two-part series by Josep Mainar, "El mobiliari a l'Exposició," Sacs's words may be interpreted as a barb at the Exposition's *Bellas Artes* exhibit that traveled between the Barcelona and Seville fairs as proof of the artistic glory and history of a united Spain. For his part, rather than covet the town's insides, the director in charge of the *Poble Espanyol*, Lluís Plandiura, valorized the exterior above all else and saw a potential for profit in its visual artificiality. In the survey, he proposed renting the space to movie producers and revealed that both Paramount and Metro studios had already made inquiries to that effect as early as May 1929 (Anon 1).

Mirador's survey provided an interesting forum for dissenting views on the value of the *Poble Espanyol*. The overall hostile response to it was in keeping with the political orientation of the journal and displayed a clear rejection of what was considered a symbol of the centrist project. The articulation of a desire to fill the town with examples of Catalan artistic production is indicative of the disconnect between the Expo and the city.[8] According to this line of thought, only once it had been imbued with some sort of culturally relevant civic life, could the *Poble Espanyol* be brought into the Catalan metropolis. This point foreshadows the journal's desire to recapture the encompassing exposition space and bestow upon it the proper sense of locality required if modern Barcelona (and hence Catalonia), rather than a unified Spain, was to be affirmed.

The sculptor Rebull's final comments provided the survey with an incisive coda. According to him, it was imperative to "Tornar les cases del Poble Espanyol a llurs pobles" (Anon 1929c: 1). Rebull's simple sentence once more invokes the idea of the *Poble*'s "impossibility" and inauthenticity in Catalanist eyes as he makes light of its pre-industrial presence in the metropolis and muses on a fanciful return of simulated stones to towns from which they never came.[9]

Integrating Montjuïc

Mirador's second response to the *Poble Espanyol* and to the usurpation of Catalan subjectivity that it and the Spain-centric Expo represented was to plan actively for the site's integration into the greater urban area. It is clear that the journal did not object so much to the ephemeral and spectacular nature of the fair as it did to the fact that the diversion for the urban masses should come at the expense of the articulation of Catalonia's historical difference. *Mirador* considered the *Poble* and the rest of the Expo through the lens of the long-term needs of the capital and its citizenry. That mass entertainment figured into these plans is evident especially in the journal's praising of Bohiga's spectacular central fountain, which they named one of the marvels of the Fair and hoped would continue to entertain after the Expo had concluded. While such importance given to a fountain may sound trivial, the concern with the Exposition's permanent physical legacy to Barcelona, both in terms of recreation and a more rational "pure" urbanism, was not idle banter; on the contrary, it was front page and headline material for *Mirador*.

The salvaging of parts of the Expo precinct notwithstanding, the encompassing space of Montjuïc came to represent the greatest recuperative potential for *Mirador*. Thus, it is significant that the editors named the Montjuïc Gardens as the Exposition's "marvel of marvels" (Anon 1929a: 1). The valorization of a stable, urbanized and tamed rural space such as the mountain clashed with the temporary nature of the architectural monumentalism incarnated by structures like the *Poble Espanyol* and the overwhelming, baroque, *Palau Nacional*. Here one sees a clear difference in the modern projects of Spain and Catalonia at the time. Whereas Primo de Rivera valorized the rural in an effort to justify historically and politically the unity of the Spanish state, Catalonia's appreciation for it was in accordance with the trajectory of a specifically Catalan modern experience, one in which language, geography and religion served as the original foundations of the *Renaixença*. What is more, aspects of the ingrained nationalist concept of *Catalunya – Ciutat* are no more closely observed than in the relationship between Barcelona and Montjuïc.

How did the paper achieve a Catalan branding of the development of the mountain? First, they made it abundantly clear that those in charge of the Exposition had not created the present gardens but rather, that they were started prior to the dictatorship. The editors stressed the fact that the city had begun to enjoy them eight years previously and they took pains to underline that a junta made up of members from various political parties had launched the planning process (Anon. 1929a: 1). One may read this claim of nonpartisan political solidarity as a further marker of an us versus them perspective, one supported by the editorial's closing paragraph in which politics and geography mix and in which Montjuïc is described as a place free from the rigors of (urban, rational) symmetry and as being both seigniorial and democratic in nature (Anon. 1929a: 1).

Although Primo de Rivera fled Spain in early 1930, the second Republic was not proclaimed until April 14, 1931. During this in-between period, censorship loosened but constitutional normality in Catalonia was not achieved. *Mirador* took up the larger question of the future of Barcelona early in 1930 in a front-page article entitled "Els problemes de la postexposició." Despite the fact that this notion had been broached before, most notably in an October piece by Nicolau M. Rubió i Tudurí, the change in the nature of the Exposition made this editorial even more salient.[10] With the International Exposition now just the Exposition, the editorial stated that a reduction in status could be beneficial to the city regardless of the danger of visitors considering the scaled-back Fair as nothing more than an event "in liquidation" (Anon. 1930b: 1). They reasoned that with the international focus gone, Barcelona had a chance to recoup its social investment and recast the Expo as a truly local event, in this way defeating any legacy of the dictatorship's imposition of the Spanish as the local and reaffirming Catalonia as subject.

As during the previous year, Montjuïc surfaced constantly as the most important part of this recasting of the Exposition. The Fair was credited with starting a process that Primo de Rivera had interrupted and that had to be continued; Montjuïc, they claimed, would be more beautiful after the Expo than before (Anon. 1930b: 1). That said, for the editors of *Mirador*, the Expo was not the be all and end all. Just as the journal considered Montjuïc in terms of the city as a whole, so too did it label other urban concerns as fundamental to the post-Expo period.[11] Apparently more urgent than questions regarding which pavilions to preserve or further assessments of the event's touristy packaging, these needs echoed in their concise analysis of the Exposition as a bluff, whose gains would only appear over the long term, a period that would hopefully fall under Catalanist control (Anon. 1930b: 1).

The Barcelona Exposition closed on July 15, 1930. Freed from the shackles of censorship, *Mirador*'s editorial two days later commemorated the Fair in its entirety but was hard-hitting in its appraisal of the overall results. First, regarding the dictatorship's initial predictions of millions of North and South American visitors, the editors scoffed and labeled the Iberian Peninsula a cul-de-sac, far removed from European mass transit. Then, in an even blunter assessment, they opined that the Exposition had been in dire need of "uns alts funcionaris més intel·ligents" (Anon. 1930a: 1). Finally, although they harped on the massive amount of public money used to finance the Fair, what seems to have rankled the most was, again, part of the optics inherent to events of this nature, namely, that the dictatorship had treated the Barcelona Exposition as an appendix to Seville's competing Exposición Iberoamericana.

Conclusion

As in international expositions in other cities, ultimately, questions of how the hosts were seen – the visual aspect of an important civic exercise in visuality and visibility – determined and conditioned the reception of the gathering as a whole. In the case of Barcelona's 1929 Fair, the *Poble Espanyol*, a draw that had become the showcase attraction, reconfigured drastically the civic dimension. Though not totally effaced, Barcelona was minimalized; the local element in the cosmopolitan mix of the Exposition did not acknowledge the industrial modernity of the host city; rather, it celebrated a folkloric, pre-industrial unity that at best stereotyped and at worst nullified the Catalan modern experience and heritage. This approach engaged a conception of the rural-as-history that was an integral part of the dictatorship's own modern process, one in which physical modernization of the state trumped any accompanying nationalist desire that contested or complicated Spanish unity.

As a mediator of both city and event, *Mirador* attempted to mitigate this effect in spite of state censorship. Through its constant focus on the past, present and future urban experience of Barcelona, the journal was able to articulate an alternative view. In the end, as the editors had previously asserted, Montjuïc, a rural space tinged with a past of urban control, emerged as the single most important aspect of the Fair in *Mirador*'s eyes. The mountain's rehabilitation through the creation of park space and limited urbanization represented a reclaiming of the area in the name of responsible urban development on behalf of Barcelona's citizens. Their ambitious plans for reform at all levels, however, ran aground on the rocks of the Spanish Republic and then sank during Franco's dictatorship, when Montjuïc's castle again became a prison and the *Poble Espanyol* stood once more as a peculiar example of regime architecture at its fanciest.

Notes

1. For a comprehensive examination of Primo de Rivera's campaign against the Catalan language and culture, see Roig Rosich.
2. This is not to say that there were not criticisms; however, press censorship often makes it difficult to judge the ambiguous tone of some of the articles.
3. The Ciutadella was ceded to the city in 1869 on the condition that the lands be developed as a public space (Julián 23–4).
4. The government approved the construction of the Poble at the end of 1926. The work team included architects Francesc Folguera i Ramon Reventós, Xavier Nogués and Miguel Utrillo (Anon. 1929b: 3). In an interview with *Mirador*, Nogués revealed that he and the others had logged some 18,000 kilometers crisscrossing Spain looking for the buildings that they eventually copied (3). An article published in June 1929 in Madrid's *El Sol* sarcastically took Utrillo to task: "dicen del 'pueblo español' que, por ser típico, hasta no tiene escuela" (Bello 1).
5. While Epps (171) considers the *Poble* a site of the uncanny – based on the effect of familiarity and displacement inherent in the experience of the town by those from other parts of Spain – he considers its political charge to be somewhat more ambivalent than I do.
6. The Països Catalans dominate one street, the stereotypically named carrer Mercaders. The majority of the buildings on that street were modeled on houses from the provinces of Girona and Tarragona, respectively.
7. One may also observe that the *plaza mayor* is more specifically representative of Castilian urban planning, since Mediterranean Catalan cities make more use of the tree-lined promenade or *rambla*.
8. An article by Josep Maria Planes highlights the apparent disjuncture between the city and the space during the Exposition. His piece, "Nit de revetlla a

l'Exposició," deals with the Sant Joan celebrations of 1929. Planes marvels at the vast numbers of people who made their way up to Montjuïc and is impressed that, finally, all of Barcelona was there and not just the elite (Planes 2). In order to convey the variety of the crowd and the intensity of a celebration of a sense of Catalan place – for one night at least – Planes offers a metaphorical mix of local specificity and Jazz Age imagery: "imagineu-vos totes les festes majors de Catalunya plegades; les que s'han celebrat d'ença que el món és món i les que vindran; tireu-les totes dintre d'una coktelera meravellosa, remeneu una mica i aboqueu el que en resulti sobre la muntanya de Montjuïc" (2).

9. The buildings in the *Poble Espanyol* are not exact copies but rather models inspired by actual buildings.
10. The editorial space of issue no. 39 was given to Rubió i Tudurí, Director of Parks for the city. He offered the readers a detailed study of his installation Futura Barcelona at the Municipal Pavilion and observed explicitly the "tilting" effect of the Exposition site on the city: "Barcelona té actualment el seu centre social entre la Plaça de Catalunya i Gràcia, però l'Exposició amb la Plaça d'Espanya i la Diagonal l'estiren fortament cap a l'Oest" (Rubió i Tudurí 1).
11. Among these figure railway problems, the prolongation of the Gran Via to Badalona, the issue of Turó-Park and affordable housing for workers.

Works Cited

Anon. "Els jardins de Montjuïc." *Mirador* 28 (1929a): 1.

—— "La paternitat del Poble Espanyol." *Mirador* 31 (1929b): 3.

—— "Què en farem del Poble Espanyol?" *Mirador* 18 (1929c): 1.

—— "La clausura de l'Exposició." *Mirador* 77 (1930a): 1.

—— "Els problemes de la postexposició." *Mirador* 51 (1930b): 1.

Bello, L. "En el 'pueblo español.'" *El Sol* (June 20, 1929): 1.

Boyer, M. Christine. *The City of Collective Memory: Its Historical Imagery and Architectural Entertainments*. Cambridge, MA: MIT Press, 1996.

Brunet, Manuel. "Per la ciutat futura." *Mirador* 84 (1930): 3.

Buck-Morss, Susan. *The Dialectics of Seeing: Walter Benjamin and the Arcades Project*. Cambridge, MA and London: MIT Press, 1989.

Epps, Brad. "Modern Spaces: Building Barcelona", *Iberian Cities*. Ed. Joan Ramon Resina. New York: Routledge, 2001. 148–97.

Gadamer, Hans Georg. "The Ontological Foundation of the Occasional and the Decorative." *Rethinking Architecture*, Ed. Neil. Leach. London: Routledge, 1997. 125–37.

Gilbert, J. "World's Fairs as Historical Events." *Fair Representations: World's Fairs and the Modern World*. Eds. R. W. Rydell and Nancy E. Gwinn. Amsterdam: VU (Vrije Universiteit) UP, 1994. 13–27.

Huertas, Josep Maria and Carles Geli. *"Mirador", la Catalunya impossible*. Barcelona: Proa, 2000.

Julián, Inmaculada. *L'urbanisme a Barcelona entre dues exposicions (1888–1929)*. Sant Cugat del Vallès: Els Llibres de la Frontera, 1988..

Lefebvre, Henri. *The Production of Space*. Oxford: Blackwell, 2000.

Mainar, J. "El mobiliari a l'Exposició (1)." *Mirador* 61 (1930): 7.

Planes, J. M. "Nit de revetlla a l'Exposició." *Mirador* 22 (1929): 2.

Read, Jan and Maite Manjón. *Paradores of Spain*. London: Macmillan, 1977.

Resina, Joan Ramon. "Modernist Journals in the *Països Catalans*." *Revista Hispánica Moderna* 8 (2000): 388–98.

Riegl, Alois. *Le culte moderne des monuments*. Paris: Seuil, 1984/1903.

Roig Rosich, Josep M. *La dictadura de Primo de Rivera a Catalunya: un assaig de repressió cultural*. Barcelona: Publicacions de l'Abadia de Montserrat, 1992.

Rubió i Tudurí, N.M. "La Barcelona futura." *Mirador* 39 (1929): 1.

–13–

Joan Miró, 1929: High and Low Culture in Barcelona and Paris

Fèlix Fanés

During the summer of 1929, Joan Miró completed a series of collages in Montroig. They involved cut pieces of paper stuck onto a paper background, technically very similar to the Cubist *papiers collés* of 1912. Louis Aragon at least seemed to think so, finding them "closer to the collages by Picasso … than anything else" (Aragon 26). Though this statement is correct as far as technique goes, it is more questionable from an aesthetic point of view. This group of collages was described by Sebastià Gasch as "work of damnable bad taste" (Gasch, "L'elogi"). For him, however, this statement was not a pejorative one. On the contrary, from "bad taste" came "intensity." One should probably look to the use that Miró made of cheap materials such as translucent paper and wrapping paper, for example, in order to find the basis for this remark. However, there are other explanations relating to the painter's "bad taste," compared in the article with French "good taste," classified by the critic as "the enemy" for "any true artist." One of these explanations can be found in Miró's interest in products of mass consumption, such as "vulgar postcards" or "lithographs on boxes of raisins or cigars," examples that were, for Gasch, of "the most regrettable bad taste" which nevertheless made a stronger impression than any of "the delicate, winged, ethereal creations by those sublime manufacturers of fine coloristic harmonies."

Gasch's vindication of bad taste through praise for humble visual materials associated with popular consumption was not some momentary whim. He had already written something very similar a few months earlier. "I love living things," he declared then; "I detest dead things." In support of his argument he recalled that he had not been to any exhibitions for a year. He found "the little chemist's window at the Arc del Teatre, the amazing illuminated sign on a boarding house in Carrer de l'Est, the disturbing paintings covering the walls of a tavern in Carrer del Migdia, the tragic – terrible – entrance to a house in Carrer del Cid" more interesting than any painting; a series of "insignificant marvels that we – Joan Miró and I – are excited to discover in our frequent visits to the Fifth District [a poor quarter of Barcelona], much more impressive than some stagnant trip around dead archeological remains" (Gasch, *Coses vives*). These ideas were not a long way from the slightly earlier writings of Michel Leiris, when he compared Miró's canvasses, "soiled rather than painted," with "destroyed buildings" and "faded walls on which generations of posters, aided by centuries of drizzle, had created mysterious poems" (Leiris, *Documents* 263–9).

But let us stay with Gasch. The collective known as *L'Amic de les Arts* group, formed by Gasch himself, the literary critic Lluís Montanyà and the painter Salvador Dalí, had been arguing in support of a form of anti-artistic poetry for a couple of years at least, finding their inspiration in the growth of individual consumption and the proliferation of consumer goods. They did not shy away from praising the banality of the modern: cars, chrome faucets, the latest dance craze, advertising. This praise, on the other hand, had recently begun to evolve, as a result of the influence of surrealist publications, towards a backward-looking admiration for surviving forms from earlier eras, things that were out of fashion, degraded, and subject to inexorable changes in taste brought on by the passage of time. It is in this context that the critic's words should be seen. For Gasch – and also for Leiris – there was something in Miró's work that came close to the detritus of urban life. Through his use of scrap materials, the painter's work gave off a stimulating intensity. Beauty in ugliness and profundity in the most superficial of things form the basis of this aesthetic approach.[1]

Of the different collages completed by Joan Miró in 1929, there is one that particularly illustrates these ideas (Figure 13.1). This collage, now in the Museum of Modern Art in New York, is very similar in terms both of its dimensions (72.2 x 108.4 cm) and the materials used (low quality paper affixed to paper) to other works by the artist during this period.[2] However, the structure of the work, which centers on a group of five circular shapes arranged around the lower part of the space, offers two innovations in respect to the other collages completed that summer. The first, a "window" with drawings on the right-hand section of the work, and the second, a newspaper cutting in the form of a circle, placed towards the centre of the piece. Given the relationship that this may have with what I have been saying up to this point, I want to analyze these two aspects of the picture in detail. Before doing this, however, I would like to remind the reader that these elements are placed on a greenish colored paper, sometimes drawn on and sometimes scratched through by Miró until other shades appear, thus permitting the creation of new forms. This paper, like the yellowish white of the "window" displays several cuts – slits of sorts – as if it had been slashed. One can also see some stains caused by the glue or other damp marks. All of this, together with the materials used, increases the impression of poverty that one gets from the work, as if we were standing, as Leiris would have said, in front of a faded wall, or, as Gasch might have put it, in front of the wall of a tavern in Barcelona's "Fifth District."

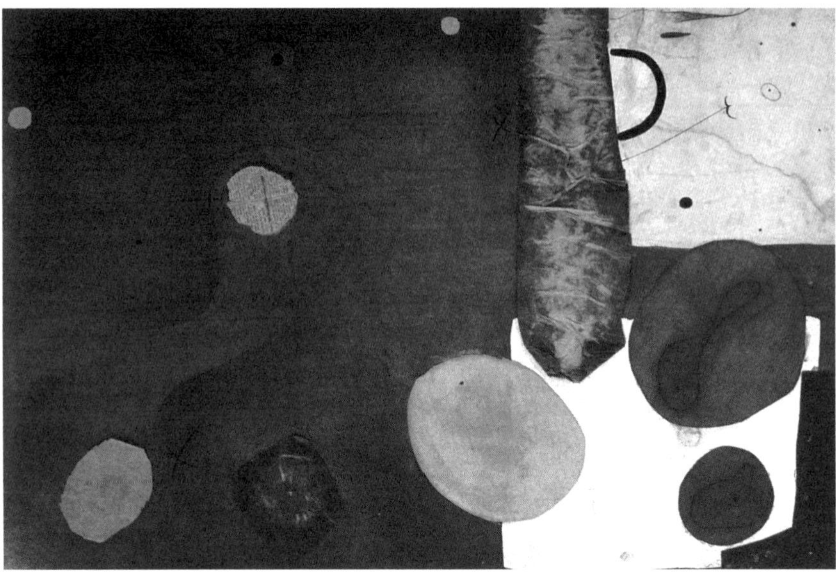

Figure 13.1 Joan Miró (1893–1983), *Collage* 1929. Pastel, ink, watercolor, crayon and pasted paper collage. 72.7 × 108.6 cm. James Thrall Soby (1307.1968). Digital image © The Museum of Modern Art/Licensed by SCALA/Art Resources, New York. © 2004 Artists Rights Society (ARS), New York/VEGAP, Madrid.

Of the whole picture, the rectangle in the top right really catches the eye (Figure 13.2). As I have already mentioned, this is a construction that includes a "window," a visual cliché used to represent spatial depth in classical European painting, though it is used here in a way that simultaneously both respects and breaks the rules. It breaks them insofar as the "window" does not form part of a deep spatial whole, though at the same time it respects them by illuminating this space (the "window" is white against a dark background) and furthermore by introducing the beginnings of a representative form. Indeed, through the "window" we see a drawing comprising four elements: a ragged shape, a semicircle, a line that ends in two semicircular shapes and a lot of black spots of various sizes, one of which is circled. The first of these elements seems to be a cloud; the half circle could be a sun or moon; the spots, depending on the previous interpretation, could be stars; in any case, if we add the circled point to the line that ends in two semicircles, we clearly see a human figure, stylized, of course, in Miró's own ideogrammatic way: the circled point is the eye, the two linked semicircles form the moustache and the line is the trunk.

Let us concentrate on the two semicircles forming the moustache. Miró's work contains many figures with this appendage, particularly around the mid-1920s. We discover it in famous works such as *The Hunter* (1923–4), *The Kerosene Lamp* (1924), *The Family* (1924) or *Carnival of the Harlequin* (1924–5). The moustache

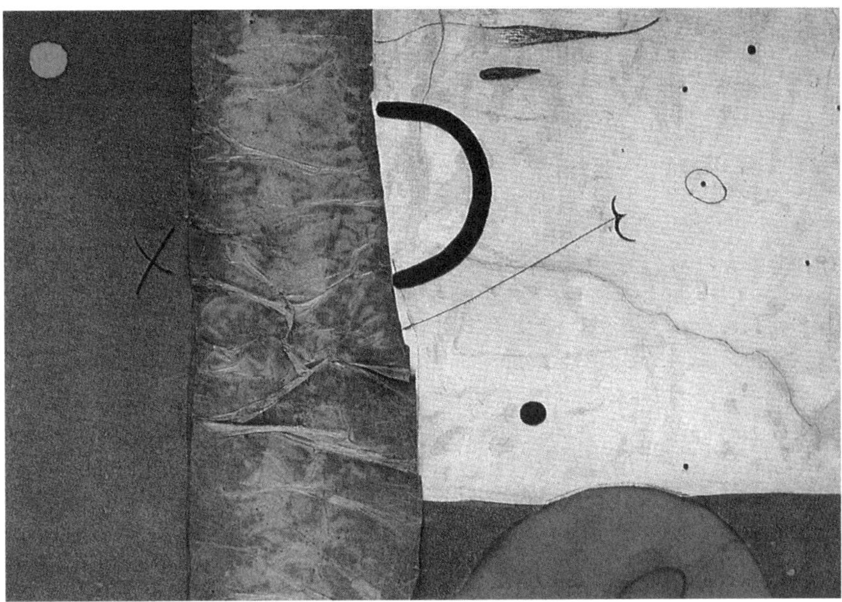

Figure 13.2 Detail from Joan Miró, *Collage* 1929. Museum of Modern Art, New York.

may actually appear as part of a human figure or on its own, symbolizing that human figure. Whichever is the case, we seem to be dealing with metonymic images that lead to a new form of representation based on signs. The method is well known. Michel Leiris had already pointed it out in 1926 as a characteristic trait of Miró's work. Among the various "components" that appear in Miró's paintings (sexual organs in the form of a spider, trees with eyes, sharply pointed breasts, etc.), the writer mentions "people reduced to moustaches" (Leiris, *Little Review*). In an article that he wrote three years later, he once again pointed out that Miró's painting "effortlessly raised and resolved all sorts of little equations", one of which was "man=moustache" (Leiris, *Documents* 263–6). Although moustaches are by no means uncommon in modern painting (we find them, for example, in Picasso's *El aficionado* (1912) and also in *Homme au chapeau melon assis dans un fauteuil* (1916), in De Chirico's *Le Cerveau de l'enfant* (1914), and in Ernst's *La Révolution, la nuit* (1923), it would seem that we should seek the origins of the graphic motifs that Miró uses somewhere else, far from any art gallery or museum; in other words, away from painting, modern or otherwise. Schematization, the act of reducing a figure to certain simplified elements, the tendency to replace the whole with a few parts that stand out until they border the grotesque, are traits that belong to caricature, an "art" that is both industrial and popular at the same time and which had already been mentioned as the basis for some of Miró's work. When Clement Greenberg refers to the synthetically caricaturesque, simplified symbols that appear in the painter's work ("an eye is inserted in the leaves of a tree, an ear is attached to its trunk, animals become toys or comic strip cut-outs"), he justifies their presence in recalling that "Barcelona has one of the richest traditions of cartooning in all Europe (Greenberg 20).

Indeed, Miró's cultural development occurred in an atmosphere that was highly favorable to the caricature. During the second half of the nineteenth century, a significant number of satirical magazines were published in Barcelona, some of which, like *La Campana de Gràcia* or *L'Esquella de la Torratxa,* could be found on the news stands for many years. The publication that began it all, *Un tros de paper,* was first printed on April 16, 1865. Josep Fontana (19) characterized its appearance as a "main event", because it represented one of the "milestones" in the growth of popular Catalan literature. The editor of this magazine went on to edit its successor, *Lo noy de la mare*, which appeared a year later, and he would subsequently be responsible for the two publications mentioned above, *La Campana* and *L'Esquella* (1870 and 1872 respectively). This meant that there was a clear homogeneity to the product, and it was offered to a readership that became loyal as the result of its use of repeated formulas. All the people working on these publications – the cartoonists and the writers were always the same. This led to the creation of a group of professionals who never stopped growing as they continually adapted their work to changing public tastes.

In spite of the fact that satirical publications also appeared in Spanish in Barcelona, sharing personnel (particularly cartoonists) with the publications mentioned above (the most notable perhaps being *La Flaca*), a common characteristic of the extensive number of humorous publications that appeared in the city from the 1860s onwards was that they were written in Catalan. This is explained by the fact that this avalanche of periodicals occurred at what has been known as *La Renaixença*, i.e. the cultural movement that brought with it the rediscovery of Catalan as a literary instrument, along with the beginnings of Catalanism as a political alternative. The overwhelming importance of these magazines lies, however, in the fact that, as opposed to the "highbrow" (and frequently stuffy) literature of the *Jocs Florals* (poetry meetings), they used an unaffected and flexible language that brought written Catalan within the range of the broader public. Although not all of these publications could by any means be called Catalanist, the majority defended anti-centralist and republican ideals and subscribed to the cultural revival of the Catalan language.

Just before the great flowering of Catalanism that accompanied the so-called *Solidaritat Catalana* of 1906, a second wave of publications began to appear, in this case supported by the most powerful of the movements involved in this political tendency, *La Lliga*, which as well as having its own newspaper wanted a broader range of publications, and so launched two large projects based on caricature, *Cu-Cut!* (a satirical publication with a political edge, 1902) and *El Patufet* (for children,

1904) (Solà' *L'Humor* 223–9). In general, the appearance of these publications, which coincided with Miró's formative years (he was born in 1893), represented a notable stylistic change among satirical artists. The most important figures from the previous generation, like Tomás Padró, practiced a realistic and very ornate form of drawing that was heavy with detail.[3] The new caricaturists, led by Cornet, Opisso, Llaveria, Junceda and "Apa," filled the pages of *Cu-Cut!* and *Patufet* with more linear, rapid, synthetic drawings, dispensing with background and the accumulation of detail. In a word, they were more modern. One new publication, *Papitu* (which was created by Feliu Elias "Apa" and appeared in 1908), would eventually swing the balance towards this cleaner, more stylized form (Solà, *L'Humor* 109–27). *Papitu* was the work of some exceptional people, like Isidre Nonell, Xavier Nogués, Manuel Humbert, Ismael Smith, Josep Aragai, Lluis Labarta, Junceda and Josep Maria Junoy, who was then living in Paris and producing some wonderful, often anti-clerical drawing (Junoy, an avant-garde poet, would write the acronymic poem that introduced the catalogue for Miró's first exhibition in Barcelona). It should be remembered that Juan Gris also drew regularly for *Papitu* during the magazine's early years, while struggling to find his way as a cubist painter in Paris (where his caricatures also appeared in *L'assiete au beurre*).

Nevertheless, Miró's cultural commitment, his Catalan cultural commitment, was probably not due to the existence, important though it may have been, of a satirical, anti-centralist, republican, democratic press. We have to look to more complex reasons (see Lubar, "Joan Miró"). However, the existence of this popular, mechanical, industrial, modern culture, although there only in the background, must undoubtedly be seen to have played some role. It is perhaps not insignificant to recall that one of the people most satirized by the publications mentioned above (particularly *Cu-Cut!*) was the politician Alejandro Lerroux, a contentious character and the source of much controversy in his day. Poorly received by the right because of his working-class demagogy, but equally poorly received by the left as a result of his alleged links with the central monarchy, Lerroux became one of the most talked about, and therefore most caricatured, individuals of the time (Figure 13.3). His pointed moustache was a distinguishing feature and became a recognizable stylized graphic element. Mention of this moustache, which formed part of the caricaturesque reality of the world of satirical magazines, brings us back to Miró, offering us another clue to the popular substrate of some of his graphic motifs. Indeed, several of his works of the time that I have already mentioned include a moustache alongside a representation of a newspaper. This can be seen, for example, in *The Kerosene Lamp* (Figure 13.4) and *The Family*, where these two elements from industrial culture, caricature and the press are intertwined.[4]

In spite of the presence of the written press in his work, and though it may seem strange, Miró rarely used newspapers in his collages until the 1930s. From the beginning of his career until 1929 he had used them in only two, *La Publicidad* and

Figure 13.3 Gaietà Cornet, Caricature of the politicians Alejandro Lerroux and Melquiades Álvarez, published in *Cu-cut!* (September 5, 1907).

Flower Vase (1917), and the collage we are discussing here. As I have already mentioned, one of the cut pieces of paper in the collage of 1929 comes from a newspaper. Though so few of Miró's collages use actual press cuttings, what we do find are newspapers, or newspaper headlines, that have been painted in, i.e. represented graphically. We can see this, for example, in *The Farm*, in which the painter applied a great deal of care in painting a copy of *L'Intransigeant* (not just any newspaper: first Apollinaire and then Maurice Raynal wrote for it).[5] This is, however, not the only case during the 1920s. In several works the newspaper has been reduced to part of a title banner, usually in French, the *jou* of *journal*. We see this symbol in *Still Life – Glove and Newspaper* (1921) (Figure 13.5), *The Tilled Field* (1923–4) and *Woman, Newspaper, Dog* (1925), among others. This text is both a generic representation (all newspapers: *journal* means newspaper in French), and a specific newspaper, *Le Journal*, well known in the history of painting because Picasso had used it very frequently for his *papiers collés*. The work of the latter painter is full of the letters "jou," "jour," "ournal," etc., though on occasion he chose, like Miró later, to paint them in directly, rather than affix cuttings. In Miró's work, however, the newspaper, the "jou," does not mean the same as it does in cubist painting.

Figure 13.4 Joan Miró, *The Kerosene Lamp* 1924. Charcoal with red couté and colored crayons, heightened with oil paint, on canvas prepared with a glue ground. 81 × 10.3 cm. Joseph and Helen Regenstein Foundation (E15488). Photography © The Art Institute of Chicago. © 2004 Artists Rights Society (ARS), New York/VEGAP, Madrid.

While in many of the works of this period the newspaper is just another element in what we could call "café" still lifes (the newspaper with bottles and wine glasses) in the Catalan painter's work it is clear that allusions to the press are metonymic references to the male gender (and therefore sometimes superimposed with a drawing of a moustache). We can see this in a drawing from the mid-1920s, which show a man, a pipe, a newspaper and an impressive sexual organ, in case there were any doubt as to what it meant as a whole.

The abundant presence of painted rather than stuck-on newspaper headlines gives us an idea of the exceptional nature of the work we are examining here. The fact that the collage of 1929 includes a stuck-on newspaper cutting is in itself a relevant point. In this case, however, the innovation does not stop here. As the note on the preparatory drawing indicates ("Newspaper/stuck on"),[6] in the summer of 1929 Miró affixed a newspaper to the brown-green paper that formed the base for the work. This was not a "cutting" from a newspaper, however, but a whole page, to the extent that in an early version of the work the newspaper would be occupying almost three-quarters of the piece (Figure 13.6).[7] This is notable

Figure 13.5 Joan Miró, *Still Life – Glove and Newspaper* 1921. Oil on canvas. 110.4 × 89.5 cm. Gift of Armand G. Erpf (18.1955). Digital image © The Museum of Modern Art/Licensed by SCALA/Art Resource, New York. © 2004 Artists Rights Society (ARS), New York/VEGAP, Madrid.

because it was not a frequent occurrence, at least not then, in Miró's work. In fact it is not usual in the history of painting. As a general rule, a collage involves the use of scissors. Artists did not just stick down, they also cut out. In spite of this lack of tradition, however, it cannot be said that there were not precedents. Picasso had already done something quite similar. In the spring of 1913 he completed a *papier collé* in Céret, with the title *Nature Morte*, showing a guitar under which a sheet unfolds: the front page of the newspaper *El Diluvio*, presented in its entirety (though cut into two pieces) (Figure 13.7).[8] As well as the surprise caused by the size of the paper included, Picasso's collage contained two more

Figure 13.6 First version of *Collage*, 1929, photographed in 1930 in the foyer of the cinema Studio 28 in Paris, where Luis Buñuel's *L'Age d'or* was premiered.

elements that attract our attention in relation to the Miró picture. It is a vertical work in which the newspaper is displayed in the position in which it would be found if we were going to read it, a position identical to the one that it would probably have had in the collage we are examining here in its original state. Second, there is the fact that instead of the usual *Le Journal*, Picasso included a Spanish newspaper in his collage of 1913, and not just any newspaper: *El Diluvio* was the most popular republican and anti-clerical publication in Barcelona. Placing it in a picture was a far less neutral gesture than using *Le Journal,* a widely circulated newspaper that lacked any of the ideological connotations of the Barcelona publication. The relevance of the selected headline seems to be a declaration of principles.[9]

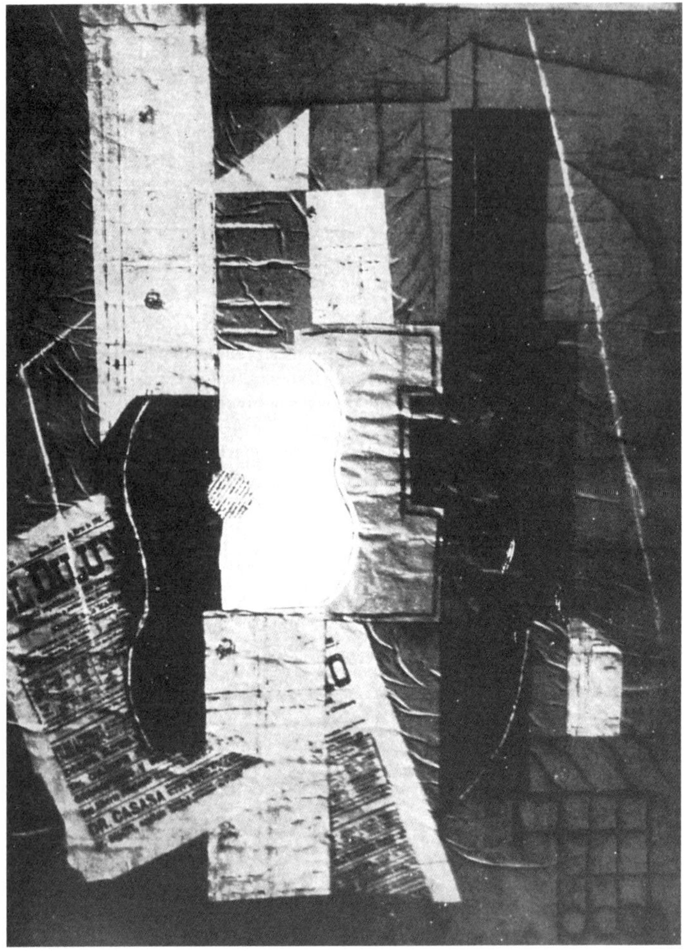

Figure 13.7 Pablo Picasso, *La guitarra* 1913. Museum of Modern Art, New York. Published in *Documents*, June 1929.

We would perhaps not pay so much importance to the existence of this precedent if it were not for the fact that the collage by the creator of *Les Demoiselles d'Avignon* was reproduced in May 1929 by a publication close to Miró, the magazine *Documents*. This would allow us to suppose that, prior to returning to Spain to spend the summer there, the painter must have seen this image which so resembled the first version of the collage of 1929. It was close to it not only structurally and formally, but also symbolically. The page chosen by Miró was from the newspaper *La Publicitat*, already used as a collage in 1917. Like the selection of *El Diluvio* by Picasso, this is a declaration of ideological principles, or at least, would seem so.

We know that Miró subscribed to two newspapers: *La Publicitat* and *La Veu de Catalunya*.[10] Both were written in Catalan and both were Catalanist. *La Veu* was the mouthpiece of *La Lliga*, the conservative nationalist party. *La Publicitat*, on the other hand, represented the ideals of *Acció Catalana*, a political party that arose as a breakaway from *La Lliga*, nourished by intellectuals who were modern, liberal and, to a point (so long as the social question was not brought up), left wing. Miró's most important connection with *La Veu* was probably his friendship with Sebastià Gasch, who worked for it regularly. On the other hand, *La Publicitat* was like a second home for the people who worked on *L'Amic de les Arts* (Miró's great defender in Barcelona). Among the people associated with one or other of these publications were J.V. Foix, Magí A.Cassanyes and Lluís Montanyà (and around the dates that Miró decided to include the newspaper page, Salvador Dalí, who published a series of articles entitled "Paris-Documental", in which he reflected on his experiences after a brief stay in the French capital, working with Buñuel on the filming of *Un Chien Andalou*).

If the choice of *La Publicitat* is not too much of a surprise, the page selected, however, is a little disconcerting. It is not the front page of the newspaper, with the title banner fully visible, as had occurred earlier, but the cinema page, in this case with the word "cinema" in a clearly visible position. More than the newspaper itself, Miró seems to want us to concentrate on the reference to the cinema. However, we don't find anything on this page that especially draws attracts attention (even the presence of a notice about Keaton and another one about a film by Murnau do not seem to be very clear reasons, given the banality of the text, just studio gossip). We must therefore conclude that if the painter chose that page, the reason for its selection should not be sought in the content but in the heading: "Cinema." The point of this would therefore be that cinema as a generic form, represented by this page. This is a little surprising, because up to this point Miró's interest in the cinema seemed to be very slight, and much less than that of the surrealists in Paris and the Catalan group of anti-artists associated with *L'Amic de les Arts*.

In any case, if Miró intended to pay homage to the cinema, then the choice of this page was an option. The cinema section in *La Publicitat* had a certain history. This page, which was initially entitled "Pall Mall Cinema," was first published on November 12, 1924. The section comprised a background article, a column about on-screen fashion, a section dealing with cinematographic techniques and a series of notes on current films, almost always from a promotional viewpoint. In addition, the foot of the page, forming a sort of base, included caricatures, comic strips, witticisms, etc. (in fact on the first day that the page was published, the comic strip was drawn by Junceda and poked fun at photography). The journalist Àngel Ferran, who would eventually take charge of this section, did not begin to work on it until May 23, 1926. At a later point, the page acquired the format seen in 1929 (a background article plus informal notes), while the sections on fashion and technical notes were published in a second edition. The original title, "Pall Mall Cinema," was replaced by the more sober "Cinema." Furthermore, the section provided a balanced analysis of the popular and at the same time modern aspects of this new art. In spite of the fact that it dealt mainly with American films, it also assessed other aspects of cinema such as technique, amateur production, etc. The observations made by Àngel Ferran combined an intellectual (though never pretentious) approach with a popular vision of the cinematographic art. The question that one would have to ask, however, would be why would Miró wish to pay this homage to the cinema in the summer of 1929? This is a question that probably has more than one answer.

That year had seen a great amount of cultural activity in Barcelona in relation to the cinema. The first two cine-clubs had been opened in the city. One of them, linked through Àngel Ferran to *La Publicitat* and managed by the journalist María Luz Morales, had been christened with the name Barcelona Film Club. This club held its sessions at the Mozart cinema, presenting documentaries and comic films alongside great recent cinema classics such as Murnau's *Tartüff* and *Sunrise*, King Vidor's *The Crowd* and Flaherty's *Moana*. The other, associated with the new weekly publication *Mirador*, held its sessions at the Rialto Cinema, occasionally showing more avant-garde films such as Man Ray's *L'Etoile de Mer* and *Emmak Bakia*.

Added to the enthusiasm for moving pictures that had been awoken among cultured circles in Barcelona were the cinematographic activities of Buñuel and Dalí in Paris (*Un chien Andalou* was presented in the French capital on June 6 of that year). Miró never concealed his fondness for these young avant-garde artists, for whom he had a great respect, as demonstrated by the letters he exchanged with Dalí at the time the painter was preparing to move to Paris.[11] Miró's friendship with Gasch can also not be discounted as regards his interest in the cinema. This art critic had combined his writings on painting with articles on the cinema, usually of a theoretical nature, from an early stage. He published various articles in *D'aci i d'allà*, *La Gaceta Literaria*, etc., in which he expressed his concerns about the techniques and expressive functionality of the cinema (particularly in America).[12]

No less important, however, is Miró's relationship with the editors of the Parisian magazine *Documents* (see Lanchner; Krauss). One of the specific traits of Bataille's magazine is the attention it pays to American talking pictures. I would emphasize both "American" and "talking," two characteristics of the cinematographic art that were not always appreciated by European intellectuals who, when evaluating film, tended to do so from an aesthete's point of view. As a result, they were inclined to value "silent" film and to be rather disdainful of "talking pictures," which were almost always viewed as something that had been imposed by the industry. *Documents*, however, took a different line. Articles, but above all pictures (i.e., "documents"), placed American talking film in a position of preeminence. This approach is no different from the radical line taken by the Catalan anti-artists (led by Dalí). It should be remembered, however, that the stance taken by the *L'Amic de les Arts* group was only a reflection of the more dadaist ideas promoted by the first surrealism. *Documents* too, though for different reasons, seized on this in a similar way. The loyalty shown by Desnos to the surrealist aesthetic of the cinema, by way of example, is total. In *Documents*, as he had done many times before, he rejects the self-styled French avant-garde cinema (Herbier, Epstein, etc.), corrupted by bad literature and false "artistry" (he classifies the films from this school quite graphically as "hair in the soup,") holding up the American cinema of Stroheim (whom he places on a pedestal), the films of Eisenstein and *Un Chien Andalou* by Buñuel and Dalí (Desnos, 385–7). Following the same line, but yet more radically, Leiris wrote several articles about the cinema, almost all of them about American talking pictures, a passion that can also be seen in the pages of his *Journal*. "Last night," he wrote, for example, on September 29, 1935, "I saw *Living on Velvet* (with Kay Francis, George Brent, Warren Williams). This film can be placed on the same level as *Hors du gouffre* and *One Way Passage*. One can think about it for days, indeed years, feeding from it, referring to it as a kind of myth" (Leiris, *Journal* 291). In his writings, Leiris lashes out at the intellectuals – "*la clique des intelectuels*" – who can only "pour scorn on a spectacle that is both simple and at the same time lacking in any pretension." Thanks to talking pictures, "from which one can expect everything", it was possible to regain the intensity, the natural eroticism that had been missing from the cinema, which now had a "burning sensuality." Perhaps less easy to understand, with the appearance of a new kind of sentimentality, American film allowed one to "rediscover the freshness of youth," a theme close to Leiris's heart (Leiris, "Fox Movietone" 388). Bataille, for his part, would take a more qualified approach. He only published one piece on the cinema, an essay about Hollywood in a new section of the magazine, deliberately entitled "Lieux de pèlerinage" (Bataille 280–1). In this piece, illustrated with pictures from the Metro musical *Hollywood Revue*, Bataille worked from the premise that all activities are carried out in order to achieve a rest, a break, and that all human actions lead towards "distraction." If Hollywood is the centre of the world it is due to the fact that it is "the only place that thinks exclusively of entertaining the rest of the world." Its status as the supplier of what is most desired turns this city of movies into a sanctuary, a sacred place, where huge amounts of money arrive every day from all over the world, so that the deities of the new religion, the stars, will not go hungry, "in the same way that people used to do with statues of gods and saints."

It may be, then, that an interest in American cinema, so clearly shown in the page from *La Publicitat* had come to Miró in various ways. One of the most important is probably represented by Michel Bataille's group. Miró's friendship with some of its members (particularly Leiris and Desnos) should be remembered, as well as the ideological closeness that developed between Miró and the people working on *Documents* around 1929. Indeed, it is in the writings of Leiris that one finds the best clues for interpreting some of the aspects of the painter's work during those years.

In two articles, written in 1926 and 1929 respectively' the author points out the following: first, in spite of the "spiritualistic" readings that one can make of Miró's work, his pictures make one think of a vulgar and prosaic reality: faded walls, covered in posters, discolored by the rain (as I have already mentioned); second, on these walls appear a series of lines ("graffiti showing the human architecture") with an ideogrammatic function: "sun=potato, file=little bird, man=moustache, spider=sex, man=sole of the foot." These "little equations," as with other painters who tended towards the abstract, are the result of a filtering, a reduction, a "subtraction" of elements, until one arrives at a "*compréhension du vide*", not in the negative sense of the "*néant*", but instead in the sense of that other term, at the same time identical and contrary to "*néant*", which is "*l'absolut*"; and third, it is not easy to take the step from the low to the spiritual, from the vulgar to the metaphysical, from the humorous to the sacred. Leiris himself acknowledged this, making the following anthropological leap in order to overcome the difficulty. The reduction, the ideogrammaticizing of shapes is merely a system of concealment in order to achieve something. "In ancient times," he wrote, "the fearful members of a tribe would bury any bits of fingernail and hair that fell out for fear of being bewitched, because they thought that these parts of them contained their entire vital spirit" (Leiris, *Little Review*). Miró was the same sort of primitive. He also buried shapes reduced to the barest minimum under a thick coating. These concealed signs correspond to an act of magic, an ancestral ritual. But what is concealed? What is buried in the collage of 1929? The materials used originate from popular culture. The moustache symbolizes the world of the Catalan satirical press. But also the world of newspapers, through which we are faced with the very explicit presence of the cinema, as an irrepressible source of images from popular industrial culture. On the other hand, we must also not forget that we are at the same time looking at a collage, i.e. an instrument that is an alternative to, if not a rejection of, the painting. Initially, as I have mentioned, the newspaper took up almost all of the work's surface. The painting is also concealed, reduced to some light inscriptions on the green-colored paper or behind the "window." Like the elements of popular culture, the art of painting has been subjected to an act of concealment.

In any case, the breaking up, the concealment of the pieces obtained, all that buried fingernail and hair explain Miró's method, but not his purpose. In 1929, by concealing popular industrial culture on the one hand, and painting on the other, what is being summoned and what is being exorcised? Caricature and cinema as opposed to the culture of the elite? Painting as opposed to mass culture?

This is not an easy question to answer. It could simply be that one finds the purpose of the project in the very act of concealment. Hiding the images was intended to preserve them. Miró's ritual recalls Benjamin's distinction between "cult value" (*Kultwert*) and "exhibition value" (*Austellungwert*) in works of art.[13] The German writer indicated that the history of western images is based on a line of evolution that runs from the predominance of one to the hegemony of the other. "Cult value" holds clear connotations of magic and religion for Benjamin, as it does for Leiris. Its strength lies in its concealment. Images do not have to be seen in order to perform their function. It is enough for them to come into contact with the priest or some other go-between. One of the most important consequences of this relationship, characteristic of a more primitive social system, relates to the images' resulting resistance to any deterioration. On the other hand, with exhibition as the basis for any relationship with the images, there is an inevitably high level of wear and tear: images tend to deteriorate, whatever their "useful" value.

Whether Benjamin's idea helps us or not, what is interesting is to see how at that time, while simultaneously concealing two opposing cultural systems (painting, refined and elitist, and caricature and the cinema, popular forms of expression associated with industrial development and mass consumption) Miró was comparing them, treating them both alike, as images that could be ritualized in order to save something. By turning them into "fingernails and hair" and giving them the same preservational value when faced with concerns about their destruction, the painter was placing these cultural systems, both high and low, on a similar, perhaps even the same level. We cannot be sure that this was the spirit of the moment. However, there is no doubt that this was the spirit of the circles that Miró was moving in at that time: the Catalan anti-artists of *L'Amic de les Arts* on the one hand, and the remaining vestiges of surrealism, through Bataille's group of dissidents, on the other. Both were resistant to barriers and hierarchies within forms of artistic expression, and both were fierce proponents of the use of "bad taste" in the search for unexpected forms of sudden "intensity."

Acknowledgments

This chapter forms part of a wider study, "Joan Miró: Painting, collage, mass culture," shortly to be published in book form. In completing this I have been assisted by a Pilar Juncosa research grant, awarded by the Fundació Joan Miró in Palma de Mallorca (Spain).

Notes

1. The existence of a third Miró, an alternative to the two most commonly accepted explanations of his paintings (a world of childlike innocence or a formal area of pictorial experimentation), has been suggested in recent years by Krauss, and by Lubar's "Miró's Defiance of Painting."
2. The work was acquired by the New York Museum of Modern Art in 1968. I would like to thank Anne Umland, curator at the museum, who allowed me to see the work and study it in detail during the autumn of 2001. The debt is also an intellectual one, in that in 1992 Umland published an interesting study of the work, "Joan Miro's *Collage* of Summer 1929: *La Peinture au défi.*" Umland is also the author of an essential work, "Joan Miró and Collage in the 1920s: The Dialectic of Painting and Anti-painting."
3. Tomàs Padró (Barcelona, 1840–77) had worked in the studio of Claudio Lorenzale, where he met Marià Fortuny. As well as being a famous cartoonist working on all the satirical magazines of the time, he was an accomplished painter whose work is on show at the Museum of Modern Art of Catalonia. See Solà, *Un segle d'humor català* and Fontbona, *Història de l'art cátala.*
4. The same combination can be found in preparatory drawings such as *The Upset* (1924), *The Trap* (1924) and *Painting* (1925), although one or other of the two elements is missing in the final work. Archives of the Fundació Joan Miró (Barcelona), identified as FJM663, FJM641 and FJM727.
5. Maurice Raynal had written an introduction in the catalogue to Joan Miró's first exhibition in Paris in 1921, at the Licorne Gallery.
6. Archive of the Fundació Joan Miró (Barcelona), FJM2601
7. Two images remain from the picture's original state. The first was published in the magazine *Ahora* (January 24, 1931), accompanying an interview with Joan Miró. The second, which forms part of a dossier connected with Buñuel's film, *L'Age d'or*, currently at the Fundació Gala-Salvador Dalí in Figueres (Spain), was first published in Bouhours and Schoeller. See also Umland, "Joan Miró's Collage of Summer 1929" 65–6 and, in particular, Umland, "Joan Miró and Collage in the 1920s," 1–5, 291–321, 382–91, 418–23, and 458–73) for an extended discussion of the *La Publicitat* sheet and the work's original state as pictured in *Ahora* and in *L'Age d'or*.
8. This work, entitled *La guitarra*, currently forms part of the New York Museum of Modern Art's collection, bequeathed by Nelson Rockefeller.
9. Richardson (274) ignores the political implications of the title banner and points out that the page selected includes several advertisements for drugs and doctors. As Picasso had had to go to Barcelona to see his father, who was seriously ill, and it was there that he would have bought the newspaper, Richardson links the two elements. Although this is a possible interpretation,

one cannot discount the idea that a person viewing the work in 1929, aware of political and cultural trends in Barcelona (as was Miró) and unaware of all those family details, would interpret the inclusion of the banner from this newspaper in Picasso's collage as a proclamation of faith (Republican and anticlerical).

10. On July 21, Miró wrote from Montroig to Sebastià Gasch that he had subscribed to *La Veu de Catalunya* and *La Publicitat* "which I have the opportunity to see every day." Letter from J. Miró to S. Gasch, July 21, 1928, Gasch Estate, Fundació Miró, Barcelona.
11. Dalí's letters to Miró can be found at the Fundacio Miró, Palma de Mallorca, while Miró's replies to Dalí are at the Fundació Gala-Salvador Dalí in Figueres. As regards Buñuel, Miró wrote to Gasch: "I met Buñuel yesterday. He is an important man and very interesting." Letter from J. Miró to S. Gasch, March 13, 1929, Gasch Estate, Fundació Miró, Barcelona
12. See, for example, Sebastià Gasch, "Fotogenia", *D'aci i d'allà*, 101 (1926) and Sebastià Gasch, "Etapas. Una: Variété", *La Gaceta Literaria*, March 1, 1928. Gasch would later work as cinema critic for *L'Opinió* (1931–34), *La Publicitat* (1935–6) and, after the war, for *Destino*. See Minguet (66).
13. Benjamin made use of this idea in his 1936 work *Das Kunstwerk im Zeitalter seiner technischen Reproduziebarkeit*. See Benjamin (482).

Works Cited

Aragon, Louis. *La Peinture au defi*. Paris: Librairie José Corti, 1930.

Bataille, George. "Lieux de pèlerinage: Hollywood." *Documents* 1.5 (1929): 280–2

Benjamin, Walter. *Das Kunstwerk im Zeitalter seiner technischen Reproduziebarkeit*. Ed. R. Tiedmann. Frankfurt: Suhrkamp Verlag, 1974/1936.

Bouhours, Michel and Natalie Schoeller, eds. *L'Age d'or: Une correspondence entre Luis Buñuel et Charles de Noailles. Lettres et documents (1928–1976)*. Paris: Centre Georges Pompidou, 1993.

Desnos, Robert. "Cinéma d'avant-garde." *Documents* 1.5 (1929): 385–7

Fontana, Josep. "L'altra Renaixença: 1860 i la represa d'una cultura nacional catalana." In *Història de la cultura catalana*. Barcelona: Edicions 62, 1994. 15–33

Fontbona, Francesc. *Història de l'art català*. Vol VI. Barcelona: Edicions 62, 1983.

Gasch, Sebastià. "Coses vives." *La Veu de Catalunya* (July 18, 1929).

—— "L'elogi del mal gust." *La Publicitat* (November 29, 1929).

—— "Etapas.Una: Variété." *La Gaceta Literaria* (March 1, 1928): 6.

—— "Fotogenia." *D'aci i d'allà* 101 (May 1926): 525–6.

Greenberg, Clement. *Joan Miró*. New York: Quadrangle Press, 1948.

Krauss, Rosalind. "Michel Bataille et Moi." *October* 68 (1994): 3–20.

Lanchner, Carolyn. "*Peinture-Poésie*, its Logic and Logistics." In *Joan Miró*, New York: Museum of Modern Art, 1993. 15–82.

Leiris, Michel. "Fox Movietone Follies of 1929." *Documents* 1.7 (1929): 388.

—— "Joan Miró." *Documents* 1.5 (1929): 263–9.

—— "Joan Miró." *Little Review* (spring–summer 1926): page unknown.

—— *Journal, 1922–1989*. Paris: Gallimard, 1992.

Lubar, Robert. "Joan Miró before *The Farm,* 1915–1922: Catalan Nationalism and Avant-garde." Doctoral thesis. New York University Institute of Fine Arts, 1988.

—— "Miró's Defiance of Painting." *Art in America* (September 1994): 86–132.

Minguet, Joan M. *Sebastià Gasch. Cric d'art i de les arts de l'espectacle*. Barcelona: Generalitat de Catalunya, 1997.

Miró, Joan. Letter to Sebastià Gasch. July 21, 1928. Gasch Estate, Fundació Miró, Barcelona.

—— Letter to Sebastià Gasch. March 13, 1929. Gasch Estate, Fundació Miró, Barcelona.

Richardson, John. *A Life of Picasso*. Vol. II, 1907–1917. New York: Random House, 1996.

Solà, Lluis. *L'Humor Català*. Vol. II. Barcelona: Bruguera, 1978.

—— *Un segle d'humor català*. Barcelona: Bruguera, 1973.

Umland, Anne. "Joan Miró's Collage of Summer 1929: 'La Peinture au défi'?" In *Studies in Modern Art 2: Essays on Assemblage*. New York: Museum of Modern Art, 1992.

—— "Joan Miró and Collage in the 1920s: The Dialectic of Painting and Anti-painting." Doctoral thesis. New York University Institute of Fine Arts, 1997.

–14–

Stages of Modernity: The Uneasy Symbiosis of the *género chico* and Early Cinema in Madrid

Susan Larson

While the emergence of early cinema has sometimes been thought of as having resulted from a technological breakthrough, the seventh art owes its existence to a wide variety of other modern technologies, spectacles, genres and modes of display. One of the goals of this volume is to seek to better understand how photography, painting, serial narrative and the realist novel, the popular press, wax museums and other visual innovations such as the diorama, the panorama and the kinetoscope shaped modes of observation employed by Spain's modern citizens. In Spain, and especially in Madrid, the production and reception of early film was aesthetically, economically and socially shaped by popular theater – more specifically, the *zarzuela* [Spanish operetta].[1] The purpose of my inquiry here is to outline the symbiotic relationship between early film and the *género chico* and, more important, to shed some light on the broader culture of modernity in turn-of-the-century Madrid, a modernity in which the traditional often existed side by side with the new, the *castizo* defined itself against the more generally European and the social meanings of technological progress were played out in the most popular forms of culture.

Vanessa Schwartz, in her essay "Cinematic Spectatorship before the Apparatus: The Public Taste for Reality in Fin-de-Siècle Paris" outlines how real life in late nineteenth-century Paris was experienced as a show at the same time that shows became increasingly lifelike. While the experience of capitalist urbanization is dramatically different in Madrid from that of Paris, what Schwartz has to say about spectatorship and representation holds true for Madrid as well. In Schwartz's mind, "it [spectatorship] must be taken as a practice whose history can be understood by examining, on the one hand, the relation between technologies and contents represented, which thus produces possibilities for observation; and, on the other hand, the discourse produced by the experiences of those technologies in a specific context" (297). With this in mind, this chapter looks at the reception of film by the popular theater and its urban, predominantly middle-class public by considering the competing discourses of modernity and vision evident in the one-act *zarzuela* entitled *Cinematógrafo Nacional* first performed in Madrid at the Apollo Theater in 1907.

Of the many theories of European modernity and vision, those of Stephen Kerns and Jonathan Crary have arguably been the most influential in cross-disciplinary research that examines shifts in modern practices of seeing. In Stephen Kern's *The Culture of Time and Space, 1880–1918* (1983), the author argues that from approximately 1880 until the outbreak of World War I, a series of sweeping changes in technology and culture created distinctive new modes of thinking about and experiencing time and space. Technological inventions including the telephone, wireless telegraph, x-ray, cinema, bicycle, automobile, and airplane established the material foundation for this reorientation. Most importantly, though, Kern says, is the fact that independent cultural developments such as the stream-of-consciousness novel, psychoanalysis, Cubism, and the theory of relativity shaped consciousness directly, resulting in a transformation of the dimensions of life and thought. Jonathan Crary's *Techniques of the Observer: On Vision and Modernity in the Nineteenth Century* (1990) takes a much different approach. His project, in his words, is "to outline some of the points of emergence of a modern and heterogeneous regime of vision, simultaneously addressing the related problem of when, and because of what events, there was a rupture with Renaissance, or classical, models of vision and of the observer" (3). Most theorists of modern vision, in Crary's opinion, suffer from an exclusive preoccupation with problems of technology and visual *representation*; he locates shifts in perception much earlier and thinks that the break with classical models of vision in the early nineteenth century was far more than simply a shift in the appearances of images and artworks, or in systems of representational conventions. Instead, he says, it was inseparable from a massive reorganization of knowledge and social practices that modified in myriad ways the productive, cognitive and desiring capacities of the human subject. Crary's contribution to the study of modern culture and visuality is key because it stresses the importance of certain bodies of knowledge and technological innovations that rarely appear in histories of art, film or modernism. One reason for this is to escape from the limitations of many of the dominant histories of visuality of the period, and to bypass the many accounts of modernism and modernity that depend on a more or less similar evaluation of the origins of modernist visual art and culture in the 1870s and 1880s. He disagrees strongly with scholars like Kern whose story of the rupture of modern vision and visuality goes something like this: with Manet, impressionism, and/or postimpressionism, a new model of visual representation and perception emerges that constitutes a break with several centuries of another model of vision, loosely definable as Renaissance perspectival, or normative. When Crary examines this visual rupture closely, however, he quite convincingly comes to the conclusion that it was considerably more restricted in its cultural and social impact than the fanfare surrounding it usually suggests. It is helpful to remember that the alleged perceptual revolution in the late nineteenth century is an event whose effects occur *outside* the most dominant and pervasive models of seeing. Thus, following the logic of the general argument of Kern and other like-minded scholars, it is actually a rupture on the margins of a vast hegemonic organization of the visual that becomes increasingly powerful in the twentieth century, with the diffusion and proliferation of photography, film, and television. In a sense, then, the myth of modernist rupture depends fundamentally on the binary model of realism versus experimentation, an opposition that is questioned when one analyzes examples of popular or mass culture, where practices of vision were frequently resisted, deflected or imperfectly constituted. "The notion of a modernist visual representation depends on the presence of a subject with a detached viewpoint, from which modernism – whether as a style, as cultural resistance, or as ideological practice – can be isolated against the background of a normative vision" (Crary 4–5). The problem then is that modernism is thus presented as the appearance of the new for an observer who remains perpetually the same, or whose historical status is never interrogated. In short, Crary's approach urges scholars of the culture of the modern, industrial period to contextualize and historicize the experience of the turn-of-the-century urban observer and to treat it as a constantly changing and evolving, even potentially contradictory subjectivity.

Modernity cannot be conceived outside the context of the city, which provided an arena for the circulation of goods, the exchange of glances, and the exercise of consumerism. From all accounts, the experience of Madrid's urban development at the end of the nineteenth and beginning of the twentieth centuries was highly contradictory. Madrid, like many cities of the time, was a monument to the conquest and subjugation of nature by humankind – the site of human progress and the wonders and marvels of technological innovation. Through its popular novelties and monuments, exhibits and museums, the modern metropolis presented a deceptive vision of past and present. In "Paris, Capital of the Nineteenth Century" and elsewhere, Walter Benjamin wrote eloquently about the city's promise of continual progress and improvement through rational planning as being one of the greatest mystifications of capitalism, one aspect of the false consciousness engendered by bourgeois ideology, the foundational myth of modernity. In Madrid, these years were known for their unbridled construction. The Paseo del Prado beautified itself with the construction of Antonio Palacios' Palacio de Comunicaciones (1904) in the Plaza Cibeles. French and British capital helped construct the area around the Plaza de Neptuno and the Ritz and Palace Hotels (1907–10) (Sambricio 33–9). The major project, the construction of the Gran Vía, would take more than fifty years, but there would eventually be a modern boulevard running from Cibeles to the Plaza de España, linking the Salamanca and Argüelles neighborhoods. New urban spaces of leisure and consumption were being constructed, often with foreign capital and foreign models in mind, to highlight Madrid's first entrance onto the stage of modernity. The neighborhoods of Atocha and Cuatro Caminos were quite another matter, however. It was in these neighborhoods that the other side of the industrial age could be felt. These parts of town grew quickly and chaotically, with no planning whatsoever. The labor necessary to build Madrid's new spaces of entertainment and leisure was housed here, and in shacks called *chabolas* constructed around the edges of Madrid. In the north were Cuatro Caminos and Tetuán; in the east, Prosperidad and Guindalera; in the southeast, the shacks of Puente de Vallecas would eventually extend all the way into the town of Vallecas; in the south, Toledo, San Isidro and Carabanchel. Much of Madrid's population lived in these areas linked by unpaved roads, insufficient plumbing, waste disposal, electricity or any municipal services, for that matter (Santos et al. 235–50). This is what Pío Baroja referred to as "Vida refinada, casi Europea, en el centro: vida africana, de aduar, en los suburbios" (A refined, almost European life in the center: African life, in run-down provisional shacks, in the suburbs) (210).

Between 1896 and 1910, however, before the dreams of the urban planners and investors for the Gran Vía had been fully realized, the vast majority of spaces where films were shown were not designed with film viewing in mind. The very first films were shown in Madrid on May 13, 1896, in the Hotel Rusia located at 34 Carrera de San Jeronimo, a location chosen by the Marquis de Reversaux, the French ambassador to Spain.[2] Earlier that year Alexandre Promio, an associate of the enterprising Lumière brothers, had come to Madrid with the purpose of introducing the new technology to the city's elite. To this end he was granted an audience with Queen María Cristina who granted him permission to film a variety of Spanish scenes, including the Queen's private guard conducting military exercises. For a period of about a month, Promio charged members of Madrid's upper class one peseta each to view a ten- to fifteen-minute program of shorts which included titles such as "Salida de los alabarderos de palacio" (a procession of the Queen's personal guard through the Plaza de Oriente), "Maniobra de la artillería" (scenes of the Queen's guard firing artillery), various takes of the Puerta del Sol, the Puerta de Toledo and a host of other more generic shorts filmed in France, such as the tearing down of a wall, the arrival of a train and workers leaving a factory. The royal family accepted an invitation to attend its own private session. The one-peseta price was extravagant for the time – many times higher than that for an entrance to even the most exclusive theater or opera – and excluded all but the wealthiest of Madrid's citizens from viewing what was considered a new miracle of science: a way of seizing continuous movement and objectively capturing and transmitting images and information on an increasingly global scale.

In subsequent years films were treated less as a new technological breakthrough and more as mass entertainment. After 1900 more democratic film viewing took place in spaces that were either previously or simultaneously dedicated to other types of business – in cafés, garages, fairgrounds, the street, and in provisional outdoor constructions called *barracones* (Pérez Rojas 70–8). These nickelodeons had flimsy facades that were pasted onto the entrances to various types of preexisting buildings, almost always with exotic or futuristic names.[3] Filmgoing during the heyday of the nickelodeon could be uncomfortable or even perilous, as Juan Antonio Cabrero describes in his telling of the collapse of one such *barracón* owned and operated by the Jimeno family during the Fiesta del Pilar de Zaragoza in 1898:

> ¡Oh, fatalidad! Para entrar en aquellos barracones era preciso subir a una plataforma de madera de medio metro en la que estaba instalado el popular órgano "Limonaire," a la que se ascendía por uno o dos escalones, y como ésta no pudiera resistir tanta aglomeración humana, por ser superior a su resistencia, en una de las esperas se vino abajo todo el entarimado con un gran estrépito, arrastrando consigo al público que, impaciente, aguardaba la entrada al barracón.

> Oh, how horrible! In order to enter one of those nickelodeons one had to step up onto a wooden platform half a meter wide where the popular "Limonaire" organ was installed, and one ascended one or two more steps, and since it couldn't hold such a human gathering, because it was too heavy, during one of the intermissions the whole thing came crashing down, crushing the other patrons who, impatiently, were waiting at the entrance. (Cabrero 38–9)

Fires were frequent in spaces such as these, due to highly flammable celluloid and overcrowding. Two of the earliest and most successful film entrepreneurs in Madrid were Eduardo Jimeno and his son, owners of the centrally located and wildly popular wax museum the Salón Maravillas on the Glorieta de Bilbao between Malasaña and Carranza streets, where films were also shown. They were among the first to acquire a film projector in order to make a profit from traveling from city to city, charging money for screenings and establishing what were the first stages of what could properly be called a film distribution system in Spain.

As Julio Pérez Perucha points out, it is in 1903 that entrepreneurs in Madrid begin to build the first more attractive and comfortable cinemas dedicated primarily (but not exclusively) to attracting a filmgoing audience. Interest in film had sharply declined by that time and would continue to drop until 1910. "[D]urante los primeros años del siglo los empresarios fueron observando con no poca alarma el progresivo descenso del número de espectadores y cómo los pocos que se iban mantenimiento procedían de las capas sociales con menos recursos económicos" (During the first years of the century the entrepreneurs witnessed with no small amount of alarm the progressive decline in the number of spectators and how the few that kept coming were from the classes with fewer economic resources.) (Pérez Perucha 45).[4] When the first movie theaters were constructed with the goal of attracting a more bourgeois public, the model used was the same as that of the theater of the seventeenth century. Like the theaters of the seventeenth century, too, clear divisions between the classes were maintained in the very organization of the buildings' spatial and price structures, offering a selection of very differently priced and located seats in an effort to cater to the desires and expectations of almost every film viewer (Diez Puertas 26–30).Theater owners also wanted to protect their investment and knew that the building had to still be suitable for a variety of entertainment purposes since in the early days of film, shorts were screened at the beginning, middle or end of other dramatic or musical presentations. Many theater owners thought that film was going to be a minor diversion and treated it as just another magic act or collective optical illusion in whose investment a certain amount of risk was involved.

Cinematógrafo Nacional was first performed on May 10, 1907 in the Teatro Apolo in Madrid. A knowledge of the history of the performance space itself is essential to an understanding of the cultural meaning of the work in its time. When the Apollo Theater was constructed in the early 1870s, Madrid's theater district extended only to the Calle de Sevilla. The theater was to be located outside of this district on the Calle de Alcalá, occupying a space that had been left vacant after the demolition of a Carmelite convent next to the Iglesia de San José – a space made available for the extension of the Calle de Barquillo.[5] The French architects Chanderlot and Festau were contracted by the Spanish investment banker Gargollo, who spared no expense in the construction of the building which was decorated with marble, bronze, velvet, paintings and sumptuous carpet. Unlike other theaters of its type, the Apollo housed 2,000 spectators. While undoubtedly luxurious, the theater was designed to seat a relatively diverse audience by offering seats at a wide variety of prices. The theater opened on November 23, 1873 with a lavish production of Calderón de la Barca's *Casa de dos puertas*. In spite of (or ironically, because of) its opulence, the Apollo Theater did a miserable business its first thirteen years, in part because of its distance from the center of Madrid's nightlife but also due to the large amount of money necessary to stage elaborate classical theater productions and a limit to what Madrid's numerically small middle and upper classes would pay to see such a spectacle. This changed, however, in the mid-1860s, when the theater's mangers Enrique Arregui and Luis Aruej became more aggressive about making a profit and the theater became known as nothing less than "La catedral del género chico." The Apollo Theater, to save itself from ruin, was one of the very first to produce shorter *zarzuelas* called *teatro por horas* because the comical musical reviews were approximately an hour in length and more than one audience could be seated every night, raising sorely needed revenue. For a time in the 1860s and 1870s, after Madrid's upper and middle classes decided that the trip to the Apollo was worth the carriage ride, *la cuarta de Apolo* was the most lively of bourgeois night activities, a place to see and be seen by one's peers (del Moral Ruiz

42–4). This was a public space dedicated to the mingling of a relatively diverse sector of Madrid's population. The reviews of the shows were almost as important as the reports in such daily newspapers as *Ahora* and *El Heraldo de Madrid* on the dress and other gossip about the previous evening. According to Eduardo Alaminos and Eduardo Salas (343–4), the evening session lasted about six hours and usually ended at dawn. Four hour-long musical revues were staged, interspersed with a wide variety of circus acts, dance numbers and various other entertainments, and allowed time for the audience to request encores of their favorite acts of the evening. Audiences were active, vocal and showed their approval or disapproval of the *teatro por horas* with their cheering or booing which could result in the prolongation, shortening or complete elimination of any act. The Apollo's patrons would eventually bring to the cinematic experience these behaviors, expectations and modes of viewing which were shaped by years of theater-going.

It is in the Apollo Theater that some of the very first short films and cartoons (some in black and white and some in color) were screened for a large, relatively diverse Madrilenian audience on November 7, 1896.[6] They were received with mild approval but with no significant fanfare. Significantly, the ticket prices for the evening were not changed. The films were slated as just another act between the main show, which still consisted of four musical reviews. The projectionist, a Frenchman named Charles de Kalb, traveled from theater to theater in Spain making a living screening these types of animated shorts and the first films available for rent in the catalogs of Méliès and the brothers Lumière. De Kalb stayed at the Apollo as part of the attractions for a period of one month. According to all accounts, after a brief period of surprise at the moving, flickering images, the viewing public of the Apollo reacted just as they would to a theatrical performance – they read the titles out loud, vocally indicated their approval, and requested of the projectionist that certain scenes be repeated.

It would be one full year before films were screened at the Apollo Theater again, this time not as a spectacle in and of itself but as part of the plot of the 1897 musical revue *Fotografías Animadas, o Arca de Noé* with music composed by Federico Chueca and a libretto by Andrés Ruesga Villoldo and Enrique Prieto Enríquez. It is significant that not only did short films work their way into the programming of the evening as diversions between the short dramatic pieces, but also brief film clips were creatively and immediately worked into the librettos of the *género chico* in an effort to surprise the audience and push the generic limits of both media. Another notable example is the 1905 one-act comic musical revue *El amigo del alma* by Francisco Torres and Carlos Cruselles in which the third scene is interrupted by a previously filmed romantic interlude shared by the two protagonists, which gives the audience the impression that they are behind the lens of a hidden camera and therefore privy to an intimate moment that gives the plot of the story a more interesting narrative structure and a lascivious slant. [7]

During the years 1896 to 1910 the established *género chico* and the fledgling film industry both suffered and enjoyed an unstable, remarkably hybrid status: both are caught in a self-conscious inbetweenness, influenced by various media and directly competing economic forces. While Madrid audiences reacted to early silent film in much the same way they did to the popular theater, however, there are several essential differences which may not have seemed immediately apparent at the time. A popular theatrical production, no matter how many times it is presented, is a local manifestation grounded in one place and reliant on the personalities and characteristics of the particular troupe of actors, the house's sets and, above all, the always changing moods and expectations of each audience. During a period of intense competition between theaters scripts, set designs and costumes for any one production would constantly evolve to better challenge, provoke, humor and titillate the audience. Film, on the other hand, is a mass produced form of culture produced for a mass audience. Especially in the silent film era, the studio could produce a film intended to be screened in a wide variety of theaters in many countries, which results in a more universally modernizing affect but is less focused on confronting national, regional and local issues and values. The growth of the star system and resultant fashions that would also result from the film industry occurs on a scale that is unthinkable for the popular theater of Madrid.

The origins of the *zarzuela* can be traced back to Italian opera of the fifteenth century but at the same time is considered to be one of the most Spanish of genres. Carlos Gómez Amat's *Historia de la música española* considers the *zarzuela* (itself an amalgam of several genres) uniquely Spanish and particularly Madrilenian (131–41). It takes its name from the Zarzuela Palace outside of Madrid, an area covered in *zarzas* (brambles) where some of the first *zarzuelas* were performed in the seventeenth century. There are two principal types of *zarzuela*: the *género chico*, a one-act comic operetta, often with a satirical theme, and *zarzuela grande*, normally in three acts and of a more serious nature, whose style approximates that of Romantic opera. Both the *zarzuela grande* and *género chico* are musical dramas whose text is alternately spoken and sung without breaking from the story line. The *zarzuela* as musical theater was considered by many cultural critics of the time to be a less sophisticated or refined form of theater. Rooted in urban folklore, made to entertain and amuse, it is a form of popular culture where language and social norms can be transgressed, where each character can reveal the truth as he or she sees it, often critiquing different aspects of Spanish society. Local and national political criticism are often present in the *zarzuela* since the plot provides the author with the opportunity and artistic flexibility to show an array of contemporary Madrid characters in situations that are either realistic, fantastic and/or allegorical. While making some political and social criticism possible, the *zarzuela* often appropriated a nostalgic view of what was considered the local color and wit of the lower classes, in particular the identity of the inhabitants of Madrid's southern, then-outlying neighborhoods such as La Latina, Lavapiés and Embajadores. The bourgeois *zarzuela* established a series of idealized and distorted popular characters or types. A nagging concern voiced by many contemporary theorists of Spanish popular entertainment is articulated by José Álvarez Junco when he asks "whether this idealized image was then adopted by thc objcct of the idealization – i.e. the popular classes – who might have gone on to imitate the stereotype" (86). To try to answer this question would be do go beyond the stated boundaries of this chapter, but suffice it to say this makes the *zarzuela* a rich cultural site to excavate if one wants to examine the economic, political, social and moral anxieties of Madrid's late- nineteenth- and early-twentieth-century citizens.

The libretto of the *zarzuela Cinematógrafo Nacional* was written by Guillermo Perrín and Miguel de Palacios (1907), and the music scored by Gerónimo Giménez, who also conducted the orchestra in the Apollo Theater.[8] All three were extremely successful and well-known artists who produced an astounding number of one-act *zarzuelas* of admittedly uneven quality.[9] They specialized in the *revista*, or musical revue, also called the *teatro por horas* or *género chico*.[10] *Cinematógrafo Nacional* opens with the hungry, unemployed, hopeless Benito walking in the direction of the Estanque (the large, man-made pool) in the Parque Retiro to drown himself. The set is described in detail, with the first scene taking place on the Retiro's Paseo de la Argentina, better known as the Avenida de las Estatuas. A very cinematic point of view is emphasized, locating the public from the very beginning in a familiar Madrid landscape full of historical meaning: "Vista tomada desde el estanque grande. En primer término derecha, la estatua del Rey Chintila. A continuación, la de Carlos II" (A view from the large reservoir. Stage right, the statue of King Chintila. Further on, that of Charles II) (Perrín and Palcios 9).[11] Both of these statues figure prominently on the Paseo, and would have been highly recognizable to the Apollo's audience. The statue of the Visigoth King Chintila in the foreground to the left symbolizes Christian Spain's initial ascent to power, with the more central Carlos II the decline of the Habsburgs and Spain's imperial strength. The comic irony of Benito's intention, of course, is that it begins to rain, and to avoid getting wet (he is carrying "un colador de paraguas") Benito hides under the statue of King Chintila. Benito would have been soaked had he jumped into the Estanque, but only from the waist down – the Estanque is only a few feet deep. Benito muses aloud that in fairytales guardian angels appear to those in need. The clumsy and highly ironic allegorical figure of "La Chispa Eléctrica" (Electric Spark) appears in the form of a lightning bolt, striking Benito and blowing the head off the statue of King Chintila, getting Benito into trouble with a nearby policeman who blames the damage on the potential suicide. Here follows the first exchange between Benito and the "Chispa Eléctrica":

Chispa:	¡Soy del progreso diosa gentil! Soy la esperanza del porvenir. Cual mariposa van las palabras *por tenues hilos* *que animo yo.* ¡Soy luz divina! ¡Potente fuerza! Todo lo alumbra mi resplandor. … ¿Quieres hacer dinero?	I am the goddess of progress! I am the hope of the future. Words float like butterflies *held by delicate threads* *that I put into motion.* I am divine light! Potent force! My splendor illuminates everything. … Do you want to make money?
Benito:	Eso no se pregunta.	You don't even have to ask.
Chispa:	Pues ya lo tienes.	Then your wish will be granted.
Benito:	¡No gastes esas bromas!	Don't joke with me!
Chispa:	Lo tendrás, si montas un Cinematógrafo.	You'll have it, if you open a movie house.
Benito:	¿Un Cinematógrafo? … ¿Y en Madrid? ¡Si los hay hasta en la sopa! Hay, Chispa, vaya una *chispa* que tienes.	A movie house! In Madrid? But the city is so full of them! Boy, Chispa, you're full of it.
Chispa:	Ven conmigo y luego me dirás si hay en Madrid un Cinematógrafo como el que voy a inspirarte … Ven y verás lo que es mi *Cinematógrafo* *Nacional*. (14–15)	Come with me and you tell me if there isn't a movie house like the one I'm about to inspire you with … Come and see my National Movie House.

What ensues is a musical and spoken farce in which Benito and the Chispa Eléctrica react to a succession of images in ways meant to appeal to the urban experiences of the audience. Benito, guided by the Chispa Eléctrica to the *cinematógrafo nacional* in question is actually led to the Congreso de los Diputados which is one the most important government buildings in Madrid and the nation. It has been transformed into a movie theater, with one long line of people filtering into the right side of the building through a door labeled Preferencia and another to the left through a door labeled Entrada General, a configuration which from the very beginning of the work mirrors the hierarchical spatial and price structure of the *zarzuela*, but also a reference to class differences on several scales (local, regional, national, international) at the same time. The double meaning of the *cinematógrafo nacional* is the driving force behind the humor of the play and relies on the premise that the center of political decision-making has been converted into the site of the selling and consumption of mass-produced spectacle. Ideologically, this *zarzuela* is fundamentally conservative in that it consistently cautions against the erasing of the boundaries between what are presented as a series of opposites: *zarzuela* and cinema, politics and entertainment, the real and the fictional, the Castilian and the European, and traditional male and female gender roles.

The organ of this whimsical *cinematógrafo* (and remember, this *zarzuela* was produced at the very beginning of the advent of the silent movie era when the instrument was essential to the success of the overall movie-going experience) "muestra las caras de hombres conocidos en la política que se irán renovando cuando el órgano juegue, con la misma precipitación que se sucede en el poder" (features the faces of familiar politicians that are changed when the organ plays, with the same frequency as they are rotated in and out of power) (16), read the stage directions. In the center, in front of the organ, is a young girl dressed like a harlequin, holding a sign that reads "POLÍTICA" (POLITICS). To her right and left are two more young girls who accompany her with cymbals and drums. The central harlequin figure symbolizing the "Political" is also flanked by two pedestals. Perched on the pedestal on the right is a stone lion on which leans a very large tambourine labeled "GÉNERO CHICO." Next to the tambourine is a woman labeled "LA PRENSA" (THE PRESS) poised to beat rhythmically on the instrument. On the pedestal to the left lies a large bass drum labeled "LO SICALÉPTICO" (meaning the erotic or suggestive) accompanied by another woman prepared to beat the drum in unison with the other stylized figures on the stage which are all powered by the Chispa Eléctrica and conducted by the harlequin to move mechanically in synchronization with the music of the allegorical *cinetagógrafo*'s organ. Below the figures already described in this highly symbolic theatrical tableau are women "colocadas en la escalinata y en actitudes diversas, mujeres representando las provincias: todas trajes de figurín y escudos y cada una con los atributos propios de cada provincia" (located on the risers and striking different poses and attitudes, women representing the provinces: all in costumes with coats of arms and each one with the attributes commonly associated with each province) (16). When the figures begin to move in unison with the music, the following exchange between Benito and the Chispa Eléctrica occurs:

Chispa:	Todo por mi fuerza moviéndose está.	This is moving all because of me.
Benito:	No en vano te llaman la Electricidad.	They don't call you Electricity for nothing.
	. . .	. . .
	¡Vaya un órgano explicando hoy las cosas como están! La política, dirige el cotarro nacional.	Imagine an organ explaining things the way they really are! Politics is running the national show.

…	…
Le zumban la pandereta	They whack on the tambourine
al pobre género chico	of the *género chico*
y el público le da bombo	and the audience hypes
a todo lo sicaléptico.	anything that is sexually suggestive.

The Chispa Eléctrica and Benito are observing and commenting on the scene in this way for a few moments, when Benito is charged by his fairy godmother to run the cinema himself: "Tuyo es. Y ahora, a ver cómo te las arreglas para que el público acuda" (It's yours. Now, let's see how you do it so that the public comes) (18). The force of technological progress embodied by the Chispa Eléctrica is what lies behind the nation's power structure, one that is presented as a benevolent or even maternal and caring entity, but one that challenges individuals to take control and structure their resources to use the new source of power in a productive way. Benito, the stereotype of *castizo* Madrid, is invited to take his place in the rational, carefully planned and mechanized power structure of modern society. The role that he is chosen to play is that of the emcee for a central component of the myth-making apparatus of modernity: the evolving, increasingly technology-driven entertainment industry.

Five seductive female performers enter the stage dressed as film reels, singing "Míranos, que somos bellas; te ofrecemos un caudal y con nuestro desarollo, ya verás, ya verás" (Look at us, we are beautiful; we offer you wealth and when we develop, you'll see, you'll see) (19). Here and throughout the play the youth and attractiveness of the women are emphasized. Through a series of double meanings such as this one, the promise of even more appealing and popular appreciation of the women as film industry lies in the future. The stage directions read: "todas llevan la rueda que se usa para envolver las cintas cinematográficas, colgadas con un cordón plateado" (they all are wearing the wheel that is used to roll up the film stock, hung by a silver cord) (19). Benito exclaims, "¡Ay, qué cintas para el Cine! Cuando empiecen a girar y le enseñen a uno todo el disloque nacional" (Oh, what trappings Film has! When they start to spin around they'll reveal a national disorder) (20). Early film was seen as dangerously seductive in several different ways. Not only did the public space of the cinema become private when all of the spectators were facing the same direction and the lights went down, but also it was thought that men and women in close proximity would be overwhelmed by passion upon viewing love scenes, and young men incited to acts of indecency after seeing so many images of beautiful, larger-than-life women on screen. In fact, pornography was one of the earliest of film genres in Madrid, introduced in short films screened between burlesque performances for all-male audiences (López Serrano 125–7). In the first years of the twentieth century the Calle de Alcalá (home of the Apollo Theater where *Cinematógrafo Nacional* was initially produced) was considered the epicenter of the nude review ("el núcleo de la noche frívola": (center of frivolous evenings) as López Serrano (126) puts it. At the same time, with the constant double entendres and symbols being utilized throughout the *zarzuela*, there is a sense that film will simultaneously bring about and document the breakdown of traditional "national" values, especially those having to do with the role of women in modern urban society.

Benito addresses the men in the audience: "Jóvenes, al desarrollo; necesito empezar una sesión en seguida" (Young men, time to get down to business; I need to start a session right away) (21). In sexually explicit terms, each film offers herself to the film manager for his personal viewing pleasure. There are five genres: the fantastic, the fairy tale, the horror film, a tourist's guide to the Vatican and a propaganda piece condemning a very unpopular municipal tax on food. Benito decides to screen the last one, which he thinks will be the most commercially successful. As mentioned above, Schwartz documents how the very first film audiences were not nearly as interested in viewing fictional narrative as seeing themselves in documentaries of everyday life. In the first decade of cinema, audiences were still expecting the popular theater, music and literature to provide them with escapist fiction. Film's role in society at that point was that of part newsreel and part scientific curiosity.

In *Cinematógrafo Nacional* one clearly sees the simultaneous existence of several genres. In much of the rest of the play one of the five actresses dressed as film reels (representing the filmic genre itself as well as a feminized film industry) stands to the left of the stage and begins to spin. A light shines on her, and in center stage are arranged a group of *zarzuela* performers playing the role of a cinema audience. To the right of the stage are placed another, distinct group of performers who act out the film that is supposedly being projected by the light shining on the human film reel. All of the three groups on stage sing and speak and the actual audience in the Apollo Theater views a human film projector, actors playing a group of filmgoers viewing a film that is actually a *zarzuela* performance within a *zarzuela* performance commenting on real-life, everyday urban places, people and situations – enough to keep a narratologist busy for weeks. *Cinematógrafo Nacional* is a hybrid, transitional genre that is part theatrical and part cinematic, part fantasy and part social criticism. The patrons of the Apollo Theater are watching a representation of themselves on the stage react to the series of short films being screened in a critical instance of self-awareness on the part of the audience and the *zarzuela* as a cultural institution on the decline, threatened by new film technology and distribution.

The first film to be "shown" is called "¡Abajo los consumos!" (Down with consumer taxes!) which comments on the politics of Madrid at the time as well as the tragic fire in a Paris theater killing more than a hundred people, the deaths of Spanish young men in North Africa, and complaints about neighborhoods in the city's center being razed to make way for the Gran Vía. The second film-within-a-

zarzuela is much more ambitious in its scope. In it there are two cities: one sad, dark, dilapidated and full of convents and churches called "Iberia" and another more dynamic, futuristic city "donde predominan los grandes monumentos, fábricas, estatuas, todo lo que indique el progreso y la civilización" (where the grand monuments, factories, statues, everything indicating progress and civilization predominates) (22). This second city is called "Europa." In between these two cities there stands a statue representing liberty and next to the stone figure a table where a series of people from different regions of Spain have to stop and ask permission to take a journey, presumably to immigrate to various parts of the world. These scenes give rise to very humorous but nevertheless biting critiques of national politics, economics, the press, Spain's seeming backwardness compared to the rest of Europe and Madrid's laws and living conditions. It also allows the *madrileños* the opportunity to indulge in some vicious stereotyping of their countrymen from other regions.

In *Cinematógrafo Nacional* there is strong resistance to film as a new visual form. In 1907, economically speaking, the larger, traditional, multipurpose theaters were beginning to lose some of their audience to the more single-purpose and modest *salones de cine* whose owners enjoyed a much lower overhead. Film was a threat to the *zarzuela*'s very existence, making its way into the spaces traditionally set aside for popular theater as documented above. Second, there is an intense concern played out in the *zarzuela* about film's potential to be used as an ideological tool. Film's supposed power to influence and persuade due to its seeming capacity to document and capture reality is commented on throughout *Cinematógrafo Nacional*. For example, in the small film audience on the stage there is an older gentleman who rants about how film will corrupt the young and debase Madrid's moral standards and then, in contrast, there is a much younger man who is fascinated by and completely transported into the futuristic world he sees on the screen. It is significant that both the old and young man are not given names – they are nameless so as to represent their respective generations. The elderly man, representing a time when the *zarzuela grande* was an important cultural presence in Madrid, harshly criticizes the appearance on screen of strong, independent women, saying they are too sexually suggestive. Since in this work film is woman and women are consistently associated with urban and technological progress, the critique of the one carries over onto the other. While these women are seen as threatening and completely unclassifiable to the older gentleman, they are obviously quite pleasing, almost inspirational to the more modern young man.

The fifth act is called "Madrid Sicaléptico," and consist of the last of the theatrical films to be shown and commented upon by the *zarzuela*'s fictional film audience. The sets indicate that the action of the film takes place in the Jardín Botánico, at the Paseo del Prado entrance, where the door is labeled "Gran

Kermesse Sicaléptica – Entrada Libre." A figure named "La Diosa del Tango" enters, followed by a chorus of young *coupletistas* dressed as nuns. They remove their habits, singing

Nos colamos en Madrid	We snuck into Madrid
y la villa es nuestra ya,	and the town is ours now,
arrojando para siempre	flinging away our mystical
nuestro místico sayal.	course wool clothing forever.
La belleza es hoy la diosa	Now beauty is the goddess
que la gente adora más	that people worship the most
y es la letra de los tangos	and tango lyrics are
el lenguaje universal.	the universal language. (36)

The "Diosa del Tango" proclaims her reign over Madrid's politics and morality, singing "Todo, todo es sicalipsis, la moral se concluyó" (It's all about the erotic, morality is no more) (37). The music and the dance of the tango were associated with dance halls where men would pay to dance with *tanguistas*, some of whom were known to grant more intimate physical contact later in the evening, for a price. Throughout this scene the female chorus repeats the refrain "armamos nosotras, armamos, armarmos la revolución" (we are preparing, preparing, preparing for the revolution) (37–8) while lifting their skirts and showing their legs, as the stage directions mandate. "¡El triunfo del femenismo es un hecho!" (Feminism has triumphed!) (42) explains the young man. In the following scene an old man in the fictional film audience on the *zarzuela* stage is seen walking around the newly occupied city, marveling at how it has changed. The theaters have all become nude reviews with shows called "La vida es tango" (Life is a tango,) "Hacer el amor" (Making love) "Dale amor" (Give love) "Toma amor" (Take love) and "El amor libre" (Free love). The street names have been changed to honor famous, seductive singers and the newspaper is called *El Madrid Verde*. In short, strong, organized, sexual and independent women seduce the male population through taking control of their objectification, an objectification made all the more complete and immediate through the new form of visual transmission, the film image. They use their recently acquired power as film stars, singers, dancers, and other roles that typically make them the objects of male desire to completely reorganize Madrid's power structure – the public space of politics, the language and names used to talk about the city and even the more private arena of individual relationships between men and women. By making this female taking of power ridiculous and comic in the extreme, *Cinematógrafo Nacional* preserves the very middle class, traditionally Catholic values for which the *zarzuela* has always been known.

After scene six, where women performers worship at the foot of the "Ara Sicalíptica" (Psycholeptic Altar) spouting green smoke and singing the refrain

Al empuje valeroso del ejército del amor, no hay valiente que resista y no rinda el corazón	To the valiant force of the army of love, no brave man can resist without breaking his heart. (44)

marching in military fashion and singing sexually suggestive lyrics about how to use their physical attraction to get what they want, the young man tells the old "[q]ue está usté soñando, que todo es un sueño. Esto es una película de un Cinematógrafo y nada más" (you're dreaming, it's all a dream. This is nothing more than a movie in a Movie House). "Pero, ¿Madrid no es Sicaléptico?" (Madrid's not Psycholeptic?) asks the old man, to which the young man responds "Todavía, no; pero quién responde del porvenir por el camino que vamos." (Not yet; but who can say about the future considering the path we're on now) (46). Yet these are two last images with which the audience in the Apollo Theater is left: in the penultimate one, the allegorical figure of Electricity, holding a film projector and surrounded by the five film reels, points the machine's light towards the back of the stage, where a coach, drawn by the mythical winged horses of the God Apollo, who points to the light projected by the film projector, in the middle of which appears one word: *Progreso*. Here the theater itself – specifically the Apollo Theater with the reference to the Greek god and the theater in general – acknowledges that progress and all that comes with it, including film, will be embraced, if ever so cautiously. This image makes abstract the very real and pressing concerns that the *zarzuela* had about its position as one of the most popular and lucrative of popular pastimes and demonstrates a grudging acceptance of the new film technology and all that it might entail. Film illuminates and makes possible the rising sun of progress and the Apollo will be forced to define itself against this potential challenge which has made its way into the very center of its space, worked its way into the beginning, middle and end of its theatrical productions and reshaped the way Madrid's classes see themselves. The piece ends with the squadrons of "psycholeptic" women kneeling respectfully and laying down their weapons. The entire cast sings in unison: "Que a nuestra España ilumine el Progreso no está mal" (For our Spain to be illuminated by Progress isn't so bad) (47). *Cinematógrafo Nacional* is self-referential in that it plays out the fears that the genre had in the face of the unknown film genre. The largely bourgeois audience of the Apollo Theater has laughed at the fear, crudeness and ignorance of the stereotyped male figures of the down-and-out Benito and the old and young men who are the film spectators within the play. They are made to feel superior but at the same time are forced to see themselves as spectators and participants in a new type of entertainment whose effects are not fully understood and therefore highly suspect.

To understand cinematic and popular theatrical spectatorship in the late nineteenth and early twentieth centuries as historical practices, it is essential to locate both in the field of cultural forms and practices associated with the burgeoning mass culture. The *género chico,* however fearful it may have been in the face of its new cinematic rival, effectively represents film as an art in its urban and political context and chronicles the reception of silent film in Madrid just as it was beginning to have an affect on a wide audience. It is clear that early cinema did not produce any new forms, concepts or techniques that were not already available in other genres, but consisted of a coming together of other aspects of modern culture, outpacing these other forms, ultimately becoming much more than just another scientific novelty. One important aspect of the *zarzuela* and early popular film in particular is its easily identifiable double nature: that of product and producer of modern, industrialized, urban society. Inextricably linked to capital, commercially successful films and *zarzuelas* both critique and document the problems inherent in capitalist society: sometimes realistically, sometimes idealistically, but always playing to and upon the emotions of a wide audience. One can't help but recognize that some of the fears and concerns expressed in the *zarzuela* about the rise of film and a perceived shift in visuality in 1907 are echoed today. Computer-aided design, synthetic holography, flight simulators, computer animation, robotic image recognition and texture mapping are only a few of the techniques that are relocating vision to a plane severed from a human observer. Obviously other older and more familiar modes of seeing will persist and coexist uneasily alongside these new forms. The evolution of ways of communicating and representing ourselves to ourselves is constant and perhaps looking back one hundred years at how one cultural form coexists with and then gives way to another can help shed some light on this ongoing process.

Notes

1. The majority of historians of Spanish film (here Pérez Perucha, Gubern, Martínez, Diez Puertas and López Serrano – Cabero is the exception) agree that the distribution, viewing and production of film in the early years 1896 to 1910 were much more dynamic in Barcelona and even Valencia than in the nation's capital. In his study of Spain's early film industry, immediately after he outlines the beginnings of film in Barcelona, Pérez Perucha (45) states unequivocally in the section of his study entitled "Madrid no existe" (Madrid does not exist) that during this time period, "en Madrid no pasaba nada, dicho sea en terminos cinematográficos. Las razón era tan simple como sorprendente: no había público para el nuevo espectáculo" (nothing was happening in Madrid, in terms of film. The reason was as simple as it was surprising: there was no audience for the new spectacle).
2. This same address on the Carrera de San Jeronimo is also where the images of Thomas Edison's patented Kinetoscope where first seen by an elite viewing

public. It should be noted that Josefina Martínez is of the opinion that the first collective viewing of moving images on a screen in Madrid did not take place in May of 1896 but a year earlier, in the Circo Parish Theater with the Animatograph, which was owned and traveled from town to town with an Englishman named Rousby.

3. In a case of trans-Atlantic cinematic cross-fertilization, Kathryn Helgesen Fuller documents how a dominant trend in nickelodeon nomenclature in the United States tied into the first wave of popularity of Spanish and Mexican architecture and culture and resulted in names such as Alhambra, Alcazar, and Valencia. Similarly, in Spain, nickelodeon owners, in an effort to draw on the public's desire for the exotic, came up with names such as Bijou, Varieté, Rouge, Campos Elíseos, Japonés, Luna Park, and Versalles.
4. Pérez Perucha (46) contrasts the interest of Madrid's population in cinema to that of Barcelona and finds it sorely lacking, due to what he believes is the stronger hold of such inexpensive and popular diversions such as the *género chico*, zarzuela, *sainete*, and bullfighting and a lack of capital.
5. The Apollo Theater was torn down in 1929 and rebuilt for its current occupant, the Banco de Vizcaya.
6. According to Martínez, Kalb's program at the Apollo Theater consisted of the following titles from the Lumière catalog: "Un famoso dentista," "Escenas en la playa," "Una comida con incidentes" and "El tíovivo de las Tullerías" as well as several from the catalog of Méliès, such as "No se permite fijar cartels," "El Boulevard de los italianos" and "Noche terrible" and another whose origin is uncertain, a seductive number called "Danza serpentina."
7. Diez Puertas points out the significance of the fact that Spanish government authorities, upon the very advent of film in Spain, subject all cinema to the "Reglamento de Policía de Espectáculos Públicos de 1886," which meant that the censorship codes for both film and theater were exactly the same. It is not until 1912 that the Spanish government would find it necessary to set up a code of cinematic censorship specific to the medium itself.
8. *Cinematógrafo Nacional* is considered to be a rather minor work. In spite of the many specific references made to the political and cultural events of early-twentieth-century Madrid, many of which would be lost on a contemporary audience, this *zarzuela* was produced again as late as 1983 by renowned producer Adolfo Marsillach in Madrid's Teatro de la Comedia. The music is performed much more frequently. It was heard as recently as July 24, 2004 when it was the required piece at the Certamen Nacional de Bandas de Música held in Campo de Criptana to commemorate the one hundred and fiftieth anniversary of the birth of Gerónimo Giménez (Portal de la Federación de Sociedad Musicales de la Comunidad Valenciana http://www.musicaypueblo.com/noticia.asp?idnoticia=58499&idioma=val).

9. Other than *Cinematógrafo Nacional*, there would be other *zarzuelas* such as *Películas madrileñas* (1908) by Pedro Baños and José Manzano, *La última película* (1913) or *Cine-Fantomas* (1915) by Ricardo González del Toro and Gerónimo Giménez.
10. Unlike other well-known librettists of their day, on the whole they tended to steer clear of scenes drawn directly from Madrid life and were best known for their plots inspired by contemporary Viennese operetta. *Cinematógrafo Nacional* is an exception to this tendency in their body of work as is their *Madrid de noche* (1897), *Bocetos madrileños* (1901), and *Madrid en el año dos mil* (1887). They are best known for their *Bohemios* (1904), based on Henri Murger's *Scènes de la vie de Bohème*, the biblical farce *La corte de Faraón* (1910) and *La generala* (1912), a farcical courtly romance set in Edwardian England.
11. King Chintila was a Visigoth who reigned from 636 to 639 and was known for, among other things, the forced conversion of the Jews in 638 and his participation in the Concilios de Toledo, where more feudal powers were granted to the Visigoth monarchy. Charles II (1661–1700) was King of Spain, Naples, and Sicily, reigning from 1665 to 1700. Son of Philip IV of Spain and of Mariana of Austria, he was the last of the Spanish Habsburg dynasty, physically disabled and mentally retarded. His mother was his regent during much of his reign. During his reign Spain continued the decline that had begun under his increasingly incompetent Habsburg ancestors.

Works Cited

Alaminos, Eduardo and Eduardo Salas. "Ocio y diversions madrileños: Del reinado de Isabel II a la Segunda República." In *Madrid: Atlas histórico de la ciudad 1850–1939*. Madrid: Lunwerg, 2001. 342–69.

Álvarez Junco, José. "Rural and Urban Popular Cultures." In *Spanish Cultural Studies: An Introduction. The Struggle for Modernity*. Helen Graham and Jo Labanyi, Oxford and New York: Oxford University Press. 82–9.

Baroja, Pío. *Aurora roja*. Madrid: Cid, 1959.

Benjamin, Walter. "Paris, Capital of the Nineteenth Century." In *Reflections: Essays, Aphorisms, Autobiographical Writings*. Ed. Peter Demetz. Trans. Edmund Jephcott. New York: Schocken, 1978. 146–62.

Cabero, Juan Antonio. *Historia de la cinematografía española: Once jornadas 1896–1948*. Madrid: Gráficas Cinema, 1949.

Charney, Leo and Vanessa R. Schwartz, eds. *Cinema and the Invention of Modern Life*. Berkeley: University of California Press, 1995.

Crary, Jonathan. *Techniques of the Observer: On Vision and Modernity in the Nineteenth Century*. Cambridge, MA and London: MIT Press, 1990.

Diez Puertas, Emeterio. *Historia social del cine en España*. Madrid: Fundamentos, 2003.

Gómez Amat, Carlos. *Historia de la música española*. Vol. 5. Siglo XIX. Madrid: Alianza, 1984.

Gubern, Román, J.E. Monterde, J.P. Perucha, E. Riamban and C. Torreiro, eds. *Historia del cine español*, 3rd edn. Madrid: Cátedra, 2000.

Helgesen Fuller, Kathryn. "At the Picture Show." In *Exhibition: The Film Reader*. Ed. Ina Rae Mark. New York: Routledge, 2002. 41–9.

Kern, Stephen. *The Culture of Time and Space, 1880–1918*. Cambridge, MA: Harvard University Press, 1983.

López Serrano, Fernando. *Madrid, figuras y sombras: De los teatros de títeres a los salones de cine*. Madrid: Complutense, 1999.

Martínez, Josefina. *Los primeros veinticinco años de cine en Madrid, 1896–1920*. Madrid: Filmoteca Española, 1992.

del Moral Ruiz, Carmen. "El género chico y la invención de Madrid: La Gran Vía (1886)." In *Madrid de Fortunata a la M-40: Un siglo de cultura urbana*. Madrid: Alianza, 2003. 27–58.

Pérez Perucha, Julio. "Narración de un aciago destino (1896–1930)." In *Historia del cine español*. Madrid: Cátedra, 2000. 19–121

Pérez Rojas, Francisco Javier. "Los cines madrileños: del barracón al rascacielos." In *El cinematógrafo en Madrid 1896–1960*. Vol. I. Madrid: Ayuntamiento de Madrid and the Concejalía de Cultura, 69–83. (Catalog of the exhibit in the Museo Municipal de Madrid March–April, 1986).

Perrín y Vico, Guillermo and Miguel de Palacios. *Cinematógrafo Nacional*. Zarzuela, 1907.

Sambricio, Carlos. *Madrid: Ciudad-Región. De la ciudad Ilustrada a la primera mitad del siglo XX*. Madrid: Comunidad de Madrid, 1999.

Santos, Juliá, David Ringrose and Cristina Segura. *Madrid: Historia de una capital*. Madrid: Alianza, 1995.

Schwartz, Vanessa R. "Cinematic Spectatorship before the Apparatus: The Public Taste for Reality in Fin-de-Siècle Paris." In L. Charney and V.R. Schwartz (eds) *Cinema and the Invention of Modern Life*. Berkley: University of California Press, 1995. 279–98.

Torres, Augusto M. "De Madrid al cine. Historia del cine madrileño." In *El cinematógrafo en Madrid 1896–1960*. Vol. I. Madrid: The Ayuntamiento de Madrid and the Concejalía de Cultura, 19–23. (Catalog of the exhibit in the Museo Municipal de Madrid March-April, 1986).

–15–

Visualizing the Time-space of Otherness: Digression and Distraction in Spanish Silent Film

Eva Woods

In the late nineteenth century, cinema played a crucial role in the representability of time. Like statistics, philosophy, and psychology, it participated in a "general cultural imperative" to structure time and contingency in capitalist modernity (Doane 3). The potential representability of time became an insistent issue as labor time and leisure time were fundamentally reconstituted by the expanded circulation of capital.[1] And as individuals found themselves subjected to rationalized, standardized time, access to a temporality that embraced affective modes of feeling, was pleasurable, even though potentially anxiety producing. Film shots, editing, and narrative could represent time through their controlled packaging and commodifying of its ongoing experience while simultaneously they embodied the contingent, chance, and the present instant (Doane 221–2). That is, while cinema tended to standardize time, it also privileged an ultimately impossible immediacy with the moment, or the instant, in a standardized world. Contingency *felt more real*. And for a nation concerned with its status as modern, there were high stakes involved in controlling what was seen as reality.

In this chapter I look at two fictional silent films, *La gitana blanca* (The White Gypsy) (Ricardo de Baños 1923) and *La Condesa María* (The Countess María) (Benito Perojo 1927) which contain temporal and spatial digressions that are central to their expositions of modernity and race. In *La gitana blanca*, the digression contains two parts: a mother is separated from her children who are sent to a "Gypsy" camp; and the mother's sister's lover is sent to Morocco to join Spanish troops in subduing Rif rebels. In *La Condesa María* the aristocratic hero is also sent to Morocco, in a digression so long that it constitutes a film within a film.[2]

In both *La gitana blanca* and *La Condesa María*, the Morocco scenes take place between the so-called "disaster" of Annual in 1921, in which the North Moroccan Riffian tribes defeated the Spanish, and the consequent revenge of the Franco-Spanish counter-offensive, which crushed the Rif independence movement of

Abdel Krim in 1925. Many of these scenes closely resemble private and government-sponsored newsreels and documentaries of the Spanish–Moroccan War. This similarity is perhaps the effect of the regular industry practice of lifting military footage from documentaries and pasting it into new films in order to create not only highly entertaining digressions but also pro-war propaganda.[3] The insertion of these fragments of reality could bring the spectator into a realistic and gripping contact with the other while allowing them to comfortably slip back into the melodramatic narrative. Contingency could be effectively simulated. Nevertheless, this filmic manipulation exposed the instability at the heart of the real, exacerbating anxieties Spaniards had about Moroccans and Gypsies.

What is the significance of these digressions into spaces of otherness, with their colonialist imperatives and racist tropes? Their meaning, I argue, derives from a confluence of events: the emergence of cinema, the loss of the colonies, and Spanish expansion into Africa (an attempt to better define the anxiety-producing Spanish-Africa border). In film, the traumatic loss of the colonies is overcome by transferring the space of otherness from the Americas to North Africa. And by visualizing the "Gypsy" population within a digression, viewers can imagine spaces of otherness as familiar, yet safely on the other side of the border. Time-based media such as film visualized Spain's perceived need to "catch up" to European time by erasing boundaries between itself and Europe, while drawing more clearly the barrier between Spain and Africa. This frontier mirage was represented through metaphors of time. As modernity has signified contemporaneity, Spain's representations of itself have hinged upon its imagined location in time: while the self occupies present time, the other lacks time. Nevertheless, control of the other requires contact, which necessitates sharing the same time, or coevalness. In order to obscure this contradiction, the encounter with the other takes place in the digression, already understood by spectators to be the representation of an alternative temporality, one of contingency, where contact is both frightening and intriguing.

The racialized digressions in these films emerge from stories of family separation and threatened social hierarchies, dramatizing fears about separation and instability on the Spain–Africa border, among the anonymous yet visible enemy. Although cinema interpellates the spectator as a unified, transcendental subject, glossing over her fundamental difference (Hansen 3), these silent deviations problematize individual and national identity. The desire for stability was logical when dictatorship, boom and bust economic trends, rampant rates of illiteracy, and an imperialist foreign policy were bound to bewilder those who saw the lunacy of a colonialist war by a country still reeling from the "disaster" of 1898. Added to anxieties over public and private identity in a time of flux was the built-in structural anxiety in films that combined fiction (simulated time) and documentary (real time). Siegfried Krakauer (249) defines the area between the actuality (i.e. documentary) and the episodic fiction film as a border region. His notion of border inevitably recalls contemporary references to borders as space-times of ambivalence: on the one hand traumatic and hysterical yet on the other constitutive of productive hybridities, unimagined utopias, and hope. In effect, the digressions in these films are "border regions" offering different modalities of time – immersion in a time not structured by capitalist modernity: contingency. The question then becomes what happens to the representation of time, as an object of knowledge within practices of looking, when it is racialized within these digressive border spaces. Equally important is how the subject inhabits this space-time's conjoining pressures and pleasures, which must be thought in relationship to the particular context of Spain's internal and external others, the "Gypsy" and the Moroccan.

Some Film Genealogy

In the earliest cinema (1896–1907) the contingent was represented by the practices of the "actuality," Tom Gunning's term for the pre-narrative "curiosity-arousing" cinema of attractions, a medium of "direct stimulation" and a "gesture of presenting for view, of displaying," akin to the spectacle of fairs, popular exhibits, the circus (73). By offering vistas of foreign, exotic places and times or filmed events that captured a sense of the ephemeral – *La vida de los gauchos en México* (The Life of the Gauchos in Mexico) (1898) or *Un tren escocés* (A Scottish Train) (1898) and *Vistas de las capitales de Europa* (Views of the Capitals of Europe) (1898) – cinema could ease the monotony of factory work or temper the over-stimulation of blasé urban dwellers, as Simmel (35) explains. Cinema's visual stimulation registered the awe and fear of new technology and machine power which were compacting the experience of temporality as life itself accelerated. Even the routine could appear novel in films such as Alexandre Promio's *La Puerta del Sol* (1896) or Ramón del Río's *Salida de Misa de doce de las Calatravas* (Leaving Twelve o'clock Mass) (1896), the latter filmed with color images. New modes of spectatorial address enabled more immediate viewing experiences, and audiences now expected to be astonished by the visuals that assaulted them in mass print, photographic reproductions and cinema (think of spectators rushing for cover when a train speeds toward them on screen). Benjamin called this experience "the shock." The receptive experience, he said, was in a state of distraction "symptomatic of profound changes in apperception" (240). Mirroring capitalist modernity's new way of perceiving the world, cinematic special effects made visible what was unseeable in everyday experience, in particular, the instantaneous shocks and accidentality of the isolated instant (Doane 133).

The desire to represent the instantaneous continued after the arrival of cinema narrative, appearing in the form of dramatizations. Residues of the actuality informed the structures of many films and were necessary to them. As Gunning notes, the actuality and the narrative are "two ways of addressing spectators [that] can frequently interrelate within the same text" (81). In silent film narratives, vestiges of the cinema of attractions appeared in the form of disastrous accidents, leaps and falls, and aerial views. My interest lies in why Spanish silent films of the 1920s – which had transitioned to full-length narrative features in the early teens – continued to rely on these spectatorial deviations. In many mature silent films, digressions invade the main narrative taking the form of comic interludes, travel sequences, documentary-like episodes, long parties, leisure activities, live performances and entertainment spectacles; sometimes documentary footage is spliced in to make the dramatization seem all the more real.[4] These digressions often follow a character journeying to distant lands which offer exotic exterior shots, using the camera's flashy features such as the pan and extreme long shots, and its ability to record live events, such as battles. Such scenes could prompt the writing of an entire narrative digression or justify surprise plot twists. Although their accidentality is mainly an illusion – except in rare shots where the director cannot control what moves into the frame of a stationary camera – these spontaneous events disrupt the otherwise predictable narrative flow.

As spectators became accustomed to sophisticated editing techniques, which ironically simulated reality far more convincingly than the actuality, they were less inclined to sit through the long interludes necessary to filming live action in real time. Dramatized live events took up less time, shocking audiences and immersing them in the instant, while also visualizing the action from an exotic location, in this case, Spain's colonial frontier in northern Africa, or the borders within the nation that marked the space of internal others, such as the Rrom.

These digressive intervals represent the true ontology of cinema: the distraction from everyday life as represented by the bourgeois dramas of romance, family conflict and patriotism, and the relationship of such distractions to the psychocultural processes of subject formation and spectatorial desire. Melodrama, central to our experience of modern world, is inextricable from this ontology of the cinema. Its etymology implies the combination of narrative and spectacle propelled by emotion. Spectacle, excess, swift turns of events and outrageous coincidence, as we see them in these two films, were part and parcel of film melodrama, a style which like its visual precedents, dramatized vision (Singer 6–7). Film melodrama was so powerful that the theatrical subgenre of the *película hablada* (talking film) began imitating its rapid succession of scenes (Díez Puertas 264). Cinema was marking out modern sensibilities that Spanish viewers recognized, smoothly folding these modes of feeling into the melodramatization of consciousness already developed since the nineteenth century, so that the viewing experience simulated actual emotional work.

The epistemological tendency – to see is to know – had characterized the spectatorial experience of the illustrated press (Martín Jiménez 375), becoming even stronger in the cinema through its creation of a subjectivity focused on "the register of the look, on processes of perceptual identification with seeing and being seen" (Hansen 2). Melodrama and the press conditioned spectators to receive mediated images of reality, and to accept "la imagen que se tiene de las cosas" (the image one has of things). Rather than first-hand images of reality, audiences came to expect visual representations of themes that constituted centers of public interest (Martín Jiménez 375). As the demand for images grew, and it was not necessarily a demand for images extracted directly from reality, a principle source for them was the archive of recorded film and photographic images dealing with the war in Morocco (375). An analysis of the viewing subject in Spain during this period therefore invites a discussion of the actuality-turned-dramatization, its relationship to melodrama, and its insinuation into later narrative cinema against the backdrop of the colonial wars in Northern Morocco.[5]

Internal Others

Los arlequines de seda y oro was shot in 1918 by Ricardo de Baños, shown in Barcelona in 1919, and then re-edited with some newly filmed sequences in 1923 and renamed *La gitana blanca.*[6] Divided into three parts, *La gitana blanca*'s complicated plot relates the adventures of two aristocratic children. Raquel and Juan de Dios are sold to a family of "Gypsies" by their father, the Count of Rosicler, in order to punish their mother, whom the father suspects has committed adultery. Under the tutelage of this surrogate family, Raquel (played by Raquel Meller) is physically and emotionally abused, but learns flamenco dance and song, and eventually escapes the "Gypsy" clan to become the famous *cupletista*, "La gitana blanca." She rockets to stardom, her family history effaced by the marketable star bio of the poor "Gypsy" girl and orphan boy cum stars. Through a series of melodramatic coincidences, the adult Raquel is rejoined with her long-lost father and brother, who all recognize each other by birthmarks on their necks. These physical signs, more distinguishable than blood, powerfully reassert Raquel's tainted racialized identity as unambiguously white and aristocratic. Raquel marries her brother's bullfighting rival in a happy ending that reaffirms the status quo, unites the family on patriarchal property, and gracefully elides the anxieties of racial mixing or class struggle.

Nevertheless, if we emphasize the digression in *La gitana blanca* that leads us to the scenes in Melilla, deeper messages surface about racial identity and its maintenance which necessarily structure bourgeois subjectivity. Within this thread, Raquel's mother's sister, Elvira, is unhappily married but in love with Captain Álvaro Valdés, who has received orders to join his regiment in Melilla. Elvira and the captain send their letters through Raquel's mother to avoid suspicions, but in a sudden turn of events, the Count intercepts the captain's letter to Elvira notifying her of the captain's transfer to Melilla. Seeking to avenge his honor, the count arranges for his butler to sell their two children to a "Gypsy" caravan.

The narrative contains two major digressions to space-times of otherness: the move to the "Gypsy" camp, set in motion by the purloined letter; and the following journey to Melilla where Álvaro battles the rebellious Riffians. Motivating the initial action is the threat of adultery, implying that the Count's children are not his – thereby affronting his honor and warranting such harsh punishment of the mother. As Singer notes, the melodramatic frame of the digression produces hyperbolic emotion and Manichean moral extremes. Like the early sensationalistic "blood and thunder" melodrama, the distracting digression is produced by non-classical narrative mechanics (Singer 6–7). Like other narratives of the bourgeois family, then, this film is structured *by* and structuring *of* filmic distraction, spectacle and shock (7). It is motivated by desire and fear, and its focus on the "Gypsy" reinforces that mechanism of ambivalence. For the original focus on potentially adulterous mothers and the tragic dissolution of family shifts to the sexually and racially threatened white woman: this motherless daughter will not only grow up with the "Gypsies," but as a "Gypsy," stigmatized by prostitution, the livelihood of even successful entertaining "Gypsies." The "Gypsy" other was also threatening because its iconic attraction was so great. The Carmen narrative, internalized by the Spanish, catalyzed an exotic, ironic marketing of this stereotype by its own inhabitants, while engendering an increased obsession with and repulsion against narratives of miscegenation. The Carmen narrative was one of the first filmic adaptations of the "Gypsies" which abound in both cinema and popular literature.[7] The spectacle of the "Gypsy" camp, coalesced with viewer's manufactured expectations of ethnic entertainers and child abusers who were displayed in the ethnographic tableau of travel novels, picture postcards and film travelogues, all of which produced a "pseudo-knowledge" about the Rrom as a people of a different temporality (Alleloula 120).[8]

As the butler drives to meet the "Gypsies," the camera advertises the myth of automobile technology by its insistent shots of the car entering and speeding away from a variety of perspectives. The scene cuts to a customs-and-manners portrait of a "Gypsy" camp, replete with wagons and campfire, recalling the rustic and ragged "Gypsies" of popular illustrations, pseudo-ethnographic photography, and travel literature – the very antithesis of the *white* "Gypsy." A "Gypsy hag" grabs money the butler offers them for the children and the audience is left to surmise the rest of the conversation which leaves the butler looking visibly uncomfortable. The scene ends with the male "Gypsy" sweeping his arm across the frame as it dissolves into a train busily making its way through the landscape. Suturing the gesture of the "Gypsy" with the same technology that shocked Spanish audiences decades earlier (remember the actuality of a train rushing toward the spectator), this editing makes a stark contrast between the primitive, seen through a pre-capitalist optic, and the modern force that slices through the land. By juxtaposing the "Gypsies" bargaining with automobile and railroad technology, the digression interprets economic disparities as opposing terms such as "preliterate vs. literate, traditional vs. modern, peasant vs. industrial, and a host of permutations which include pairs such as tribal vs. feudal, rural vs. urban" (Fabian 22). These dichotomies are strengthened as the film cuts to a shot of the butler looking through the train window at the passing geography.

As traveler, the butler is the subject par excellence of middle-class identity, the interpellated protagonist of the new technologies emerging in the nineteenth century. Decades earlier than the cinema, the railroad had ruptured traditional frontiers between spaces, forging an intimate connection between the body, time and space. Clearly, "[t]he railroad journey anticipated more explicitly than any other technology an important facet of the experience of cinema: a person in a seat watches moving visuals through a frame that does not change position" (Charney and Schwartz 6). For many viewers, however, references to railroad technology could have evoked the Spanish civilian workers who died attempting to install a railroad in sacred territory of a *morabito* (Marabout), a Muslim shrine. The violent resistance from the Riffians was an invitation for the Spanish government to send even more workers, this time from Barcelona. The incident spawned Barcelona's Tragic Week, and was remembered as the infamous battle of Barranco del Lobo. It is often equated with Annual in the list of colonial disasters in Morocco (Martín Corrales 93–4).

As the butler peers out the window, the film directs our gaze to a match shot in which the butler's cigarette smoke parallels the train's puffing stack, identifying him with the iron juggernaut dynamically cutting through the landscape. Indeed, he becomes the train: the middle class *is* the modern and serves the upper classes as does the machine. The scene's focalization through the working class yet professionally dressed and aspiring bourgeois butler evokes contempt for the "Gypsy" pariah, while soliciting solidarity for the count's vengeance. Scapegoating the "Gypsies" for buying the children overlooks the real culprits – the unscrupulous Count, but also the class structure which requires that marginalized groups resort to such practices. The final shots of this journey to the demonized "Gypsies" show the "bad step-parents," the antonym of the heterosexual, non-racialized couple, struggling to control the children while leading them to a caravan headed for an unknown destination.

External Others

Instead of finding out the fate of the children, the digression in *La gitana blanca* takes us even further into the heart of darkness, prolonging the experience of disjuncture. The last shot of the "Gypsy" camp is followed by the intertitle,

"MELILLA," a jolting spectatorial address that evokes Sergei Eisenstein's montage theory of thesis, antithesis, synthesis: two very different images are juxtaposed and thereby conflated to produce an entirely new meaning. Here, the digression to the contingent time of the "Gypsy" camp precedes the rational time of the military sequence in Melilla where the most current technology of the Spanish army, propelled by the flood tide of Western modernity, subdues the wild frontier. The abrupt intertitle with its official weight of capital letters strengthens the comparison between Melilla and the "Gypsy" camp, the more so because "Melilla" had immediate resonance with Spanish audiences in the 1920s. As the military seat of Spain's closest extra-national territory, and the point of departure for penetration into Morocco, Melilla had become synonymous with war and suffering, the antithesis of progress, and a source of collective angst over the safety of its Spanish civilians and military personnel (Díez Sánchez 51). After 1911, it was normal for war events in the eastern region of the protectorate to be generically referred to as "sucesos de Melilla" even though they occurred hundreds of kilometers away (Díez Sánchez 50–1). As a Spanish film historian put it, "la mayoría no sabía leer y África era todo un mismo sitio."[9] The Spanish protectorates of Ceuta and Melilla were metonyms for Africa. In silent film production, it was common practice to edit newsreels by cutting and pasting from several different shorts, and it was understood that certain images might not be from the same battle being described. In this particular film, the events in Melilla could have evoked the battles of either Barranco del Lobo in 1909 or Annual in 1921. At Annual, the Riffians retook most of the Melilla region, forcing the Spaniards into urban confines of Melilla city. Not until the 1925 battle of Al Hoceima did the Spanish finally put down the Rif rebellion.

The defeat at Annual was so disastrous that it took on a mythical quality. Between 8,000 and 12,000 Spanish soldiers died. According to Sebastian Balfour, it was a "national tragedy on a much greater scale than any other military defeat suffered by Spain, including the war of 1898" (70). That the Rif saw Annual as the crowning victory of a holy war is understandable: their growing antagonism to colonial penetration, exacerbated by the errors and abuses of Spanish officers (looting, raping, disregard for local customs, disruption of the local economy), finally resulted in an explosion of violence. But for the Spaniards, only the ruthless extermination of the Riffian race was sufficient to avenge the enormous casualties that remained on the battlefield, mutilated, unburied, and half eaten by vultures after the panicked retreat. Later came the bitterness and anger over military incompetence and the hordes of Spanish prisoners of war. This loss of face for the Spaniards was exacerbated by a wave of racism in the media that reactivated myths of Arab cruelty and savagery, fueling the obsession with recuperating their masculinity.[10] During this time, media objects such as *literatura de cordel*, chocolate wrappers, match box covers, song lyrics, and comic strips promoted a banal version of orientalism exhibiting extreme racist caricatures.

But it was mainly the gruesome photos and film footage of Spanish soldiers that won support for the war. The Spanish military explicitly supported this colonial cinema between 1909 and 1927 in order to justify the draft to the working class. The emergent cinema companies sent droves of cameramen to capture battle scenes, which were then shown all over Spain, and sometimes this footage quietly found its way into film melodramas. In *La Condesa María*, for instance, the digression to Morocco is comprised of footage filmed in the exteriors of Tetuan, Chauen, Mogado and the surrounding desert. Perojo obtained the full collaboration of the army based in the Rif for the shoot of the war scenes (Gubern 143–4). Perojo seemed to have spent every resource to glorify the army, directing 2,000 extras at a time, and coordinating military parades through the narrow streets of Tetuan.

Slavery, revenge, and racialized scapegoats drove these melodramatic film plots, and such topoi were easily translated to the mediatized invasion of Alhucemas. Newsreels, documentaries, the digressions to Morocco in both *La gitana blanca* and *La Condesa María* – all make use of similar structures of feeling, similar scenarios of revenge and victimization. In the second digression in *La gitana blanca*, it is unclear what the relationship is between Álvaro's suspected adultery and his abrupt transfer to Melilla. But his apparently unwarranted punishment of being separated from his lover and sent to Morocco is unavoidably associated with the unjust draft that sent workers to die in Africa. For the war not only brings death but also tears apart families. Loyal to melodrama's strong pathos, the film consolidates these different scenarios, strengthening the need for revenge, simplifying the Manichean morality, and economically channeling the emotion against a single enemy. The cloudier the origins of the revenge, the easier it was for film, and other ideological vehicles, to continue spreading revenge propaganda (Martín Corrales 127). In fact, the majority of the Spanish population was against the war, due to the devastating loss of Spanish lives. To counteract this antiwar sentiment, the government, the military, upper-class colonialist interests and the conservative mass media launched a massive publicity campaign that cast the Moroccan as inherently blood-thirsty, traitorous by nature, and in need of annihilation if civilization was to be saved (Martín Corrales 127). In the end, the marketing of military footage and melodrama together appealed to both male and female audiences – there was "something for everyone." That appeal, combined with the inflammatory need for revenge, enabled the colonial enterprise in manufacturing compatible notions of personal and national identity.

After the brusque announcement that the spectator has arrived to Melilla, the camera pans slowly from left to right across the rocky promontory of this port city. In early cinema, pans created the unstaged, on-the-scene actuality that converted the spectator from passerby to witness (Doane 153–4). From its first use, the pan has been synonymous with this effect – as if the cameraman happened to be there at the right time to "capture" an event (Doane 154). Negating distance and enhancing the appearance of instantaneity, the pan denies the frame as boundary, destabilizing the binary perspective of newsreel and dramatization, and making the passive spectator a participant. The power of this scene, as with panoramic camera views in general, is its latent dynamism: "not man posed in landscape but man poised to move in landscape; for in a moment, the figure will ride down the cliff and across the plain" (Marantz Cohen 72). As André Bazin (148) wrote of the western film: "perhaps the cinema was the only language capable [...] of giving it [the West] its true aesthetic dimension. Without the cinema, the conquest of the West would have left behind, in the shape of the 'Western stories,' only a minor literature." Without film, many landscapes "would not occupy such a prominent place in national mythologies" (Marantz Cohen 72) and Morocco, bereft of natural resources needed to be made more attractive. Because photography had unwittingly revealed the unsavory side of Morocco, its poverty-stricken barrenness and lack of technology, it behooved colonialist visions to find an alternative mode of visualizing landscape. Film could remedy this lack through montage and the carefully chosen pan, manipulating images to provide a cohesive, albeit illusory vision. Morocco thus became Spain's West, a notion that Alex de la Iglesia cleverly employed in *800 balas* (2002).

During this pan, the viewer becomes witness as barely discernible insect-like people run across the streets of the town. The slow, methodical encroachment of the camera onto this unsuspecting coastline ironically echoes Primo de Rivera's reference to the war as Spain's colonial conquest. As Balfour describes it,

> eschewing the parallel frequently made with the Reconquest against the Moors, [Primo de Rivera] implicitly compared the Moroccan wars to the conquest of the New World, which in traditional discourse was the struggle to convert pagan and barbarous peoples of the Americas to the true faith. Thus mixing traditional and modern images, he implied that the army had had to conquer an ignorant semi-savage people in order to bring them the benefits of civilization. (Balfour 117)

Yet graphic representations of Moroccans depended on the success or failure of the Spanish colonial apparatus, with its need to project either a paternalistic civilizing mode or an all-powerful war machine that used any means necessary to quell the enemy (Martín Corrales 84). The image of the Moroccan thus tended to oscillate between the naïve primitive other and the brutal, cruel savage, the latter predominating between the disasters of Barranco del Lobo (1909) and Annual (1921).

Exaggerating the power of the Spanish by fetishizing technology through visual technology, *La gitana blanca*, *La Condesa María*, and documentaries such as *Alhucemas* contain virtually identical action scenes of troops which celebrate military organization, efficiency and speed through geometrical visions of space and mass.[11] Striving to re-enact, or construct, an image of military order and invincibility, these ostensible recordings nevertheless betray an anxiety about their transitional status between the actuality and the narrative film, which corresponds to other anxieties about the mirage of impermeable strength that they try to project. Indeed, many historical accounts (Balfour, Fernández Colorado, Martín Corrales, for instance) attest to the absolute chaos and unregulated barbarism of the Spanish forces. And despite Spain's foregrounding of technology in representations of its encounters with Morocco, its actual technological capabilities lagged far behind those of other European countries, feeding insecurities about its modernness that bled through the visual representations of its supposed technical superiority. (see Elena and Ordóñez).

In the documentary *Alhucemas*, the camera slowly pans across the bay of Ceuta to rest upon the loading crafts and warships carrying convoys of forces. The film becomes an inventory and a cataloguing of the quantities of men, machines, and fire power. Spanish spectators identified with these scenes replete with technology that most had no access to, as it was normal for filmic fantasies of travel, technology, and modernization to gloss over the realities of Spain's illiterate majority population. Of course, when the intertitles announce that we are seeing "las barcazas K," we cannot know that in reality these vessels had been used in the Gallipoli landings and were bought from the British in Gibraltar; according to Balfour (111), these aging vessels broke down as they approached the shore.[12]

In *La gitana blanca*, the initial pan of the city stabilizes into a stationary view which obsessively documents the movement of troops in a lengthy sequence where the soldiers cut across the frame from a variety of directions, alternating with shots of boats docking and columns of men marching in and out from right and left and from frontal and rear perspectives, reversing the movement in every other shot. After informing us that Melilla's strategic situation is critical, the film records the regiment landing, engaging in combat, then rushing towards targets, climbing and descending the terrain, rising up from kneeling positions, crouching down to shoot, and loading cannons. The attempt to represent instantaneity, time unfolding before our eyes, privileges the movement of bodies and machines over land, so that the numerous shots appear as parts of a machine, avoiding uneventful time and productively moving us through the narrative of military advance. This vision denies coevalness (shared temporality) to the Riffians, conceptualizes Spaniards as a logical system, an ensemble of machines, characterized by its expediency of procedure. The quick, numerous cuts allow for more action, even though we see less of each shot, ensuring an economy of time that will not allow one wasted moment.

In *La Condesa María*, the dominant narrative is the romance between Luis, the son of the Countess, and Rosario, a seamstress. Luis' cross-class relationship with Rosario is threatened by his parasitical cousins, who fear his Luis' relationship with Rosario will jeopardize their degenerate existence, enjoyed at the expense of the Countess. Just before Luis is ordered to Morocco, Rosario falls ill (a euphemism for pregnancy out of wedlock). In an expressionistic scene, Luis and Rosario bid farewell and receive marriage rites, framed by a play of shadows, silhouetted profiles and crisp images which contrast sharply with the white walls of the convent-hospital. The digression begins about thirty minutes into the film. Immediately following Luis and Rosario's austere demonstration of faith, we cut to a pan of Tetuan and its chaotic urban menagerie. The clean lines of the hospital contrast with the urban montage of unmanageable excess, where chance elements and scurrying robed individuals mill around the camera, emerging apparently at random from streets, houses, suks. These unnarrated frontal and rear shots of the citizens of Tetuan add up to a sequence of eleven takes which provide an ethnographic tableau of everyday life in the bustling city. The camera archives the activity at various urban intersections and plazas while people and animals rush past from all directions. Vendors in the suk and in the street, veiled women sitting in groups, children and adults are shot against the architectural idiosyncrasies of the city, its arches, tunnels, doorways and windows, and decorated walls. Spectators are inundated by a wealth of detail, in sharp contrast to the *castizo* severity of the convent hospital.

Abruptly, high angle long shots of a linear, orderly regiment marching through the narrow Tetuán street displace the shots of anarchic inhabitants clumped together against the buildings. As the column slices through this chaos, the camera takes medium angles of Luis, the protagonist, mounted on his horse, methodically capturing the symmetrical column from all possible angles and distances, while it documents the regiment's exit from the walled city. Emerging from the crowded metropolis, the troops are flanked by vast expanses of desert, the effect of which turns the troops into a geometric play of shapes, giving these quasi-documentary scenes a surrealist aesthetic (the surrealists were fascinated with the accidental and the impossibly describable). Like ants marching across the sand, the troops scar the frame in series of zigzagged lines in 11 shots of about 1 minute each, mapping the landscape in pulsing geometric diagrams.

In *La gitana blanca*, the incessant movement of troops slows down to a brief medium shot, providing a suspenseful gap that shows Álvaro discussing plans with commanders of the Foreign Legion, the fanatical military organization that was instrumental in avenging the Spanish cause. Established in 1920, the Legion's "stellar role" in cinema of the 1920s (Martín Corrales 134), aided in its mythification as the barbarous fanatical Spanish troops who would even surpass the enemy's savagery. Cut to a line of cacti, from behind which the armed Riffian enemy emerges leads to an opposite point of view from which Rif men shoot from crouched positions from behind the plants. References to the Andalusian's patient vegetable-like existence, ready for penetration by the northerner, would be noted by Ortega y Gassett in his "Teoría de Andalucía" (1932). But more immediate to viewers of the time would have been the postcard and newspaper images of

Moroccans lying in wait behind rocks or desert flora (Martín Corrales 128). Even the Legionnaires deeply feared these snipers, or *pacos*, who shot Spanish soldiers from the back from hidden positions, feeding the already popularized myth about the traitorous nature of the Riffians. The inexpertness of the Spanish troops, who were primarily peasants with little or no experience with arms or military instruction, made them easy prey for what the press labeled *ataques de traición* (treacherous attacks) (Martín Corrales 127), a term that drew attention away from the ineptitude of the military and sharpened the border between enemy and hero.

As we near the enemy positions among the cacti, a lone fighter is captured so closely by the camera that we detect the whites of his eyes and even a fake beard. The illusion of the real again breaks down when he points his rifle and fires directly at the camera. In a point-of-view shot, we switch to our hero, Álvaro, wounded by the shot, then reverse to the Riffian who retires to the cacti and disappears from the narrative. This relatively long take of the Riffian sharpshooter completes a sequence in which the shots become longer, the distances between camera and object narrows, and the intertitles cease to intrude, especially during scenes that show the enemy. As with train technology, cinema broke down space and eliminated previous barriers of time and distance. And as seeing the world became inseparable from the awareness of speed, acceleration or deceleration (Virilio 21), the viewer was brought closer to the other. Such a collapse of time-distance, however, provokes the viewer's desire to re-enter the different time of the other. Intertitles dissect the action of the film, then, structuring the narrative, and ascribing (Western) meanings to the image. Yet when the camera remains fixated on the enemy rifleman, we are immersed in duration, forced to engage with the image, unmediated by the cut. Suddenly we are overwhelmed by wasted time with its unstructured meaning and its disturbing feelings of contingency.

Anxiety over the real and its representation belongs to a revolutionary change in the regime of vision that Paul Virilio locates in the "fusion-confusion" of the eye and the camera lens. Such eye/camera fusion marks the completion of the passage from vision to visualization – that apocalyptic deregulation of perception that occurred when "the mass of Americans and Europeans could no longer believe their eyes, when their *faith in perception* became slave to faith in the technical *sightline*: in other words, the visual field was reduced to the line of a sighting device" (Virilio 13). We have moved from vision to visualization when the camera no longer gives us long shots (as if we were free to direct and focus our vision), but rather focuses on this one image. We trust the camera's truth because if we doubt its veracity, we become visionless; for we have already conceded that we can see only through this sighting device. The desire to believe in the truth of the dramatization is thereby rendered all the more intense.

Nevertheless, the close-up of this Rif fighter recedes as he disappears into the brush and the film cuts to new images. The cut simulates the experience of real time, productively eliding the need to wait for the event, which would be necessary in an actual extended take. By reasserting the Riffian's status as representation, the economy of edited cinematic discourse confirms our subjectivity through its ability to render invisible the lacks in film (the spaces between frames, the separation between off-screen space and screen space), positing a real behind the representation, and thereby consoling the spectator's anxiety about the inherent instability of the real.

In the combat scenes of *La Condesa María*, against a background of tanks firing, explosions, soldiers scrambling for cover, and montages of heavy cavalry attacks, we see the figure of Luis, edged with glowing light. The image of Luis in this montage bears witness to what Virilio's terms a phatic image, "a targeted image that forces you to look and hold your attention," as only specific parts of this image are defined or illuminated, while the context mostly recedes into a blur (Virilio 14). Overwhelming us with Luis' "enlightened," struggling figure, the film blurs death and barbarism, focusing only on the male subject's heroism. We are forced to accept the outward representation of Luis' inner-desire to lead his men to glorious victory as the meaning of colonial war. The reality that the working classes are the ones to fight wars (the riots in Barcelona in 1911 during the Semana Trágica were rooted in the anger of the urban proletariat who was being sent to Morocco) is pushed back by the aristocratic Luis' nationalistic heroism. But Luis falls to the ground, slumping against a canon, and we realize that he has been shot. As he looks up, the film cuts to a second glowing montage that silhouettes him against scenes of destruction. But this time Luis is the spectator of his own hallucination, signaling that he might not live to enjoy the fame. The last shot brandishes a white flag against the sky, symbol of the Rif surrender yet also a return to whiteness, which fades to black. The dominant romance narrative reopens onto the close-ups of a rocking baby carriage and Rosario's face as she leans against the cradle, mourning the absence of Luis.

Identity and meaning are not merely affected by the digressions but fully located within them. The time-space of otherness lures us to its different temporality, and despite our fear of confronting the other, the digression encourages our identification with this difference. According to the logic of the film, what made Raquel Meller able to become a star rather than a housewife, was precisely the time gap and confrontation with the other in the "Gypsy" Camp and in Morocco. And in *La Condesa María*, Luis becomes a hero rather than a simply a guard soldier and father of a bastard child, thanks to his journey to Morocco. Both bourgeois protagonists, Luis and Raquel, gain from such experience a more exciting, fuller existence, unhampered by the exigencies of work or domestic life.

To conclude, cinema not only reflects but also constructs the very substance of modernity. The digressions, many of them produced in direct collaboration with the Spanish military, advertise the modernity of Spain. Hardly an unconscious or subliminal industry, cinema at this time is fascinated with itself, constantly aware of its power both to represent the state and push the state forward, realizing through its art the drama of war. A driving force in the state, cinema is a motor of modernity, and its digressions are not mere diversions, but focal points of cultural disparity, from which the viewer can trace the trajectory from the pre-modern to the modern. Film, as it is thrust upon the public by the developing national cinema, is thus a performative example of the movement towards modernity. Its transportability and translatability (lack of sound), enabled its massive dissemination throughout the West, demonstrating Spain's arrival to the world market. The films we have discussed trace the passage from an internal border to a redefined, and more remote, external one, a progression also seen in stardom narratives, another dominant story line in early Spanish cinema.

Notes

1. The intensification of interest in dissecting and reunifying time in the nineteenth century, in manipulating it in order to produce both the possibility of its record/representation and the opportunity to construct alternative temporalities, is not some reflection of a perennial psychical order, but a reflection of a quite precise historical trauma. The subject is no longer immersed in time, no longer experiences it as an enveloping medium. Through its rationalization and abstraction, its externalization and reification in the form of pocket watches, standardized schedules, the organization of the work day, and industrialization in general, time becomes other, alienated (Doane 221).
2. Throughout the chapter I will refer to fictional representations of *gitanos*, Rrom, and Calés as "Gypsies." Although the quotation marks are tedious for the reader, I would argue that the difference between the depiction and the reality of these individuals can not be overstated.
3. There is a marked similarity between many of the images in the digressions I discuss and a 1925 military propaganda film entitled *Alhucemas*. This news film narrates the final stages of an extremely long and drawn out counter-offensive by the Spanish military and their subsequent reassertion of control over the protectorate, culminating in Franco's troops' amphibious landing at the bay of Alhucemas/Al Hoceima.
4. A few examples not mentioned in this chapter are: *La Venenosa* (1928), *El sexto sentido* (Eusebio Fernández Ardavín and Nemesio Sobrevila, 1929), *El abuelo* (José Buchs, 1925), *El misterio de la Puerta del Sol* (Francisco Elías, 1929), and *La sin ventura* (Benito Perojo and E.B. Donatien, 1923).
5. Cinema produced in Spain or by Spanish directors was no different from other cinema of this period in terms of its necessarily cosmopolitan nature. This is due to lack of resources, paucity of state interest in promoting cinema either

through economic or legislative means, and the reality that cosmopolitan themes were in demand, spurred on by popular erotic pulp fiction published in the weeklies. Many of these novels were later adapted to the cinema, most notably *El negro que tenía el alma blanca* (Benito Perojo, 1926). Spanish cinema thus needs to be seen as part of a larger historical and geographical phenomenon that participated in shaping Western practices of seeing.

6. This second, "modernized" version was largely an effort to resell the film, since Raquel Meller, who starred in both versions, had experienced considerable fame since the release of the first version. I reference this second version of which only a 1925 Dutch copy survives.
7. For lack of space I forgo a lengthy discussion on the history of representations of Rrom in Spain. See Lou Charnon-Deutsch for an excellent analysis of images and general history of the "imaginary Gypsy." For interpretations and history of the Carmen narrative see Gonzalo Troyano.
8. For more on the different temporality of the "Gyspy" see Katie Trumpener.
9. Margarita Lobo, email correspondence, November 24, 2003.
10. I rely on Martín Corrales' analysis of these events in Chapter 5, "El traidor enemigo (1909–1927)," of his *La imagen del Magrebí.*
11. Films that offer similar presentations of troops in Northern Morocco are Benito Perojo's *Malvaloca* (1926), *La Guerra de África* (1925–6), *España y Francia en Marruecos*, and Florián Rey's *Águilas de acero* a.k.a. *Los misterios de Tánger* (1927). This does not include the numerous Spanish documentaries filmed in Morocco between 1909 and 1927. For these, see Alberto Elena.
12. We can picture in our minds an absurd image which never made it onto the newsreels: the landing craft runs aground just before the shore. The high command orders the crafts' commander to withdraw, but Franco ignores the order, and he and his men leap into the water up to their necks (!), holding their arms above their heads, and like the troops that had launched the first military action of the war in 1908, wade to the beach under heavy fire (Balfour 111). This was far from the military efficiency depicted in cinematic renditions of troops running down the ramp of a K-boat onto the beach.

Works Cited

Alleloula, Malek. *The Colonial Harem.* Minneapolis, MN: University of Minnesota Press, 1986.

Balfour, Sebastian. *Deadly Embrace: Morocco and the Road to the Spanish Civil War*. London: Oxford, 2002.

Baños, Ricardo de. *La gitana blanca.* 1923. producer: Royal Film. Based on Armando Crespo Cutillas; adapted by and written by Josep Amich I Bert ("Amitachis"); Photography: Ramón de Baños.

Bazin, André. *What is Cinema? Volume II*. Trans. Hugh Gray. Berkeley: University of California Press, 1971.

Benjamin, Walter. "The Work of Art in the Mechanical Age of Reproduction." *Illuminations*. Trans. Hannah Arendt. New York: Schocken, 1985.

Charney, Leo and Vanessa R. Schwartz, eds. *Cinema and the Invention of Modern Life*. Berkeley: University of California Press, 1995.

Charon-Deutsch, Lou. *The Spanish Gypsy: The History of a European Obsession*. University Park, PA: Penn State University Press, 2004.

Díez Puertas, Emeterio. "Del teatro al cine mudo." In *De Dalí a Hitchcock: Los caminos en el cine. Actas del V Congreso de la AEHC*. Ed. Julio Pérez Perucha. Asociación Española de Historiadores del Cine. Centro Galego de Artes de Imaxe, La Coruña, 1995. 261–70.

Díez Sánchez, Juan. *Melilla y el mundo de la imagen*. Cuidad Autónoma de Melilla: Consejería de Cultura, Educación, Juventud y Deporte, 1997.

Doane, Mary Ann. *The Emergence of Cinematic Time: Modernity, Contingency, the Archive*. Cambridge, MA: Harvard University Press, 2002.

Elena, Alberto. "Notas sobre el documental colonial en España." *Imagen, memoria y fascinación: Notas sobre el documental en España*. Eds. Josep Maria Català, Josetxo Cerdán, and Casimiro Torreiro. Madrid: Festival de Cine Español de Málaga/Ocho y Medio, 2001. 115–24.

Elena, Alberto and Javier Ordóñez. "Science, Technology and the Spanish Colonial Experience in the Nineteenth Century." *Nature and Empire: Science and the Colonial Enterprise*. Ed. Roy MacLeod. Chicago: University of Chicago Press, 2000.

Fabian, Johannes. *Time and its Other: How Anthropology Makes its Object*. New York: Columbia University Press, 1983.

Fernández Colorado, Luis. "Los expositores del imperio." In *Imagen, memoria y fascinación: Notas sobre el documental en España*. 65–74.

Gubern, Román. *Benito Perojo: Pionerismo y superviviencia*. Madrid: Ministerio de Cultura/Filmoteca Española, 1994.

Gunning, Tom. "'Now You See It, Now You Don't': The Temporality of the Cinema of Attractions." *Silent Film*. Ed. Richard Abel. New Brunswick, NJ: Rutgers University Press, 1996. 71–84.

Hansen, Miriam. *Babel and Babylon: Spectatorship in American Silent Film*. Cambridge, MA: Harvard University Press, 1991.

Krakauer, Siegfried. *Theory of Film: The Redemption of Physical Reality*. Princeton, NJ: Princeton University Press, 1997 (Oxford, 1960).

Marantz Cohen, Paula. *Silent Film and the Triumph of the American Myth*. New York: Oxford University Press, 2001.

Martín Corrales, E. *La imagen del Magrebí en España: Una perspectiva histórica, siglos XVI–XX*. Barcelona: Bellaterra, 2002.

Martín Jiménez, Ignacio. "El cine de los años 20 y su relación con el espectáculo popular." In *De Dalí a Hitchcock: Los caminos en el cine. Actas del V Congreso de la AEHC*. Ed. Julio Pérez Perucha. Asociación Española de Historiadores del Cine. Centro Galego de Artes de Imaxe, La Coruña, 1995. 375–84.

Perojo, Benito. *La Condesa María* (Benito Perojo 1927). Artistic director, Alexander Kamenka; Producer: Julio César-Albatros; Script: B. Perojo. Based on the theatrical comedy by Juan Ignacio Luca de Tena. Photography: Maurice Desfassiaux, Nicolas Roudakoff and Marcel Eywinger.

Simmel, Georg. "The Metropolis and Mental Life." *Metropolis: Center and Symbol of our Times*. Ed. Philip Kasinitz. New York: New York University Press, 1995.

Singer, Ben. *Melodrama and Modernity: Early Sensational Cinema and its Contexts*. New York: Columbia University Press, 2001.

Troyana, Gonzalo. *La desventura de Carmen: una divagación sobre Andalucía*. Madrid: Espasa Calpe, 1990.

Trumpener, Katie. "The Time of the Gypsies: A 'People without History' in Narratives of the West." *Critical Inquiry* 18(4) (1992): 843–84.

Virilio, Paul. *The Vision Machine*. London: British Film Institute: Bloomington, IN: Indiana University Press, 1994.

–16–

Modern Anxiety and Documentary Cinema in Republican Spain

Geoffrey B. Pingree

Proclamación de la República, a little edited motion picture from April 1931, registers the public enthusiasm that greeted the birth of Spain's Second Republic and forecasts the excitement that would surround cinema in the early Republican years. This silent actuality film, shot in and around the overflowing Plaza del Sol by the Spanish Movie Information Company, depicts government leaders parading in top hats and tails; soldiers marching briskly; citizens waving Republican flags; young people dangling from buildings, cheering; and couples dancing and holding hands. *Proclamación*, the first movie of the new republic, premiered in Madrid at the Principe Alfonso theater on April 17, 1931, just three days after the events it portrayed had occurred (Gubern, "El cortometraje republicano" 35, all translations mine unless otherwise indicated).[1] Even now, the film invokes the romance of that celebratory moment, recalling an excitement that would not last, as the Republic, within a few short years, would be crushed by civil war and dictatorship.

Undone by malignant internal strife and a wave of aggression from the right, the Second Republic failed politically. Recent work investigates this failure's cultural dimensions and emphasizes how the Republican government, unable to articulate a comprehensive program of land reform, to separate Church and state without alienating the clergy and ruling elite, or to sufficiently improve living conditions for the working classes, *also* failed to develop a symbolic vocabulary with which it could communicate a distinct national vision, – essentially because it never resolved its own ambivalence about the nation's past. Carolyn Boyd (231, xiii), for example, notes that in its educational reforms the government exhibited a "profound ambivalence" that inhibited a collective sense of "origins and destiny," while Pamela Radcliffe (2–3) suggests that the Republic's inability to generate "a unified set of symbols" or "totalizing vision" of nation invited the "festering, unresolved conflict over the parameters of Spain's national identity" that became civil war.

If the collapse of thc Rcpublic was, at least in part, a failure of cultural forms, what part did film play in that failure? When *Proclamación* premiered, cinema – a medium that was innovative, popular, and especially venerated in its non-fiction mode – would have seemed a persuasive and reliable means to generate a new vision of Spain and provide the kind of unifying cultural idiom that Boyd and Radcliffe claim the nation lacked. But despite the promise it heralded, in the end Republican documentary film did not offer a "totalizing vision." There is no question that the Second Republic witnessed the beginnings of a socially ambitious documentary film tradition. Yet as if to embody Boyd's profound ambivalence, the Republic's documentary cinema, and the public discourse surrounding it, also betrayed an unsteady view of the nation's past and often reflected uncertain attitudes towards film itself as an industry, as an aesthetic form, as a moral and educational tool, and even as a political and cultural language. In this chapter, I will consider this ambivalence. Rather than provide an historical investigation of the Republic's collapse, or even a comprehensive narrative of Republican documentary film, I will draw on several cases that suggest a way of thinking about this cinematic mode's curious fate during the Second Republic. Though my discussion may add some understanding of the Republic's political failures, I offer it primarily to illuminate Spain's complex relation to the currents of modernity and to Modernism itself.

From 1896, when they first arrived in Spain, motion pictures occasioned some speculation about their function and influence within the country, but with the advent of the Second Republic thirty-five years later, movies took on genuine importance as a means of social reform. Political movements in 1930s' Europe often unfolded around questions of nationalism, and in Republican Spain, cinema was central to public debates over what the nation was and how its identity ought to be forged. For those who supported social reform, the nascent Republic stood to gain legitimacy as guardian of Spain's future if it could use this powerful medium to help replace old notions of Spanishness with new ones and project a national identity distinct from the one embraced by past monarchies and dictatorships.

It certainly made sense that so modern a medium as cinema – with its rapid growth, innovative technology (sound film was barely older than the Republic itself), and mass influence – would entice those seeking to replace a religious, conservative Spain with a secular, liberal one. Yet cinema's appeal was, politically speaking, actually quite broad: when critic, filmmaker, and onetime government official Manuel Villegas López declared in 1933 that "the cinema is … among the most powerful forces of our time: a nascent art; a medium of culture; a political, economic, and social weapon," he voiced an enthusiasm towards film shared by many throughout the Republic, even among segments of Spanish society traditionally at odds over political, educational, economic, and religious issues (Villegas López 7). The very idea of cinema drew great interest from across the political landscape, especially outside the government; it circulated among popular as well as elite audiences, appearing in the rapidly expanding number of specialized periodicals (no fewer than twenty-two new film-related publications appeared between 1931 and 1936), as well as in mainstream newspapers, "low-brow" magazines, and even some government documents. Film also blossomed during the Republic in novel forms and at new venues; unmatched numbers of amateur filmmakers used low-end equipment to explore new ways to communicate with moving images, while the country's loose network of diverse film clubs expanded as never before.

Many considered film to be inextricably bound up in society itself. "To deny cinema's social nature is to deny cinema itself," claimed César M. Arconada (90) in *Nuestro Cinema*. And much like the Soviets before them, those supporting revolutionary change in Spain saw film as a political weapon. Radical filmmaker and critic Mateo Santos argued in *Popular Film* that the Republic ought to use the instruments of technology to build culture where the traditions of religion, military and monarchy had oppressed it. He claimed that such technologies, and especially cinema, were both means and measure of public enlightenment, the bearers, even the saviors, of culture (Santos, "La cruzada" 1). But more politically moderate figures also embraced cinema as a social tool. Luís Gómez Mesa (109), for example, a film critic and vigorous proponent of a pan-Hispanic film industry, insisted that film's mission was "always to teach". While the government's official actions initially reflected a limited interest in cinema, individual Republicans of all stripes – including many affiliated with the administration – were enthralled by a "mass art that seemed to carry the essence of modernity … and could serve as a potent ideological tool," and they seemed to share the conviction that film could genuinely transform Spanish society (Gubern, "El cine sonoro" 161).

Fuelled by diverse schemes of social progress, the broad interest in film's power during the Republic was accompanied by a growing demand for a distinctly and authentically Spanish cinema. While the arrival of sound had transformed the film industry worldwide in the late 1920s, Spain – lacking the financial and technical means to upgrade its production and exhibition equipment – had lagged behind, continuing to make silent movies, which it often synchronized with poor-quality audio recordings or sent abroad to obtain better results. In that state of crisis, Spain's cinema had been easy prey to rapidly expanding foreign film industries, especially Hollywood, which was already seeking to gain control of the Spanish-language film market (Martínez-Bretón 25–6). By the time the Republic was established, moviegoers in Spain had come to depend heavily on foreign – especially American – films, and much public discussion of cinema focused on this dependence. As critic Julio Escobar (1) insisted in a typical editorial, "we can, and we must, make movies, good movies of high caliber, not what we're fed by the Americans … , [so] alien to our [Spanish] taste and temperament."

Hollywood was not solely responsible, however, for the abundance of films that affronted many Spaniards' sense of national identity. For years the country's movie industry itself had impeded an accurate vision of Spain, producing *españoladas* whose embellished caricature of Spaniards' actual experiences and perspectives kept the nation's public image planted firmly in a fanciful past. Santos, too, acknowledged Spain's tendency to portray inaccurately its own cultural character, but he insisted that cinema could nonetheless move the nation forward, and he urged the Spanish film industry to turn to artistic, documentary, and other alternative modes of representation and focus less on commercial gain, in order to create popular interest in what was *truly* Spanish (Santos, "Llamamiento a los aficionados" 1).

This wish to renew Spain's public image by thus reordering its cinematic priorities appeared to draw wide support early in the Republic: the Hispano-American Cinema Congress convened in Madrid and discussed ways to transform the nation's film industry; the government changed its tax structure to favor local films and penalize imports; and both elite and popular cinema periodicals ran more articles on cinema-workers' unions, expanded their coverage of movie stars to include Spanish performers as well as Hollywood actors, and reported more extensively on the state of the country's film industry. And by expanding their treatment of German, Italian, and French cinemas, these publications also revived a trope, traditionally deployed by those who would reform Spain, to "join" more fully with the rest of Europe; challenging Spain's traditional isolation, this strategy signaled a confidence that Spanish cinema might actually fortify the nation's own emerging modern character by supporting – and thus strengthening its own place on – the continental stage.

Yet for all of its apparent promise to help Spain move beyond its benighted past, during the Republican years cinema more often than not seemed ambivalent towards that past, playing a curiously hesitant – if not contradictory – role in efforts to further such a transition. In 1933 the Republican government, for example, despite having publicly championed progressive social change, responded with a notable uncertainty when given an opportunity to use film to refashion the nation's image across Europe. In response to a request from its consul in Toulouse for help in developing "Spanish films" that could be used to export the idea of the Spanish nation to France, the Republic's Ministry of Culture recommended creating pictures built around the actress Raquel Meller. This suggestion might seem reasonable, for Meller was both a Spaniard and a beloved figure in France; her *Violettes impériales* (1932) had recently played to enthusiastic audiences in Toulouse. Yet Meller earned much of her fame by appearing in *españoladas* and folkloric films – works that exploited bullfighting, gypsies, and other "typical" themes to convey precisely the kind of familiar yet misleading image of Spain that Santos and other proponents of reform had publicly decried. As if to dismiss this contradiction, the Ministry of Culture, in later correspondence with the consulate in Toulouse, actually acknowledged Meller's well-known affiliation with the old, conservative regime, but insisted nonetheless that she was credible as an emissary for the new Spain. This incident, while not conclusive in itself, signaled the Republican government's somewhat surprising willingness to compromise with tradition – even as it charted a cinematic program many hoped would help renovate the nation's image ("Asunto").

The government's regulation of film provided even more compelling evidence that it was willing to make similar compromises with the past it sought to transcend. In a 1912 royal decree, Spain had become one of the first countries in Europe to restrict cinema, and the country pursued a pattern of repression for the next two decades. When the Republic arrived, armed with its progressive ideals, expectations were high that it would loosen restrictions on all forms of public expression. But while the new government made general pledges to greater freedom of expression, it did not take any concrete steps to unleash cinema. As time proved, in fact, the Republican government largely replicated the previous regime's censorship of cinema – an especially disillusioning surprise to politically progressive Spaniards who had anticipated expanded opportunities to use film in the country's social transformation.[2] Before the year was out, *Popular Film* voiced the frustration of many over the Republic's continuation of censorship, imploring the government to discontinue this legacy of arbitrary control and allow Spain's citizens themselves to construct a set of norms to supervise cinema. By extending the preceding regime's authoritarian relationship with cinema, the otherwise progressive Republican government was implicitly confirming the reactionary belief, long held in Spain, that film was potentially dangerous and had to be supervised carefully (the country's original 1912 decree was inspired by a fear of the "pernicious influence that cinematic projections exercise on the public, especially the youth") (Martínez-Bretón 39).

That this traditional anxiety about cinema's moral influence on spectators would continue to guide both audience tastes and government regulations during the Second Republic is not remarkable; no society, regardless of its ambitions for social change, operates wholly free of its past traditions. Moreover, the Republican government, continually plagued by internal tensions and conflicts, was politically vulnerable from the start, unsure of its own stability and authority; its retention of existing regulatory norms was likely born, at least in part, of political need – as a way of placating the more conservative elements of Spanish society, for example. The 1933 national elections, which pushed the government to the right, certainly underlined the validity of this concern. Nonetheless, both its decision to censor film, and the ways in which it carried out that decision, are difficult to reconcile with the Republican government's stated ideals. In much the same fashion as its predecessors, the Republican government exploited general legislation to exercise specific control over film, relying primarily on two of its own ordinances, the Law of Defense of the Republic and the Law of Public Order – neither of which made any specific reference to cinema. The government also continued the previous regime's hostile stance towards Soviet cinema, arbitrarily imposing impossible standards on films coming from Moscow. This meant, wrote Piqueras in *Nuestro Cinema* in early 1932, that Spanish movie-goers could "dull their minds" watching a multitude of Hollywood and other imported films, but were prohibited from seeing innovative Soviet work – and revealed the Republican government to be "just like the dictatorships of Primo de Rivera … , Mussolini, and Hitler …."[3] This only intensified the atmosphere of intolerance and deepened a mood of uncertainty regarding film's place in the new society (Martínez-Bretón 16, 68).

The government's overtly paradoxical relationship with cinema was matched by subtle contradictions within the public conversation about film itself. The movie magazines and journals of the early 1930s in Spain, for example, routinely characterized the most popular films of the day (Hollywood-style narratives) as feminine leisure props. And many journalists, movie critics, and filmmakers, while they wrote, on the one hand, to promote cinema as a means of social transformation, often made use, on the other, of gender tropes that – rooted in Spain's most traditional conceptions of men and women – were anything but forward-looking. In October of 1931, for example, Méndez-Leite, writing enthusiastically about film's place in the new Republic, encouraged Spaniards to read *Cinema*, the magazine that he himself edited, by likening it to a woman audiences could turn to as "your girlfriend, your lover," thus characterizing spectators' relationship with cinema in the traditional language of heterosexual affiliation and romance (Editorial 7). Neither the prominence of gender analogies, nor the sexual hierarchy that such analogies implied, were unique to Spain's film culture or even to its more conservative figures. In 1932, for example, the Anarchist Santos wrote that "Spanish cinema has been born without a sex. If we abandon it to the arms of its godparents [the theater impresarios who first disparaged, then embraced, film for its commercial potential], very illustrious but very indifferent as well, it will be female cinema [*cine hembra*]" (Santos, Editorial 1). Even this outspoken Anarchist seemed comfortable deploying the patriarchal terms typical of previous, conservative governments to champion film's transformative powers, highlighting again a subtle ambivalence towards past ways and ideas that appeared to permeate the Republic's cinema culture.

Though using a traditional, conservative taxonomy of gender, he nonetheless seemed intent on rousing Spaniards from their complacent view of film so that the country might deploy cinema for radical purposes and transform movie-going from a soothing, passive experience into a more politically provocative one. Consider the rest of his comment: "And what we need here is a masculine cinema [*cine macho*], strong, vigorous, with impudence and popular grace, the dramatic soul of our people, even a little rough around the edges, because courtesies and finery don't sit well with those who try to cheat their pain and their hunger with songs and wine" (Santos, Editorial 1).

Extending his retrograde gender analogy, he called for a cinema that would present more than alluring artifice, a cinema that, however gritty, might grasp more deeply the authentic realities of Spain and its people. In this, Santos expressed a clear commitment to help move the country forward – beyond an erroneous and static view of itself.

Despite his contradictorily chauvinistic analogy, in this instance Santos was somewhat visionary. Amending Méndez-Leite's ("Cinema nuevo" 32) earlier, dreamy description of film as the "world's new theater," Santos pointed towards a cinema that would follow its scientific, rather than its theatrical, ancestry, that would utilize its powers of lucid observation rather than exploit its talents for dramatic embellishment. Hence his paradoxical invocation of cinema as an hermaphroditic orphan whose survival depended on its eventual maleness, a child who could be trusted to enlighten the masses about Spain's authentic identity only if its parents (the citizens of the new Republic) nurtured its rational (masculine) qualities rather than encouraging its whimsical (feminine) charms.

Santos' view underscored the precise dilemma facing those serious about using film as a tool of reform in Spain. Certainly the cautious hesitation that seemed to mark government actions towards, and public discussion about, film in the Republic can be read as a simple failure to back up strong talk of cinema's transformative powers with resolute action. Yet no amount of progressive ambition would have allowed Spain to simply sever its ties with its past, and Santos' provocative claim embodied an essential problem facing the reform-minded in 1930s' Spain who sought to bring about political change using deeply rooted languages, to realize new purposes using old forms. Republican cinema was entangled in a complex sphere of contradictions, and the uncertainty evident in film during the Second Republic was actually fed by two opposed "anxieties": first, a cautious fear of letting go of the past – a separation anxiety; and second, an impatient desire to move forward – an achievement anxiety. And despite using backward-looking cultural images, continuing moral censorship at home, or relying on popular if clichéd Spanish performers abroad, both individual Spaniards and an unproven government nonetheless appeared determined to use film – in one way or another – to support forward-looking social action, gain legitimacy from a politically divided Spanish populace, and establish credibility with a doubtful international audience.

Yet to actually deploy film, on a widespread basis, to perform different, contradictory tasks such as offering authentic – if unsettling – views of Spain that might challenge and help transform a conservative society, would surely encounter much resistance. During the three decades previous to the Second Republic, film in Spain had become primarily a leisure spectacle, providing the country with visually pleasing and politically reassuring narratives. And during the early Republican years this established mode of cinematic production and reception would, of course, continue to hold sway over filmmakers and spectators alike, – despite any progressive hopes for film that were publicly expressed. Indeed, at this critical political moment in Spain's history, a moment framed by competing anxieties, it might make sense for someone like Santos – someone who recognized the crucial role film might play for filmmaker and spectator alike in the Republic's struggle to transform the country into a modern, progressive society – to argue, if somewhat impudently, that film must be vigorous and forceful in order to break the entrenched habits of passive reception and effect real social change. And it is not hard to imagine how, at this point in time, Santos' type of gender distinction would appeal to readers, for the split dramatized, in familiar and accessible terms, the difference between perception and action, between mere appearance and genuine power. Moreover, despite its capricious tone, Santos' scheme actually had substantive roots; like many others agitating for change during the Republic, he was drawing on the Enlightenment-revived distinction between reason and emotion, an intellectual tradition that largely had been absent in the "old" Spain of the nineteenth-century (a Spain relatively isolated from "civilized" Europe moving towards modernity), but a tradition that in recent years had, nonetheless, begun to shape Spain's own sociological debates over education, culture and social progress. And so while Spaniards had come to depend on a cinema whose stories provided cultural and political resolution, there were – as Santos insisted – alternatives. As an established material medium, film – a radiant technology and visual spectacle – might provide spectators with exciting and pleasurable sensations, but it had to evolve as a conceptual mode, to move beyond its function as a reassuring narrative apparatus if it were to become a trustworthy means by which the masses could apprehend the actual world, become educated about what Spain really was, and thus be moved to take action and change their society.

Documentary, possessing cinema's material power as a medium but embodying a different mode of presentation and reception than traditional narrative film, seemed an answer. Indeed, many of the calls for more authentic "national" representations of Spain in film, as well the gendered depictions of cinema, pointed to documentary, as Santos had done, as a serious, masculine alternative to the feminized *españolada* or flirtatious Hollywood feature film. Within this implicit gender hierarchy, Santos' assertion that film-as-document could best capture genuine "Spanishness," and the cinema periodicals' common references to non-fiction cinema as a potent tool of reason for political reform, articulated a new rhetorical path for the nation, one that seemed to suggest that documentary as a mode was capable of turning film's gaze – traditionally focused on the female, and on her body in narrative cinema – to "the people," perceived as masculine.

As a form of representation documentary carried an authoritative aura of objectivity that might help the nation see itself clearly and thus move beyond, and dispel its ambivalence about, a mythic past; in contrast to both Hollywood films and contemporary Spanish feature films, documentary cinema, rather than exploiting clichéd notions of *flamenco* dancers and bullfighters, might faithfully depict the nation's actual events and experiences and convey the "real" Spain envisioned by Santos. Moreover, in comparison with the feature film industry, documentary was a relatively independent means of production – in both economic and aesthetic terms. Much of the pioneering documentary activity during the Republic, in fact, relied on small production budgets and the fresh ideas of individuals – like Carlos Velo, a Gallegan biologist, or Fernando G. Mantilla, a Madrid radio critic – who came to filmmaking from other fields or professions. Documentary could actually strengthen Spanish cinema, by diminishing the nation's cultural dependence on Hollywood or other national traditions, and by anchoring the industrial and creative origins of films within Spain itself. Adding rational strength and industrial independence to cinema's now familiar technology of illusion, documentary thus seemed well positioned to help the country move forward.

Spain was not the only country probing documentary's potential. Political nonfiction film traditions were gaining force in the Soviet Union, England, and Germany, among others, and despite supporting diverse public agendas, these movements all emphasized cinema's social impact over its individual artistry. By mid-decade, documentary film held a prominent place in the languages of local and global politics, as individual filmmakers and national governments alike – exploiting cinema as a medium of social exchange and documentary as a mode of reliable depiction – sought to frame events and issues in ways that would generate political credibility and public support. It makes sense that as Spain engaged further with the continent's intellectual traditions, and as it shared its neighbors' aspirations for social change, it would also embrace documentary.

Yet even as it gained currency in the Second Republic as a cinematic mode, documentary too bore clear traces of ambivalence, both about the country's past and about the role that film might play in conjuring a new future; in key instances when documentary seemed poised to help transform the nation's imagination and effect social change, it fell short. Late in the spring of 1931, the Republican government fully acknowledged the medium's importance when it included a Cinema Section in its prized Pedagogic Missions. The brainchild of Manuel B. Cossío (who had long advocated taking culture to the country's rural folk), the Missions were formally created to educate the Republic's citizens and implant "modern democratic principles" (Holguín 55–6, "Patronato" 1). Relying on volunteer workers, and attracting many reform-minded young artists and intellectuals (including poets Luis Cernuda and Rafael Dieste, the painter Ramón Goya, and the photographer and filmmaker José Val del Omar), the Missions traveled the country, using theater, music, mobile museums and libraries, and public readings in a campaign to bring civilized learning to the rural masses (Sáenz de Buruaga, "Las Misiones Pedagógicas" 214).

But the Missions gave film – especially documentary – a special place in this cultural project.[4] Convinced that the Cinema Section could use film not only to carry new ideas, subjects, and sights to the rural populations, but also to introduce them to modern technology, the Missions provided their volunteers with portable motion picture equipment, which the workers used to transform the country's tiniest towns into public theaters of instruction.[5] Led by Val del Omar, Gonzalo Menéndez Pidal, and others, the Cinema Section's volunteers soon discovered that in the villages "the movie screen always attracts the most interest and elicits the greatest emotional response" ("Patronato" 12). As if to illustrate Santos' claim that "moving images strike more directly and profoundly at the uncultured mind," the Missions offered cinema to the peasants not as a passive pleasure, but as an active learning experience, an invitation to emerge from the shadows of the past and help forge a new Spain (Santos, "La Cruzada" 1). In their accounts, Missions workers often recalled film's sharp impact on the rural audiences, noting how the movie screen seemed to awaken even the most indifferent or suspicious spectators (Otero Urtaza 125). Among Val del Omar's hundreds of Mission photographs, in fact, the most striking (and the most commonly used to publicize the Missions' work) were those featuring enraptured rural film spectators who – eyes sparkling, mouths joyfully ajar – appeared ready to rise up to meet the movie screen.

The Second Republic's decision to include a film division in its Pedagogic Missions clearly signaled an ambitious and unprecedented effort to use the cinema as an educational tool. Drawing on the Missions' collection of films, which included mostly 16 mm documentaries about agriculture, geography, history, science, sanitation, and industry, the Cinema Section's volunteers ambitiously spanned the country, screening anywhere from a few to several dozen movies in each town or village; between 1932 and 1933 alone, the Missions registered almost 2,400 screenings in more than 200 towns and villages, and their film collection grew from 174 (all silent) in 1933, to 411 (including 21 sound movies) a year later (Cabra Loredo 85–90; Gubern, *Val del Omar, cinemista* 14–15).[6] Yet while the very effort to take film to the people was, in itself, a bold and innovative strategy of distribution and exhibition, the Cinema Section produced little work of its own, and the movies it actually screened were mostly produced and imported from abroad.[7] The Missions' movie collection, in fact, came largely from Eastman Kodak's Pedagogic Films archive. A sampling of the films shown in the villages – *Plant Development*, *Animals that Hide in the Sand*, *Volcanoes*, *Great Expeditions to New Guinea*, *Typical Industries of Japan*, *The Kingdom of Carbon*, *From the Tobacco Leaf to the Cigarette* – suggests that these documentaries had been produced to instruct general audiences about nature's marvels, or to show them new parts of the world, or to educate them about industrial achievements (Government Receipts). Despite the Missions' noble aspirations, the movies themselves did little to broaden the uneducated and illiterate rural spectators' knowledge of Spanish culture and thus draw them into a more collective sense of national identity. The documentaries that did focus on Spain were in the minority and tended to emphasize geography.[8] It is not surprising that the cartoons were widely reported to be the most popular movies screened.[9]

Though the Missions at first considered its repertoire of films to be "adequate for its purposes," the need for original material, for work targeted specifically at the Missions' audiences – was increasingly evident (Cabra Loredo 1992: 85). Val del Omar was the only prolific filmmaker among the few Missions volunteers who took any part in making movies, but the quantity and character of his work made him an anomaly and only underscored the overall lack of cinematic production within the Missions.[10] By late 1934, the now conservative Republican government had radically cut the Missions' budget, and in the absence of new and original material, the Cinema Section sometimes re-edited imported films, to make them more comprehensible to the peasant audiences, or relied more heavily on slide shows, which were easier to understand (Gubern, *Val del Omar, cinemista* 15). But these were stopgap measures, and by 1935, some of the Missions' own officials had acknowledged that the problem was a "scarcity of good films, especially films that could help the Spanish people come to know their own country." Yet even as they avowed that the Missions needed to produce their own films, they conceded that there simply were not sufficient funds to support such a complex undertaking (García Lorenzo 17). Without adequate support, the Missions, in the end, were unable to take advantage of cinema's power to educate the country's rural populations and help them envision a new Spain, and the Cinema Section itself came to embody the Republic's broader hesitation about what the nation was, and what it could become.

Unable to make use of cinema's revolutionary potential, the Pedagogic Missions heralded the country's own imminent fate. Caught in a precarious balancing act, its leadership passed back and forth between left and right, the government never achieved political stability. The elections in early 1936, which seated a Popular Front regime, further disrupted the Republic's fragile equilibrium and left the country vulnerable to the military uprising in July, which quickly became full-scale civil war. As the country descended into violence, notions of traditional past and progressive future soon became antagonistic, all-encompassing ideals by which opposed sides sought to define themselves. Public debate over what made up the "true" Spain continued, but the possible answers to this question were quickly reduced to just two; though comprised of a complex array of political and cultural conflicts, the war took on a simplistic, binary shape – both as a military battle and as a set of competing representations. While Nationalists crusaded to save Spain's soul and protect its time-honored values against a faithless popular revolution, diverse groups on the left gathered under the Republican banner to counter a fascist military uprising and free the country from the ruinous influences of a traditional military, Church, and monarchy.

With the outbreak of war, cinematic production, until then dependent primarily on private companies, initially came to a halt, but rival political factions, seeking authority and popular support, soon took control of the film industry's resources. The Republic possessed the country's centers of production (Madrid, Barcelona, and, to a much lesser extent, Valencia), which forced the Nationalists to turn for help to the cinema industries in Lisbon, Berlin, and Rome. Despite its nominal control over Spain's main production centers, however, the Republican government's dominion actually diminished as locally controlled political syndicates exerted far greater influence over the film industry's workers. The war drastically reduced cinema's market, dispersed its employees along political lines, disrupted its material resources, and inhibited its financial resources (Gubern, "El cine sonoro" 164–5).[11]

When the Republic's long-held political tensions boiled over and helped ignite the civil war, the stakes of its indecision rose dramatically. As Spaniards were forced to choose sides, cinema's resources were diverted away from fiction film and towards documentary production, and the ambivalence that had surrounded cinema earlier during the Republic was absorbed into the war's hardened political polarities. Even as war altered Republican cinema's previously ambivalent relationship with the nation's past, however, it did not resolve it. The Spanish Pavilion at the 1937 World's Fair in Paris, where the struggling government had a rare chance to use films and other cultural materials to define itself clearly to the outside world, represents what is perhaps the culminating illustration of the Republic's ambivalence. Organized around a theme of "Art and Technology," the Fair was held when cinema was at the vanguard of both artistic expression and technological innovation, and the Republic eagerly included film with other artistic media at its pavilion. But selecting materials to exhibit was difficult, for while the pavilion afforded the Republic a valuable public relations opportunity, it also represented a dilemma: on the one hand, the government wanted to appear politically stable and forward-looking; on the other, it somehow had to address its urgent need for foreign assistance against Franco's Nationalists. To meet these competing interests, the Republic assembled a body of work that was both formally traditional and innovative, both politically reassuring and strident. It selected certain pieces intended to affirm Spain's stability, others to articulate the government's political vision, and others still to inform the international audience about the civil war (Gubern, "Exhibiciones" 174). Hoping to use the pavilion to affirm its roots in Spain's grand cultural traditions and illustrious artistic past, the Republic featured a variety of classical musical concerts and flamenco performances. Wishing also to highlight its progressive, dynamic character – Spain's first modern regime to attempt sweeping social change and seek a place among the democratic nations of the world – the government showcased strikingly innovative work by Spanish avant-garde and modernist artists. And to make a statement about its difficult military situation, the Republic deliberately included a variety of works, in different media, whose primary subject was the civil war.[12]

The pavilion's films also pointedly addressed the civil war, but artistically they were considerably less daring.[13] Often highlighting Spain's distinct history and heritage, these movies appear to have been chosen, for the most part, to buttress an image of the Republic as the legitimate steward of Spain's cultural heritage and political future – an image likely to play well to the Fair's international audience. Though no comprehensive record is available of the movies shown in Paris, there is general agreement about the presentation of twelve films.[14] These included one commercially successful feature-length fiction film, *La hija de Juan Simón* (1935); three movies that specifically addressed the war, *Guerra en el campo* (1936), *Espagne 36* (1937), and *Madrid* (1937); seven ethnographic documentaries presenting cultural, historical and social themes, *La ruta de Don Quijote* (1934), *Guadalquivir* (1935), *El Escorial de Felipe II* (1935), *Castillos de Castilla* (1935), *Almadrabas* (1935), *Sinfonía vasca* (1936), and *El tribunal de las aguas* (1937); and one older, politico-social work, *Reforma agraria* (1935) (Gubern, "Exhibiciones" 174). With this group of films the Republic seemed intent on portraying itself as a country that appreciated its past cultural traditions, that met its social problems head-on and yet looked to a better future, that was ruled by a freely elected government, and that – despite contending with an illegitimate military uprising – was functioning reasonably well. And by relying almost exclusively on the credible documentary mode, the government apparently wished to emphasize the authenticity of its self-portrayal.

The one feature film screened at the pavilion provided entertainment, implied social normalcy, and stressed cultural continuity, but *La hija de Juan Simón* did little to distinguish the Republic's vision of Spain. *Guerra en el campo*, *Espagne 36*, and *Madrid*, on the other hand – all movies that graphically depicted certain aspects of the civil war – seemed to signal that the Republic might finally be ready to dispel the ambivalence that previously marked its cinema. Sharing a clear if somewhat idealistic view of the war, the movies portrayed a democratically governed people bravely resisting Fascist invaders. And though only three (perhaps to avoid making the war seem *too* important) the films – whose explicit purpose was to show the world the unsettling realities of a war-torn Spain – were, unmistakably, political weapons. Even so, they were carefully deployed political weapons – all produced by one of the two groups (the Spanish Communist Party and the government itself) then controlling Republican Spain. It was not coincidental, for example, that films made by, or reflecting the views of, other leftist groups such as the Anarchists, were excluded from the pavilion, for such works could only jeopardize the Republic's efforts to appear politically unified.[15]

Guerra en el campo (1936), produced by the international, Communist-backed Alliance of Anti-Fascist Intellectuals for the Defense of Culture, and directed by Arturo Ruíz Castillo, linked military survival to the land itself, emphasizing the profound patriotism of the country's largely agrarian population and blending documentary footage with dramatized scenes to depict how readily and naturally

Spain's peasants took up arms to defend the Republic's vision of the nation. The other two war films screened at the pavilion were sponsored by the Republican government itself. *Madrid*, made by the Cinematic Division of the Subsecretary of Propaganda and built around the intense fighting that enveloped Spain's capital in 1937, chronicled the city's beseigement, emphasized the indomitable spirit of the Spanish people, and suggested that despite Fascist aggression, the will of the *madrileños* was unbreakable. *Espagne 36* or *Espana leal en armas*, produced under the direction of Luis Buñuel at the request of the Republican government, was the most formally innovative of the war films shown in Paris.[16] Opening with a shot of the equestrian statue of Philip IV being turned on its head, the movie recounted the 1931 fall of the monarchy and the rise – amid great popular enthusiasm – of the Republic, emphasizing the legality of the elected government and highlighting its many social reforms, describing the 1936 elections that led to the outbreak of civil war, and calling attention to the Nationalists' subsequent reliance on foreign military assistance in their effort to take Spain by force. Despite its noticeably subtler political rhetoric (one sequence pairs a somewhat detached voice-over narration with horrifying, graphic images of women and children lying dead after a bombing), *Espagne 36*, like both *Guerra en el campo* and *Madrid*, was most memorable for taking the kind of hard, unambiguous political stance that was so rare in Republican cinema before the war.

By contrast, most of the other pavilion documentaries, though occasionally exhibiting innovative strategies, characterized Spain in reassuring cultural terms, relying heavily on an established, compliant idiom to underscore the Republic's ties to the nation's honorable traditions.[17] Ramón Biadiu's *La ruta de Don Quijote*, for example, offered a tour of picturesque sites in La Mancha, the setting for Cervantes' famous novel, using the personae of Don Quijote and Sancho Panza to structure distinct points of view and conflicting visual perspectives of the land. Despite this mildly challenging formal strategy, the film nonetheless focused on subjects – roadside inns, windmills, flocks of animals – that merely illustrated well-known details from the book. Screened at an exhibition featuring boldly experimental art, *La ruta de Don Quijote* catered primarily to a view of Spain that, for foreigners, was already shaped by Cervantes' novel and decades of stereotypes delivered by Spanish film. By simply reaffirming the traditional customs and heritage of one of the country's most stereotyped regions, *Salamanca, monumental e histórica* also depicted Spain retrospectively. The Communist-produced *El Tribunal de las Aguas*, directed by Angel Villatoro (known for pursuing cultural and folkloric topics in his films), sought to present a public image, notes Gubern, of normal civilian life in the context of war by revisiting the ancient, Arab-influenced Valencian juridical rites that occurred weekly before the city's cathedral door to mediate local disputes. And *Guadalquivir* and *Sinfonía vasca* were both picturesque portrayals of local regions (Gubern, "Exhibiciones" 178). By telling a story of Spain that essentially could have come from the Golden Age, these films, despite occasional structural inventiveness, appear to have been ineffectual in helping the Republic convey a progressive national vision.

Among the pavilion's films, only *El Escorial de Felipe II*, *Castillos de Castilla*, and *Almadrabas* showed genuine promise to articulate a distinct view of Spain. Made by the revered Velo and Mantilla, the films addressed both traditional and everyday subjects in innovative and sometimes challenging ways. Begun before the establishment of the Second Republic, *El Escorial de Felipe II* was, as Gubern notes, Velo's effort to demystify the work and philosophy of the Hapsburg monarchy. Critic Antonio Guzmán Merino noted the movie's originality when he reviewed it in *Cinegramas* in May 1935, claiming that it exceeded the usual "post-card" treatment of cultural monuments and revealed El Escorial's "spirit … , which is the petrified dream of a Catholic conception of the world" (Gubern, "Exhibiciones" 176).

Yet in 1939, when Velo and Mantilla had fled the country after the civil war ended, the film's original voice-over was replaced with a commentary that rooted Spain's national identity squarely within traditions of Church and crown. The new voice-over, – which declared that "only God is great, only Spain is great" – described El Escorial, the austere monastery built by the country's crusading King Philip II, as a symbol of and repository for the nation's true history and spirit. Once intended to defy the centuries of absolutist Catholic rule that created this well known and traditionally beloved historical landmark, Velo and Mantilla's film now exalted it. In 1967 Velo himself called *Felipe II y El Escorial* "very innovative" for its time and confirmed that it had "been changed considerably" – given a "narration that has nothing to do with its visual images" – and thus transformed into "an offense to the original."[18] *Castillos de Castilla* suffered a similar fate when it, too, was re-edited after the civil war. Velo meant for this film – which addressed conquest, another conservative trope in Spanish history – to defy Spain's status quo as well; he later verified that the movie's current version, burdened with a new voice-over narration, conveys "a completely different meaning" than its original. Indeed, today's *Castillos de Castilla* presents numerous shots of medieval castles that, framed by the altered voice-over, not only highlight the defensive architecture of castles, but also implicitly glorify the military past that required such defenses. *Almadrabas* was Velo and Mantilla's only film shown in Paris that appears to have remained intact after the civil war. An exploration of the daily life of tuna fishermen, it was also the only pavilion documentary that focused on a contemporary subject. The film traced in detail the fishing expeditions and the conserving industries in Barbate, following the journey of the tuna, from procreation to marketable product, then returning to the factory as workers finished their work for the day. This efficiently narrated investigation of human labor, clearly indebted to the British documentary tradition, achieved its simple authority using an unsentimental and probing camera (Gubern, "Exhibiciones" 176–7).

Yet while Velo and Mantilla's films stood out among the documentaries shown at the pavilion, their contributions to a progressive vision of Spain were somewhat compromised. Even in their original, subversive forms, for example, *Felipe II y El Escorial* and *Castillos de Castilla* were more reactionary than revolutionary, challenging the nation's past by returning to subjects that, by their presence, would subtly reinforce links between the Republic and a tradition of conquest it wanted to shed. And *Almadrabas*, the most impressively crafted pavilion film, betrayed a hint of ambiguity about Spain's past when it cross-cut shots of the tuna industry with footage of the town's tradition of bullfighting, preserving a certain folkloric flavor as it drew explicit comparisons between fishermen and *toreros*. For all their innovative intent, then, Velo and Mantilla's works carried traces of the uncertainty towards the past that was more explicitly evident in the other pavilion documentaries.

Given a crucial opportunity to represent itself to the world through a national pavilion in Paris, the Republic was nonetheless burdened by the competing demands to appear as Spain's politically steadfast and culturally modern leader, while acknowledging its own besieged status in a civil war then being fought over how the nation should address its past and chart its future. As the Republic sought to meet these demands by deploying cultural and artistic materials to convey political continuity and stability, communicate a modern vision, and reflect a commitment to defending progressive ideals against hostile attack, it seemed of two minds. And it appeared to split in two the public relations task as well: while it selected works of fine art for the pavilion that powerfully articulated a provocative creative vision and a fierce political determination, the Republic chose films that were noticeably cautious in both subject and style, that often reiterated "folkloric" topics and themes, and that revisited, in mostly traditional ways, the longstanding customs and heritage of some of the country's familiar regions. Even when a film like *Almadrabas* took up previously unexplored social issues, it could not seem to resist drawing, if only a little, on the traditional store of symbols that had represented Spain for centuries. To be sure, familiar images need not, in themselves, impede the development of public consciousness; any genuine social change would have to engage with such established symbols. But presentation is not the same as examination, and the pavilion movies' references to Spain's grand traditions of crown, church, and conquest were largely static. It is hard not to wonder if those films might have encouraged a more dynamic, progressive view of Spain had they examined their subjects more critically.

In retrospect, the Republican cinema program's ambivalence at the 1937 World's Fair reveals a number of telling ironies that help explain the Second Republic's overall demise. For example, the man who assembled that program was Luis Buñuel, working in his official capacity as Spain's cultural emissary in Paris (Gubern, "El cine sonoro" 173). Buñuel's own poetically subversive *Land Without Bread*, which he had shot in 1932, under the Republican government, would have provided a highly innovative documentary offering at the Paris exposition. One can imagine how this grim "study in human geography" – a complexly ironic piece of ethnography that implied a profound cultural and political critique of, among other things, Spain's economic and racial divisions – might have supported the Republic's stated program of liberalization and social reform. Thc film might have helped establish, in Radcliffe's words, a new and unified set of cultural symbols that could interrogate and revise the nation's hierarchical past (the *hurdanos* were, after all, considered to be the descendants of Jews persecuted by Spain's past Catholic Kings).

Yet shortly after it was first screened in Madrid, with Buñuel himself reading narration through a microphone, the film was banned and prohibited from being shown within Spain or through its embassies in other countries. Like the innovative Soviet films, *Las Hurdes* appeared to frighten the Republican government, which decisively censored it.[19] That this film was repressed as a threat to the government's reformist mission discloses – perhaps more than any other example – an ambivalence in the years leading up to the civil war, both *in* and *about* documentary cinema, an anxiety that was at once an enthusiasm *for*, and a concern *about*, the emergence of a new social discourse of imagination and action. Even if we recall that *Las Hurdes* was censored during the two-year period during the Republic when elections had given the balance of power to the conservative CEDA, it is difficult to fully account for the sense of contradiction that surrounded the fate of this troubling and innovative film. The Republic's inexperienced censors may have been unsettled by the film's disturbing subject, whose existence at least hinted that the government had done no more than its predecessor to alleviate the sufferings of rural Spain. But Buñuel's film was not only disquieting in its choice of subject matter, but also jarring in its formal presentation – utilizing startling camera angles, for example, or setting its appalling vision of the impoverished *hurdanos* to a detached voice-over narration and incongruously reassuring classical music soundtrack. Indeed, the most lasting of the film's subversive effects may have been its sly acknowledgement that there was a "form" to documentary at all. By imitating, and then skewing (so slightly, but so significantly) the instructional documentary's classic rhetorical structure (in which image, sound, and information had a rigidly determined relationship), *Las Hurdes* posed a radical challenge to established hierarchies of knowledge and categories of information.

As the selections of films for the Paris Exhibition encapsulated the government's tensions and ambiguities, so *Las Hurdes* may have symbolized best the paradoxical fate of documentary cinema in the Second Republic, for it arguably stood as the documentary that most explicitly attempted to achieve social impact *and* (indeed *through*) artistic innovation. Whatever else Buñuel may have been doing with *Las Hurdes*, he was documenting a particular social reality in order to spur some kind of public response to that reality. The government was – at least at this moment – still reluctant to embrace a radical vision of the nation, preferring instead to retreat to the safe harbor of tradition.[20] For all its talk of fundamental change and revolutionary agendas, the Republic behaved as though it feared the possibility of radical transformation. And the government's decision in Paris to use mostly documentary only amplifies this irony. The Republic appeared to have learned little from its episode years earlier with *Las Hurdes*, or even from its experience with the Pedagogic Missions, for – perhaps too enamored of film's rapidly advancing mechanical powers – it seemed to embrace documentary cinema as though it could, of its own accord, function as some kind of "truth-teller," allowing the new, democratic Spain to be seen for what it "truly" was and would become. The Republic's innovators, it seemed, believed too much – too literally – in documentary's ability to give them "reality," failing to treat documentary as a mode, a *kind* of window on reality that frames a particular, though incomplete, way of seeing, understanding, and believing. Yet the backward-looking films shown at the pavilion made clear that no amount of technological innovation in itself could provide a coherent national vision.

Notwithstanding the heightened political stakes, then, the Republic's documentary cinema in Paris conveyed a national vision strikingly similar to the one that the country's native cinema had perpetuated since its inception, a vision that – marked by historic grandeur and entrenched in folkloric cultural formations – mocked the fledgling government's aspirations. Even in civil war, the Spanish Republic was still torn between clinging to the old and promoting the new, still ambivalent about how it should see and project itself as a nation. While it makes some sense, then, to ask whether the Republic "failed," the question is misleading. It is too simple to say that the Republic simply squandered its golden chance to transform the nation; if anything, its case seems less to embody an active failure than to illustrate a dilemma facing any new government attempting to effect wholesale change in a society entrenched in old habits. Fresh national visions do not easily bloom from the soil of established political orders; new vocabularies do not readily emerge from old languages. Any major transition in power seems destined – in various and repeated ways – to fail along the way. Concerning the Spanish Republic, then, it may be less useful to wonder what it did wrong than to consider what it discloses about the general nature of political change.

As a point of inquiry, cinema can provide a telling perspective on this issue, because it lays bare the often subtle *process* of cultural negotiation regularly obscured by political or military conflict. The hierarchical relationship between gender roles and film genres in Republican cinema reveals sexual stereotypes of a given time and place, for example, but it also illuminates broader political meanings. Documentary film in the Second Republic was asked to exploit the "masculine" power of the camera's gaze but shift focus from its traditional subject ("woman") to a politically expedient one ("the people"), thus performing a progressive ideological move using a retrograde gender distinction. Just as it is necessary to rely somewhat on a traditional worldview when developing a progressive one, so the Republic's embrace of documentary cinema as a tool of liberation in terms contradicting that liberation may suggest that its ambivalence was less a concrete failure than an illustration of a general process of (and of its own) social transformation. In the end, it may make more sense to think of Republican cinema's ambivalence towards the past as a symptom of a necessary and unavoidable burden, evidence of an inevitable set of contradictory pressures. Bound paradoxically to the idea of documentary's power, the Republic acted as if simply *showing* documentary films was enough to transform society. It is tempting to imagine the effect that a film like Vertov's *Man with a Movie Camera* (1929) might have had at the pavilion, yet it is likely more useful to contemplate the causes of its absence. In privileging documentary cinema at its national pavilion, the Republic appeared to be getting more than it bargained for; though it utilized the medium, it did not fully exploit the mode. Thus did the Paris World's Fair mark an unfortunate continuity: documentary cinema, saddled from the start with contradictory expectations, bore its ambivalence from the Republic's first, optimistic moments in April, 1931, through its last, despairing ones in the same cruel month eight years later.

Arguing ambivalence is a curious task, and I do not want to make too much of the kind of contradiction or inconsistency I have identified. But the pattern is suggestive. The ideals of progress, experimentation, and change so often championed during the early Republican years certainly raised expectations that an innovative documentary film practice would flourish, nourished by a committed government and supportive public. As a material technology of production and exhibition, cinema was powerful enough to reach the masses with notions of radical social change and political salvation; as a conceptual mode, documentary seemed sufficiently trustworthy to anchor those notions in the "real" life and experience of Spain; as a symbolic cultural language, documentary cinema appeared poised to help the nation articulate itself anew. That in practice documentary did little to support this crucial task – especially in light of the remarkable formal developments in, and political involvement of, theater, painting, sculpture, and other media – and in fact functioned as a guardian of traditional, narrowly envisioned ideas of the nation, is a ripe contradiction (and a disparity that certainly supports the notion, noted by Boyd and Radcliffe, that the Second Republic's political collapse was linked directly to its failure to create a distinct, unified symbolic identity). Yet the contradiction suggests another story, one that revolves around documentary as a particular kind of character, one that begins with *Proclamación de la República*. To be sure, the film symbolized the Second Republic's embrace of cinema and hope for a new political landscape. But as it both imagined *and* documented a bright future for its audience, this short movie also evinced a fundamental rhetorical ambivalence. The film engaged its audience's social aspirations through the sheer visual power of motion pictures, while communicating a powerful immediacy by speaking in a "realist" language whose terms those spectators implicitly understood and accepted. With just three days between event and representation, *Proclamación* projected images of a nation in dramatic upheaval using a traditional, straightforward, and relatively unadorned mode of address; it seemed to encourage its viewers to dream of the Second Republic's future while witnessing its birth.

That the film can be read as both normative creative vision and descriptive factual record of a key moment in the nation's history foreshadows the ambivalent mission of cinema itself, especially documentary, in the Second Republic. In theory, the wish to transform and the desire to reflect – both linked with traditions of documentary representation – need not stand in conflict.[21] Yet in practice, as Bill Nichols suggests, these rhetorical aims have distinct histories and sometimes uneasy relations. Distinguishing between film as *document* and film as *documentary*, Nichols argues that the latter, the documentary film as we know it today, came to be as "an actual practice [only] in the 1920s and early 1930s" when it combined four elements: "photographic realism, narrative structure, … modernist fragmentation [and an] emphasis on the rhetoric of social persuasion" (Nichols 582). It makes sense that the Republic, with its urgent needs for legitimacy and unity, would have navigated the tensions implied in Nichols' scheme (the tug between neutral presentation and interested representation, the pull between artistic innovation and political action) by using documentary cinema first and foremost to affirm its own authority. By recording and displaying – by memorializing – the epic public events surrounding the Republic's emergence, *Proclamación* appears to have done just that, and we might regard it as part of the burst of documentary practice that Nichols believes appeared during these decades when cinema became part of "already active efforts to build national identity" Yet by serving the aims of national unity in this way, the film may have paid a different political price, for such a cautious adherence to the conventions of actualities or newsreels (a strategy Nichols observes in other European film traditions of the time) likely diluted documentary's "activist goals" (Nichols 582).

Illustrating Nichols' claim that documentary essentially "affirms, or contests, the power of the state," governing bodies across Europe and around the world in the 1920s and 1930s employed documentary as a political instrument. Yet since its ability to both challenge and support the state made documentary "an unruly ally of those in power," these efforts predictably met with different results (Nichols 582). Indeed, the Second Republic's apparent wish both to document itself as a legitimate state and to transform itself as a progressive society seemed to make its documentary film practice more impotent than powerful. As these dual purposes clashed, Republican documentary's power to conjure a vision of a new nation was ultimately compromised by its unwillingness to relinquish images of the old one. Yet the Republic's documentary discourse offers more than a mere reflection of the larger political tale of divided ambitions leading to incoherence and breakdown. Indeed, *Proclamación* – because it is both a *film* and a *documentary* – further illuminates the connection between this ambivalence and the broader relationship between cultural forms and political failure in the Second Republic. Like other actuality films of its time, *Proclamación* was both a descendant of an early cinematic medium (as a public spectacle employing technologies of mechanical reproduction and display that for decades had provoked evolving styles of wonder and belief) and a representative of a nascent documentary mode (as a public declaration utilizing those same technologies, epistemological conventions known through actualities and newsreels, and an expanded narrative scope – all to achieve particular rhetorical ends). But the film not only embodies this duality, but also *displays* it – not as an overt conflict, but as a brooding tension.

Proclamación emphasizes the appeal documentary film held in the Second Republic as a symbolic means to articulate a legitimate and coherent national identity, but it also highlights the complex, often contradictory role spectators play in this process. Characteristically postmodern in its capacity for deceptively reliable (or reliably deceptive?) depiction, documentary is also a tool commonly utilized – that is, relied upon as authoritative (because visual) evidence – in ideological debate. In Spain in 1931, *Proclamación*, as an emblem of public excitement both for an actual scene and for a way of envisioning that scene, embodied this tension: it both registered *and* conceived a political hope for its viewers. To the *madrileños* seated in the Príncipe Alfonso Theater in April of that year, in other words, or to those gathered in theaters throughout the rest of Spain in the days and weeks that followed, the film issued a call both to witness and to participate in the figural founding of the new Spanish republic. With dramatic images of the near-past, *Proclamación* framed a dynamic present for its audiences and invited them to imaginatively construct a history with which they could live – indeed, a history within whose narrative trajectory they *would* live. By both documenting and symbolizing a legitimate and coherent national identity, the film positioned its spectators in a complex and somewhat contradictory relation to the symbolic vision that it projected.

A birth proclaimed, a proclamation exhibited, and an exhibition circulated – *Proclamación* prefigured, in a curious way, the complex tension between technologies of representation and political action that has marked much modern and postmodern art. While it is not possible to know how documentary film might have shaped the nation's fate in the early 1930s, the rhetorical ambivalence surrounding Spanish documentary cinema at that moment does elucidate the striking anxiety that beset the Second Republic. We might use this ambivalence to read the

Republic's collapse as a "modern" phenomenon in both the senses that this chapter's title, "Modern Anxiety," implies (as an anxiousness that *is*, or is *about* something, "modern"), and to re-examine Spain's place in "Modernism"'s broad amalgam of attitudes, ideas, and movements. During the Second Republic, the "modern" was a vibrant and fluid set of ideas and terms that were disputed, embraced, and rejected within the larger context of art's relation to ideas of nation. Much of this complex public conversation over the meaning of "modernity" and its relation to Spain's national identity centered on the notion of "culture" itself. It is no surprise, then, that many discussions about film's proper role in the process of Spain's becoming modern featured claims about cinema's power to shape and even create new forms of culture. This notion of culture as the equivalent of liberated political consciousness suggested that the "modern" aspects of cinema were not essentially modernist in the broad artistic sense, but rather reminiscent of the Enlightenment view of secular education as the basis for social and political progress (a view that would, understandably, be experienced as more "modern" in a country as conservative and tradition-bound as Spain). Documentary – lauded as the rational and objective masculine to fictional film's emotional and subjective feminine, a clear window on true Spanishness in contrast to the dreamy, Hollywood-clouded views of the nation – was the cinematic form that most clearly embodied this contradiction, as it faltered under the expectation that it could both capture Spain's essential past and imagine its progressive future.

But again, reconciling proclamations about cinema's technological power and documentary's epistemological credibility, on the one hand, with the strikingly bland and conventional documentaries that were actually produced, on the other, may be less important than thinking about the broad cultural anxiety that generated this contradiction. For it was as if the Second Republic was locked in a paradigm that nurtured enthusiasm for using emergent technologies to effect cultural and political change while it stifled the imagination of symbolic or cultural means necessary to pursue such change. This inability is more than a mere confirmation of what has been described countless times as an essentially political breakdown. The Republic's sense of social mission, specific to the conditions and realities of 1930s' Spain, differed in important ways from the visions that other European nations followed into modernity. Yet the Republic's efforts to build a more progressive society were "modern" in the essential sense that they opened a break with the past. And its failure of imagination, its inability to conceive of a future except in terms of a past, was a "modern" tension surely not unique to Spain. There is no question that the Second Republic, for all its activist rhetoric, at times seemed more reactionary than revolutionary. But perhaps the particular nature of the Republic's collapse – so quickly and dramatically transformed into a public spectacle of tragic violence – too easily obscures the broader insights it might offer to those seeking to understand political and social change in general.

Phrased a bit less majestically, the Second Republic's use of documentary cinema reflected one of modernist discourse's more common contradictions – between a distrust of, and challenge to, Enlightenment ideals of reason, logic, and progress, on the one hand; and an enthusiastic embrace of developments in science and technology that were the result of those Enlightenment ideals, on the other. Anxious to promote a new, more genuine vision of itself as a nation, anxious that this vision might not be sufficiently different from what had come before, perhaps the Republic was not such an anomaly in twentieth-century Europe. The Republic's documentary cinema – local and idiosyncratic a case as it may seem – may have borne publicly an anxiety that other societies carried in less apparent forms. Is it possible that this anxiety – consciously expressed as ideological enthusiasm, unconsciously transmitted (in figural discourses like documentary cinema) as fearful hesitation – was not solely a Spanish disposition, but a cultural mood harbored as well by other nations, struggling apprehensively, like the Republic, to navigate the precarious web of political, cultural, and economic tensions we call "modernity"?

Notes

1. Throughout this chapter I am indebted to Román Gubern's influential work on cinema in the Second Republic. Gubern refers to this film as *La proclamación de la República*; the Filmoteca Española in Madrid archives the movie simply as *Proclamación de la República*.
2. Though the Republic made free expression its constitution's central principle, in fact, it nonetheless censored cinema and other media by continuing a tradition that used vague laws to capriciously regulate specific practices. See Martínez-Bretón Chapters 1 and 3.
3. The Popular Front victory in the February 1936 elections led to the removal of the Republic's restrictions on Soviet film, if only for a brief time.
4. The Missions made the Cinema Section the second highest priority in their proposed overall budget (Cabra Loredo 85; Gubern, *Val del Omar, cinemista* 13; Fernández et al. 193).
5. By 1933, the Missions had twenty-six 16 mm and two 35 mm projectors; 1934 saw ten more film projectors (one sound), portable generators, three film and six still cameras, and two slide projectors (Cabra Loredo 85–86; Gubern, *Val del Omar, cinemista* 14–15).
6. Gubern notes that in 1933 the Missions had 156 16 mm and 18 35 mm films; 123 of the 16 mm and all the 35 mm films, were documentaries. The rest were animated films (including Felix the Cat cartoons) and comedies (including Charlie Chaplin movies).
7. In 1934 the Missions for the first time counted fifteen original documentaries.

8. Holguín suggests that geographical films might have helped serve at least one of the Missions' purposes – to link those in isolated rural areas with their urban compatriots (126).
9. *Memoria del Patronato de las Misiones Pedagógicas (septiembre 1931–diciembre 1933)* notes that "when … [the villagers] are watching … films, they are interested in the familiar rather than the exotic; if a great city appears on screen, but there's a cat in a window, they look at the cat. And above all they like … the animated films, which at first they never understand" (31).
10. Val del Omar shot dozens of documentaries and hundreds of photographs, yet as a visionary filmmaker and technical innovator, he was representative of neither the Missions nor the Republic (which did not have the will or wherewithal to pursue a vision like his). Unfortunately, virtually all of his films from the Republican era were lost, though recently, through the efforts of Val del Omar's son-in-law, Gonzalo Sáenz de Buruaga, three have been recovered: *Estampas 1932*, *Fiestas cristianas/Fiestas profanas* (1934), and *Vibración de Granada* (1935) (Gubern, *Val del Omar, cinemista* 13–16; *The Galaxy* 7–9). For more on Val del Omar and the Pedagogic Missions, see, for example, Fernández et al.; Gubern, *Val del Omar, cinemista* 13–17; Sáenz de Buruaga "Las Misiones Pedagógicas"; *Val del Omar y las Misiones Pedagógicas*.
11. Here "documentary" refers to films that pass (or wish to pass) as non-fiction: actualities, so-called propaganda, compilation documentaries, etc.
12. The pavilion's groundbreaking collection emphasized the Republic's bold cultural imagination and political vision while articulating a distinct position on the civil war; it included, for example, Alexander Calder's abstractionist *Spanish Mercury from Almaden*," dedicated to miners under attack by Franco's forces, and Picasso's chilling *Guernica*, depicting the bombing of the Basque town of the same name.
13. The Spanish Pavilion also featured a photomontage of the Pedagogic Missions' activities. For more on the Republic's use of film at its pavilion, see, for example, Gubern, "Exibiciones"; Martín Martín 198–201; Mendelson, "Contested Territory" 241–20.
14. Gubern, in the most recent and explicit treatment of the pavilion's films, refers cryptically to the "list of twelve screened films that was given to us." Gubern told me that when the *Pabellón Español* catalog's general editor, Josefina Alix Trueba, asked him to contribute an essay on the pavilion's films, she answered his question about which movies were shown by mailing him that list of twelve, without providing further explanation. In his earlier book, Martín Martín discusses these same twelve films but also quotes the French daily *L'Humanité*'s 1937 write-up on the pavilion as saying that "Among the (films) that will be shown, and that total more than forty, are": before it lists the same

twelve films. Martín Martín also notes that Joris Ivens' *The Spanish Earth* (1937) may have been shown, and it is generally agreed that the Pedagogic Missions showed films as well. Despite the uncertainty, most concur that this frequently named list of twelve movies is representative of what the Republic screened (Gubern, "Exhibiciones" 174; Interview; Martín Martín 200–1).

15. Although the diversity of competing political factions – whose strife in 1936 had contributed to the government's breakdown – was eventually compressed into the two-sided military structure of the Spanish Civil War, the left remained politically fragmented well after the fighting had begun. By the time of the Paris Exposition in 1937, the PCE-controlled Republic, attempting to unify itself and to crush the left's non-Communists, had become adept at putting a harmonious public face on a society that remained internally fractured.
16. Despite being attributed a central role, Buñuel told Max Aub that his contribution to the film was limited to "supervising" Jean-Paul Dreyfus' editing of the "material sent by the Subsecretary of Propaganda" (Gubern, *La guerra de España* 25; Sala Noguer 156–64; Aub 93).
17. *Reforma agraria* could be an exception, but it is impossible to say, since it is the film among the twelve about which the least information exists (Gubern "Exhibiciones" 174).
18. It is unclear whether the film's image track was re-edited with its sound track, yet the extant version of *Felipe II y el Escorial*, combining reactionary voice-over narration with expansive shots accenting El Escorial's architectural grandeur, undoubtedly conveys a different message than Velo intended when the film was shown at the pavilion.
19. Except at clandestine screenings, *Las Hurdes* was next publicly presented in Paris in late 1936 or early 1937 (Martínez-Bretón and Gubern give different dates), with a soundtrack, a French voice-over, and a coda of intertitles supporting the fight against fascism as a means of eradicating the very misery the film revealed. As the war progressed, the Republican government, once adamantly opposed to Buñuel's subtly subversive film, now willingly exploited the politically strident version of *Las Hurdes* in its increasingly desperate efforts to gain international support, calculating, it seems, that as anti-fascist propaganda it would no longer reflect poorly on the government (Gubern, "Interview", "El cortometraje republicano" 39, and *La Guerra de España* 24–25; Martínez-Bretón 73–9).
20. Mendelson suggests that *Las Hurdes* was excluded from the pavilion because it already included Missions' photographs depicting rural Spain in a way quite different from Buñuel's film, whose "ideological content … was … ambiguous." She also notes that Buñuel, "recognizing the transformation that *Las Hurdes* underwent during its various moments of reception," and

"[p]erhaps recalling the ability of photographs from *Las Hurdes* to operate as revolutionary documents when released from the film's structure and the film-maker's name," might have supported the exclusion, choosing "instead to edit a film [*Espagne 36*] about the Civil War for the Pavilion" ("Contested Territory" 241–2).

21. Indeed, these aims, generally reconciled in histories of cinema, are in some sense inseparable, and can be complementary (much documentary work in the United States in the 1930s, for example, recorded social misery in order to help transform it).

Works Cited

Arconada, César M. "Posibilidades sociales del cinema." *Nuestro Cinema* (8–9) (1933): 90.

"Asunto: sobre proyectos cinematográficos artista Raquel Meller." Government Correspondence. Madrid/Paris: March 24, April 22, May 2, 1933. Archivo General de la Administración (Alcalá de Henares). Petición 65, Sección A.E., Caja/Leg. 11271.

Aub, Max. *Conversaciones con Buñuel*. Madrid: Aguilar, 1985.

Boyd, Carolyn. *Historia Patria*. Princeton, NJ: Princeton University Press, 1997.

Cabra Loredo, María Dolores, ed. *Misiones Pedagógicas. Septiembre de 1931–Diciembre de 1933. Informes. I*. Madrid: El Museo Universal, 1992.

Escobar, Julio. "España y sus heroes del cinema." *Cine español* 3 (1934): 1.

Fernández, Isabel, Juan Carlos Ibáñez Fernández and Teresa C. Rodríguez. "El cine en las Misiones Pedagógicas. La figura de Val del Omar." In *Actas de las IV Jornadas Internacionales de Jóvenes Investigadores en Communicación*. Barcelona: Universidad Autónoma de Barcelona, 1997. 193–5.

García Lorenzo, Luciano. *Las "Misiones Pedagógicas" en Zamora (1933–1934)*. Zamora: Cuadernos de Investigación, 1991.

Gómez Mesa, Luis. "Alcance del cinema educativo y cultural." *Nuestro Cinema* 8–9 (1933): 109.

Government Receipts (Pedagogic Missions films). Madrid: December 3–31, 1933. Archivo General de la Administración (Alcalá de Henares). Petición 65, Sección A.E., Caja/Leg. 11268.

Gubern, Román. *1936–1939: La guerra de España en la pantalla*. Madrid: Filmoteca, 1986.

—— "El cine sonoro (1930–1939)." In *Historia del cine español*. Eds. Román Gubern, J.E. Monterde, J.P. Perucha, E. Riambau and C. Torreito. Madrid: Cátedra, 1995. 123–79.

—— *El cine sonoro en la II República 1929–1936*. Barcelona: Editorial Lumen, 1977.

—— "El cortometraje republicano." In *Historia del cortometraje español*. Eds. Pedro Medina, Luis Mariano González and José Martín Velázquez with Francisco Llinas. Alcalá de Henares: Festival de Cine de Alcalá de Henares, 1996. 34–55.

—— "Exibiciones Cinematográficas en el Pabellón español." *Pabellón Español. Exposición Internacional de París 1937*. Madrid: Ministerio de Cultura, 1987. 174–80.

—— Interview with author. January 27 2004a. Barcelona.

—— *Val del Omar, cinemista*. Granada: Editorial dc la Diputación de Granada, 2004b.

Holguín, Sandie. *Creating Spaniards*. Madison, WI: University of Wisconsin Press, 2002.

Martín Martín, Fernando. *El pabellón español en la Exposición Universal de Paris en 1937*. Seville: Universidad de Sevilla, 1982.

Martínez-Bretón, Juan Antonio. *Libertad de expresión cinematográfica durante la II República Española (1931–1936)*. Madrid: Fragua, 2000.

Memoria del Patronato de las Misiones Pedagógicas (septiembre 1931–diciembre 1933). Madrid, 1934.

Mendelson, Jordana. "Contested Territory." *Locus Amoenus* 2 (1996): 229–42.

—— "La imagen de España el la década de 1930." Trans. Sara Font. *Val del Omar y las Misiones Pedagógicas*. Murcia: Residencia de Estudiantes, 2003. 61–73.

Mendez-Leite, Fernando. Editorial. *Cinema* October 7 1931a: 7.

—— "Cinema nuevo teatro del mundo." *Cinema* October 7 1931b: 32–3.

Nichols, Bill. "Documentary Film and the Modernist Avant-Garde." *Critical Inquiry* 27 (Summer 2001): 580–610.

Otero Urtaza, Eugenio. *Las Misiones Pedagógicas*. A Coruña: Ediciós do Castro, 1982.

Pabellón Español. Exposición Internacional de París 1937. Madrid: Ministerio de Cultura, 1987.

"Patronato de Misiones Pedagógicas." *Residencia*. February 1933: 1–21.

Piqueras, Juan. Editorial. *Nuestro Cinema 11 (1932).*

Radcliffe, Pamela. "Representing the Nation." Unpublished paper, "Nationalism and Spain" conference, Tufts University, 1996.

Sáenz de Buruaga, Gonzalo. "Las Misiones Pedagógicas y la utopía cinematográfica de Val del Omar." *Cinematògraf* 3 (2001): 211–20.

—— and M.J. Val del Omar. *Val del Omar sin fin*. Granada: Filmoteca de Andalucía, 1992.

Sala Noguer, Ramón. *El cine en la España republicana durante la Guerra civil (1936–1939)*. Bilbao: Mensajero, 1993.

Santos, Mateo. Editorial. *Popular Film* April 14, 1932a: 1.

—— "La cruzada de la cultura: Misiones Pedagógicas." *Popular Film* February 11 1932b: 1.

——— "Llamamiento a los aficionados para constituir la Agrupación Cinematográfica Española." *Popular Film* February 4 1932c: 1.

The Galaxy of Val del Omar. Madrid: Instituto Cervantes, 2002.

Val del Omar y las Misiones Pedagógicas. Murcia: Residencia de Estudiantes, 2003.

Villegas López, Manuel. *Arte de masas*. Madrid: GECI, 1936.

–17–

The Last Look from the Border

Joan Ramon Resina

The eye opens the subject to the world. If I close my eyes, the world is no longer there and I am no longer in the world. The other's gaze, the flicker in her eye lets me know that I am a presence. That flicker betrays her awareness that I see her; it is the awareness itself. Because seeing and looking are intertwined, everything visual is loaded with affect. The eye is the organ of transcendence, and seeing a transitive occupation. Merely by lifting our eyelids we come onto the threshold of the objective world. And the range of our vision, by defining the visual field, suggests that there is more than meets the eye, that experience is self-transcending. The bounded nature of perception is expressed in the notion of horizon. A subjective byproduct of the objectivity of visual experience, the horizon is not only the condition of possibility of all acts of perception but also a melancholy sign of the viewer's finitude, a marker of his confinement and thus of his exposure. It is Finis Terrae, the end of the world as seen by an embodied subjectivity.

To see an object means to accept the boundary between that object and the rest of the world. Seeing presupposes the object's determination. Seeing, then, is synonymous with knowing, for to know is to ascertain the limits of the object. I "see" something insofar as I can make it out, detaching it from its surroundings. But seeing also implies re-cognizing, for how could I trace the object's boundary unless that object already exists for me? In the case at hand, "seeing" the nation depends on the existence of a boundary, or more precisely, a political horizon. Although today many assert that nations are imagined, I will argue that they are eminently visual and reveal themselves to a particular form of attention.

Before me is a black and white photograph of an urban space, a square perhaps, or a wide street (Figure 17.1) Although the scene is unmistakably urban, the background blur makes it nearly unidentifiable. It could be any city, and the time is equally nondescript. The subdued light (low winter light?) makes the moment ambiguous. Is it early morning? Dusk? In the foreground, a woman and a dog run across empty space. Nothing in this image suggests Spain; nothing claims my attention particularly. And yet my eyes turn to it with insistence. Something in the picture buttonholes me, demands the concourse of my subjectivity. In my effort to re-

Figure 17.1 Robert R. Capa (1913–64), "Barcelona, January 1939." Black and white photograph. In *Spain. Spanish Civil War (1936–9).* ICP 281 (CAR1936004W00009/ ICP281). Running for shelter during the air raid alarm. The city was being heavily bombed by Fascist planes as General Franco's troops rapidly approached the city. © Magnum Photos.

cognize this image, I look instinctively for analogies. The dynamic subject reminds me, in the first place, of a futuristic representation of movement, such as Giacomo Balla's painting *Leash in Motion*. But this only means that images always call for a space of reverberation, that I can "see" something only in relation to a horizon of visibility defined by the history of my visual experience. In principle, the nature of that horizon is undetermined, although in practice it will depend on the system of relevances operating at the moment. Those references may be political, as they may be metaphysical, cosmological, entomological, or culinary. In the Middle Ages religion was the ultimate horizon of meaning, to be replaced by scientism in the nineteenth century and economicism in the twentieth. Hence, I must dissent from Fredric Jameson's superfetation of the political in his claim that the political is "the absolute horizon of all reading and all interpretation" (17). Such an inflated notion of the political undermines the rational foundation of politics, displacing its basis in public discourse and turning it into the pre-discursive premise of human reflexivity. By disseminating the political perspective throughout the symbolic sphere, Jameson dissolves its specificity. As a metalanguage at the limit of symbolic action, politics becomes for Jameson the master trope for every possible experience.

This clarification was necessary because I intend to assign political relevance to acts of seeing that are as ambiguous as the photograph I have just mentioned. But I do not want the reader to "lose sight" of the fact that it is my intervention, my set of relevances, that constitutes that particular horizon of interpretation, and that other horizons could claim competing pertinence. What if the Spanish Civil War were, for once, stripped of its political shroud and considered a huge sadomasochistic performance? What if Spain were an eidetic image resulting from the historical materialization of the death drive? Whereas the acts of seeing that I will discuss and the images they produce are, I believe, most productive when "regarded," or, in other words, determined, as political, such determination would be impossible if the political were the ultimate ground of all discernment. The eye establishes the existential conditions of the real before the political intervenes. Hence, if "seeing" the nation presupposes a political horizon of interpretation, it is equally true that this ideal "boundary" attains concrete existence in the nation's borders, from where we can both catch and lose sight of the nation. Borders may be the expression of political arbitration of conflict, but they are also scenarios of personal and collective dramas, which can be contained within political exegesis only at the cost of severe reduction. Furthermore, although borders are usually thought of as spatial, and even as natural geographic demarcations, they are essentially historical. Borders are the temporary crystallization of innumerable dramas, the thickening of a formerly fluid relation of people to the territory, the political precipitate of a reality that formerly existed in underdetermined suspension. Hence, it is within the logic of the relation between politics and drama that the border turns into a stage for significant action whenever the state is shaken to its foundations.

The state exists in space and in time by virtue of the border, with the political subject in the role of transcendental subject. The border, then, is the nation's horizon of possibility, the perspective from which that political reality can be observed. A virtual line created and sustained trough the most strenuous and costly efforts, the border is constitutive of the perspective from which any object of experience is promoted to the status of a metonymyc representation of the national. Yet, unlike the Kantian subject, the political subject can overstep her ideal bubble and expose herself to a different regime of visibility. She can discover the gap between the state's ideal border and the nation she actually spies from her dramatic standpoint.

Whose horizon?

Let us look again at the photograph of the running woman and dog, this time identifying the reference. This image in silver gelatin of dimensions 25.6 × 40 cm.

belongs to Robert Capa's "Barcelona" series, taken in January 1939. The reference provides us with spatial and temporal coordinates and thus with a more precise point of view. Slowly, the background shapes up as my mind refocuses. The woman's fast stride becomes more familiar as I gradually recognize the space involved. I re-cognize it means, in this instance, that it begins to look familiar, that it starts falling into place with a pre-existing image: is it the Gran Via or the lower end of the Rambles? Could it be Passeig de Gràcia? One thing is certain: it is January 1939. The picture's subdued illumination had already suggested the possibility of winter. Now we can add the date's dramatic overtones, masterfully captured in the plate's chiaroscuro. The woman rushing across the street during an air raid succinctly displays the emergency of an entire population. On the 26th of that month, in the afternoon, Navarrese and Moroccan divisions, the most brutal troops of the fascist army, marched into Barcelona. With that action, the Spanish Civil War was effectively over.[1] Franco's army would quickly proceed to shut the French border and then move south to Valencia and Alacant, to lock the last remaining gates of egress by sea. Madrid, placed on hold during the last phase of the war, fell like ripe fruit after the collapse of the eastern front. On July 18, 1936, Barcelona had signaled to other cities that resistance was possible. Likewise, its fall in January 1939 sealed the Republic's fate. Capa's photo, therefore, brims with significance. The running woman and dog are a limit-image of Republican Spain. Frozen in movement against the blurry background, the two bodies are an epiphany of life on the verge of disappearing. And that is exactly what a horizon is: the line over which things vanish, but also the condition of visibility that orders the relations among the things that one can see.

To where is this woman rushing? Capa's photo shows her fleeing but gives no hint of her destination. It displays the essence of flight, and therein lies its power. In mid-January the dominant feeling in Barcelona was one of impending doom. People knew it was a matter of days, maybe hours before the enemy would arrive. For many, leaving the city was a matter of life or death. Urgency altered the spirits and conditioned sight. In one of the best documents of the Catalan exodus, *Els darrers dies de la Catalunya republicana*, Antoni Rovira i Virgili recorded the correlation between the experience of the end and the consciousness of the eye.

In the early hours of January 24, the Generalitat dispatched a car to Rovira's house, in the suburb of Horta, to evacuate his family. As the chauffeur waited while the household gathered their essentials, Rovira's wife kept saying: "Let's run! Quick, quick!"[2] In the anxiety of those words, it is possible to recognize the pathos of Capa's photograph. Both are iconic moments of a city waiting for the blow that will smash it. And they are simultaneous. Same city, same time. Only the media are different. In both, a woman strides over quotidian space into the unknown. It is precisely at this moment that Rovira becomes conscious of looking for the last time on a world that suddenly appears temporally circumscribed.

> I hardly have time to direct a final regretful look at the house, whose outline I can vaguely trace in the shadows. A throng of impressions, memories and images assault my spirit and present themselves to my imagination like a film. Silently, I take leave of the rooms, the furniture, the books, and the domestic animals, of the plants and trees in the orchard and in the garden. I always had a tender look for the animate or inanimate companions of my daily life. I think that no other living being watches the night scene, but I am wrong. At the very moment when the car starts, I see through the fence, deep in the darkness, four phosphorescent eyes. The house cats have noticed our departure. (Rovira i Virgili 49)

Emerging from the Republic's defeat as dimly as the house's silhouette from the surrounding umbra is a historical boundary. On this boundary, images and affections are projected as on a screen, and Rovira watches while the house, ensconced in darkness, serves as a backdrop for the experience of flight, like the street in Capa's photo. In this case, though, only humans are running. The house cats sit in the darkness and look on their owners' stealthy departure. It is a scene of abandonment. Pets are left behind; the Republic is left to its fate. This realization, weighing heavily on Rovira's glum leave-taking opens another perspective on Capa's picture. Suddenly, we realize that the dog we see cavorting ahead of the woman turns a seemingly ordinary scene into a scene of fright. Capa has centered the picture on the dog, letting everything else recede toward the vanishing point somewhere among the hazy buildings. By focusing on the animated figures while blurring the background, Capa skillfully conveys the impression of movement. But it is all based on trompe-l'œil. It is the spectator, not those figures, who "feels" the motion. Like Rovira's cats, Capa's dog is frozen in the posthumous life of a thing seen from the standpoint of a historical catastrophe. And although it does not stare back at the spectator, it too is a silent witness of doom.

In the quoted passage, Rovira is aware of leaving behind a temporal order, not just a familiar space. In point of fact, the distinction is merely conceptual, for in practice both are equivalent. The time that is running out, making his wife exhort the family to a brisker departure, is, in his own words, the quotidian time spent in private rooms, among his furniture, his books, his animals, the plants and trees in the orchard and the garden. Like a camera in the dusk of a projection room, his eye illuminates the memories that run through his mind before rushing back into the dark places where he will never venture again. The phenomenon is well known by those who have ever been keenly aware of a disruption in their lives. Walter Benjamin has written about rooms in which we spend months without imprinting them in our memory until "one day from an alien source [the necessary light] flashes as if from burning magnesium powder, and now a snapshot fixes the room's image on the plate." Those moments of "sudden illumination," as Benjamin calls them (115), divide the self into a habitual, everyday self that is involved in the external world, and a deeper self that responds to the shock of the extraordinary event, lighting up and bringing the image into relief in the brain's dark chamber.

Steeped in the emotion of loss, Rovira's last look at the nooks of his ordinary life is the opposite of his habitual perception of those same places. That illuminating look ratifies Bakhtin's definition of the everyday as an ambit that is insufficiently lit. For the Russian critic, "Everyday life is the nether world, the grave, where the sun does not shine, where there is no starry firmament. For this reason, everyday life is presented to us as the underside of real life" (Bakhtin 128). Bakhtin is speaking, of course, about novelistic time, which is by definition the time of exceptionality, but his insight applies to the experience of the exile, whose life has become the antithesis of the routine and customary. Even so, for the fugitive who lacks every reassurance, the everyday is not "deprived of its unity and wholeness," as Bakhtin (128) asserts, but, on the contrary, is the melancholy source of the meaning and continuity in his life.

On the Edge of History

Phenomenology establishes time as the condition of perception. For Husserl, "This world now present to me, and in every waking 'now' obviously so, has its temporal horizon, infinite in both directions, its known and unknown, its intimately alive and its unalive past and future" (Husserl 102).[3] According to this view, at every moment the subject contemplates the world from a temporal limit. But phenomenology's time is still ideal time. It is not shaped by events or by the dramas that twist abstract time into distinct eras. Upon leaving his house, Rovira knew that he stood at a historical threshold, and from that vantage point the intimately "alive" past glimmered in the consciousness of its dissolution. Infinity, in Husserl's sense of the unfathomable duration of the world, invades his consciousness in the vision of the house receding into the shadows. And as the familiar becomes indiscernible, history emerges into visibility, as the collective drama that smashes private lives creates a new horizon, a new inroad into the world's infinite interpretability. Objectified in the land, Catalonian history appears to Rovira as a live orography running off into an "unalive" future. And once more, the affects are spatialized and viewed like a film.

> Now that Barcelona is lost, the Catalonian mountains in front of me, the sky above me, the Catalonian land under me, seem to flee, to vanish, to end like a ribbon when it comes to its end. At every turn of my short walk I verify the presence of the mountains, the sky and the earth, which are Catalonia's material presence. An agonizing presence, though. I fix my eyes on the landscape with the eagerness of the person who watches the face of a dying loved one. (Rovira i Virgili 118)

In its simplicity, this passage is remarkable. It calls up an image of the nation's permanence only to underscore its instability. *These* mountains, *this* earth, *this* sky are

Catalonia: a finite stretch of the planet's surface contained within precise topographical limits. Knowable therefore. And yet, this permanent object, this material presence is perceived in the act of vanishing. The world cannot retain its image. Under extraordinary historical pressure, Rovira is spontaneously performing a phenomenological reduction, detaching the image from the object it replicates. The landscape remains in place while the nation fades from perception and becomes a pure image. A naïve nationalist, an essentialist, would mistake the image for the object, endowing it with ontological reality. Then the nation would *be* the mountains, the earth, and the sky that intuition grasps in many different forms and circumstances. Unlike the mountains, though, the image does not impose itself on the subject through a set of pragmatic demands. You cannot climb the image of a mountain. The image does not exist outside the consciousness of the observer, or even in it. Husserl distinguishes between an imaging act of consciousness and the material that the intention acts upon. It is important not to confuse this material of consciousness or *hyle* with the object of perception, which remains in the world, in its radical otherness.

Rovira's "agonizing presence" refers to the *hyle* or material of his image of Catalonia, not to the geological accidents that remain securely in place. The nation's "agonizing presence" is not "imagined" in Benedict Anderson's sense but imaged in Husserl's. A fiction, yes, in the sense of the phenomenological object of consciousness, not in the constructivist's sense of a fabrication or an engineered experience. Above all, a fiction seen, correlated, that is, with the external world through everyday links of different affective intensity, and subject to exhaustion when consciousness is unable to sustain its imaging intention. "I fix my eyes on the landscape," says Rovira, but his gaze no longer animates the image, which pales and dims like the face of a dying person, while the mountains, the earth, and the sky detach themselves from consciousness and return to their purely geological condition.

Far from anchoring the nation in cosmic eternity, the permanent accidents of the land verify that the nation can be ravaged by history. Destroyed by its secular enemies, Catalonia seems to disappear not just as society but even as territory. The impression of a receding country is, of course, an effect of the viewer's progress toward the horizon, which in this case involves not merely a spatial but above all a historical boundary. The dramatic events put pressure on Catalonia's physical existence to such a degree that Rovira sees geography in the light of the fate that pushes the nation off its existential limits. It is from the vantage point of utter loss (of country, possessions, citizenship, profession, and even language), that he and Carles Pi Sunyer (Minister of Culture in the Catalonian government) evoke Catalonian history as they train their eyes on the Empordà shortly before reaching the border:

> Our gaze traces the landscape with leisurely fruition. The bright, clean air brings the hills, the mountains, and the valleys nearer to us. It gives sharpness to the profiles, perspectives, and details. It shows clearly the ribbon of the road, the twisting of the pathways, the crimson roofs of the village house and the white frontages of the nearby country houses.
> – The mountains over there – I say, pointing with my arm – must be the Alberes.
> – They are – concurs Pi.
> Having started this conversation, Pi traces with his eyes and points out with his arm the hills, ravines, villages and hamlets, the ruins and beaches of this farthest reach of the High Empordà.
> …
> While my friend is naming the geographical markers and the towns, both of us evoke episodes from Catalonian history. Pi, who has studied in depth the Franco-Spanish war during the period of the French revolution, explains to me the movements of both armies in this border region. When his explanation is over, I compliment him on his knowledge.
> – You know the region very well.
> – It's my region – he replies.
> And slowly, in a tone that is not dejected but rather courageous, he adds:
> – Perhaps I will never see it again! (Rovira i Virgili 132–3)

The loss of even the expectation of future vision endows present vision with special sharpness. "What we know that we will soon no longer have before us, this is what becomes an image" (Benjamin 1974: 590). Prescience of the disappearance of the world is at the root of the aesthetic experience. Only because it will pass away, does the world settle in our retina. And not only the external world. Foreknowledge of impending loss also opens the gates to the images stored in the preconscious. Pi's last view of the homeland teems with images that had been arrested at different levels of temporality. The crisscrossing movements of spectral armies from former wars transform the spatial relations among villages and hamlets, hills and ravines. In the same way, the Catalonian exodus, the second in the span of two centuries, changes the way Pi and Rovira look at the barren country roads leading to the southern slopes of the Pyrenees. What they see from their vantage on the terrace of Can Perxers, a farmhouse in the village of Agullana, is not an inert tract of land but the nation affirmed in its visibility. At this moment of extremity, hope gathers the entire country into a synecdoche furnished by the eyes:

> – I believe that we will see this district again and all the other Catalonian districts. I believe that those who are about to go into exile will see again the Empordà, the Camp, the Vallès, the Segarra, the Penedès, the Urgell; that we will again see the Montseny, Cadí, Montserrat, Montsant; that we will see once more Figueres, Girona, Olot, Vic, Lleida, Manresa, Tarragona, Barcelona. All the districts, all the mountains, all the

> rivers, all the cities of the fatherland, which has not died, which shall not die, which cannot die. (Rovira i Virgili 133–4)

But nations can and do die, as Rovira is plainly aware of when he mentions the landscape's agonizing presence. Nonetheless, bracketing natural contingency permits the mind to reveal essences, and these, like scientific laws, are eternal. It is not just a matter of internalizing the empirical data that make the landscape, but as Sartre (140) explained phenomenological reflection requires yet another step from the empirical to the general. Looking at Catalonia from this temporal horizon, Rovira's consciousness first turns from the empirically seen to the data fixed by introspection and then to a pure form of temporal protension. Consciousness ventures into the future through an act of faith in the face of destruction. Hope implies the reversal of fate, the looping of time, the return of images to their objects. Hope teases the eye with the possibility of regaining a lost perspective. "When I return to Catalonia – I do not say 'if I return to Catalonia' – I shall come to Can Perxers and ask the farmers to let me climb to the terrace to look at this same landscape that is now before our eyes" (Rovira i Virgili 134). As it happened, Rovira continued to live in his native Catalonia (he never left it), although he would never cross the border again. He died in Perpinyà on December 5, 1949 without having fulfilled his vow of returning to Can Perxers. Blake's dictum that the eye sees more than the heart knows proved right on this occasion. Feasting his eyes on the landscape of the Empordà, Rovira eagerly absorbed the last images he would ever get on this side of the border.

> I have turned my gaze toward the West, where the sun swoons in a golden explosion of light. Silently but fervently I take leave of the beautiful landscape … Tomorrow, when the sun sets, I will be on the other side of the border.
>
> The star has fallen behind the mountains. The sun has set in Catalonia. (136)

The date was January 30. The next morning Rovira crossed the border through the Pertús. Unlike his wife, he did not look back at the moment of crossing. Instead, he looked at the conventional line, tempering his political skepticism with the pragmatic observation that at least this time the official fiction had saved their lives.

> We know full well that this part of France into which we have just entered is still Catalonia. But at this moment the official line has real meaning. We leave one state and enter another. We leave a country that is at war and enter one that is in peace. We escape from the enemy's persecution and come under the protection of a different sovereignty. For this reason I renounce all reflection about the fact that the Roussillon is Catalonian and the state line is, in some regards, fictitious. For our group the psychological transition to another country takes place at the moment we enter into the territory of the French State. (158)

In reality, Rovira is looking at the same landscape as the day before. Outside the political perspective, paramount at this moment, nothing much has changed. For a while, he can see villages and traditions similar to those on the other side. Common genealogies and a common language reveal a cultural continuity slowly broken by state interference.[4] Yet the state imposes its reality. The French government has sent 50,000 men – troops and gendarmes – to police the refugees (Villarroya 20), as they reach the border with Franco's army close on their heels. Had Pi not recalled, just the day before, the maneuvers of eighteenth-century armies in this area and how their movements settled the line that Rovira has just crossed? Now both armies are about to meet once more along this fateful limit.

Ordinarily inconspicuous and ultimately arbitrary, the horizon of state sovereignty looms momentously under extreme circumstances. From the standpoint of this horizon, the long condensation of everyday life, the language formed over the centuries, the labor that founded villages and shaped the landscape, and the memories that took hold of the terrain must all be overlooked – renounced, says Rovira – in order to survive state violence. Seen from this perspective, the land becomes merely territory. And the exile, at the moment when a state voids his everyday horizon, has no choice but to acknowledge the alternative horizon emerging from the ruins of his elemental world. "On the hard asphalt of the French route our feet have a feeling of safety. The old Canigó protects a stretch of Catalonian land that will not be tramped by the enemies of our fatherland and our language, the same language as the Rousillon's" (161).

As in the Middle Ages, when Catalonia came into existence as Europe's outpost on the western frontier with Islam, Mount Canigó constitutes a horizon of invulnerability. Yet, in 1939 it is not a natural fortress but French asphalt that keeps Catalonia's enemies at bay. Man-made political realities take precedence over organic traditions. Asphalt, a modern invention sung by Baudelaire,[5] helped considerably to absorb northern Catalonia into France (Sahlins 282–4). Asphalt is not merely contemporaneous with the nation-state; it stands for it. Like the gendarmes encountered along the road and the *préfet* of the Pyrénées Orientales, as the French have renamed Catalonia, the roads are emblematic of the state that now confers on the fugitives the status of refugees in their ancestral homeland.

Rovira's twofold perspective arises from overlapping heterogeneous spaces, each ringed by a different horizon. From the standpoint of the state, space is territory, and borders mark the cessation of jurisdictional turf. Cultural reality, however, persists unbroken on either side of the border, and Catalonia stretches along a thinning continuum of traditional practices and resilient historical memories. This way of being in the state without coinciding with it turns Catalonia into a heterotopy. Foucault defined heterotopies as spaces where the official determinations of space could be contested. It only remains for us to add that such spaces depend on the availability of alternative perspectives, in short, on the existence of disparate horizons.

The Road of Sorrow

"The exodus toward the border attains incredible proportions." With these words, Carlos Rojas (292) begins his account of the Republican evacuation from Catalonia in January 1939. It was the exodus of an entire people, says Villarroya (14). And more than that, because, as he points out, around 1 million people from other parts of Spain had taken refuge in Catalonia by the end of 1938 (14). Many of them were also bound for the border. The droves fleeing the Francoist army walked many miles against the north wind and under the rain, harassed by enemy aviation, which routinely machine-gunned the roads. The lucky ones covered the distance from Barcelona in automobile, but near the border they found themselves immobilized for hours by the crawling throngs. The German ambassador to the Burgos government, Von Stohrer, referred to the Catalonian road into France as "that road of sorrow" (Rojas 293). On January 28, several hundred thousand people, cars, horse-drawn carts, and mules packed the roads in the neighborhood of the Pertús under heavy rain. Didkowski, the préfet of the Eastern Pyrenees, had ordered the border shut to all vehicles except official ones, and now only women, children and the wounded on stretchers were allowed to cross. Twelve babies died from the cold on that day.

Footage of the exodus was first shown to audiences in Frédéric Rossif's film *Mourir à Madrid* (1963). Images of weary, ill-clad civilians trekking the snowy Pyrenees effectively communicate the emotional abyss of a forsaken people. From the close-up of a child fingering another child's espadrille, a peasant's shoe unfit for trudging in snow, the camera cuts to a view of the fascist columns marching to the border. Such effects are frequent in *Mourir à Madrid*, which relies heavily on the contrasts produced by montage. At the outset, the camera tracks the slow gait of a peasant riding to the fields at dawn just before the voice over scrolls a series of quantitative facts. The film ends with a peasant emerging from the diffuse light of dawn and walking toward the camera with his hoe on his shoulder. The placid images are not there to speak for themselves but to anchor the political message, namely the arresting of history in a false timelessness through brutal repression. It is not incidental to that message that *Mourir à Madrid* was produced with the support of the French Communist Party. The subordination of the image to a political narrative is commonplace in the film history of the conflict, and it may be one reason why there is no great film about the Spanish Civil War.

Things are altogether different where photography is concerned. In the pre-discursive sensuality of the photographic image lurks a modality of experience that language cannot fully render. Among the documentary arts, photography furnishes the highest degree of what Jacques Leenhardt has called "the violence of the image" (9). He refers to the stubborn refusal of the visual to be appropriated by discourse. I have already mentioned how, in Capa's photograph of the running woman, the context's uncertainty, underscored by an indistinct background, depletes the foreground of all epistemological coordinates.

Now I would like to look at another photo, also from Capa's "Barcelona" series (Figure 17.2). It is a well-known picture of a young girl sitting among bundles and leaning on a rice bag. Her body, seen at a slant, takes up most of the upper-left triangle created by the diagonal section of the frame. This triangle is obscured by the girl's roomy coat, which is too large to be her own, and by her coal-black hair, which veils a good part of her face. The girl's dark mass, combined with that of the bundles, fills up this half of the picture, contrasting with the comparatively unburdened lower-right triangle. A segment of bare floor, an empty bottle and a smaller bag do not balance the weight on the opposite side of the top-heavy picture, which induces a certain anxiety in the viewer, as if it were about to topple.

From this phenomenological description of the image, it is possible to proceed in two different ways. One way would be to take the aesthetic route that Pierre Bourdieu associates with codified rituals of enjoyment. The stress would fall on Capa's narrow framing of the image so as to isolate the girl from the surrounding group of people, which an enlarged camera angle would have revealed (Figure 17.3). From all the possible aspects of the scene, Capa has chosen one that, on closer inspection, turns out to emerge from an elaborate perspective. The close-up, eye-to eye position of the camera that is slightly raised above the subject involves the viewer in visual intimacy with the girl, who looks back from her iconic timelessness. Treated as an aesthetic object, the photo sheds all external references and takes its place in the hierarchy of formal achievements.

Another way to proceed is by stressing photography's power of illusion, the impression that nature stands directly before our eyes. But what kind of nature is this? The flash of consciousness in the girl's look has been excised from the continuum of her life by the action of the shutter. Photo-time is time-out, the unalive time of Husserl's unknown. Much of the magic of the photographic image comes from its defamiliarization of the everyday. It will be noticed that in commenting this photograph I have not resorted to narrative. I have not advanced any story about this girl's origin or destination, nor have I speculated about her social class, although plenty of information in the picture would justify my doing so. Nevertheless, an analogy offers itself. The excision of the habitual and routine through Capa's intervention parallels the suspension of the everyday in Rovira's account of his departure. Supporting this analogy is, of course, the title and the date of the series to which the photograph belongs. While the minimalist title preempts any attempt to narrativize the image, tension arises nonetheless between the image of the girl among bundles and the aesthetic expectations associated with a

Figure 17.2 Robert R. Capa, "Barcelona, January 1939." Black and white photograph. In *Spain. Spanish Civil War 1936–9.* ICP 289 (CAR1939005W00001/ICP289). A refugee transit center during the evacuation of the city, which was being heavily bombed by Fascist planes, as General Franco's troops rapidly approached the city. © Magnum photos.

modern city. The image is somehow out of joint, but the date, January 1939, corroborates its objective character by referring to its dramatic exceptionality. Time and place markers, realism's traditional pillars, reintroduce history into the image.

There is another way of saying this. If, as Bourdieu claims, frontality suggests the atemporal (112), then, by refusing the status of photographic subject, the girl rejects eternity. Frontality, says Bourdieu, is a means of objectifying oneself (120). Disdaining the dignified manner of traditional portraiture, the girl retains a paradoxical agency. By remaining one more bundle among the other bundles, she

Figure 17.3 Robert R. Capa, "Barcelona, January 1939." Black and white photograph. In *Spain. Spanish Civil War 1936–9*. ICP 290 (CAR1939005W00002/ICP290). A refugee transit center during the evacuation of the city, which was being heavily bombed by Fascist planes, as General Franco's troops rapidly approached the city. The white circle shows the location of the young girl in Figure 17.2. © Magnum photos.

refuses to produce herself as a transcendental meaning. She is not an allegory (of the defeated Republic or of fascist inhumanity), embodies no idea, and conveys no message. To read her as such is to tame the image, subduing its intrinsic violence. Violence inheres in the ambiguity of the visual, in the fatal remainder of reality which consciousness cannot process. As Leenhardt puts it: "The photograph is not a *document*; it is a *symptom* of whatever escapes the work of discursive encoding, and this symptom *behaves like a sign*; it is not a *sign*" (13).

Resisting language's eternizing thrust, the girl takes her place in the image as a symptom of a past that words cannot bring back to life. The image's historicity rests on its irreducibility to language, not on the meanings it may accrue through exegesis. Unlike the sign, which is always determined by the code, a symptom cannot be reduced to meaning. It is a material event – the photograph's ocularity, its eye-to-eye effect, depends ultimately on a chemical process – whose "truth" remains somatic through and through.

The Mystery in the Eye

Looking at Capa's photograph, one is struck by the fact that its vanishing point is located precisely in the girl's eye. Not only does her eye open up a perspective in the picture's crammed surface, but it also provides the missing balance for the mass of the objects concentrated in the photo's upper section. By nailing the viewer's attention, the eye stabilizes the otherwise decentered picture and injects temporality into the image. By virtue of the gaze something comes alive in the midst of the cargo that is obviously too heavy for the girl. That burden is all that remains of her past, which becomes ours the moment her eye draws us into her perspective. In itself, though, the past is dead weight. If it comes into our purview, it is because its effulgence was fixed on the film's silver gelatin, like a butterfly nailed on cardboard. It is in and through the gaze that history stirs on the photo's surface. Our gaze, in the first place, but also the girl's, an anonymous gaze anchored in time. Whether dead or alive today, to us she is only a trace of receding memory. A trace, first of all, in the chemical sense of a faintly perceptible concentration of an element, but also in the sense of the mark left on a medium by the passage of an object or by an action that has long ceased.

Thus we must face up to the possibility that the images of a nation that are etched in consciousness cast that nation as something lost or about to be lost. I do not mean the banality that the nation is a utopian projection of desire for wholeness in the past and can be experienced only in a melancholy mood of supposed bereavement. I mean, rather, that the act of consciously looking at a vanishing object is the privilege (or the fate) of a subject who is itself receding into history. From the temporal horizon of a subject that knows itself projected toward death, the nation is no more than the reflexivity of the experience of loss. Far from offering redemption from biological time, the nation is always experienced under the sign of Saturn. For Rovira, looking from the terrace of Can Perxers, or for Capa, looking through the lens, chronological change is grasped in spatial images. Pierre Mac Orland wrote that the power of photography consists in creating sudden death, and Eduardo Cadava (8) glosses this sentence as follows: "the photographic event reproduces, according to its own faithful and deathbringing manner, the posthumous character of our lived experience." Capa's photograph of the evacuee girl owes its intensity to the overlap between the life surprised in it and the medium's "deathbringing" effect. It owes its power, that is, to its redundancy. If all photographs announce the impending absence of their subject, this one mesmerizes by objectifying the medium's subliminal statement. It is a picture of a departure that we assume to be definitive. In the last analysis, though, the finality in the girl's look does not arise from the mediated conditions of *our* looking but from the excision performed in the temporal continuum by the camera. The camera's mechanism transforms an otherwise ordinary moment (a girl waiting in front of what looks like a bus station) into a last-time experience.

Although consciousness must indeed be imputed to the eye that looks at us from the other side of the lens, we may not legitimately attribute any particular emotion or thought to that look. When narrative supplements vision – as in Rovira's reflections on the reversal of fate – the words colonize the visual field without revealing its secret. Exposing the mystery of the look at the limit is the ostensible purpose of Javier Cercas's bestseller, *Soldados de Salamina* (2001), a novel that mimics historical reportage. The book is based on a real event that took place during the retreat of the Republican army toward the French border in the last days of January 1939. A few miles from the border, at the Catalonian shrine of El Colell, Republican troops received the order to execute a group of prisoners. Among these prisoners was Rafael Sánchez Mazas, co-founder of Spanish Falange and the most prominent fascist leader still alive at the end of the war. The focal point of Cercas's narrative is the moment when Sánchez Mazas bounds from the firing squad and hides himself in the forest. Cowed and dirty, Mazas digs himself in the mud to escape his pursuers. All is in vain. A militiaman finds him, and then time freezes while the hunter and the prey look at each other eye to eye. A thin line separates Sánchez Mazas from death, but it is doubtful that the myopic fascist sees anything through his mud-spattered spectacles, except perhaps those other eyes in which his fate balances at that moment. A few yards back, another soldier asks the militiaman if he has seen anything. "Nothing," replies the latter, then turns around and leaves the scene. This, in few words, is the kernel of Cercas' story. The remainder of the book is split between the account of Sánchez Mazas's lying low while waiting for Franco's army, which reached the border on February 9, and the narrator's search, some 60 years later, for the surviving witnesses of Sánchez Mazas's reprieve. Ultimately, the narrator is after the *meaning* of the look that graced a posthumous Mazas.

A silly project, but its absurdity did not prevent the novel's success. Cercas owes his instant popularity to the novel's affectation of political aloofness and its vindication of fascist writers on dubious aesthetic terms. The book drives home the message that agency is irrelevant since the truth is mired in a morass of fragmented discourses undistinguishable from myth. Incidentally, the fact that the narrator is a man named Cercas suggests that the author, by erasing the distinction between fiction and historical reportage, renounced his answerability to either category. Cercas's aesthetic argument is specious. It does not vindicate the eye or seek to dispel the ideological shadow that falls upon his narrative world. And although much in the novel turns around the issue of visibility, of seeing and being (or not being) seen, the author appears insensitive to the localization of sight. The genuine tension packed in the eye-to-eye confrontation between the fascist ideologue and the anonymous militiaman unravels in a narrative that spotlights the former while leaving the latter in the shadow. That is to say, it leaves matters as they stood under Franco.

Disavowing the image's violence, Cercas inflicts violence on the militiaman's look. For it is not the case that the novel acknowledges the look's incommensurability with what Cercas might report about it. Rather, the novel insists on allegorizing it, and it is the promise of that "truth" that sends the narrator over the border in search of a look from the border. Cercas's horizon of visibility, or ours, is hardly reconcilable with the militiaman's. To put it in different terms: we are not entitled, as he was, to reprieve a fascist, and much less on aesthetic grounds. But if we cannot step into the magic circle of history, we can still situate the militiaman's look and frame it, as it were. While he stands in the forest with his weapon trained on the cowering fugitive, the militiaman is looking from the threshold of expatriation on a man who looks back at him from the threshold of death. Both are enthralled with visions of finality, and thus in some sense both see the reflection of Spain in eyes that already look beyond it.

Cercas's search for the meaning of the militiaman's gaze is absurd because, even if he could recall it faithfully, the former soldier would not be able to verbalize that trance-like moment without inflicting violence on the image. And violence is precisely what he renounces by keeping silent. With language laid to rest, the ideological categories drop out of sight, and only a crouching living thing remains. Granted, even this curt description of the look *per via negativa* introduces abstraction into the sphere of the unrepeatable event. Nonetheless, insisting on the local conditions of sight can qualify the scope of Cercas's allegory. In his novel, the mystery in the militiaman's eye functions as a narrative blackhole into which the ethics of memory lapses. Enlisting the militiaman's look as a stand-in for the Republican soldier's gaze is an instance of bad universality and reintroduces ideology into a professed aesthetic framework. At the end of the novel, the failure of sight through the miscarriage of the narrator's benighted project implies a *sacrificium memoriae*, the ultimate defeat for those who measure their losses by the impossibility of reconciling lived experience with public truths.

Cercas's fabrication of a former militiaman[6] who freely chooses oblivion suits the prevailing mood in a country, Spain, where, from the horizon of a "peaceful transition to democracy," some of the most hideous crimes of the twentieth century were gentrified into a "fraternal conflict" and a breakdown of *convivencia*. The novel seduced a large audience that was predisposed to close the account book of history without disturbing the war's long-term distribution of injuries and rewards or lifting the general amnesty which the murderers extorted from the victims as the price for the transition they themselves engineered. Voluntary amnesia, however, does not prevent Cercas from vindicating memory in favor of fascist figures, whom the current political conditions make once more suitable for history's limelight. Concurrently, the ex-militiaman's skepticism toward the articulation of the past under these conditions passes over as a generous or perhaps simply ironical capitulation. The faulty logic of this outcome exposes the novel's ideological stripe, which underlies the confusion of horizons. The specific conditions of "seeing" that led the militiaman to renounce revenge on the last stage of the road to exile do not warrant his relinquishing justice on the last stage of his life's journey. Yet Cercas transposes the militiaman's long-forgotten look to the present horizon and, drawing a moral lesson from his silence, defrauds his readers of the mystery in his character's eye.

It is always possible, of course, to restore that mystery by stressing the silence over the ideological inference, which readers, however, do not fail to draw. Perhaps the old militiaman considers Cercas unworthy of sharing his past or simply beyond understanding. But even this interpretation transgresses the boundary of the self and violates the precincts of intimate experience. It also violates the image by sublimating it into something noble, above the narrator's mediocrity. The violence of the image, its mystery, does not depend on the pathos with which Cercas surrounds it, but rather on the fact that "seeing," as opposed to "perceiving," precedes any moral or aesthetic codes. The eye brings us into immediate contact with the world by producing that world as an object for us. We are not what we see, and vision is the ultimate source for the sense of separation and exile.

If we ask now: what did the exilic eye see in January 1939? we cannot expect to produce a satisfactory answer, at best a sympathetic estimate based on iconic mediations and our own experiences of loss. What did Rovira i Virgili's cats see from the darkness of the fence? What did the girl see as she turned her eye toward Capa's objective? What did the militiaman see when he stared at a sentenced fascist whose identity he might not have known? All these looks are in close temporal and spatial proximity to each other. Yet, each keeps its meaning to itself, and we cannot presume to disclose its intimacy. What we can do, giving up the pretension of decoding them as signs of something that transcends their immediate situation, is to see them as symptoms of an alterity that inheres in vision itself. Each of these sentient beings is looking from beyond an insurmountable horizon (a fence, a camera's lens, the barrel of a rifle) at the receding gaze of other beings who cannot and will not accompany them in their fate. And neither can we, even if we stubbornly insist on re-experiencing, as trace, the open secret of what they saw.

Notes

1. The French Governemnet understood it so. In Paris, Daladier told the Spanish ambassador, Marcelino Pascua, that after the fall of Barcelona France considered the Spanish Republic defeated (Rojas 299).
2. Translations of quotations are mine, unless otherwise indicated.
3. I owe this reference to Husserl's stress on the temporality of experience to Enrique Lima in his article "Of Horizons and Experience," in a special issue of

Diacritis, "New Coordinates: Spatial Mappings, National Trajectories," 2005.

4. For a history of the creation of this border, see Sahlins.
5. In "perte d'auréole," *Petits poèmes en prose (Le Spleen de Paris).*
6. The status of this character as militiaman is central to the fabrication. After May 1937, The militias were abolished and militiamen integrated into the communist-controlled Republican army.

Works Cited

Anderson, Benedict. *Imagined Communities: Reflections on the Origin and Spread of Nationalism*, 2nd edn. London: Verso, 1991.

Bakhtin, Mikhail. "Forms of Time and of the Chronotope in the Novel." In *The Dialogic Imagination.* Ed. Michael Holquist. Trans. Caryl Emerson and Michael Holquist. Austin: University of Texas Press, 1981: 84–258.

Baudelaire, Charles. *Petits Poèmes en prose (Le Spleen de Paris)*. Paris: Garnier, 1962.

Benjamin, Walter. *Berliner Chronik.* Frankfurt am Main: Suhrkamp, 1970.

—— *Charles Baudelaire: Ein Lyriker im Zeitalter des Hochkapitalismus. Gesammelte Schriften*. Eds. Rolf Tiedemann and Hermann Schweppenhäuser. Frankfurt am Main: Suhrkamp, 1974. I.2: 509–690.

Bourdieu, Pierre. "La définition sociale de la photographie." In Pierre Bourdieu, L. Boltanski, R. Castel and J-C. Chamboredon. *Un art moyen. Essai sur les usages sociaux de la photographie*. Paris: minuit, 1965.

Cadava, Eduardo. *Words of Light: Theses on the Photography of History.* Princeton, NJ: Princeton University Press, 1997.

Cercas, Javier. *Soldados de Salamina*. Barcelona: Tusquets, 2001.

Foucault, Michel. "Of Other Spaces." *Diacritics* 16. (1) (1986): 22–7.

Husserl, Edmund. *Ideas: General Introduction to Pure Phenomenology*. Trans. W.R. Boyce Gibson. London: Allen and Unwin; New York: Humanities Press, 1931.

Jameson, Fredric. *The Political Unconscious: Narrative as a Socially Symbolic Act*. Ithaca NY: Cornell University Press, 1981.

La Guerra Civil Espanyola: Fotògrafs per a la història. Barcelona: Museu Nacional d'Art de Catalunya, 2001.

Leenhardt, Jacques. "L'écrit et la violènce de l'image." In *Texte-Image/Bild-Text*. Eds. Sybil Dümchen and Michael Nerlich. Berlin: Technische Universität Berlin, Institut für Romanische Literaturwissenschaft, 1990: 9–15.

Lima, Enrique. "Of Horizons and Experience." *Diacritics*, 2005. [forthcoming].

Rojas, Carlos. *La guerra en Catalunya*. Barcelona: Plaza y Janés, 1979.

Rovira i Virgili, Antoni. *Els darrers dies de la Catalunya republicana: Memòries sobre l'èxode català*. Barcelona: Proa, 1999.

Sahlins, Peter. *Boundaries: The Making of France and Spain in the Pyrenees*. Berkeley: University of California Press, 1989.

Sartre, Jean-Paul. *L'imagination*. Paris: Presses Universitaires de France, 1981.

Villarroya i Font, Joan. *Desterrats: L'exili català de 1939*. Barcelona: Base, 2002.

Index

Abdel Krim 284
advertising 29, 46, 150, 197, 223, 226n20, 260n9, 296
Africa 5, 8, 15, 128, 206, 286–7, 289–92, 296, 298–9
agency 341, 344
Albareda, Rafael 167, 175n11
Alliance of Anti-Fascist Intellectuals for the Defense of Culture 313
Álvarez de Sotomayor, Fernando 219
anarchy 13, 113, 121–5, 127–32, 136, 138n8, 306, 313
Andalusia
  Alhambra 153–4, 156–7, 209–10, 280n3
  Cartas de Andalucía 13, 142
Andersen, Hans Christian 209–10
Anderson, Benedict 117, 226, 335, 346
Arco, Ricardo del 219, 225n16
authenticity 26, 39, 71, 75, 91, 144, 146, 152, 154, 194, 216, 307–8

Baena, Ernesto 170
Bakhtin, Mikhail 334, 347
Balfour, Sebastian 20n3, 290, 292–3
Balla, Giacomo 330
Baños, Ricardo de 287
Barcelona (*see* Catalonia)
Barthes, Roland 13, 112–13, 118, 125, 127, 137n3, 187
battle(s)
  of Annual 283
  of Barranco del Lobo 289, 292
Baudelaire, Charles 338, 347
Bazin, André 292, 299
Bécquer, Gustavo Adolfo 118, 210–14, 216
Benjamin, Walter 1, 6, 94–7, 101–2, 107n1, n4, n6, 108 n7, n8, 109–11, 144
  and the Age of Mechanical Reproduction 2, 4, 20n17, 299
  aura of the work of art 4, 13, 101, 109n18, 146, 148, 234
  and the city 265
  cult value 16, 259
  display and collecting 95, 108n9, 109n17
  materialist history 97, 108n7
  and modernism 20n17
  and modernity 1, 6, 8, 96, 105, 341
  and museum 85
  and shock 285
  and vision 12, 16, 19n3, 95, 96, 333, 336
Benlliure, Mariano 219
Bentham, Jeremy 7
Biadiu, Ramón 314
Black Legend 117
Blake, William 337
Blay, Miguel 219

blindness 13, 59–60, 109n22, 118, 124, 128, 131, 140
Bonaparte, Napoleon
  invasion of Spain 25, 119, 209
border(s) 329, 331–3, 335–9, 341, 343–7
Bourdieu, Pierre 70, 79, 340–1, 347
Brennan, Gerald 95, 107n4, 109–11
Bryson, Norman 120, 131–132, 140
bullfighter(s) 179, 308
Buñuel, Luis 253, 255–7, 260n7, 261n11, 314, 316–317

camera obscura 7, 12, 57–60, 94–6, 105, 107–8, 120
Capa, Robert R. 18, 119, 330, 332–3, 340–3, 346
capitalism 1–13, 16–17, 24–5, 27, 108n7, 263, 265, 279, 283, 285, 288
cartoon(s) 35, 198–9, 269, 310, 323n6
Casado del Alisal, José 11, 64–5, 80
Catalonia
  Barcelona
    international exposition(s) 16, 207, 228–40
    World's Fair(s) 229, 242n10, 312, 316, 319
    modernisme 117, 132, 151, 230
    Montjuïc 232–4, 236–42
    noucentisme 230
    Tragic Week 296
censorship
  film 8, 280n7, 305, 307
  press 14–15, 26–7, 30, 178–81, 186, 192, 197–9, 202, 232, 237, 241n2, 248–9, 303–4, 306, 308
  Francoist 134, 344
Centelles, Agustí 13, 113–14, 116, 119–20, 133–40
Cercas, Javier 18, 344–6, 347
Cernuda, Luis 309
Chakrabarty, Dipesh 5–6, 20n10, 107n6, 111
Chiaroscuro 332
cinema
  animation 269, 323n6, 324n9, 333
  of attractions 285–6, 299
  distribution 3, 98, 267, 275, 279n1, 310, 345
  documentary 8, 17–18, 26, 36, 134, 284, 286, 293, 301–5, 307–9, 311–13, 315, 317–27, 339
  and melodrama 76, 79–80, 286–8, 291, 300
  and morality 277, 291
  Soviet 306, 309, 317, 323n3
    Eisenstein, Sergei 257, 290
    Vertov, Dziga 319
citizenship 7, 11, 25–6, 34, 46–55, 60–2, 64, 70–2, 76, 133, 208, 214, 232, 236, 241, 263, 266, 301, 305, 307
  and democracy 1, 11, 77, 79, 345
class
  difference 13, 111, 134, 151, 153, 189, 192, 228–9, 238–9, 284
  distinctions 3, 94, 234
  formation of 7–8, 207
  struggle 17, 54, 66, 92, 133, 136, 207, 287, 292, 308
Clifford, Charles 26, 167, 176, 182, 209
Clifford, Jane 167
collage 4, 16, 245–7, 250–4, 258–62
colonialism
  Africa 5, 8, 17, 183, 275, 284, 286, 290–1, 298
  Latin America 19n8, 22
consumerism 12, 33, 265 (*see also* Luxury)
contingency 111, 132, 283–5, 295, 299, 337

Coromina, José 209
cosmopolitan(ism) 119, 149, 208
Cossío, Manuel B. 309
Costumbrismo 26, 41n8, 43, 45, 101, 103, 209
Coup d'oeil 131
Crary, Jonathan 2, 48–52, 57–9, 62, 85, 92, 264–5
Cruz Cano y Olmedilla, Juan de la 208

d'Ors, Eugeni 230
death 116–20, 138n8, 166, 291, 296, 331–2, 243–5
delusion 61, 123
democracy 17, 66, 84, 86, 133–4, 239, 249, 266, 309, 312, 318 (*see* Enlightenment)
Derrida, Jacques 13, 129, 131–2, 139n12
La desheredada (*see* Galdós)
dialectical thought 110, 154
Dieste, Rafael 309
digression 17, 283–4, 286–91, 294, 296
display 26, 66, 68, 71, 83–4, 87, 89–90, 95–6, 98–100, 103, 179, 214–15, 233, 263, 321
dress
  as costume 210, 212, 215, 223n1
  folk 15, 64, 103, 166, 208, 212, 215, 218, 309

Elkins, James 2, 19n3, 21
Ellerbeck, J.H.T. 169, 175n13, 177
Engels, Fredrick 7, 22
England 151, 159, 231
engraving 14–15, 28, 164, 178–83, 185–95, 197, 199
Enlightenment
  as model for democracy 1, 11, 77, 79, 345
  philosophy in Spain 11, 13, 31, 39, 49, 52, 150, 231, 239, 265, 274, 290, 307, 309, 322, 330
Episodios nacionales (*see also* Galdós)
Escobar, Julio 303
Españolada(s) 161n8, 308 (*see also Cuplé*)
Euskadi 230
exhibition(s) 3, 11, 15, 16, 22, 64, 66–70, 72–5, 78, 82, 84–5, 87–91, 98, 145, 160, 233, 238, 265, 282, 285 301, 303, 310, 312–15, 317, 319, 321, 325n14, n17
  diorama 244n9
  dress and costume 43, 45–7, 68–75, 78, 83, 88–9, 102–3, 126, 178–9, 197, 207–24 passim, 253, 256, 258–9, 263, 265, 267, 269–71
  international 3, 13, 15–16, 64, 119–20, 207, 213, 228–30, 232–4, 236–7, 239–40, 312–13, 325n14
  magic lantern 26
  photography 175n8
experimentation, aesthetic 69–70, 249, 256–7, 312, 327

Fabian, Johannes 46, 63, 289, 299
Falange 18
fascism 311, 313–14, 332, 339, 341, 344–6
  and aesthetics 84–5
  and architecture 152, 232, 234
  and censorship 8
Ferdinand VII 209
film (*see* cinema)
flamenco 158, 160, 287, 308, 312
folk
  dress 15, 83, 89, 126, 197, 207–25, 227, 269

music 206, 214, 236, 269–77 passim, 309, 317
and regional culture 5, 15, 26, 104, 118, 151, 154, 173, 207–11, 215–27, 234
types 9, 26–7, 54, 61, 122–3, 125, 181, 221, 268, 278, 308
Foreign Legion 294
Fortuny Madrazo, Mariano 92, 154, 160, 220, 227, 260n3
Foucault, Michel 7, 22, 89, 338, 347
Franco, Francisco 8, 105, 120, 133–5, 138, 170, 223, 241, 297n3, 312, 332, 338, 344
Franz, Joseph Gall 122

Gadamer, Hans 236
Galdós, Benito Pérez
La desheredada 12, 81, 84–93
Episodios nacionales 11, 46, 61, 63
realism 4, 14, 16, 70–2, 74, 97, 170, 187, 265, 320, 341
García Mercadal, Fernando 219
Gardner, Alexander 112–13
Gasch, Sebastià 16, 139, 244–5, 255–6, 261n10, n12
Gaudí, Antonio 123, 126, 131, 140–1
gender 2, 3, 48, 56, 130
and cinema 5, 8–9, 17–18, 51, 63, 69, 96, 216, 222, 226, 255–7, 263–70, 274–80, 291, 306–8, 318–19, 333–4, 339, 343
feminine 3, 6, 11, 77, 197, 211, 218–19, 273–5, 277
feminism 198
masculine 95, 290
and modern concepts of family 121, 198, 222, 291
and nation 11, 64–75, 77, 79, 262, 302, 327, 346
Generation of '98 215
Género chico (*see Zarzuela*)
Germany 5, 20n16, 32, 181, 194, 199, 309
Gómez de la Serna, Ramón 12, 94, 96–103, 107–9, 111
Gómez Mesa, Luis 303
Goya, Francisco 117, 119, 161n8, 309
Graham, Helen 19n7
Granada 67, 140–3, 150–62 passim, 209, 327
Gunning, Tom 9, 22, 285, 299
Gutiérrez Solana, José 78n5, 117, 126–7, 129, 140–1
Guzmán Merino, Antonio 315
gypsy (*see* Rrom)

heliograph 192, 204n5
Herrera, Juan de 43 (*see also* fascism and architecture)
heterotopy 338
historical
materialism 1, 108n7, n9, 150
modern understanding of 1, 18, 29, 32–3, 50–1, 56, 61, 71, 128, 187, 215, 235, 295, 329, 334–5
painting 64, 66–9, 74–8, 87, 94, 118, 120, 132–3, 139–40, 179, 182, 186, 211–12, 215–16, 246–7, 250–2, 256, 262–3
Hollywood 222, 226n19, 257, 303–4, 306, 308–9
horizon
political 329–31, 337–9, 344–5, 347
temporal 18, 228, 233, 283, 332–4, 337, 343, 346
of visibility 330
Huntington, Archer M. 215–16, 226–7
Hurdanos 317
Husserl, Edmund 334–5, 340, 347

Iglesia, Alex de la 292
illustrated magazine(s) (*see* magazines and periodicals)
illustrated periodical(s) (*see* magazines and periodicals)
image
  eidetic 331
  immediacy of the 49
  mechanical (re)production of the 27–8, 35, 39, 45–6, 48–9, 69–70, 85, 100, 102–6, 112–13, 120, 143–4, 150, 178–82, 263–4, 285, 288–90, 292–3, 295, 299, 302–3, 307–9, 311–12
  phatic 296
impressionism 143, 264
Industrial Revolution 144, 209
Inquisition 117, 129
Institución Libre de Enseñanza 215
intaglio 180–1
international Fair(s) (*see* Catalonia)
Isabel II 26, 43, 70, 168, 176, 209–10
Islam 152, 289, 338
Italy 75, 94, 101, 125, 270, 304

Jackson, William Henry 168–9
Jameson, Frederic 4, 18, 22, 330–1, 347
Jay, Martin 7, 19n6, 20n9, 110–11
journalism
  military 17, 113, 189, 207, 232, 266, 278, 284, 303, 311–15, 318
  and style 82, 171, 316

Kern, Stephen 8, 19n6, 22, 264, 282

La gitana blanca 17, 283, 287, 289, 291–4, 298
La llegada de un tren 9
Labanyi, Jo 11, 13, 19n7, 50, 159
Lahuerta, Juan José 121–31 passim, 137n2, 140
landscape 14, 26, 58, 123, 143–4, 149–50, 155, 159, 163–78 passim, 212, 217, 220, 271, 288–9, 292, 319, 334–8
Laurent, Jean 182–3, 185, 205n11, 213, 224n5, 227
Leenhardt, Jacques 340, 342, 347
Lefebre, Jules 186–7
Lefebvre, Henri 236, 243
Legros, Alfonse 183, 185
Leiris, Michael 16, 245, 247, 257–9, 262
leisure 2, 6, 15, 222–3, 229, 265–6, 283, 286, 306–7
Lekuona, Nicolás de 176
Lerroux, Alejandro 249–50
lithograph(y) 4, 164, 180, 209
Locker, Edward Hawke 166, 175n9
Lombroso, Cesare 122, 130
luxury
  and fashion 143, 153, 155, 169–72, 265, 270, 316
  goods 30, 34–5, 69, 244–5, 259, 265, 273

Madrid
  as capital 24–7, 30, 32–4, 39–40, 59, 64, 66–79, 115–22, 126, 128, 156–7, 194, 207–8, 211–38 passim, 255–6, 274–6, 286, 290–2, 301–5, 327, 329, 331, 334–6
  and urban planning 24–6, 33–4, 70, 81–4, 86, 90–1, 148–50, 179, 208, 210, 229, 231–4, 263, 272, 275–6, 289–90
magazine(s) and periodical(s)
  L'Amic de les Arts 16, 245, 255, 257, 259

Blanco y Negro 15, 178, 194, 196–203, 205n15
Diario de Avisos 10, 25, 30–1, 33, 43–4
Documents 254, 256–8
La Ilustración Española y Americana 44, 178, 186, 197, 203–6
La Ilustración de Madrid 211
Impresiones de arte 13, 142–57 passim
El Mirador 5, 15, 16, 228–44 passim
El Museo Universal 14, 178, 182–3, 198, 211
Popular Film 303, 305
Semanario Pintoresco Español 10, 24, 44–5
magic lantern 10, 26, 29–30
mannequin(s) 215, 220
Maragall, Joan 117, 126–8, 141
Marey, Étienne-Jules 2, 19
Marraco, Joaquín Gil 171
Martínez Campos, General Arsenio 125
Martínez Sanz, Vicente 171, 177
Martorell, Francesc 169
Marx, Karl 6–7, 22
Melilla 191–2, 287–8, 290–1, 293, 299
Meller, Raquel 287, 296, 298n6, 304
Menéndez Pidal, Ramón 310
Mesonero Romanos, Ramón de
chronicle of Madrid 24–45 passim, 73–5, 78–85, 89–97, 99, 103–5
Manual de Madrid 10, 25, 41n3, 43, 79, 93
military battles (*see* battles)
Mir Escudé, Adreu 171
Mir, Joaquim 123, 126, 171
Miró, Joan 4, 16, 88, 139, 244–62
modernism 4, 8, 14, 17, 19n7, 20n12, n17, 97, 101, 223, 225n16, 264–5, 302, 322
modernisme (*see* Catalonia)
modernity 1–19, 19n7, 20n12, n17, n18, 24, 37, 76, 96–7, 104, 118–20, 143–4, 211–13, 223, 263–6, 274, 283–5, 290, 296–7, 302–3, 322
of Catalonia 229–37 passim, 240
and race 283–4
resistance to 3, 5, 52, 149–50, 259, 276
Moliné, Manuel 167, 175n11
monument(s) and monumentality 32–3, 106, 234–6, 243, 265, 276, 315
Morocco
Moroccan War 284
representation of 17, 20n13, 128, 187, 283–290 passim, 298n11
Mulet Gomila, Antoni 169
Mulvey, Laura 51, 63
museum(s)
Museo del Prado 3, 11, 12, 26, 33, 64–89 passim, 91n3, 93, 217, 265, 277
Museo del Pueblo Español 15, 221
Museo del Traje 15, 224n7, 227
Museo de la Trinidad 211
music
folk 15, 64, 103, 166, 208, 212, 215, 218, 309
popular 19n7, 186, 244, 247–9, 253, 256, 258–9, 263–77
regional and national 161n5, 214, 236–7, 262, 302, 327
Muslim (*see* Islam)

Napper, R. P. 165–6, 168, 179, 186–7
nation(alism) 22, 24–5, 32, 59, 64–75, 106, 116–20, 122, 136, 144, 190,

207–8, 212–13, 218, 262, 274, 283, 286, 301–2, 304–5, 308–9, 311–13, 346
naturalism 97, 121, 198
neo-classicism 8
newspaper(s) (*see* magazine(s) and periodical(s))
newsreel(s) 275, 284, 290–2, 298n12, 320–1
nostalgia 26, 102–3, 120
novels
  avant-garde 102, 145, 179, 312, 314
  and cinematic technique 51, 222, 255–7, 263–70, 333–4
  naturalist 27, 128
  realist (*see* Galdós)
  serialized 3, 12, 31, 33, 128, 198

objectivity 14, 61, 112, 119, 124, 127, 137n1, 186, 308, 329
ocular(ity) 8, 20n9, 128, 342
orientalism 150, 156, 158, 186, 290
Ortega y Gasset, José 8, 222, 227
Ortiz Echagüe, José 14, 171–3, 175n15, 227

painting, historical 3, 64–77 passim
Pallàs, Paulí 125–6
Pannemaker, Adolphe 181, 186n6
panorama(s) 29, 263
parador(s) 236
Paris 78, 80, 138–9, 142–54, 197, 224n5, 243–4, 260–3, 275, 312–19
patriotism 209, 217, 286, 313
Payne, Lewis 112–13, 118, 127
perception 18, 32–3, 50–61 passim, 71, 117, 119, 235, 264, 295, 329, 334–5
perceptual identification 287
Pérez de Villa Amil, Genaro 166, 176
Perojo, Benito 291, 297n4
perspective 7–8, 129
photography
  album(s) 179, 182
  chronophotography 2, 19n5
  ethnographic 288, 294, 313
  studios 133, 179, 182–3, 214, 238
  technology 45, 48–9, 102–6, 263–4, 288–90, 302–3
photojournalism 179, 191, 199
photomontage 187, 324n13
phrenology 113, 122–3, 127, 132
Pi Sunyer, Carles 335
Picasso, Pablo 118, 244, 247, 250, 252–4, 260n9, 324n12
Picatoste y Rodríguez, Felipe 181
picturesque 26, 35, 167, 176, 211–22 passim, 224n14, 226n19, 314
Planes Peñalver, José 220
planography 180
Plato 7
Poble Espanyol, El (El Pueblo Español) 15, 73, 219, 221, 223, 233–42
popular
  dress 64, 103, 166, 208, 212, 215, 218, 309
  Front 27, 135, 237, 239, 245, 273, 311, 323, 332, 334, 343
  music 206, 214, 236, 269–80 passim, 309, 317
  theater 126, 263–80 passim, 301, 306–7, 309, 319, 321
portraiture 113, 123, 179, 188, 341
positivism 113, 121, 138
postmodernity 2, 4, 6, 22, 321
Pradilla y Ortiz, Francisco 11, 64–5, 79
Prado Museum (*see* museums)
Prat de la Riba, Enric 230
preservation 16, 212, 230, 237

Primo de Rivera, Miguel 229–43 passim, 292, 306
Promio, Alexandre 266, 285
propaganda 17, 20n16, 45, 133, 136, 208, 275, 284, 291, 297n3, 314, 324n11
punctum 127

race 2, 5, 17, 215, 283, 290
railroad(s) (*see* train(s))
Ramón y Cajal, Santiago 97
Rastro, El 12, 96–103, 108n13, 111
realism 4, 14, 16, 70–2, 74, 97, 170, 187, 265, 320, 341
representation
 metonymic 104, 247, 251
 of women 8, 48, 50, 53, 57, 61, 198, 216, 223, 275, 314
reproduction
 bichromatographic 196
of the image 47, 58, 64, 96, 127, 164, 198, 208, 292, 296, 334–5, 339–40
 mass 2, 6, 11, 15–16, 29, 33, 43, 46, 64–75, 80, 127, 145, 178–80, 231, 234–40, 244, 259, 265–6, 270, 279, 285, 291–2, 295, 302–3, 340, 342
republican government 67, 70, 133–6, 226n21, 231, 237–41 passim, 301–25 passim
Retiro 33, 81, 83, 86, 91, 227, 271
revolution
 of 1868 6, 66–70,
 in Barcelona 113, 127, 131, 133, 230 (*see* Catalonia)
 French 71, 336
 Industrial 144, 209
Riegl, Alois 234–5, 243
Rif 283, 290, 294–6
Roberts, David 166–7, 175n9
Rojas, Carlos 267, 282, 339, 346–7
Roldán, José 219
Rossif, Frédéric 339
Rovira i Virgili, Antoni 18, 332–4, 336–7, 346, 347
royalty 71, 179, 199, 205n12
Rrom 286, 288, 297n2
Rubió i Tudurí, Nicolau M. 239, 242n10
Ruiz Castillo, Arturo 313
Rusiñol, Santiago 113–15, 118–34, 136–8, 140–62 passim

Saavedra, José María 169
Saboya, King Amadeo de (King Amadeus I) 167, 175n11
Salvador, Santiago 121–3, 125, 139n11
Sánchez Mazas, Rafael 18, 344
Sartre, Jean-Paul 107, 337, 347
scapes 164–7, 169, 171
scenography 191
Schmidt de las Heras, Inocencio 171, 176
science 7, 91n3, 103, 127, 266, 310
Second Republic (1931–36) (*see* republican government)
serial
 printing 40, 45, 179–81, 197, 209 (*see* magazine(s) and periodical(s))
 novels 12, 46–8, 52–4, 61, 63, 72, 198, 208, 288, 298n5 (*see* novels)
shock 1, 107n6, 285, 288, 333
silent film (*see* cinema, silent)
Simmel, Georg 19n4, 23, 285, 300
simulacrum 99
Singer, Ben 69, 80, 286, 288, 300
skepsis 139
Sociedad Española de Antropología y Etnografía (Spanish Society of

Anthropology and Ethnography) 221
Sontag, Susan 13, 118–20, 141
Sorolla, Joaquín 215–17, 222, 224n9 n10, 226–227
Soviet cinema (*see* cinema, Soviet)
Spanish Civil War 6, 8, 13, 113, 119, 134, 138, 140, 325n12, 331–2, 339
spectacle 15, 49, 64–5, 67–79 passim, 83, 229–30, 233–4, 268–9, 273, 279
star system 222, 257, 287, 303–9 passim
Stephens, John L. 163, 177
stereoscope 50, 181n10
Subirats, Eduardo 6
subject
  formation 7–8, 71, 97, 136, 207, 221, 286
  political 331
  transcendental 68, 220, 284, 331, 341
surrealism 96, 245, 255–9
surveillance 7–8, 72, 88–90
symbolism 143

Talbot, William Henry Fox 164–5, 204n3
taste 16, 32, 49, 69–70, 73, 79, 82, 160, 181, 197, 244–5, 259, 263, 282, 303
technology
  of photography 2, 14, 41n7, 133, 163, 165–7, 169–71, 173
  of representation 9, 11, 29, 48, 53, 94, 101, 112, 119–20, 163, 209, 216, 247, 249, 275, 284–5, 296, 304, 308, 321, 330–1
  of reproduction 94, 112, 192, 205, 209, 299
telescope 12, 96, 101, 105–6
terrorism 119, 123, 131
  Hipercor bombing 137
  March 11, 2004 137
  Orsini bomb 125–6
theater
  popular 3, 263–81 passim (*see Zarzuela*)
  musical 186, 257, 268–72, 312
time
  biological 97, 343
  cinematic 111, 263, 269, 271, 275, 282, 285, 296–314 passim, 321–2
  novelistic 334
  and photography 14–15, 25, 112, 120, 163, 178–81, 209, 221, 288
  quotidian 47, 145, 332–3
  standardized 17, 283, 297
timelessness 339–40
torture 113, 117, 123, 220
tourism industry 149–50, 256, 270, 274–5, 302–4, 308, 310–12
train(s) 1, 9, 13, 149–50, 285, 288–9, 295
Trapiello, Andrés 117, 140–1
travel 25, 42n18, 72, 143–5, 147–50, 155, 177, 213, 221, 286
Tugores, Adalberto Benítez 169, 175n13
typography 182, 190

urban
  planning 13, 34, 39, 150, 233, 239, 241, 265–6
  reform 10, 15, 24, 30, 36, 39, 219, 301–2, 304, 307–8, 317
Utopia 81, 104
Utrillo, Miguel 142, 152, 155, 157–8, 162, 241

Val del Omar, José del 309–11, 323n5, 324n10
van den Wyngaerde, Anton (Antonio

de las Viñas) 163, 176
Vega Inclán, Marqués de la 219, 227
Villegas López, Manuel 302, 328
Virilio, Paul 19n6, 20n9, 23, 295–6, 300
visual 1–23, 46–61, 68, 71, 76, 82–4, 94, 101–9, 132, 139, 167, 207–19 passim, 228, 234–5, 238–40, 263–5, 276–86 passim, 295, 308, 314–15, 320–1, 329, 340–3
  culture 1–2, 10–11, 15–18, 19n2, 25–6, 47
  field 46–7, 51, 58, 295, 329, 343
  mediation 164
  practices 2–4, 36, 208
  primitivism 164
  studies 6, 19n2
  representation 87, 144, 164, 202, 264, 288, 293
war
  journalism 142, 144, 181, 198, 205
  of Independence 25, 209
Watkins, Carleton 168
wax
  museum 71–7, 78n5, 263
  works 64, 71–87 passim
Wolf, Reinhart 172–3, 177

xylography 180–1, 194, 204n8

zarzuela(s) 16, 102, 263, 268–80
zoetrope 50
Zuloaga, Ignacio 142, 149, 151, 157, 160, 224n9